Peregrinations

per·ĕ·grĭ·ná·tiŏns

CONVERSATIONS WITH
CONTEMPORARY ARTISTS

•

ROBERT ENRIGHT

Bain & Cox, Publishers
Winnipeg • Buffalo

First published 1997 by Bain & Cox, Publishers
an imprint of Blizzard Publishing Inc.
73 Furby Street, Winnipeg, Canada R3C 2A2

Distributed in the United States by General Distribution Services,
85 River Rock Dr., Unit 202, Buffalo, NY 14207-2170.

Cover art by Robert Pasternak.
Design by Otium Productions.
Printed in Canada by Friesen's Printing Ltd.

All the interviews appearing in this book were first published
in one form or another in *Border Crossings* magazine.

Blizzard Publishing gratefully acknowledges the support of the
Manitoba Arts Council and the Canada Council to its publishing program.

Cataloguing In Publication Data

Enright, Robert
   Peregrinations: conversations with contemporary artists
   ISBN 0-921356-67-4
1. Artists – Interviews.   I. Title.
NX163.E57 1997   709'.2'2   C97-920074-1

Contents

Photographies

Musicalities

Looking at Matisse

To Meeka,
still counting the ways

Introduction

As a child growing up in the prairie flatlands of Saskachewan, all I could see wherever I looked was open space, and my compulsion then, as now, was to fill it up with something. It was a huge canvas, white—for six months of the year, anyway—unprimed and open to mark-making. Prairie-dwellers often share a verbal reticence, a penchant for plain speaking, if any speaking at all, but silence suited neither my temperament nor my personality. I began to ask questions if only because the answers I got back were at least something. It turned out I was intent on making sounds and listening to others who had a similar need. I am sure my interest in the interview as a form of communication had its origin in my response to those big, white, unarticulated spaces.

But interest is too uncommitted a word. The truth is I've been enamoured of the interview and have been carrying on a love affair with it for almost twenty years. It has been an experience as rewarding and as exasperating as any other relationship which we enter with our heads full and our hearts pounding. The thirty-two interviews in this book represent an equal number of significant encounters in a three-way conversation among interview subject, interviewer and interview form. They are none of them the same because none of the artists is the same.

In each case I began with an idea about the shape of the ideal interview—my notebooks are full of questions that never happened in the way I imagined they would—but often from the very get-go the interview took the shape the artist wanted it to take. From that exhilarating moment on, my job was simply to hang on and attempt to exercise a little pressure for a turn here or a change of pace there. It's not exactly being on a runaway horse but sometimes it felt that way. Interviewing is an exhausting activity; you have to listen hard to every word and watch every body movement, you have to be attentive to where the interview starts to run on its own fuel and in its own direction. In an important way, the interview is the opposite of a legal interrogation. A lawyer is advised never to ask a question to which he or she doesn't already know the answer; an interviewer talking to an artist should *only* ask questions to which he or she doesn't know the answer. I am not normally surprised by my questions but to my ongoing delight I am constantly surprised by the answers they elicit.

The interview is a private encounter shaped by an awareness of its ultimate public disclosure; it is two people talking in order for a lot more to listen in. Robert Motherwell fully understood the seriousness of what we were doing. In 1980 I was the newly appointed visual arts critic for a national radio program on the CBC called *Stereo Morning*, and one of my earliest assignments was to go to New York to interview Motherwell.

I was terrified. What I had seen of the *Elegies to the Spanish Republic*, Motherwell's great ongoing body of work, had moved me profoundly and the opportunity to talk to its maker was challenging in every way imaginable. Motherwell also had a reputation for not suffering fools gladly and so I read everything I could get my hands on and my mind around: books on American and European Art, on art and psychoanalysis, on automatism, on anything that would give me insights into the cultural context from which Motherwell had come.

The train ride from New York to Greenwich, Connecticut was one of the longest trips I have ever taken; all the while I rehearsed in my mind the interview I planned to conduct. By the time I got to the large door of the converted carriage house where Robert lived with his wife, the photographer Renate Ponsold, I felt I was as ready as I would ever be. Motherwell was friendly, if a bit wary and as I was setting up my tape recorder he said, "There's something I'd like you to read," and he handed me an article Dore Ashton had written on his work and its connection to modernist culture. It was a test.

I began to read the article and while I can't recall exactly what it was that got me onto the subject of Ezra Pound's poetry, I soon found myself reciting *Canto CXX*, the last of the Cantos and a fragment that always seemed to me an apologia for Pound's wayward indulgences with Fascism. "I have tried to write Paradise," the poem opens and goes on, "Do not move / Let the wind speak / That is paradise. / Let the Gods forgive what I / have made / Let those I love try to forgive / what I have made." When I finished, Motherwell fairly snatched the article out of my hands saying, "You don't need to read this. Let's start." It turned out my cultural border crossings—before becoming a cultural journalist I had been working towards a doctorate in American literature—had been the right primer for interviewing the artist who knew more about the culture of modernism than any member of his generation.

He always said it was the best interview he had ever done, which hardly relieves the anxiety I feel as I recall the moments just before it began. (For the record, the interview which opens this book is not the one done in Greenwich but a conversation recorded about a decade later in Provincetown where Motherwell took his summers. By this time we were friends and the interview seemed harder on him than on me. He knew me well enough to disclose some things he regretted the next day and, as a friend would do, I removed them from the published version). It may have been presumptuous of him to take my measure in the way he did but today I'm grateful. Now when I go out to interview an artist I'm my own Robert Motherwell, demanding as much from the interview process as he did from me in that initial encounter.

All of the interviews included in this book were done for *Border Crossings*, the arts magazine with which I've been associated since it began publication fifteen years ago. The name of the magazine is a description of its orientation, its interest in crossing the boundaries of artistic practice; and so filmmakers, composers, theatre artists, photographers, even a choreographer, an art critic, a novelist and a politician-porn star have legitimately worked their way onto its pages and subsequently into this peregrinating collection. And these really are wanderings; there has been nothing systematic about the choice of subjects. What is interesting to me is how coherent is the picture of contemporary art-making that emerges from these random journeys.

The Canadian writer David Arnason has said that just as the letter was the essential form of considered communication between human beings in the nineteenth century, so the interview is that essential form in the latter part of the twentieth. I think he's right, and in that respect I'm reminded of Gertrude Stein's observation that the letter-writer writes what the hearer wants to hear. Does the interviewer, then, always ask what the interviewee wants to be asked? I pose this question because these interviews were not conceived as confrontations, and while I hope they are entertaining—who wouldn't be captivated by the best artists being encouraged to talk about what they do?—nor were they conceived as entertainments. My purpose in conducting them was neither sensational nor investigative, but came out of a genuine wish to understand what makes artists do what they do. I wanted to get inside the creative process to try and discern (from the outside in) the thoughts and processes that result in something being made. Robert Duncan, the American poet, said that if you don't enter the dance you mistake the event, and I would say that my entire strategy has been to enter that generating dance. I'll leave it up to readers to determine whether or not I understood what was going on once I got there.

Robert Enright,
Winnipeg, September 1997

Singularities

Robert Motherwell

The Monumental Diarist

Robert Motherwell is the only painter I've ever talked to who understands fully what ravishing means. The word comes out of his mouth with the "r" almost growled, as if his throat had a serrated edge and then, as his understanding gives over to wonder, it rises to a voluptuous prayer. He also knows what the word looks like and is able to recreate that look in his art. The dazzling beauty of the *Red and Black* series, or the stately presence of the *Night Music Opus*—both bodies of work Motherwell completed in his seventies—gives the viewer important insights into the state of ravishment. Any contemplation of his work involves being taken over, led by the eye to an encounter with our most elegant and most brutal selves. In this sense he is Spanish by adoption and certainly so by artistic temperament.

He also understands the multiple dimensions of black, a pigment that in his hands seems less an absence of colour than the presence of all colours. "It's possible," says Motherwell, "to think of black not as simply the darkest tone but as a colour as vivid and luscious in its way as lemon yellow or magenta or ultramarine blue or alizarin crimson." And then he goes on to describe black by way of an analogy which underlines the workings of his eclectic imagination. "If you thought of the picture as being a string quartet then in a sense the black is the cello. And in most of my work, the cello is necessary."

The composition of Motherwell's life is well known: he was educated in philosophy and art, studying at Stanford, Harvard and then at Columbia under the legendary art historian, Meyer Schapiro, who encouraged him to make art rather than study it. He arrived in New York in the early '40s and became associated with a number of leading European artists in exile, including Fernand Léger, André Breton, Piet Mondrian and Max Ernst. Motherwell immersed himself in the culture of modernism, becoming its most devoted acolyte and its most articulate spokesman. He had his first one-man exhibition at Peggy Guggenheim's Art of This Century Gallery in 1944 and the same year the Museum of Modern Art in New York purchased an early painting called *Pancho Villa Dead and Alive*.

He was the youngest member of the Abstract Expressionists, a myriad group of artists including Mark Rothko, Franz Kline, David Smith, Jackson Pollock and Willem de Kooning, which was to steal the distant thunder of pre-eminence from French art and to make the New York School the most influential group of artists in the twentieth century. But Motherwell's sense of modern art was discrete and not tribal. "What modern art is, both its greatness and its limitations, is an art of individuals," he says. "A modern individual is faced with inventing a whole culture by himself, and in some ways, it is impossible."

This attention to his self-limitations is characteristic—"what I would like to emphasize is that I don't know how to paint" is how he sums up his ability—a judgement that seems perverse in the face of his extraordinary achievement. His *Elegies to the Spanish Republic*, some two hundred paintings and drawings in all— constitute one of the most significant bodies of work in the history of American art. The *Elegies* are monumental, elegant and chthonic at the same time, contemporary paintings that inexplicably have about them a patina of timeless dread. Motherwell has also turned his exquisite sensibility to making automatic drawings, collages and prints which are unequalled by any artist of his generation.

His collages are his most personal works to the extent that they come out of fragments of earlier work. "Collage is my lucky medium," says Motherwell before he goes on to insinuate an element of the primitive. "One behaves like a raider in collage." He is by this measure a "raider of the lost art": the echoes in his work connect less to the pastoral lawns of Connecticut where he actually resides than to the caves of Altamira where his imagination lives. Here is the essence of Motherwell's modernism: he speaks a language of refined violence and he is a masterful linguist.

Motherwell's work is compelling because he possesses the rare gift of sensate intelligence. He is a thinking man's painter who would no doubt agree with Stanley Kunitz, his friend and fellow Provincetowner, that "a tear is an intellectual thing." Kunitz is, of course, borrowing his epigraph from that wily innocent, William Blake. But for Motherwell the reverse is equally tempting. "Or" and here I'm duplicating his favourite rhetorical device, "let me put it another way." An idea, for Motherwell, is a visceral thing; it has a body and a pulse. Everywhere in his work I catch intimations of what Baudelaire called "the universal ecstasy of things"; it is his openness to the realm of sensation, to what the artist has elsewhere called "the skin of the world." "The picture is finished," he says talking like a satiated lover, "when the original emotion has exhausted itself."

The emotion might be over but the work that comes out of it isn't. The consistently high standard of what Motherwell achieves on blank canvas or page, and out of the litter of fragments that serves as the raw material for his collages, is astonishing. At the time of this interview in his seventy-fifth year to heaven (to appropriate a notion from Dylan Thomas), Motherwell continues to produce art that pulls inexorably, and in an almost primal way, to "the foul rag and bone shop of the heart," that secular netherworld Yeats so ravishingly describes as the place "where all the ladders start."

The following interview was conducted in Provincetown, Massachusetts, in Motherwell's summer home in August 1989. It was a three hour conversation punctuated by phone calls and a tour bus which intermittently drove by on Commercial Street. Even inside the house you could hear the tour guide saying, "on the left is the house of Robert Motherwell, the internationally respected Abstract Expressionist." It was an unambiguous reminder that Motherwell is not only "a walking witness to history" as he describes himself, but an integral part of the history to which he so eloquently draws our attention.

ROBERT ENRIGHT: I'm curious about what provoked your initial interest in art?

ROBERT MOTHERWELL: It was always there. I was put into kindergarten when we moved from Aberdeen, Washington where I was born, to Seattle. I'm physically very awkward and tone deaf. I can't recognize a tune although I've listened to classical music all my life. I can, for example, tell who's conducting but I can't recognize the tune. In kindergarten there was much dancing and I couldn't dance because I couldn't hear the beat of the music. There was singing and I couldn't do the singing either, and when I was four or five some lovely teacher said to me, "Bobby, you seem to like painting and colouring books. When the others are singing and dancing, would you rather paint?" I said, "Would I!" and I started painting. Also, the Pacific Coast of Washington is very rainy and one of the rituals in this kindergarten was to depict the sun with orange chalk, or blue rain with grey clouds in front on a blackboard and these abstract symbols were more real to me than if they had been realistic.

RE: Do you mean at four years old you had a recognition of the language and shape of modernism?

RM: Absolutely. Shortly after we moved to Southern California into a housing project I met some kids two or three houses away who had Raggedy Ann and Raggedy Andy dolls. I remember one of my first pitched battles with my parents—by this time I was six—was because I wanted to have them. Again, Raggedy Ann and Raggedy Andy were much more real to me than girl's dolls—largely from Germany—which were porcelain and had eyes that moved. They repelled me while I absolutely went for the abstraction of the Raggedy Ann things.

We had been living in San Francisco then and with the fog and the dampness I became violently asthmatic, and was sent to a prep school in central California where it was very dry. Actually it was very like Provence or Catalonia. From there I went to Stanford University. I was a very good tennis player when I left prep school and one day after a game the fellow I had been playing with said in a most casual way, "I'm going to a cocktail party, would you like to come?" And I said, "Oh, I don't think so." I've never been very sociable and parties mostly either bore me or torment me. "I've heard you're interested in pictures," he said. "Well, these people have some pictures." I said, " In that case, I'll come," because in San Francisco in those days there were no pictures at all. Behold, it turned out to be the Michael Stein collection. I saw Matisses and they went through me like an arrow and from that moment I knew exactly what I wanted to do.

RE: Did you get much encouragement at home to move towards art?

RM: My father was a very prominent banker and when I graduated from Stanford he said to me, "Is it going to be law or business administration?" My heart froze because I'd never thought of the future. When I was in prep school there was a huge study hall in which we were forced to work for two hours every afternoon. I could literally do the work in five minutes, but I was not allowed to leave. The library there was a non-library—the school was very new, having started in 1928 at the peak of the stock market. Then in '29, with the crash, it was suddenly in a very precarious position and couldn't buy books. It couldn't do anything. In those days there used to be little pocket books published in Rome: the Great Masters, the Sistine Chapel, Rubens, Rembrandt. They were a dollar a copy and I would save up and when I had a dollar I would buy one and then simply copy it from beginning to end. But always my own temperament would come through. I spent three years drawing all the time. And when I ran out of my little books, one of the few books the library had was the latest edition of the *Encyclopedia Brittanica*. I looked up art and there were more Rubenses and Michelangelos and at the end it said, "see Modern Art, Art Modern." So I went and got the volume and pulled it out, and there was a colour plate of a late Cézanne and *it* went through me like an arrow. I should also say that in the '20s—when it was almost unheard of—my mother was a collector of French Provincial furniture. She used to take me to auctions before I was fourteen and there was a moment where I could tell what region and within fifteen years the date of any piece of French Provincial furniture. It was a tremendous training for my eye because, in one sense, the subject was always the same—a chair or an armoire—but in another sense it taught me to look for discriminating differences.

RE: You seem to have had from the beginning an almost epiphanic relationship to art. You talk about seeing the paintings in the Stein collection and then a reproduction by Cézanne and about the electrifying effect they had on you. Has your interest in art always been generated out of other art, rather than out of life?

RM: Well, yes and no. All culture comes from other artists. But equally important is to get at core experiences by stripping away all visual influences from everyday life. In the *Times* today there's an article about brain research. They're beginning to think that the brain doesn't work quite the way they thought it did. In mammals there is an emotional response before there's a signifying response, and that's why there are certain psychoses because the emotion goes into action before rationality does. In that sense I've always bet on the "before reflection" response.

RE: In the making of art, too, not just in reflecting on its making?

RM: When I paint, I don't paint in front of the canvas all the time. I walk around it or stare at the ceiling or whatever. Most often the inspired elements come when

I'm doing something else and out of my peripheral vision I suddenly see something, pick up a brush, and do what I see.

RE: One of the things that fascinates me about your work is the constant dialogue between gesture and structure. Has that been an informing notion for you, finding some kind of balance? How do you know when you've got it?

RM: I don't. Once every ten days I have fifteen minutes of clarity and can make a judgment, otherwise I'm simply making marks or not making marks. My ultimate heroes are Zen masters on one side and Piero della Francesca on the other. Obviously Zen calligraphy is the acme of inspired gesture and it's almost instantaneous. A Zen masterpiece takes anywhere from five minutes to forty minutes to compose and it's wrecked if one brush stroke is wrong. Piero is the opposite; he's so systematic. At the end of his life he gave up painting altogether to write treatises and perspectives on mathematics. And yet in Piero and in Zen, there's equally something mysterious.

RE: Have you consciously tried to orchestrate a dialogue along the gesture/structure spectrum or is it something that just happens? I guess I'm trying to get inside the creative process itself.

RM: Well, everybody tries but nobody succeeds, including artists. But maybe because I was trained as a professional philosopher I've guarded too much against rationality. Nevertheless, there's a part of rationality that is built into my eye. I think people investigating creativity look too much for a one-to-one correlation and it's not that at all, anymore than a physicist's character is involved in the problem of physics. But that's too extreme. The medium is both a collaborator and an enemy and the ultimate judge. And it's not about you in the sense that you felt inspired that day or felt melancholy or whatever. An artist is in one sense the authority on his work and in another sense he's the one who least knows what he's doing and what its general effect is.

RE: I wanted to ask you about the whole notion of locale. Have there been highly significant places for you in the making of art? I would guess we're sitting in one now.

RM: Well, except for the light, Provincetown has nothing to do with the way I paint. This place is on a meridian with Barcelona, with the Côte d'Azur and Rome so I would say maybe latitude has something to do with it. But all of that was ingrained in me in California which was a kind of arid, sunlit landscape.

RE: I'm thinking of the splash works which you called the *Beside the Sea* series. They clearly came out of your perception of what happens in this place.

RM: Actually those splash drawings came when I was trying to buy this house. It was the summer that Helen Frankenthaler and I were painting in Day's Lumberyard. The house was unoccupied and sometimes after the day's work I would come and sit on the step and look at the sea and also look at the building and begin to figure out what I would do with it. On several occasions on a very windy, stormy day the waves would pound at high tide and spray up. Normally I never look at landscape in the sense of thinking how to use it but that did strike me. Maybe I was also thinking of the practical difficulties—it probably would need a bulkhead. Anyway, the story of my trying to paint it is well known. I realized I had to use the same activity as nature and really hit the paper with my full force, like a hammer blow, and when I did that the English and French rag papers would split. Then I discovered five ply, American rag paper, which like plywood is glued in layers and is so strong that I can't even tear it.

RE: I hear in the way you approach the making of art a kind of sensate intelligence, or to come at it another way, it seems to me that you have always engaged in passionate thinking. It's that you care desperately for the physical act of painting and you also care for the process that allows you to think through the painting. You respond with the gut and the brain.

RM: Above all, it's physical and then it's sensuous. When I talk about painting, I mean literally breast strokes on the surface with brushes, and from that standpoint illusionism or representation is totally irrelevant. The great lesson I learned from my prep school copying of the old masters was that at a certain moment one didn't look at a model and then evolve Baroqueness, for example. It was the opposite. Painters were schooled in Baroque drawing and applied it to the model. I realized how simple-minded it was for students to sit in front of a jug or a plate and copy it and try to evolve some kind of a style. You start with style, you don't end with it.

RE: You've talked about your painting being of two kinds: the kind where you get down on your knees like an animal and enter the cave of painting and about painting in what you call your "street clothes." Do they actually happen at separate times?

RM: At separate times and in separate moods. I'm something of a manic depressive and in my manic "phase" everything pours out. In my depressed phases, sometimes it will take a month for me to make three or four marks.

RE: I want to talk a bit about your enigmatic titles. What was the source of *In Plato's Cave*?

RM: The origin of that title comes from several things. As you know, they're very dark, shadowy pictures and there is something womb-like or cave-like about them. It so happened that at the time I was painting them I was also reading a novel by Saul Bellow, who is exactly my age, about a poet named Delmore Schwartz who died disastrously, at exactly my age as well. He wrote a poem called "In Plato's Cave" and the picture came out of nowhere. I was trying something technical that I'd never tried before and literally cradled the picture—it was a very fluid picture—on the floor, rocking it back and forth, hoping it would dry before it would drip too much. And the first one caught exactly at the magical moment so it was a totally unpredicted picture. I always name my pictures afterward, trying to give them a title that may be a lead into the kind of universe they belong to. But certainly never as the Surrealists often did in giving titles that lead you in the opposite direction.

When one's a so-called abstract painter, then one can't say it's a still life or give it a mythological title. The real secret is to have a title that is a metaphor, that is not literal. The rule of the game is to give a title that is not misleading. I remember being in the Museum of Modern Art one day with André Breton and there was an Yves Tanguy called "Mama, Where's Papa?" or vice versa. I remarked what a stupid title it was and Breton looked at me and said, "I gave it." I also remember Matta telling me once that the Surrealists were looking at a show of Miró's at Pierre Matisse's Gallery. They were looking at some picture and trying to give it a title and they couldn't come to any conclusion. Breton's daughter, who was six or seven, was tagging along and one of them turned to her and said, "What do you think this picture's about?" And she said, "Oh, it's easy, it's the way it is when it's sunny inside when it's raining outside," or something to that effect. She was so on the beam about the general character of Miró's simple, direct perception. Something that's not generally known is that the Surrealists in New York in the early 1940s were still very dubious about Miró.

RE: Was Miró too decorative? Why would the Surrealists initially have responded unfavourably to him?

RM: Most of them had no visual sense really. And Miró is a radical painter, much more radical than Matisse or Picasso were in the beginning. Cubism still carries a lot of tradition, but Miró is a bolt out of the blue. Now of course, we're very used to him.

RE: Let me ask you about the first of your *Elegy* images. Did you have any idea at the time that it would have the kind of visual resonance, both personally and culturally, that it's turned out to have had?

RM: No.

RE: Where did it come from?

RM: Harold Rosenberg and I were working on publishing a magazine of which only one issue ever appeared because one of the two publishers was killed in a transatlantic plane crash. I was to illustrate a very savage poem called "The Bird for Every Bird." I was making an automatic drawing and I wanted it to carry the same violence as Rosenberg's poem; I was also thinking in terms of black and white because the magazine couldn't afford to print in colour. I did the drawing and it was printed and then I forgot all about it. I was living in East Hampton, Long Island when I did the drawing and a couple of years later I moved to New York. I'm the sort of person who, when I move, takes two years to unpack. After a couple of years I pulled out a little package and here was the original drawing for the Rosenberg poem. At first glance I realized that clumsy as it was, there was something remarkable about it, and I realized too that it was not intimate. It was a monumental thing from conception.

RE: Even in small scale?

RM: Yes. One of the few gifts I have is a sense of scale. I can make a small thing that is meant to be big, or a big thing that could be smaller. So I made a second one—twice as big—and then I made a much larger one and it was more and more right. And I realized that my instinct was correct. And at a certain moment the problem became—what is it? I thought to myself, what public things do I really care about? You see, to western intellectuals and artists the Spanish Civil War had a universal quality of empathy, sympathy and frustration with a tragic undertone. I was exactly twenty-one in 1936 when the Spanish Civil War began, living in California, a place as remote from Europe as North America can be. And I think it was the first time it had ever occurred to me that the ideas of democracy and progress and a better life for Western civilization could be stopped absolutely dead. And then as the war developed and one saw the Germans and the Italians trying out new military techniques, it also became very clear to us that this was the rehearsal for the Second World War. I'm sure there've been other situations, but I really can't think of another period where there was a three-year prelude to a World War that we thought would be as ghastly as the First World War, which in many ways broke the back of Western civilization and from which I think continental Europe never recovered.

RE: What intrigues me is your continual involvement in extending the unique formal language of the *Elegies*.

RM: After I discovered the image I realized it was the most important image that I had ever discovered, and I think, maybe even half suspected (though one never likes to think that as a young man), maybe the most important one I ever would. It had an extra-aesthetic quality. I know from personal experience that there are many people who are moved by those *Elegies to the Spanish Republic* who are indifferent to modern art in general and who often actively dislike abstract art in particular. To this day I don't know why, which is one of the reasons I can still paint them. I'm still trying to find out why, and sometimes I make bad ones because I don't understand it. But they do have a special significance in relation to my own body of work. They're my private Stonehenges, if you want to put it that way. A lot of my work is very personal, very private; a lot of it is almost a diary, but these were more public, more monumental, something outside of myself. In naming them I tried to generalize and externalize my experience and make it more public, out of one of the deepest concerns of my life up to then, which was the defeat of the Spanish Republic. So the *Elegy* series is tragic: it is filled with death and it is also filled with sexuality. In those days I used to think that those were the two major themes, not only of painting but of life itself. I still do to some extent. Lot's of critics describe the *Elegies* in sexual terms but the first complete one was called *At Five in the Afternoon*, after Federico Garcia Lorca's "Lament for the Bull-fighter." Also there was something Spanish about them: the blackness, the death quality, the directness of the paint.

RE: Yours is a career that spans a considerable number of decades now and I was interested to hear you say that last year was the most productive you've had in that long career. What compels you to make art?

RM: It's the only thing that interests me. In the twenties the Surrealists had a mock contest about what led one to create and they gave the prize to Knut Hamsun who replied that he created out of boredom. To put it in more positive terms, painting interests me more than anything else does. I think one of the reasons my wife, Renate Ponsold, is so marvelous is that she's creative herself and I don't mean only as a photographer. She's creative in everything and understands perfectly that my whole psyche is dependent upon how my work is going. So although I passionately love her, at times I am oblivious to her existence and she regards it as perfectly normal. She divides the world into creative people and diplomats, has total contempt for diplomats and is absorbed by creative people of whatever medium.

RE: You've never been accused by anybody of being a diplomat have you?

RM: No. A critic who knows my work and knows me very well remarked one day, "Everybody's always talking about your culture and that you were reared as a gentleman. They don't seem to see that underneath is a real Nordic barbarian." And there is. Maybe painting is a way that barbarism can come out. What I mean is there's a streak of Celtic caveman in me that would just as soon have Lascaux as the Sistine Chapel. And I regard them the same way—as whole matrices.

RE: One of the things that has fascinated me in your work is the central place that James Joyce has occupied. What is it that you respond to so completely?

RM: Well, it's the texture of his writing. It's also that even though it's Thomistic, he had a first-rate philosophical mind, the operation of which he regarded as natural as going to a whorehouse. And of course my basic creative principle is what the Surrealists call psychic automatism, which in everyday lingo is doodling of one kind or another. I can give thirty psychoanalytic arguments for the validity of it and Joyce, instead of beginning automatically, ends that way. He starts with a straight narrative and slowly transforms it. But I suppose it's the sheer beauty of the surface. I agree with Kierkegaard that art *qua* art is the purely sensed, what I call the skin of the world. Another thing that I identify with in Joyce is belonging to something and yet being in permanent exile. I understand perfectly how he could leave Ireland while writing the greatest Irish epic. Of course, it's also true that he took his Nora with him. We could say that he took Ireland right with him. If you read her letters, they're Joycean—without punctuation, just straight out.

RE: T. S. Eliot said that art was an escape from personality. He clearly was trying to get away from self-indulgence, but his comments also set the tone for a lot of great modernist literature. Is that a notion that you would subscribe to as well?

RM: The only way one can describe these things is negatively. Sensibility, sensitivity, subtlety—many of the most valuable human feelings—are expressed in furniture or in automobiles or in walking habits. And from that standpoint most people's lives are essentially gross and I simply don't feel at home with them. At the same time I'm not at all an aesthete, in the sense of an interior decorator or something of that sort. Everybody thinks I've been influenced by Baudelaire's Theory of Correspondences but that's simply a way of making legitimate my perception that everything "speaks." Chairs speak, sidewalks speak, dresses speak, and either one is very sensitive to those things—on many levels and to many degrees—or one is not. And yet a world in which there were not objects that expressed genuine sensibility would be almost like the animal world. You strip away the aesthetic and what is there left but the survival of the species? I suppose the only aesthetic experience that is fairly universal is sexuality.

RE: It's hard to sustain the ecstatic. One of the things that I see in the best art is the maintenance of some kind of balance, the search for something solid, that seems to hold.

RM: But one could say exactly the same thing about sexuality.

RE: That it's transitory …

RM: But at the same time it will come again.

RE: What I'm saying is that the natural impulse for a poet is to have the greatest lovemaking he's ever had and then immediately get up and write a poem about it because the experience has somehow got to be saved from this fleeting thing called time.

RM: But it's not a poem about it, it's *itself* and in that sense the subject matter is not the issue. It's the domain of feeling that also brings in lots of knowledge and perception. I once wrote a speech for a psychoanalytic association saying that a work of art is the only thing that is as subtle, complicated and meaningful as a human being himself. And it's in that sense that all other human activities are essentially impoverished. When you listen to Mozart or read Joyce you're totally satisfied. Human life in many ways is an endurance contest and if it weren't for those kinds of things I think it is certain one would get fed up. There's some dogged faith in me that is indestructible. The human expression when it's transcendent is what makes life endurable. It can even be something childish for example. I remember when my daughters were four and six. I'd come home exhausted from teaching and they used to love me to throw them up in the air and catch them. They came running up and said, "Daddy, throw us up in the air!" And I said, "Oh, I'm too old for all of that." And in unison they said, "That's right, you're old and we're new." And it suddenly occurred to me that if instead of young the word "new" were used in contrast with old, then reality itself would be much more clear.

RE: You've sometimes been accused, not of being too new, but of being too elegant.

RM: In North America I'm often criticized as being too tasteful. I never am in Europe. It would never occur to a Spaniard that my work represents good taste. To them it's sheer aesthetics, like everything else that they admire.

RE: Has the North American continent some innate suspicion of the whole notion of taste and refinement? Surely we've grown up enough not to let that bother us.

RM: No. American culture is still populist. This whole topic is so loaded. It goes back to Rosenberg's essay on "Coonskins and Redcoats." I would say the issue is not at all populism versus elitism. It's about civilization, again a sensibility of subtlety and complexity. On the damn TV everything is resolved by a shoot-out or by a car crash. Well, that's not how human life is resolved. It's sometimes resolved by one person looking at another person and there being a sudden comprehension of what really happened, of what both endured.

RE: There was a period when your work wasn't very popular, wasn't there?

RM: The other day I was talking to my accountant and he said, "Do you remember 1971?" and I said, "Very well, it was when I met Renate." And he said, "I didn't mean that. That was the year I became your accountant and you sold one picture that year—probably it would have been for $15,000." In February of this year I sold a picture, four by five feet, for $1,200,000. All the money I have has been made, basically, in the last six years.

RE: You're not very comfortable under public scrutiny are you?

RM: Well, my myth is a counter-myth and it's an unappealing one. You know, banker's son, WASP, Harvard educated, wealthy, private schools. But the anxiety of making something living and true never leaves a creative person and is basically so deep, so insatiable that after years of it—and again I say this partly jokingly—I can imagine a person very well saying to himself, "I've had it. I can't face another ten years of wondering if what I'm doing even makes sense, let alone whether it's any good." The private life of a creative person is almost intolerable. It's as difficult to make a painting now that satisfies me as it was the first year I painted. I have no virtuoso capacities at all. I was never schooled in technique. In one sense of the word, I work quite primitively, quite directly—as directly as a child. But there's a compensation in not being a virtuoso. I can't fake a picture, really. It either authentically comes out or it's nothing and I just throw it away. So in that sense painting remains an eternal challenge to me. I think that partly keeps me going. But I would think probably in the end most people simply could not take this amount of anxiety over a lifetime. Who would want to live the life of Franz Kafka and become immortal? It's too great a price.

RE: That anxiety never really leaves, does it? Is there doubt about every canvas as it's being done?

RM: Always, about the canvas itself and also about the audience. Because there's no such thing as a permanent history. There were even a couple of centuries where Rembrandt was regarded as a minor, uninteresting painter.

RE: You still look at a blank page or canvas with trepidation?

RM: Absolutely. No more than everyday life is easier, or my relations with my wife or with a friend. At times everything goes haywire, at times everything is as smooth as honey. But there's no way I can control any of it, except in social relations. I'm more peaceful than I used to be. But being peaceful is no help in painting, because painting is supposed to be the opposite, an act of passion.

RE: I want to end with a large question. Why does art matter to you?

RM: The importance of it is to make one feel less mad, less alienated and less ill-at-ease in the universe. I mean if one hears an early Divertimento by Mozart, one immediately feels, "Yes, I'm sane, I understand what he's talking about, there's another person in the world whose feelings match my feelings, I'm not some isolated creature wandering around in a foreign, uncomfortable, frightening, unreal universe." Basically my interest is to communicate and to have a medium that's as expressive in its complexity as is a human being. It's an inexhaustible problem, and also an inexhaustible interest. What could really be more interesting, or in the end more ecstatic, than in those rare moments when you see another person look at something you've made and realize that they got it exactly, that your heart jumped to their heart, with nothing in between.

Jim Dine

Regarding Jim Dine

Jim Dine is fiercely intense. He comes at the making of art like a street-fighter, willing to pull out any dirty compositional trick he knows to get the job done. And he's been at it so long, and with such conviction, that he knows all the tricks. There's a telling sequence in *Jim Dine: A Self-Portrait on the Walls*, one of a trilogy of films made on his art and life by Nancy Dine, his wife, model, muse and now public chronicler. Dine is making nine site-specific drawings for a temporary exhibition at the Kunstverein Ludwigsburg in Germany, a process he describes as "a kind of smoky fight against the wall." Everything for him is adversarial and so at various times he kicks and pokes his drawings, he cuts away pieces, he erases them with his hands or with chunks of bread that he tears from loaves, he attacks them with a broom, a screw-driver, a wooden handle. He even throws Pepsi at one and watches with satisfaction as the corrosive liquid bubbles up on the drawing surface. His is no less a compelling performance than a dizzying act of creation. The energy that goes into it is commonplace for Dine, one of America's most engaging and gifted artists. From his performances in 1960 in New York, through his brief flirtation with Pop Art and finally into the paintings and drawings of a cluster of familiar objects (tools, bathrobes, hearts, gates and still-life elements) that he would thoroughly claim as his own, Dine has remained an artist of apparently limitless imagination. Crossed with a relentless work ethic, these characteristics have resulted in bodies of work that are among the most significant produced by any American artist of the post-war generation.

In the best sense of the term he is a conservative, in that his impulse is to respect the past. So complete is his engagement with what he has called "the romance of the ancient world," that he regularly initiates projects which are ultimately acts of homage to the continuing relevance of Greek and Roman art. But as with everything Dine's hand touches, the past becomes a point of departure for a scrupulous examination of his own personal relationship to the meaning of his sources. "These people left something," he writes in the introduction to his *Drawing from the Glyptothek*, a series of forty images produced from 1987 to 1988 in response to the sculpture in the Munich museum. "It is a gift from them to us. And it remains and it reaffirms who you are. It's like looking in a mirror, it's like painting yourself." Dine's tendency is to transform everything he does into a form of self-portraiture, some of which is disguised, while other aspects are sore-thumb blatant. The inanimate world has been a storehouse of surrogates for him, filled with objects waiting to be chosen and then nominated as a subject in the visual autobiography Dine has been composing for almost four decades. Always, the need is to transform his sources into something that belongs to him, whether he's meticulously drawing nudes or inventing from classical sculpture, so that he can carry his own museum with him wherever he goes.

In the following interview a clear picture emerges of an artist who is passionate, exasperating, utterly committed to making art, and a highly articulate analyst of his own achievement. Making work is his pleasure, as he says, and so is talking about the influences—painful and celebratory—which compel that making. I spoke with Jim Dine in New York over two days in June 1993, once in his studio surrounded by drawings and sculptures for *The Ape and the Cat* series he was then working on, and the second time in his Soho apartment.

ROBERT ENRIGHT: How seductive did you find the modernist prescription to "make it new"?

JIM DINE: That never came up when I was a child because I wasn't aware that's what Modernism was. I thought Modernism was Picasso distorting things. I aspired to it, but I was always taken by the painterliness of the nineteenth century painting I grew up with in Ohio. It wasn't until I was in college that I realized the mission of American artists was to make something new. If it wasn't new, it was no good. They were even apologetic about people like Fairfield Porter who wrote so well about newness yet painted in this post-Vuillard way. But he was a good guy because he was a friend of de Kooning and wrote the great review of Jasper John's first show. By the time I came to New York the whole point was to be new. Yet somewhere in my body I knew that I wasn't prepared to make something new before I was able to do anything I wanted to do.

RE: It's interesting to hear you talk about newness in light of the performance art you did in the early '60s. Those performances have become legendary. How good were they when you think back on them?

JD: Oh, they were really good. But that was because they were not about what we know as performance art. They did not come out of anything except my ability as an actor and my ability to get my bad dreams out into art. So they were quite frightening at times and dismaying for a lot of people. Everybody's performances were different: [George] Whitman's and Red Grooms were different from mine and [Claes] Oldenburg's. Although Allan Kaprow seemed to start it, I liked him better as a painter. He made about six paintings in his life and they were really pretty good. But the other people made plays. That's what I was interested in, making these plays, this painter's theatre.

RE: How technically good were you as a performer?

JD: Good. Everybody was, though. Lucas Samaras was great as an actor and Red Grooms was just fantastic. Everybody made a play that suited them.

RE: This was deeply autobiographical work then?

JD: Totally autobiographical. I would say everybody's was other than Kaprow—who was not in touch with his autobiography. Except for *Car Crash*, for which I needed other people, mine only had me in them because I didn't trust anybody else. I needed to make these one-person things.

RE: In looking at photographs of your performances—in *Car Crash* for example—there are times when you look demonic.

JD: Yes, it was about obsession. Had we more money it would have been better in terms of the productions. It was a bit raw. Not amateurish, so much as raw. There wasn't money for lights and things like that so everything had to be improvised. They had a feeling of the spirit of the time, which was this assemblage time. We were able to make these things with very little money. I don't recall ever spending more than ten or twenty bucks.

RE: Let me ask you about *The Smiling Workman*. There was a point where you actually drank what people thought was pig's blood—it was tomato juice—next you poured paint over yourself and then you jumped through a painting on stage. Did you intend the audience to draw the conclusion that you had a certain aggression towards the idea of painting?

JD: What I had in mind was so total an obsession with painting and being involved with the painting that I had to be in it.

RE: A variation on the philosophy that you are what you eat?

JD: Yes, when I jumped through the painting I didn't want to destroy it; I jumped through the painting to *become* it.

RE: You've been vaguely dismissive about the performance work, I think, because you've said they seemed too easy?

JD: I was dismissive about them because I was eager to get on with my painting life. Everybody wanted so much more of this, as people do of performers, not of painters. That's why I went back and did *Natural History (The Dreams)* in 1965 with Alan Solomon at the First Theatre Rally. It was different; I was different. It was more serious and more minimal, stolid. It didn't have a lot of humour.

RE: I also can't imagine you having any sympathy with Kaprow's notion that performance was going to be the death of painting?

JD: That was ridiculous, just part of his personal ambition.

RE: I don't want to let the phrase "assemblage time" get out of my head before I get you to elaborate on how you would describe its spirit.

JD: I was always totally at home with the detritus of the city and when I came to New York it was a vast palette for me. Claes Oldenburg felt exactly the same way and was able to articulate it better than me. I just took it as a natural phenomenon and picked up everything as I went along. Many of the shows which we made at the Judson Gallery and at the Reuben Gallery were made from garbage in the city. It was a different kind of garbage then, very different. In the first place you were able to pick things up without looking like a maniac. Sometimes Claes and I would go out at night with a cart. Everything we made was from found things which we then elaborated with paint and collage. We didn't have any money but more to the point was to use the garbage, to use the city. Claes had been very influenced by Dubuffet and by Art Brut. He used to speak a lot about Céline and Dubuffet.

RE: Were you much attracted by Dubuffet?

JD: I only knew him from "Jean Dubuffet Paints a Painting," done by Thomas Hess in *Art News* around the middle '50s. I had been stealing the magazine from the Ohio University library: that's how I got to know about New York and what was going on. I was always really a fan of Dubuffet's but I didn't realize he had made himself into an Art Brut artist after being classically trained. Anyway, William Seitz curated this show called The Art of Assemblage in 1961 at MOMA [Museum of Modern Art, New York] and he left all of us out. And we were really cooking down there. He did include a photograph of an environment or a Happening of mine. But as I said, it was a time of assemblage. After all, Seitz was able to mount a show, however inappropriate were the people he chose. He used a lot of people no one ever heard of again. Ettore Colla for instance. Who the fuck is that? Some Italian sculptor who constructs his pieces out of gears. So what.

RE: Like a bad Tinguely?

JD: Yeah. Tinguely was a great man, although, we were not impressed by his blowing up that thing at the Museum of Modern Art. We had already been doing this stuff and here's this guy who gets the Museum of Modern Art Garden. But no one realized what a fabulous hustler he was. We were just too naïve and too young to pick that up yet.

RE: You really do like junk though? Didn't Arman do a piece called *Jim Dine's Dustbin* out of the detritus from your studio?

JD: Yeah. It was in the Pop Art show in Montreal curated by Marco Livingstone. But that piece has been entirely misinterpreted. Here's what it is. Arman was an amazing hustle. His dad had been a dealer in Nice and he himself was a dealer/ artist. He moved to New York in the early '60s which was brilliant. And he traded brilliantly with everybody. He traded a painting with me and he said, "What do you want?" I looked at some things and one was like a glass bell and in it was the contents of his wife's bathroom waste basket. When I brought that home, Mrs. Dine said, "Are you crazy? You gave him a gorgeous painting and what is this?" It was horrible in a way. It was tampax and pubic hair and kleenex and stuff. It really was quite revolting, but I thought beautiful. Truly beautiful. Of course, it wasn't just Mrs. Dine; it was my friends too. A lot of them would say, "What the fuck are you doing? It's so repellent that if it breaks you and the kids are dead."

RE: Did you know the Fluxus people in the early '60s?

JD: A lot. We were very close with some of those guys—Dick Higgins and George Brecht.

RE: What made the stuff that you, Oldenburg and Grooms were doing different from what the Fluxus artists were doing?

JD: Our things had a narrative line and we were interested in the emotions of people. Fluxus were interested in putting together decks of cards and things. I thought it was a sad bit of chance art, sort of second-rate Duchamp. The nicest thing I ever saw by any of those people was a little book by Emmett Williams in the '60s called *Sweethearts*. I thought the typography and everything in it was just beautiful.

RE: What made you so disenchanted with New York? You left the city in 1967.

JD: I was disenchanted with myself and I took it out on New York. New York was no different then than it is now. Europe wasn't so competitive and it was easier to be friends with people. I was thirty when I went. Never been overseas at all but as soon as I got there I felt totally at home and never questioned why until later. I still move easily in Western Europe and have rarely found a place I don't feel comfortable in. I speak no other languages and I never have. One of my kids met me for a drink at the Café Flore in Paris about three years ago—he's a musician and was on tour—and he said to me, "Thirty years and you can't even order a drink." It never bothered me. In fact I enjoy the silence, not having to talk all the time. I like to look at things and walk a lot of the time. For me Europe was a gift. Still is. Not that I want to live there all the time. After a while I get pissed off and want to go home, so-called home. Then I get back here and I go over in my mind how wonderful it was in Europe. I'm more comfortable in my body there. I'm only here because my wife and children and grandchildren live here. That's the only reason I live in America. And also it made me. But I really feel at home in Europe. I'm a great fan of Scandinavia.

RE: Not for its art surely?

JD: That too. I made a little film on Edvard Munch last year. I'm very proud of it. I've been going to Norway for years to look at Munch. In my guts he's the painter I feel closest to; I'm very moved by his art and his life. So I go to Scandinavia a lot. I attribute all this to my love of darkness and to cold weather. I flew into Helsinki and I thought to myself I've seen this before even though I'd never been there. The sky seemed so familiar, but then my people were all from the Baltic so maybe there's something in the DNA.

RE: Do you find yourself being attracted to place?

JD: I have an affinity to nature and to land, but not necessarily to the Ohio Valley where I was raised. The river's very beautiful and quite charming. But the memories are so horrible for the most part that I'd just as soon not go back. Still, I'm torn because I go back trying to grasp at my childhood. I do carry my landscape on my back. I can be anywhere. I'm very happy travelling; I'm an itinerant that way. I'm here six months of the year maybe, but never over a longer stretch and I'm in London at my studio for three or four months. I can paint in any hotel room you put me in. I'm very lucky that way. Most artists need their fancy studios or their home. I don't. My home is on my back. I feel that very strongly. In fact, sometimes I prefer hotels. I prefer the anonymity. I love room service, a hotel bar, I love reading a newspaper in a hotel bar. I often find myself standing off from humanity. It's about being uncomfortable in your skin, about not walking comfortably in this world. I don't necessarily think what happened to me is any worse than what's happened to anybody else, but it's just what it did to me. So there's a shock and then you invent yourself and you slip through the world. Somehow you find some crooked route to get through the world. You are constantly looking over your shoulder. You just are.

RE: You said that by 1971 you'd learned something very significant from living abroad that you could bring back to America. What was it you found there?

JD: I brought back a sense of myself that I hadn't had before. I was no longer a "pop" artist. I was just me. I had gone off on a very circuitous route and thought of myself in the line of those singular European artists of this century like Balthus and Giacometti and Morandi and Munch. I felt part of a tradition of loners. I consider all those people loners.

RE: Is that a tradition that you choose out of its inherent eccentricity, or is it an inclination of personality?

JD: It was chosen. It was a way that I could identify and say, "you're not a complete maniac, you're not completely alone. Other people have gone this route too."

RE: Now what's the route?

JD: Let's take Morandi because he is very uneven. I don't like his drawings; I love his prints. Except for the masters, Matisse and Picasso, I think he and Munch are the two greatest print-makers of the twentieth century. But here's Morandi, living in Bologna all those years with his two sisters. He sits in a room and he paints bottles. It's an enviable position to be in, it's really relaxing. I aspire to it but I'll never do it. Or Francis Bacon. He was my neighbour in London and I would see him cruising boys last year—he was eighty-two or something—in the subway. South Kensington tube station was our stop. I'd always meet him down there and he would walk away. But then you'd see him in a bar and he'd send over champagne. He was a real sport. I found the idea of Bacon living this lie in the London underworld and being a grand European painter something to aspire to.

RE: I assume it's the work and not the man which initially attracted you?

JD: The person too because you've got to live in this life. I was attracted to the work but not in the later years. He repeated himself in a way that isn't so amusing or interesting. But I would say the paintings from '50 to '65 are something grand, especially the *Van Gogh on the Road* paintings.

RE: I'm not surprised you seize on that body of work because you've done your own drawings in homage to van Gogh.

JD: I'd been thinking about it for a long time. I spend a lot of time looking at pictures in books, sometimes picking out a phrase for a title or looking at something that would grab me and then getting into it. If it did not grab me I would go on. And van Gogh would just keep on like that. He is never *not* on my mind now. I always think of his sad life.

RE: It's astonishing how much you invest in the painter and not just the things the painter makes.

JD: Half the time I don't care about the objects at all. I like the life in art. It means a lot to me, therefore, it makes it difficult to be friends with painters sometimes. I'm like a disappointed fan.

RE: So you refuse to divorce life from art?

JD: I cannot do it. I don't believe there's a bridge between life and art and that's my struggle. I've raised a family and I come from rather an eccentric, crazy old family that can show up on my doorstep and still haunt me. I love all these people yet I also try to paint and make a life in art. It's a sometimes difficult juggling act.

RE: When you left America you talked about a "defection." You really reacted strongly against the pressure on you here to be a performance and Pop artist didn't you?

JD: I probably overreacted. I just couldn't take it because I wasn't ready to be so public. But the handwriting was already on the wall. I don't think I've ever really gotten a good review, a review where I consider that the critic has actually understood what I was doing. It was always something backhanded. I pissed a lot of people off. I still do, and I don't really like that. Some people might think that's a badge of honour but I don't. I think it's a misunderstanding.

RE: Do you sense it's your directness that they can't handle?

JD: I believe that, yes.

RE: It's funny you should say that. One of the stories you tell in *Childhood Stories* is about your grandfather not allowing you to look directly at the television, so you had to look at things from the side. There's a poem by Emily Dickinson where she writes about "seeing things slant," a way of looking which becomes an aesthetic strategy for her. You also came at meaning indirectly. I'm thinking of the bathrobe as a surrogate self-portrait.

JD: Absolutely. I had to use metaphors and come from the side to stop the frontal attack that is in my nature. You see I invented myself. After my mother died, which is not said in the film, I was truly on my own. Here I was in the midst of this quite natural Oedipal conflict and I never had an opportunity to react against it or to succumb to it. It was a clean cut. And so then I invented myself. I had to in order to survive. I was struggling to find out who the hell I was and what I was going to do. When I was sixteen I went to the Art Academy in Cincinnati and I never looked back. I never was going to be anything else. Finally, I just did what I had to do. I've always done what I had to do to get the art out.

RE: You're ruthless at that level?

JD: Ruthless at getting the art out. I don't think it has ever hurt anyone. But I would hate for anyone to stand in my way. I mean that.

RE: One of the things you do say in the film is that your self-image as a child was as a Dolby screen on which your mother projected all of her anxiety. I found that both a very moving and a frightening recognition.

JD: Tell me about it.

RE: So it was anxiety-ridden?

JD: Yeah, but it was also great. We were in the midst of the great mythic drama, being wooed, being seduced. It was textbook stuff and it was really exciting. As I said I don't know how it would have ended, but I would have loved the opportunity, as most people have had, to rebel against it, to give in, to work it out.

RE: And your relationship with your father was obviously more troubled?

JD: It was almost nothing. He was a cipher and was jealous of me and, I gather, vice versa. I was the daytime husband and he was the night-time husband.

RE: When you talk about your father in the film you can actually see your face harden. Your contempt is readable.

JD: He was a real asshole. I wanted it to be different, but it never changed. I saw him a year before he died. I hadn't seen him in twenty years. I thought I ought to because I was having that drawing show at the Contemporary Art Center in Cincinnati. I flew out to see him and I asked, "Would you have dinner with me?" He asked if he could bring his girlfriend. He was a tremendous swordsman, as they say. He gave us up for that. I said, "No, I don't want you to bring your girlfriend, I just want to see you." And he said, "Well I can die a peaceful, happy man, now that my famous son has called."

RE: Dripping with irony?

JD: Yeah. So he comes and I asked him things. I said, "What did you think of me as a kid artist?" He said, "Nothing." I said, "Weren't you proud?" He said, "Don't be ridiculous, it didn't mean anything to me. I only used it as a social lever. I could say my son goes to the art museum for classes." That was how loony he was. But it was nice to hear that he didn't care about me; it validated exactly what I imagined. This guy was a real loser. And he went on to have three more sons by the evil stepmother. He should have left her almost immediately. She was a psychopath. The middle son was going to university and she had it all planned that he was going to be a doctor, and he came to her and said, "I want to be a nurse." She said, "I'll kill myself." And he said, "I'm sorry, but that's what I'm going to do." So my father and this boy watched her take pills and she died. They say they thought she was kidding but it's so typical of my father's passivity. The whole thing is like a terrible version of the Jewish mother joke.

RE: Is that a true story?

JD: Yeah, absolutely. She was a maniac, probably the most evil person I ever met, except for my father.

RE: So in a sense you reconciled yourself with your father, because no reconciliation was possible?

JD: I realized what he was. But I didn't have to challenge him. I let him talk. My brother is quite contentious and confrontational.

RE: As opposed to you?

JD: You have no idea really. Honestly, I'm like Winnie the Pooh; I'm Christopher Robin next to my brother.

RE: Did your father explain why you weren't allowed to say goodbye to your mother after she died?

JD: I asked him. He said in those days we just thought it was bad for children to see dead people or to go to funerals. He checked with the Rabbi who agreed with him.

RE: He sent you to a ball game? That was meant to compensate for the death of your mother?

JD: Yeah. He was really a headcase.

RE: I understand the compulsion to construct yourself coming out of that kind of experience but it also has its humorous side. Let me give you an example. In the film there's a segment where you're overlooking Cincinnati. You're outside, wearing a parka and a toque, it's so cold you can see your breath and you say, "This is a southern city."

JD: Right.

RE: Except that it's not. It's your romance through memory that makes the city southern for you.

JD: Sure, that's my myth. Now, it's not like that at all. But it was when I grew up. See, my grandma was southern. She was from Virginia. And my mother was born in Georgia so we had all these relatives down south. There was always talk about the L & N Railway and we always went *down* to Knoxville. We went to Florida twice, and we drove through the South. It was full of romance for me. I was raised by my grandma on Stephen Foster songs.

RE: But there were no mint juleps?

JD: There's no mint julep in our family, I can tell you that. They were as afraid of the Southerners as black people were. My grandma was obsessed with the Ku Klux Klan. She'd say, "Baby, they're gonna get you, the Ku Kluxers."

RE: In the film you said that losing your mother was like an amputation. Have you reconciled yourself to her death yet?

JD: I've reconciled myself to the fact that she will never come back and I will never have the opportunity to say goodbye. I'm totally clear about that.

RE: You've done a very powerful, multi-panelled painting with text that actually deals with your relationship with her. Have you used painting as a way of resolving these things?

JD: No, I've resolved it and I'm still doing it through psychoanalysis. I have tried to be analyzed for thirty-three years, on and off. It never worked until five years ago.

RE: Why would you be receptive to it now?

JD: In those last thirty years it worked as a stopgap measure to keep me from going nuts. It's worked now because there is a certain pressure to make it work. When I was fifty I said I was going to give myself a present by starting again. The process of psychoanalysis and the talent of the person I work with is to get me to understand what I am and how I can turn sand to gold. It has made me able to bring forth the art in a much easier way these days.

RE: Is it the work that tells me who you are, or does the work tell you who you are?

JD: Both. When I said that *The Ape and the Cat* found me I meant it. It told me something about myself and it's still doing that. I have a lot of trouble with the idea of showing this new work. I've never felt that before. I feel that it's self-revelatory in a way that nothing else is. I think it shows there are things about myself that I'm not even clear about. People will get things that I'm not sure I want them to know. I don't know what that is even. I'm not being coy or anything.

RE: Why do you think this work makes you more vulnerable than previous work you've done?

JD: Because it's not a heart that you can hang a landscape on. It's not a metaphor. It is some sort of realism.

RE: You describe yourself as a realistic painter, but you say what you're painting realistically is the inside, not the outside. Is this the outside *and* the inside being painted realistically?

JD: No this is the inside *really* painted realistically. But it's specific, it's this ape and this cat. It's not a bathrobe, it isn't these big overall topics, you know. I don't even know what to title it, other than *Ape and Cat*. And I can't call every one *Ape and Cat 1, Ape and Cat 2, Ape and Cat 3, Ape and Cat 4*—and go to forty or something. That's ridiculous. But if I put a title like I have done in all my other work, then it looks like I'm explaining it, like I'm giving too many clues. Initially, I wanted someone to write something for the catalogue, then I thought I would write something and now I've come to not wanting anything. I don't want people to have a preconceived notion of what it is. I don't want to spoil it.

RE: It's going to be a shock, isn't it?

JD: At the lowest end of the scale there will be dopey people who will make comparisons with Jeff Koons; but that really doesn't make me too nervous because there's too much hand involved.

RE: Where did *The Ape and the Cat* come from in the first place?

JD: I was with one of my pottery dealers, a woman who I am very friendly with. She's been very kind in that she will hold things back for me. She's quite an interesting woman in her own British way. And there was this little Parian figure of people in the guise of an ape and cat, but the man and the woman were actually in mid-nineteenth-century evening clothes. It said: "Picture of a Man and Woman in Ape and Cat Masks," but they weren't because the ape had ape's feet and hands. I don't know why I was moved but I kept asking about it. I would have bought it but it didn't strike me artistically. It was ugly. I asked if I could borrow it and she said "Of course." So I borrowed it for a year and I went to Paris and I made three little drawings. I can't find one now. That summer I went to the foundry at Walla Walla where they photographed it and pointed it up for me in clay. It looked like chocolate and I hated it. So I drew from it. Big. Five or six of the drawings that you saw are drawn from it directly. I pinned them up—I'd just moved in here actually—and people started to comment. Dear friends, people whose eyes I trusted, kept saying there's something going on here. I just kept them for a year. Women in particular were moved by them, which always gets me because I'm very much in awe of women. They then found me, that's all I can say.

RE: Have you always been interested in anthropomorphism? In your second Happening you didn't appear in the second act but what did appear were inanimate objects—vegetables actually—which you manipulated.

JD: I love anthropomorphism.

RE: Because you can invest the whole world with a kind of humanism?

JD: Sure. Including inanimate objects. I loved the way artists in the early twentieth century—Picasso and Schwitters—found things. The glass of absinthe, with the real spoon on this bronze thing. To make a still life that comes off the canvas like that. I had no problem with it at all. As a teenager I thought it was the perfectly right thing to do. It wasn't avant-garde, it wasn't *Les Demoiselles d'Avignon*. This was a real bit of realism.

RE: This seems like a good time to ask you about specific painters to whom you've been attracted. You did a work after Derain. I'm interested to know what it is in his painting that captured your interest?

JD: It was just one of the figure studies that I could copy. That's about it. I wanted to include it in a group of drawings that Connie Glenn curated. I wanted to include it as a way of giving some heft to my new reputation as a figurative drawer. I'm an enthusiastic fan of Derain's up to a point. Firstly, he's a terrible Fascist, and he was a collaborator during the war, so that put me off, but the fact that Giacometti and Balthus and Bacon thought he was great really turned me on. I'm a terrible snob that way. So I looked closer and realized, if nothing else, he is what you would call a painter's painter. He just went and did very intelligent paintings. It's hard looking; that's what gets me about Derain. Sometimes you'll see a Derain that's so dumb and off-centre and awkward, then you see another and it's perfect. He never cared for colour either. It's very hip painting.

RE: Do you know the Balthus portrait of Derain in the bathrobe?

JD: I think it's one of the two great Balthus portraits, the other being of Miró with the suede shoes. The way he painted the suede shoes on Miró is amazing. They're also dandy painters and I like that. I'm very much involved with clothes. It doesn't often look it, but I'm involved with tailoring, have been all my life.

RE: Is Warhol also in that same category of fashion painter?

JD: No. While I don't like the turn art has taken because of Warhol, I consider him the most important influence in painting in the last thirty-five years, without a doubt. He's certainly *the* painter of the '60s, and then some. I think he's taken Duchamp and the art of non-feeling to the "nth" degree, but I think you get what you want. It's like Reagan. We got Warhol and we got Reagan because we wanted them. Who am I to fight nature, except in myself? I'll do what I want, but the rest of the world deserves Warhol. I really do feel that. I went to see Cy Twombly in

Rome in '68 because I was working on a film down there. I was broke and some-body got me a job making paintings for the movie. I hadn't really known Twombly, except to meet him at parties a few times in New York. So I called him and he had me to lunch. He lives like a Cardinal. I don't say that idly; he lives in a Cardinal's apartment from the seventeenth century. He was a very wealthy man even then—his wife was wealthy—and he's very fancy. And he had all these damaged Warhols that he bought very cheaply from Leo Castelli because he knew already what was fashionable. He knew it was very chic, hip-looking. Somebody had put a pencil through one and he loved that look.

RE: I don't want to leave Balthus entirely quite yet. Are you attracted to his ability to draw?

JD: Nobody's ever asked me, so let me think about it. I have to tell you that it's not a new obsession with me. When I was very very young, I knew the drawings from *Wuthering Heights* that looked a bit like Edward Gorey. And I knew the portrait of Miró and his daughter because I had seen it at MOMA when I went there for the first time when I was eighteen. It's almost like something untouchable. Born to this refined family but being befriended by Rilke when he was twelve years old. It's the Walter Mitty in me; it's the upwardly mobile Jew from Ohio in me that said, My God, to start out life like this, to have choices like that. And to choose to live this elegant life and just to make a few paintings. I once went to see some Balthus drawings at Claude Bernard's in Paris and Bernard said, "Oh yes, Balthus wants to buy another castle so he just made these." And I thought, What an amazing thing to do. Art is currency; it's all about supply and demand. I hate to take it to such a crass, sheeny level but that's it.

RE: People might think your attraction to him would be on the basis of the danger involved in the explicit sexuality of his work.

JD: That doesn't interest me at all. I don't think it's dangerous in the first place. That's not brave. He's just a realist painter. He's a very good artist who's way out of his league in the century but that's part of the charm. No, it's something else. It's the elegance, the life. And it's the sense of history: he knew what was great in all painting. Piero della Francesca understood completely and he shows it. Balthus shows how much he understood these people. He understands every little mark too. Unlike Johns, who I often think is just beautifully done masturbation. Johns—as they would say in the underworld here—knows how to pull his meat. But Balthus is something else. He knows about every mark relating to history, not relating to his personal pleasure. He learned about the marks. A very elegant, dandy painter. And its about tailoring. What I like about Balthus and what I like about tailoring is the attention to detail. I like that there's still somebody who would care to do that, to make it finer.

RE: Ezra Pound said that, "technique is the test of a man's sincerity." I mention it to get at the question of what I think you call craftsmanship and what Pound would probably have called technique. Is it a touchstone for you?

JD: It's a pressure, an aspiration and an ambition of mine, but I do not discount the craftsmanship Rauschenberg talked about when he said, "I conceive a great drawing when a tire goes over a piece of paper." I really do believe in that too. I was in my bank the other day and there were these ten Basquiat's, who I don't even consider an artist—but I have to admit I thought they were great. I've never admitted that to anybody. It was what I call second-rate ghetto art that brings down the culture and I don't mean that in a racist way. Here was something; the marks were beautiful, the way the oil formed around them on the paper. I liked the way the dopey words were written. I just liked everything about them.

RE: I don't think he has any middle range. The cartoonlike drawings in the Whitney Retrospective were wonderful and I admired his large scale works. But the entire middle range seemed banal and flat.

JD: He was lionized and deified before he produced a really mature body of work. Maybe he was Rimbaud. Who knows what would have happened. Maybe nothing.

RE: I want to ask you about a particularly fallow period in your early career. From 1966 to 1969 you hardly did any painting or drawing.

JD: Just a little bit of painting. Otherwise I just wrote a lot of poems, corresponded with a lot of people and went out at night.

RE: Were you a very good poet?

JD: Not too bad. I like some poets: Olson and Creeley and Ted Berrigan. I was always a big fan of Walt Whitman. I've had a lot of pleasure from poetry because it was easier for me to read than novels. Because it's shorter.

RE: I've always felt that one of the greatest inventions of American poetry was Walt Whitman. He invented the barbaric yawp. Do you feel close to him as a poet for that reason, does the largeness of his personality appeal to you?

JD: No, the romance appealed to me. The same way with Emily Dickinson; it's the romance that gets me.

RE: You use that word a lot. You say you go where your romance takes you.

JD: That's what I really feel. And it never lets up with me either. I've never lost it. And that's what I love about Munch too. He's a great romantic painter.

RE: David Shapiro says an interesting thing in his monograph about you. He contrasts you with the luminous Hudson River School and says you represent the dark side of the American sensibility. Do you go along with that?

JD: Yes, absolutely. That's my pleasure. That's why I like Scandinavia in the winter time. I like it when it doesn't get light very much. I like skiing in the dark; I like walking on a street in Oslo, looking in people's windows and seeing they're not watching television.

RE: But is the darkness also part of your sensibility?

JD: The primary subject matter of my art is being able to call up the darkness.

RE: Do you have to call it up or is it there waiting just below the surface?

JD: It's pretty much the natural way it takes me. If I were to follow my nose I would go down the dark corridor, not into the light.

RE: Are there things that you won't go near as an artist, things that you don't want to expose?

JD: You mean things in me? Not that I know of. At least, they haven't been revealed to me. All of it's difficult to do because—first and foremost—I want to make art. I don't want to get out my soap opera. So it is difficult sometimes to walk this fine line. And sometimes the confrontational nature of my work puts people off and is embarrassing to me. I let my work sit around me a long time before I let it out. Then I can get it before it happens.

RE: You started the drawings for *The Ape and the Cat* three years ago?

JD: Yeah. I've kept them around and I fuck with them. Like I noodle around and I enhance things, or I bring things back and then get rid of them. That's my method; erasing and correcting. I like chopping and rebuilding, putting things back together.

RE: In talking about the van Gogh drawings you referred to the sense of fear you had when you started. At the same time you have enough confidence to know that you can erase a fabulous drawing and then do it again because you know you can make it better. That strikes me as either stupid or incredibly courageous.

JD: It's how I teach too. Whenever I've taught—and it's usually drawing—I always insist that my students erase whatever they've done that's good. Because I believe you can do it again. It isn't stupid. Plus you get a dividend. You get the pentimento. So you get your history *and* you get something to build on.

RE: There's no risk that you can lose it?

JD: Of course there is. That's the deal and that's the fun of it too. It's always there; it's like walking a wire. It makes the work itself—not the content of the work—all the more interesting.

RE: One of the things I've admired about Hemingway is that he used to stop writing when he was really hot because he couldn't face the blank page the next morning. He always knew where he was going the next time he sat down to write.

JD: I have no fear of the blank page. Maybe it's also a lack of confidence to be afraid to leave something so fresh. How could it possibly be any good if you did it the first time? Lately I've noticed that there are certain things I've left that ordinarily I would have gotten rid of.

RE: You can be sentimental then?

JD: Don't you think? I don't mind sentimentality.

RE: You've used that telling phrase, "the pentimento of destruction." Clearly it draws attention to a submersion and a revelling in the darker side of your sensibility.

JD: Right. It's staying down in the depths with the pentimento. In the basement. Always my dreams are about the basement. That's when I'm the healthiest.

RE: In this connection—the world of darkness—I'm interested in the theatre work you did on *A Midsummer Night's Dream* and in *The Picture of Dorian Gray*. Were they useful projects in helping you get to the figure? In doing costumes I assume you were dealing with the figure in a fairly direct way?

JD: That was part of how I came to be a figurative artist. It's funny but nobody's ever asked me that before. One of the pleasures of those two works was making costume drawings because I was able to be a figurative artist without being called revisionist. It was a tremendous well of material. I did the drawings in two days. This goes back to the beginning of our conversation about the newness of things. There was this thing against the figure. Now Red Grooms was a wonderful figurative artist in the circle of Lester Johnson, the American figurative expressionist who painted very dark figures with lots of paint. So much better than Frank Auerbach because it's not bullshit; it's not *sturm und drang* for no reason other than to tell you how serious the painter is. Johnson was a wonderful American painter whose best paintings were in the '50s, I think. They're not so good now. There was a very strong thing around the Hansa Gallery too. And while Jan Müller wasn't a very good artist, his paintings spoke to me as a student, more than so-called abstract art. But when I came to New York, abstraction was all around us. Oldenburg had also been a wonderful figurative painter before he was a sculptor. He painted like Lovis Corinth, really glib and with a great touch.

RE: Is that what you meant when you said he had the potential to be the greatest draftsman of the century?

JD: I think so. I don't really feel that now because he's gone another way. Drawing means a lot to him. He's a terrific draftsman but as Wayne Thiebaud once said to me, "He didn't draw deeply enough." So even though Lester Johnson spoke to me, I felt I had to go my own way. I had to make something that was new. That's what we all felt. We were these careerist, ambitious young men who were trying to find ways to have a camaraderie but also become known at the moment when Abstract Expressionism ended and something else began. No one quite knew what was going on but it did happen in 1953 when de Kooning and Rauschenberg and Johns started to do these things. We came out of that. It's as simple as that. Now when I made my first bathrobe I really did want to make a drawing of myself. I just couldn't allow myself to do it. Moving to Europe really got me into the figurative tradition. I heard the harangue from Kitaj and from Hockney. I was not friendly with Hockney but I thought he was a really interesting, inventive painter at that time. Around 1967 or 1968 he had a show in Kasmin's. It was full of ideas, terrifically funny and very gay and I thought he was very brave. Like he had no problems. And I thought that was also a product of being from Europe. It was not American bullshit. I thought he was a terrific draftsman too. I was very respectful of him and Kitaj. But I also was not a dope. I knew what I wanted out of art. I already knew Giacometti and I had seen a lot of Balthus's paintings. In 1973 it looked to me like I was becoming a colour-field painter with objects. I was at a dead end and I just thought I've got to stop what I'm doing and just draw from the figure. And immediately I was good because I had been looking all this time and looking very hard. Then it got bad because I was trying to draw deeper. I had to learn how to invent the invention. I had to invent a way to rebuild the figures and I did it by drawing myself, my wife and my neighbour, Jessie Heller. I hardly drew anyone else but Jessie and Nancy—mainly Jessie.

RE: Because you knew them or because they were close at hand?

JD: They were close at hand and it was very practical. With Nancy it was also an emotional thing. It was somehow important to our relationship at that time that I draw her. With Jessie it was strictly business. She was slightly anorexic, but she was also a great skier and runner, so everything was very articulated. She was very weird and she could stay still forever.

RE: So those were the drawings where you "regarded" her, to use your word, for hours and hours?

JD: I looked at the articulation of her muscles, which was very moving to me. I swear every day I thank God for the opportunity to draw like that.

RE: Have you always been a regarder, a careful looker at things?

JD: Totally. I remember everything and I remember looking at everything. I make people around me—people who are close to me—nervous a lot of the time. Nancy, who's known me for forty years, will say "What are you looking at?" I'm not even aware I'm doing it, but it's about drawing.

RE: I like "regarding" because it's a more subtle word than "looking." It means looking with care, to have regard for the thing looked at.

JD: Absolutely, that's why I use it. It's the way I draw. That's what the looking is about. That's why I was able to arrive full-blown when I started figure drawing in '74. Then the doubt set in and I retaught myself.

RE: This is the period during which you only did twenty drawings a year, drawings which you worked and reworked and reworked?

JD: Over and over again. I kept on erasing, took it out, brought it back, took it out. There was plenty of other good stuff that I got rid of, but it was really worth it to do that.

RE: In a number of those drawings *eros* and *thanatos* seem to commingle rather easily. When you use the skull, Jessie either seems to be giving birth to it, or the skull is performing a sexual act on her. You don't read those images neutrally.

JD: It's hard to read them neutrally now but when I did them I was unconscious about what I was doing. I just thought, take the skull, hold it because it looks historical.

RE: Come on, you're too aware of the metaphoric possibilities of the object.

JD: I tried to keep it at bay. I didn't even want to deal with it. And I just thought it makes me more like an artist if there's a skull in there. It's the way I became involved with the Venus de Milo too. I bought it in an art store and painted it in the still life because I wanted to feel more like a real artist. My idea of a real artist was a before-the-twentieth-century European artist.

RE: So part of your interest in antiquity was a way of validating your own art-making?

JD: Sure, it's a validation. The drawings from antiquity are meditations on the culture, on the fact that I didn't come from nowhere.

RE: But in a drawing like *Jessie Dreaming the High Life* you heighten the genitals so much so that it seems an image out of Boucher. You're aware of the effect of focusing on certain areas. You'll give more weight to the breasts, or you'll pull the nipple out into a red pout.

JD: It's not about me thinking about doing that, though. It's like a meditation and suddenly I'm fixed on that. I realize it can piss people off. Riva Castleman came up and saw those drawings and she was shocked. She hated all those high-lights. Whereas for me, I couldn't get it high enough. I was so enthusiastic that I had power in my hands to do what I wanted. I wasn't in there totally neutral. It was always an erotic situation. Without that tension, there would have been no drawings. Otherwise I would have drawn landscapes.

RE: William Faulkner said that he wanted to get the entire world into one sentence. It occurs to me that one of your compulsions is to get the entire world into one drawing?

JD: I want them full and dense. I envy Matisse's being able to make these single line drawings. I really envy that but I could never sit with it. That's like five minutes right, and then I just would have to screw around with it. I'm a fanatic, like Khomeini, except it's about painting.

RE: I'm always interested in knowing how Americans think of themselves in relation to European tradition. You've been fairly straightforward in assigning yourself to the great tradition of European draftsmanship.

JD: Who am I going to look to? I mean Albert Pinkham Ryder is a good painter but he's not William Blake. If you're talking visionaries you're not talking about Pinkham Ryder. I know Winslow Homer's a wonderful artist but he isn't Courbet. He isn't as good as his peers in Europe at the same time.

RE: But at the same time you say you still paint like a Cincinnati painter and you figure you always will. Are these contradictions?

JD: They aren't contradictions because Ohio made me and that's where I experienced Europe first. In books, in the museum and in my grandpa's front parlour, with his accent, his tales of eastern Europe, his superstitions and his deep, deep primitive culture. He had no schooling whatsoever and he came here when he was eighteen. He spoke German and Yiddish and English very well and he played the violin. He was a smart guy who was a European. He wasn't a Philistine; he didn't put down great music. It wasn't just a work ethic.

RE: Are you serious when you say that a day doesn't go by when you don't pull out a book and compare what you're doing with something that one of the master's has done?

JD: You've got to face yourself. I look in the mirror every day. I mean I don't specifically go and pick up Piero della Francesca every day, but I'm surrounded by books about art and archaeology and I look at them all the time. Also because of my learning disabilities—I'm dyslexic—I prefer looking at pictures to reading. I often read backwards. In a bookstore I'll stand and read something that I wouldn't get in my living room where I have to sit by myself. One of the hardest things about being me is to sit with myself. I get hyperactive and claustrophobic. The drawing has also taught me to sit and to erase and to go back and to sit again.

RE: Are you constantly having to contain yourself?

JD: I constantly have to contain myself, period. Otherwise I would be too destructive. And I'm not interested in that. I'm interested in constructive things. I'm interested in building on one's gifts, on what you've got and making it better.

RE: You've mentioned de Kooning a fair amount. Tell me about him in the early years and what influence he had on you?

JD: He was a sensational man. I first met him in 1962 when I had just gone with Sidney Janis—he was still with Janis as well. Sidney had this show called New Realists and de Kooning came to it with Philip Johnson. When he was introduced to me he said, "You know Dine, you're a real painter." It was a very generous thing to say because Rothko and Guston had left the gallery when Sidney took on me and the other realists. But before that he had meant a lot to me. *Asheville* meant a lot to me and *Easter Monday* at the Metropolitan Museum. He had some way of blotting the white with newspaper in which he wasn't just blotting the white, he was leaving the imprint of the city on it. He was aware of what he was doing, probably the most intelligent person I've ever met.

RE: Obviously that would appeal to your sense of urban romanticism?

JD: Not only that. It appealed to my sense of collage and of found objects. What he was really doing was leaving a found object on this painting. No one talks about that. But it certainly appealed to *his* sense of urban romance. He and Franz Kline were always talking about that.

RE: When he said "you're a real painter" it must have been like having the clouds part and hearing God voice his approval.

JD: It was a generous thing because I was surrounded by so many ungenerous people. The art world is full of ungenerous people. He didn't need to say it and I'll always be in his debt. It didn't validate anything. I knew I was a real painter. I knew I hadn't become an artist to my satisfaction yet, but I knew what he meant. He meant I had the touch.

Roy Lichtenstein

Pop Goes the Tradition

The Roy Lichtenstein Retrospective, organized by the Guggenheim Museum in 1994, caught me off guard. I had expected the show, overall, to be characterized by clever, graphically engaging paintings, then punctuated by specific works which had legitimately attained a reputation as Pop Art icons. The exhibition delivered on both these counts. Paintings like *Look Mickey* (1961), *The Engagement Ring* (1961), *Popeye* (1961), *Blam* (1962), *Takka Takka* (1962) and *Hopeless* (1963) define Pop Art in ways that most people who have seen them in reproduction would be unable to articulate but in ways they would certainly understand. What I wasn't prepared for was the range of paintings and sculpture, and their consistently high quality. In the almost thirty-five years since he painted *Look Mickey*, Lichtenstein has produced a body of work of remarkable visual and conceptual vigour. He emerged from this show not merely as the singularly most important Pop painter in America but as one of the singularly most important painters of his entire generation. How he went from his self-description as "a mid-western teacher coming to New York and looking at the scene from a distance" to his leading role as a painter at the centre of one of the most influential movements in the history of contemporary art, is an amazing transformation. The change seemed abrupt even to Lichtenstein: "I was doing Abstract Expressionism the moment before I did Pop" is the way he recalls the sequence of events and while he admits that the rejection of Abstract Expressionism was "a little traumatic," it's something he did with a sense of no-turning-back exhilaration.

Who would have thought that turning the page of a comic book would fundamentally alter the content and range of American painting in the sixties? Lichtenstein had done some paintings and drawings using comic book and cartoon characters as subject matter prior to painting *Look Mickey* but they were rendered in the style of the New York School. If you cover any distinguishing feature of *Donald Duck*, a 1958 India ink on paper drawing, it looks like it could have been done by Philip Guston. Lichtenstein recognized there was something unnecessarily evasive about his style and he decided "to do it more like the thing I was copying from." Pop went the tradition.

By ransacking images from cartoons, comics, advertising and from other artists (he does his first quotational painting from Picasso as early as 1962) Lichtenstein was able to produce work of surprising inventiveness and enviable visual clarity. He possessed an impeccable sense of which objects would make good subjects— a golf ball, a magnifying glass, an advertisement for a honeymoon lodge, a cheaply printed still life, a romance or a war comic, even a single word—all of these printed sources were enlarged, simplified and recast as paintings which celebrated the quotidian no less than they celebrated the act of painting what—only moments before, to use his own telescoped sense of time—had been marginalized and disregarded.

I'm emphasizing the celebratory aspect of his work because Lichtenstein remained uninterested in investigating the darker dimensions of the imagery of Pop. There was nothing in his sensibility—as there was in Andy Warhol, the other colossus in the Pop pantheon—that drew him towards the disastrous, the spectacular or the macabre. Lichtenstein is unapologetically cheerful and bright without ever giving over to the banal or the superficial.

I want to be careful, though, not to portray Lichtenstein as a kind of genial naïve wandering through the candy store of popular culture and nominating one *bonbon* after another to the status of "high" low art. His flawless judgment underscores an abiding intelligence that seems from the distance of three-and-a-half decades to be inevitable, even canonical. It's a virtue he has always sustained, even as his later art became progressively more concerned with his own earlier art. From the beginning Lichtenstein was a quotational painter; he developed into a self-quotational painter. So *Look Mickey* is reprised as a painting on the wall in *Artist's Studio No. 1* (1973); in *Still Life with Goldfish Bowl* (1972), Lichtenstein keeps the red fish from Matisse's famous 1912 still life *Goldfish and Sculpture* but he replaces the sculpture with a looming golf ball that is appropriated from his own sixties work. That the original golf ball painting in 1962 was both a tribute to and a play on an early Mondrian abstraction called *Composition in Black and White* (1917) will give you an idea about how layered, witty and complex is Lichtenstein's painting process. (It's worth pointing out that he was a lender as well as a borrower. His audacious word paintings from 1962—like *IN* and *ART*—where the piece consists of a single word realized in massive black letters, anticipate the work of later artists like Jenny Holzer and Ken Lum.)

Lichtenstein forces us into a world of painting, a world that while it unabashedly quotes from other painters and from popular sources, is now so thoroughly his own invention that he seems its sole proprietor.

This interview with Roy Lichtenstein took place in his New York studio in June of 1994.

ROBERT ENRIGHT: Back in the early '60s, did you have a sense of the significance of what you and other artists were doing?

ROY LICHTENSTEIN: The problem is that the same lack of insight judging the era is producing the paintings, so it's really hard to know. Yes, I thought it meant something and I'm surprised at how long the influence has been. It did change the era for better or worse and I do think in retrospect that it was important because Minimal and Conceptual Art really had their roots in the early part of the '60s.

RE: Was there a sense of aggressive rejection of the tradition you had inherited through Abstract Expressionism?

RL: I think I was pretty conscious of that, although I loved the Abstract Expressionists. And it was an era that I was brought up in and it meant a lot. Everything I was taught wasn't Abstract Expressionism but it implied that kind of painting. I just felt it had gone on quite a while. The idea of changing it altogether was a little traumatic and I wondered whether anybody would accept the art. But in a way I didn't care because for the first time I really thought I had something and whether people accepted it or not wasn't really that important.

RE: Did you feel a sense of exhilaration and freedom?

RL: Yeah, I did. And actually there were quite a few people who did like it, although most of the criticism was against it.

RE: Why did you go to school in Ohio?

RL: Well, there were very few schools that gave degrees in studio art in 1940. I thought it would be good to go away and there was no New York scene that I knew of. So it was a combination of wanting to see more of the country, getting out of New York, wanting to study art and my parents wanting me to have a degree.

RE: Were you living in a kind of exile there? Did you feel out of touch?

RL: I did finally when the New York School became more obvious. That was after the war in '46 and then I felt I should really be in New York. My first show was in 1951 but it was from Ohio. I would come to New York every chance I got, but I was still a mid-western teacher looking at the scene from a distance.

RE: You came to Douglass College in 1960 when Allan Kaprow was teaching there. Was there a sense of excitement back then?

RL: Yeah, there was. I'd been teaching up in Oswego—which wasn't the centre of the world—and trying to get to New York. But I had children and a wife and so I had to have a job. Through a lot of luck Reginald Neal, who was head of the department, came up to visit a friend and invited us both to come down. It turns out my friend had already gotten a job at MIT, so only I came down. Luckily it was a bit of a centre and it put me right near New York. There were a lot of Fluxus people and Kaprow who was an entrée into Happenings.

RE: Did you have much in common with the Fluxus sensibility?

RL: Nothing. But I was interested in the Happenings and Environments of Oldenburg and Kaprow and Dine. It seemed like an expansion of painting. I was looking at the idea of expanding painting from Pollock into the whole room. It had an Abstract Expressionist feeling about it which I was still into. But it had objects that were American—like Kaprow's tires and some of Oldenburg's things, things that looked like signs in stores.

RE: Were you going to Judson as well? Were you seeing all of the Performances and Happenings?

RL: A lot of them. Although it still wasn't really what I wanted to do. I never thought of doing it. I was painting Abstract Expressionist versions of Mickey Mouse and it suddenly occurred to me to do it more like the thing I was copying from. At the time it didn't seem to tie into anything, but of course the vernacular attitude of the Happenings must have played into it.

RE: You said they were using American themes. Was part of what they were doing a repatriation of the act of art-making?

RL: Maybe I'm reading into it, but I do think that a part of what they were doing was to put objects into these things that were not European. I think they wanted to de-Europeanize it.

RE: Were you all aware of making an American idiom? Was that a conscious thing?

RL: Everyone said it right from the beginning, except that I would like to think of it as industrial rather than American. The US was the industrial nation and we had all of the junk that people think they need. Europe was in shambles still.

RE: Léger had an industrial idiom as well.

RL: Yeah, but it still had the hand even if it was trying to be mechanical. But then my earlier things did too. I thought they were mechanical but in retrospect they seem rather crudely drawn. Léger also had an optimistic sense that you could build things for workers and farmers. Mine are much more ironic. But there certainly is a relationship between Léger and me.

RE: I want to talk about your famous declaration that you wanted to make a painting so "despicable" that no one would hang it. The British critic Lawrence Alloway says you were given that word by a critic. I guess a better way to pose the question is to ask how ugly you wanted your paintings to be?

RL: Well, "despicable" really is a pretty harsh word to use. I didn't want people to think my work was really despicable, although a lot of them did, and do. But there was a thing at the time that allowed people to hang almost anything—anything except commercial art—and the more abstract and the more expressionist the better. But I don't think I really decided any of this. I just had an impulse to do it one day and the rest was rationalized after the fact.

RE: A painting like *Look Mickey* was a sea change in a way. Did you know it was a radical painting, or had you already been playing with the subject matter enough that it didn't seem so preposterous?

RL: It seemed preposterous to me because it was different from anything I had done. I thought nobody would even look at them, but I liked the idea very much and I thought I had something. It wasn't that it was vernacular so much as it was about precision. Not being expressionist wasn't so unusual. I think it was probably that the whole cartoon thing couldn't be art.

RE: Was there also a compulsion to distance yourself from what Rauschenberg and Johns were doing because they had used some Pop imagery in a few pieces? Did you feel it necessary to make two leaps in order to find your own idiom?

RL: I had seen their work but I wasn't thinking about it really. I was aware of certain things but not enough to know that Jasper had done things that were really cartoons and that Rauschenberg had used Coke bottles.

RE: Had you seen *Rebus*, which Rauschenberg had made as early as 1955?

RL: Yes, I had. It just seemed to me that all I was doing was trying to reconstruct a cartoon and use a two-dimensional subject. I've always used two-dimensional subjects. Then later I realized what the influences were.

RE: Once you started there was no stopping you. It seems that from '61 right through to '65 you produced an enormous amount of work which consistently employed cartoon imagery.

RL: Cartoon or yellow pages or things printed on boxes. Something printed. And it was that kind of bad drawing or what you think of as "how-to-draw" drawing that I was interested in doing.

RE: What's so intriguing now is the sheer energy and the volume of it.

RL: I was very excited.

RE: Were you consciously haunting the shops where you would buy material? Did you go and buy romance comics?

RL: I did.

RE: So did you become an aficionado or were they just a source for you?

RL: They were just the source. I found out a lot of people knew a lot about comics, things like when Popeye had his first spinach can. I knew absolutely nothing.

RE: What was the appeal they had for you? The subject matter itself?

RL: It was the humour, mixed with the possibility of making a painting that had a different tonality. The dots and the unmodulated areas could result in a tonality that was different. Because of the contrast it was very strong to look at and it seemed to say a lot about printing and what information is given. It said that it's a fake and it's either copied or printed matter or it symbolized the fact that it was worthless. All of that. Maybe that has its own pretension but it seemed unpretentious. I think it was very hard for people to see where the art was and I liked that.

RE: But it wasn't hard for you to realize where the art was? You were always trying to make good paintings.

RL: Most people thought I was just being Dada, or that by bringing a cartoon into a museum I was making a statement. People were upset that it wasn't transformed, that I was really redoing the cartoon. I think they were thrown by the subject matter being two-dimensional which had certain ramifications: it wasn't a picture of a cartoon lying on a table, it was the cartoon right up front. No matter what the perspective was, the dots and diagonals would keep being on the surface because they were all the same size. So I was making a thing more than a picture of something. Of course within the cartoon is a picture of something. But I'm only painting the cartoon. I really think that's important and it's true of all of the things I do. I also believe that all art really comes from two-dimensional sources. When you think you're drawing from nature you're really drawing your version of Titian already figured out by somebody else.

RE: You're sounding like a Greenbergian here.

RL: Well his point of view is pretty good although I'm not so fond of the art he picked out.

RE: What about scale? I mean scale obviously played importantly into this whole process. Were you aware of the necessity of making art that had a certain presence on the wall?

RL: Yeah, but I don't think that my paintings from that time were really so big that the subject matter seemed enlarged. It was big for a magnifying glass but compared with Abstract Expressionist paintings—or certainly Renaissance painting—mine really weren't that big.

RE: What about this question of personality and style? Was your work about objectivity, or was there a fair investment of yourself in it?

RL: I think it's me. I don't think you can put two marks together, for better or worse, that aren't you. And it has a lot of personal characteristics that, in retrospect, weren't really suited for Abstract Expressionism. I'm rather tidy and irony is part of it. But I hate to think there's no emotion in my work just because it's portraying something that has no emotion. I'm allowing for more change than it seems. I use a lot of collage. All of the black on that painting over there is tape; I just take it off and move it. It'll be paint when I'm done but at this stage it makes an exacting line. The line can get bigger and smaller and move very easily. I usually use methods like collage that can be changed, but then when it's painted it looks as though I must have thought this all out beforehand. Even if the process—collage or painting—starts out as a mess, it winds up being tidy.

RE: There's a way in which your career seems to have been intelligently conceived and orchestrated. Is that going too far? Is that making you too tidy?

RL: I don't think about that really. I think one thing comes out of another and I have no idea why. Sometimes I get more and more complex as I seem to be doing in the studio work here and then I'll do something extremely simple. It seems to alternate that way.

RE: There's an interesting process of reduction that goes on in your work. I'm thinking of the mirrors and the entablatures and a painting like *Like New* which is a canvas with a hole painted on it. Your bodies of work ultimately reduce themselves to an essential, minimal statement.

RL: I think I might have just got the idea from something I saw. That particular painting was a diptych—which is usually a religious image—portraying something mundane. But I could also visualize that it would be interesting to do images that were very minimal.

RE: The landscapes are relatively reduced; the mirrors become that. Everything gets pared down.

RL: The mirrors came because I had a brochure on mirrors. And there's no way to portray a mirror because it just reflects the room. It doesn't really have diagonal stripes. It's just obviously funny to look into a painting and not be able to see anything.

RE: There's a small mirror that looks like a tribute to Mondrian. It has a little bit of red on the rim along with a yellow and white palette.

RL: They often had rims on them because they would reflect light. It made it interesting through peripheral stimulation. You still have to tell people it's a mirror because they don't look anything like a mirror. We are used to those diagonal lines in comics as standing for a mirror.

RE: You actually take insubstantial things and make them substantial.

RL: I'm always like that. I mean the explosions are like that. Some of them are porcelain on steel and you could make them even harder. But the cartoonists already had made a beautiful bouquet or something out of it. And water glasses and then sculptured lamps that were held up by their rays. Cartoonists invented this process of realizing something that really has no form. I just don't think they were struck by its irony.

RE: Your sensibility has a strong sense of play which keeps curling back into irony. Is that an essential tone of your character?

RL: Basically it is. I don't know that everything I've done has been like that, but almost everything.

RE: I want to go back briefly. By '62 or '63 you're already doing paintings which could be called quotational. Where did the impulse come so early on to do a kind of meta-art?

RL: I don't know. I guess I was struck by the idea of a Picasso which you could do easily. Something that looked like a Picasso and yet you would know it wasn't. I was always very influenced by Picasso.

RE: I just assumed that the first *Brush Stroke* would have come directly from Abstract Expressionism. So I was surprised to find out that it also came from a cartoon source.

RL: It was in a comic book, I just don't know which one. Somebody was painting a fence and it had a hand and a brush in the painting. I realized it would be more interesting to do it without the hand and the brush and just use the brush strokes. Because the brush stroke symbolizes art and besides, it's a bravura statement done very painstakingly. I knew it would look like Abstract Expressionism but it wasn't really supposed to be anti-Expressionist. It was just that it had its own contradictions. But even then I thought it inevitable that it would be taken as a statement against Expressionism.

RE: How do you keep interested?

RL: Sometimes I think up something that is interesting as a way to go, then each painting has its own problems. It's always interesting to try to get it together so it works.

RE: Each painting also generates its own continuing genealogy. Is there a way in which your paintings are now at the stage where your own art is feeding itself?

RL: There's a lot of my putting my own pictures into it, but that's not unusual. Matisse and everybody did that. But I think it's funnier when I do it. I don't mean funny just because what I do is funny. When Matisse portrays his own work it's done with a certain atmosphere, but with me it's just pasted on. It isn't any different from the rest of the painting. It has just the same amount of contrast, there's no modulation to give you any sense of atmosphere or remove from the work. It's just put on. There's something about that that I like.

RE: But by the time you do *Studio No. 1* with Mickey in the background you're entirely aware of your own history?

RL: Yeah.

RE: What about the *Large Interior with Three Reflections*? The *film noir* figure with the girl in the background and the hand curving around is vaguely threatening. There's something going on there, and then when you paint the reverse of the female figure it becomes even more problematic.

RL: That particular one looks like a plot to a story, as if something happened in the room. I didn't start out with that idea but it got to look that way with little clues and various things. But the cigar is there because the man who bought the painting is the head of a cigar company. A completely mundane reason for being there.

RE: But it establishes a narrative?

RL: Yeah, which isn't usually the case. I mean there was no sign of a human, except for a used ashtray.

RE: I notice that you've been eroticizing the work in the last little while. What's the reason for that?

RL: It started out as my idea of mixing chiaroscuro—done with dots and shading—with flat areas of colour, which is a complete inconsistency. Nobody I know has used it. Now with a nude the surface is curvilinear. You can put any kind of a shadow on it and it takes its place somewhere. But I found that it doesn't really make any difference whether it's a nude or a jar of something. You can do it with anything. So it originated with an art problem rather than with the nude. But then I also thought that the nudes would disappear because this idea I had in my head was so strong. It isn't that way at all. If you draw three lines that look like a nude, people see a nude. And the nude is just too ...

RE: Loaded ...?

RL: Loaded, yeah. I don't mind that it is. It's kind of amusing that you just paint them and leave the clothes off and it means something much different. It's more riveting.

RE: Are you still bewildered by what you end up making?

RL: I've got the idea by now.

RE: I wasn't asking if you're stupid.

RL: Yes, some of that. I'm sure everybody else has the idea too. I keep looking at the paint to reaffirm that what I'm saying actually has something to do with this work.

RE: Pierre Restany wrote an early article on the New Realists where he talked about the necessity of appropriation. I wonder how influential that notion was?

RL: We were appropriating things from commercial art. It wasn't appropriation in the way that you couldn't tell the difference. But it isn't much different from artists using the work of other artists. It's been done a lot. We might have been a bit more ironic and maybe we did more of it.

RE: Did you think of it as an act of homage too? They weren't parody, which carries with it a certain sense of disregard and disdain for the source. I sense in your work something that is closer to respect and care.

RL: Well most of the people I did I like a lot. But I don't think it was homage. It's really just redoing it in my style, which makes it then fake and ordinary along with all the other things it's supposed to symbolize. It isn't that different from Picasso doing Velasquez. It was probably considered vernacularizing and denigrating when he did it. But now they're both viewed as masterpieces.

RE: I suspect that Picasso's impulse was to declare himself a *modern* master in the same tradition that viewed Velasquez as an *old* master. I guess I'm asking a question about the scale of ego in your case.

RL: I don't think it has that scale of ego. I hope it doesn't. Because it's not supposed to look as though I did it any good, or that I added to it in any way. I just made it more accessible.

RE: How do you decide which artists to choose?

RL: I couldn't find a way into many artists because they simply wouldn't look either like mine or like themselves. But I thought Picasso would work out well and I did Mondrian very early on. Léger would have been a little too close at that time.

RE: And then you felt you could go back and claim him when you were more secure?

RL: Yeah, I don't have any that's purely Léger though.

RE: Were you surprised by the Guggenheim show?

RL: First of all I thought it would be very hard to show at the Guggenheim because of the way the museum is designed. But I was really happy with the way it looked. And it's terrific to see paintings you haven't seen for a long time.

RE: Did it tell you anything at all? Did you learn from the show?

RL: I don't know. It meant something to me but I don't think I could say that I thought of any particular way to go because of it.

RE: Your work has been so much about your own work for a long time so it's not as if you needed a prod to take advantage of what you've already done.

RL: Maybe that's why I didn't expect to find a way of proceeding by looking at the show. But I'm sure its going to have some influence in some way I don't know yet.

RE: Do things percolate for you?

RL: Very much. I get an idea that I don't follow through and then it comes up again in my mind. The early *Brush Strokes* looked like bacon or something. I couldn't make out what they were and finally I figured out how to do it. When I was trying to make landscapes out of brush strokes—which I thought could say something about what a landscape painting is—the first things looked like objects with melted wax on them. It didn't portray what I meant; it just took awhile to get into it. I don't know what I did that made it work. I get ideas in the middle of the night that in the morning seem just ridiculous.

RE: You don't seem to run out of ideas. Your imagination seems fairly fertile.

RL: I don't want to jinx it by saying anything. So far so good I guess.

RE: Some of your works on one subject are complicated; others are simple. In a compositional sense, have you always been able to move across that spectrum?

RL: That's what I seem to do a lot.

RE: Is it just temperamental and not something you plan?

RL: It just happens. It may be relief that I've finally thought of a simple thing to do.

RE: Other than what won't work, I gather there's nothing you won't do. I mean there's nothing you don't feel you can give yourself permission to do.

RL: Only if I can't think of any way to make it into "art." I hate to use that word; I would love to think of something else.

RE: Does taste matter to you? I know this would be a strange question back in 1961, but since you've been making elegant, beautiful paintings, it seems an appropriate question.

RL: I was tasteless you mean?

RE: I mean you're a tasty painter. Is the whole idea of beauty something that concerns you?

RL: Well, I think you've got to transcend your own level of taste. That's part of how you go on and I don't think I continue to do that. I think I did that once and that brought me into Pop Art. They probably become tastier because they weren't particularly elegant at the beginning. I don't know. It wasn't my original intention. If something had obvious taste, or was too beautiful in a certain way, I would think it would be nauseating. Or too "pop" without any substance—which is true of a lot of Pop.

RE: Do you have to obliterate something to reuse it? I'm wondering how much of a compulsion there is to deconstruct a thing so that you can find ways to continually reuse it and keep yourself interested?

RL: Because I'm reusing a lot of images, or images I might have done, it does look that way doesn't it? I never thought of it. Some of them just appear because I need red over here and so I just put some marks down. It might become a woman or it might become a picture. When I'm sketching I'm just wondering and I just put something down and see what it develops into. I don't know if I'm answering your question. I'm not sure it's a good idea because you don't want your paintings to be built on taste exactly. It could be part of it but it's not enough.

RE: You've mentioned the word "reuse" before. The question for me is: what's involved in the process of making something out of something already made, and how much does the remake have to alter, or destroy, the source?

RL: What I liked about putting Mickey into that artist studio painting was that there wasn't any change. You have to change other things to make the thing work. You really can't just plaster the painting on it. But I want it to look that way. Of course, I just made up these other things while I was doing the composition. They may look like individual things but I say they're paintings because they have frames around them. I can use almost anything if I bend it around enough. It's better to keep thinking of the whole painting and change the things you're putting in.

RE: You always see the whole painting?

RL: Yeah. It's really important. It's more than important; it's just the whole thing.

Larry Rivers

The Juice and the Joy of It

Larry Rivers has raised irreverence to the level of art and because his art and life always have been inseparable, he has concurrently elevated it to the condition of a virtue. We shouldn't be surprised, then, to find the tone and content of his 1992 autobiography, called *What Did I Do?*, outrageous and irresistible. It contains references to a wide-ranging inventory of taboos, mostly involving sex: from unsuccessful proposals to sleep with his mother-in-law; to diaristic wishes to do the same with his sister; from successful encounters with both men and women; to an attempted act of "petophilia" with his dog, Amy. "She howled and I stopped," he matter-of factly reports, "and we remained just good friends." *What Did I Do?* amounts to a late-twentieth-century secular equivalent of *The Confessions of St. Augustine*, although Rivers's lack of repentance makes him an unlikely candidate for any kind of canonization. *What Did I Do?* could as easily have been called *Who Did I Do?* and it's all the more delightful for its candour. It's also vaguely disturbing to think that the book contains only a small portion of the tales deemed tellable. "Three-quarters of the stories didn't get in," he says and you can hear sighs of collective relief rising above the New York skyline.

It's characteristic of Rivers's impishness that a book in which he played a central role (it was written "with" Arnold Weinstein, the artist's longtime friend and a poet, playwright and stage director in his own right) would be called an "unauthorized autobiography," as if such a thing could exist. But the sub-title points to a quality that no one can ignore in reading this piece of life-writing: it is full of rambunctious good humour and anarchic wisdom. So it's easy to imagine Rivers's recognized career—which now spans over forty years—as being less about work and mostly about play. But even a cursory list of his indispensable paintings makes it clear that his unseriousness has been a very serious and productive pursuit indeed.

The exhibition of *Washington Crossing the Delaware* in 1953 brought Rivers serious attention, not all of it positive. The painting—his reinterpretation of an 1851 patriotic work by the German academician Emanuel Leutze—was seen as a challenge to the reigning Abstract Expressionist style whose court painters—among them Jackson Pollock, Willem de Kooning and Philip Guston—drank and talked art at the Cedar Street Tavern where Rivers himself was a regular. A figurative painting with no centre, littered with blurred figures representing some kind of disconnected narrative and with an attitude to boot, didn't sit comfortably with High Church aesthetics. Rivers explained his approach in an interview conducted in 1959 by poet and curator, Frank O'Hara:

> Luckily for me I didn't give a crap about what was going on at the time in New York painting … I was energetic and egomaniacal and what is even more important, cocky and angry enough to want to do something no one in the New York art world could doubt was disgusting, dead and absurd. So, what could be dopier than a painting dedicated to a national cliché.

Rivers continued to paint what pleased him and what was familiar—nude portraits of his wife, Augusta; Berdie, his mother-in-law; and his friends, notably Frank O'Hara. This latter portrait, painted in 1954 with the subject wearing only leather boots and with his hands sitting on his head, remains as potent and undeniably homoerotic today as the day it was painted. But these portraits were also beautifully rendered, the flesh tones putting you in mind of Gerard Manley Hopkins's "glory be to God for dappled things." For the remainder of the '50s and throughout the '60s Rivers applied his graphic and colourist gifts to a wide-ranging body of work that included Camel cigarette packs, the front grill of a 1960 Buick, playing cards, Civil War veterans, vocabulary lessons in various languages corresponding to various body parts, the contents of his studio, not to mention the contents of other painters' paintings. While the work may have been drawn from a dizzying list of sources, it had in common a feel that came out of Rivers's apparently insatiable quest for life. In a letter to O'Hara, he argues a shift in their relationship by including the rhetorical question, "Would you throw away such joy and juice?" The phrase comes from another Hopkins poem called "Spring"; an explosive May Day of a poem—a sonnet actually—bursting with weedy lushness, the "little low heavens" of thrush eggs and glassy pear trees that brush the descending blue of the sky. The sestet opens with these lines: "What is all this juice and all this joy? / A strain of the earth's sweet being in the beginning / In Eden garden." "Spring" might have been written for Rivers, the irascible gardener. His art and life have been juicy and joyful and in their openness have taken on the character of a proximate Eden, the being of almost innocence.

The following interview was conducted in Larry Rivers's New York apartment in June, 1993, surrounded by his painted intimates, including Augusta and Frank O'Hara.

ROBERT ENRIGHT: In your autobiography, *What Did I Do?*, you say that in the '50s everything was like being inside a novel.

LARRY RIVERS: It was a novel. Everybody's life is a novel. Every evening is a short story. All you need is a kind of enthusiasm for it. If you're a writer, why not use it?

RE: But what I'm getting at is a sense that you constructed your identities, that you made yourselves up as you were going along.

LR: Life was unfolding and what was also unfolding was our view that someone was looking over our shoulder, that we were part of history. Something like that. Childish, but it turned out to be partially true.

RE: Was there a point when you realized that you really were making art that was historically significant?

LR: When I did collaborations with Frank O'Hara we'd name ourselves; I would be Matisse and he would be Paul Eluard. We were in our twenties, getting to be in our early thirties. So I think I was self-conscious about it. You should read some of my pompous writings from the '50s. It was just so disgusting. As if I were Gide. I don't know what I thought I was.

RE: But what gave you permission to think that way? I mean, you were pretty young guys and there was already one generation ...

LR: The question really is: how can you put it into a shape that will be accepted by others? I'm sure that every Tom, Dick and Harry associates himself with dreams of being Cézanne, di Chirico or whomever.

RE: Your wife Augusta said you dreamt of immortality from the word go.

LR: If she said it I'll take her word for it. It's possible. She knows me quite intimately.

RE: De Kooning and Pollock's generation was already pretty fully formed. I have a sense that by the time you and your bunch came along it was necessary to create an identity for yourselves that responded to what was already in place.

LR: They acted as if they were revolutionaries, as if they were doing things for the advancement of art, but it didn't take me very long to figure out what they were up to. There was a revolution but they had to be counted as its leaders. I began to see that they hung onto those positions very strongly. They'd gladly accept followers because we just solidified their identity. When people eventually started paying money and writing about them they got interested in careers like everybody else. I didn't know them that well. The only one I knew slightly was de Kooning. He's a very strange man you know.

RE: Was there more generosity in the early years among your contemporaries? Was there more of a sense of community?

LR: I think so. We were all poor. No one knew us. Where was there to go?

RE: It's what you didn't have rather than what you did have that made you a community?

LR: Yeah, as soon as people started getting prizes, then you'd ask, "How come I didn't get a prize?"

RE: De Kooning said a lovely thing about you earlier on: "Looking at your painting was like putting your face in wet grass." Do you recall how you felt when you heard about his praise?

LR: Very good. And it was in a good magazine. I think Lotte Lenya had a gay husband who ran a magazine called *Park*, and it was in one of the first few issues. When I appeared in it de Kooning was already Mr. Hero. Sure I liked him. I liked his work. I thought he was a good artist, very good. I guess he gave me a plug.

RE: And when Clement Greenberg compared you favourably to Bonnard?

LR: I got a lot of good reviews. There's something about my art that makes people trust me. I don't understand.

RE: But it must have mattered in the early years. Was it pretty competitive?

LR: When there's a little success, you want more, and when you get a little more you want a little more again. It takes you out of oblivion. Earlier you asked how come we were nice to each other. It was just that you felt no one knew you were alive. So when someone paid attention, it had an attraction that was hard to resist.

RE: Were you having as much fun back then as *What Did I Do?* seems to imply? It's a book full of raucous good humour.

LR: It was rather rambunctious. Somebody handed me a review from a Los Angeles paper that said, "There's enough in this book to offend everybody." I feel now that I should write the sad version: *What Did I Do?: The Dark Side*. Although there are some sad moments—when I'm ignored in love—this book is a bit on the lighter side. Actually, I felt a certain enthusiasm in writing it and that's what I had hoped to convey. The spirit of my feelings are there in the telling. But as soon as you get into sex and numbers then you're up against a real problem because there are people who are simply offended by it.

RE: The essential puritanism of America persists.

LR: You're right. These guys are puritans. They're intelligent, witty but it's a mean wit. I don't know what the problem is.

RE: In some senses it's a kiss-and-tell book. You must have known that it was pretty outrageous.

LR: From a feminist point of view I was awful. At the time I thought I was very normal. As a matter of fact, in relation to other young men that I knew, I thought I had a special sensitivity. I was embarrassed by the way they spoke to women on the streets. They would come on in really dumb ways and I never did that. I realized when I wrote it that it wasn't going to please the feminists. But everybody has this kind of beginning and then as you get older you realize you're wrong. I thought of myself as having courage just to do it and hope that as the book proceeds you see some growth. Betty Freidan said that I should put in a whole sociological thing which would rationalize the way I talked but I felt that would take away from the book. I mean if I'm talking about what did I do, this is what I did.

RE: There's a section in the book where you confess that you were prepared to sleep with Berdie, your mother-in-law. That's going about as far as American society will tolerate.

LR: I'm in my twenties and a woman in her fifties is an old lady to you at that stage. But it was on my mind all the time because psychoanalysis was full of everybody wanting to sleep with their mother. You know, the Oedipus complex. So I thought I can't sleep with my mother but I'll do the next best thing, as it were—I'll sleep with my mother-in-law. It has the word "mother" in it. So I called her up from a party. I said, "I'm going to come up there and we're going to do it."

RE: She just seemed to take all this in stride?

LR: She was a saint. She was a little stupid, but extraordinary.

RE: But you had no hesitations at all?

LR: I think it was absolutely hilarious. What the hell is wrong with it when you're twenty years old? You call up your mother-in-law and say, "listen, we're going to do it. Don't tell your daughter, we're going to do it." And I'm stoned. She was sort of a juicy lady—grey-headed and totally disfigured. When I say disfigured I don't mean that she was awful. She just had a lot of meat.

RE: Was there anything that you considered taboo at the time?

LR: I was thinking about it recently. What could children do, what could I do, what could a friend do that wouldn't be okay? One of my sons put an earring in his ear at about sixteen years old. I was embarrassed by it. It's so stupid on my part. Do you understand what I mean? But other things don't bother me—sexual things don't and funny things and failures. Three-quarters of the stories didn't get in.

RE: How did you escape American puritanism, its fear of sexuality and the body?

LR: You know what is right for you. It's not a matter of escape; you just don't bother with it. I felt perfectly happy not to know America.

RE: I'd like to talk about the double portrait of your mother-in-law. Were you aware in painting it that you really were beginning to change the shape of American art?

LR: I didn't think so at all. As a matter of fact, I thought it was in some ways a step backwards. Don't forget Jackson Pollock was living down the road and I was seeing Franz Kline in the Cedar Tavern. Even *Washington Crossing the Delaware* was considered revisionist by these people. I didn't think, "I'm now bringing American painting somewhere." I was just interested in stories as part of my life. I was also interested in the old masters. I knew what everybody I was involved with thought was modern painting. So I didn't want to lose that identity; I didn't want to be considered some sort of academician. After all, *Berdie* is an all-over painting. There isn't an inch of the painting that doesn't have something going on, just as those abstract works did.

RE: Except for de Kooning and a handful of others, there weren't a lot of artists who were working figuratively. You seemed to be doing a species of personal history painting.

LR: Well, I was teaching myself things too. I wanted to see if I could get it. In certain ways it was also bound up in a moral issue. My father got up at five o'clock in the morning and I had a certain affection for him because he was a hard worker. So how could I consider anything to be anything if it took me five minutes? Now

I see the silliness of that but I felt it at the time. I try now to do a painting in four hours. But at the same time I was criticizing my father. His generation was ignorant and backward and conservative. You know they couldn't help it. But it took too long to get what I wanted. I wasn't very good. I went for something I couldn't get in five minutes.

RE: It's interesting you should say that because *Washington Crossing the Delaware* and the double portrait of *Berdie* are such good paintings. You must have figured that out pretty quickly?

LR: I didn't actually know, as a matter of fact. For a very long time after I did it people told me they thought that mine was after the Leutze painting. It wasn't at all. It came out of my response to *War and Peace*. I was reading Tolstoy and I was going to do a work of art that had to do with the history of America. So I picked on this very funny thing, *Washington Crossing the Delaware*. I could have talked about the opening of the West. But I hadn't seen the Leutze painting. I worked from children's illustrations because I'm so lazy. I work very hard and then on the other hand there are certain things I'm lazy about. I would have had to go to New York and look up uniforms of the Revolution and stuff like that. Luckily I ran into a cache of children's illustrations in the library in Southampton and I managed to make them into serious looking drawings. There were about a dozen for the painting. I think it's an accomplishment that no one knows about. It's quite peculiar to look at the sources and realize what I got from it.

RE: What was the reaction to it among people like Franz Kline and other gestural, abstract painters? Did they take you seriously?

LR: They didn't say very much. Anyway, they thought they were onto what was really important because they were being looked at by museums and magazines.

RE: But they liked you?

LR: Some of them. Jackson Pollock didn't but the others liked me. You know, I'm social and don't start too many fights, and I'm willing to talk about anything. So they didn't say much. Elaine de Kooning said it was *Pascin Crossing the Delaware*. She was talking about my style. I wasn't put off by that remark at all. Some people said it was corny.

RE: You started out as a musician and had a real interest in poetry as well. In 1950 you went to Paris, and I gather you wanted to be a poet. Were you having trouble deciding which of the arts you wanted to commit yourself to?

LR: By then I was pretty well finished thinking of myself as a professional musician. I fought to get gigs but I didn't have that high an opinion of my playing.

RE: Were you a good saxophone player?

LR: I played with bands. I didn't think I was that good, but I was competent. There were certainly guys who were better but you couldn't stop me. I was interested in playing at sessions. I started out getting club dates and jobs in the Catskills.

RE: Wasn't your name—Irving Grossberg—changed by an emcee? He said you had to be named something that had to do with The Mudcats, the name of your band?

LR: We never discussed it; he just said it one night when he was up there emceeing. So when we lost that job and went to another place I was able to get rid of some Jewish baggage. The second your name was mentioned in a room people would say here comes a Jew. It was hard in those days.

RE: Anti-Semitism was a given?

LR: Sure, sure. Don't forget Hitler. We're talking about the '30s and the '40s, and while I myself wasn't being attacked, there were many awful situations. School kids would be attacked. You would simply be surrounded by a gang of people.

RE: So was *The History of Matzoh* an attempt to respond to your background and Jewishness?

LR: It was a commissioned work.

RE: I know about the commission, but you also committed yourself to it in a fairly major way. Were you trying to say something about your cultural background in it?

LR: No, I'm not as deep as a well. I went to an historian and said, "Name me ten things that you think are important in Jewish history." The guy was a Columbia professor, actually a Marxist philosopher. Right after Benjamin Cardozo, his father was the head of the Zionists of America. So he lived in the professional Jewish arena his whole life. He was very smart.

RE: So he gave you these ten things. One of which was matzoh?

LR: Well, the matzoh was my idea.

RE: It's a great idea for an all-over painting. It really works.

LR: You're not too long into the thing and you realize the physical evidence that Christ existed is pretty meagre, and so is the history of the Jews. There were temples that were spoken of and things like that, but there wasn't a fucking brick left. So I decided to call it *The History of Matzoh, The Story of the Jews*, to indicate that the story is made up. But I definitely was interested in it.

RE: I want to ask about your notion of history, because you also did a painting in 1965 called *The History of the Russian Revolution: From Marx to Mayakovsky*. Do you have any particular political interest in the Russian Revolution?

LR: Again, it was personal. Isaac Deutscher wrote a trilogy on the life of Trotsky. My parents were Russian Jews and my mother actually came to America after the Revolution. So they hated the Communists. They killed her brother. I heard all these stories but I didn't pay much attention. The Russian Revolution is one of the great events. In a certain way it's like the French Revolution. The Czar was overthrown; it had world-wide influence. If you wanted to be against the United States you were a Commie. So there was a lot of power there and I tried to cover it. I did research myself. I had luck. All of these things were always associated with crazy little stories. I ran into a guy who was connected with *Sov Foto* (Soviet Photograph), so I had access to archives because this guy heard what I was doing and he thought—and so did everybody else—that I was honouring the Russian Revolution. I wasn't. I didn't like it, but it interested me, it definitely interested me. And the Isaac Deutscher trilogy filled in certain things. It made the path.

RE: Did you have an idea about what history was? I'm asking a philosophical question. There's a line in James Joyce where Stephen Daedalus says that history is the nightmare from which he wants to awake. You seem to use history in a very different way. It seems to be a thing which you can use, something with which you feel comfortable.

LR: To me it's stories and great events, and it seems to account for lots of the things that come down to us. They're full of irony and interest and cruelty. I'm just interested in history. I did things on Blacks when I was younger too.

RE: Did you have a lot of tolerance and interest in people who weren't part of mainstream society?

LR: Well if you're born a Jew you grow up avoiding sticks and stones so you have some kind of natural sympathy. That's why I think Jews were the biggest supporters of Blacks in the earlier days. It's a little different today. But that's why I didn't look at prostitutes and drug addicts as the biggest criminals that ever existed. I found conservatism and right-wing cranks much more of a drag in life.

RE: Where did the portrait of Frank O'Hara come from? Do you remember what you were thinking when you did it?

LR: I was simply trying to get it to look like him. Nothing more. And the boots had to do with knowing many homosexuals who either pretended, or actually were, attracted to cops. You know, uniforms. They'd see this wonderful sailor, or whatever. I think that crept in. I also think that maybe I wanted to be like Gericault, who died young.

RE: Did you model the composition on Gericault?

LR: Well, there was a Gericault in the cellar of the Met where a guy is hitting a gong. It was wonderful. The flesh was so fantastic. So I really tried to get that.

RE: Actually, the flesh is beautifully painted in the portrait of Frank O'Hara too.

LR: It's a very peculiar portrait. I thinks he was better looking than what came out but that was the best I could do. Instead of cutting the canvas I just let the canvas unroll. I never cut it until it was all finished. I would keep it on a roll. Then I would have to keep opening it up if I needed more and more and more footage. He posed in the cellar, Berdie too. I painted them in the cellar of this house that I lived in, because they were nude and there were kids running around.

RE: You loved O'Hara. What was it about him that everybody was so attracted to? He's become a bit of a legend.

LR: He was just a very enthusiastic, intelligent and talented nut. In a certain way he was very affectionate. He liked me and made a fuss over me all the time, and I made a fuss over him. That's really what it was. We went our separate ways, then we would come together. It was also at a point at which I was trying to see what homosexuality was.

RE: Was it something you consciously wanted to investigate?

LR: Yeah, that was one of the things about my generation. I think we wanted to try all these new experiences—sex and drugs and all sorts of things. I don't know exactly how I managed the whole homosexual thing. It was later on, as I was writing the book, that I realized I left the most space for my involvement with Frank O'Hara. What was that telling me about myself? I was pretty confident that I had sexual feelings for women. Jane Freilicher was a pal; and Frank was a pal. We went places together, we talked and observed things. You wouldn't do that with a woman. Somehow what attracted me sexually didn't contain that. In a way, I guess, I was a real corny, macho guy because I didn't search out women who were brainy, except for Jane. She was very nice, I liked her. What can you do about it?

RE: You quote Oscar Wilde about regretting the things you *don't* do in life. I know this is a corny question but do you have any regrets about that early period?

LR: There are lots of things I didn't do. For about thirty years I had been promising myself to go up to forty-second street and see what was going on, but I never did. There were very beautiful people there, people I was physically attracted to. And I just wanted to go up and see what it was about. I wonder why I didn't? But that's a silly thing. There are other things, too, that I regret that I didn't do, choices that I made.

RE: But as far as your relationships with people are concerned, there aren't things you wish you hadn't done?

LR: It's the opposite. It's the things you didn't do. I'm talking about choices. I regret certain decisions I made, like abandoning my dealer, John Bernard Myers, who was both in love with me and gave me my start. I just went for what I thought would be more glamorous and successful. It wasn't very nice. He was a smart guy, not a regular dealer. He wasn't a businessman like these guys are now.

RE: What about your early painterly interests? What was it about Bonnard that you were so attracted to in those early years? Was it because he was a fleshy, figurative painter?

LR: Yeah. The first things I was attracted to were Bonnard's and things like that. I never knew what Cézanne was about. It took me five years to begin to see something. You know when you begin you're a baby, you're crawling.

RE: Bonnard did some great bath paintings and bedroom paintings. Are those the ones you were attracted to?

LR: Yeah, when I painted I used to tack up a painting and steal passages from it. I liked him better than Matisse. Then I changed everything. I think probably Matisse is more related to the modern me. I have a show where I did quite a few Matisses, I didn't do a Bonnard. Matisse is easier.

RE: But you did somebody like Léger. You did all kinds of people, including Max Ernst, Mondrian, even Delacroix.

LR: Yeah, but they weren't hard. The ones that were hard were Balthus and Hélion. I got a wonderful letter from his widow. Somehow she got wind of what I had done.

RE: Why would you have chosen Hélion?

LR: I liked him. Nell Blaine, my first mentor used to talk about him. He was a French soldier who had been captured, and when the war was over he declared he didn't want to do any more abstract painting. It just suddenly seemed an immoral thing to do. I think then I got interested in him because suddenly he was regretting his past. He was man enough to say that. Also, it struck me that abstract paintings were getting so much attention that any little tidbit I could find, from a painter whom I respected, which put that attention in a certain perspective was something I enjoyed.

RE: Sam Hunter has this wild phrase about you. He says, "you're a creature of impulse with a whim of iron." Now with critics like that you don't need enemies.

LR: What's so insulting?

RE: Well "whim of iron" is a phrase some political pundit applied to Governor Brown in California. It wasn't meant to be favourable. A whim of iron means you're capricious.

LR: Oh, it's capricious.

RE: I guess I'm asking whether you feel that you operate entirely out of instinct and impulse?

LR: Well, the actual painting, the brush work, where things go and all that, is a combination of instinct and also some sort of aesthetic.

RE: You have a lot of fun with your art and I gather you want the viewer to have a fair amount of fun too.

LR: I hope so. But the directors and the elite people who write seem to think that they can get very serious. They're taking art too seriously. I don't see it that way. I don't see it that way at all.

RE: Let me ask you a question about the painting called *The Burial*. There are critics who argue that you were consciously burying Modernist abstract art, that you were flying the colours of the ascendant figurative art. It was your version of an erased de Kooning.

LR: Listen folks out there, I'm a really serious artist. I'm doing a death scene. Didn't Courbet do a death scene? Childish, childish, but that's what I was doing.

RE: Your art has been involved with what's called today quotational or paraphrased or appropriated issues. Were you aware that you were practising a species of postmodernism?

LR: Until two years ago I'd never even heard about any of that. I was thinking about those guys from day one. In 1951 I wanted to do something as serious as the Courbet, that fantastic painting with these guys and their great outfits. I did the same thing if you remember. I mean, the hole is right at the edge of the painting, so I did it in my own way but I did it.

Yoko Ono

Instructions in the Marital Arts

If you mention the name Yoko Ono to anyone over thirty-five you can almost guarantee they'll associate it with John Lennon and the Beatles, the most highly visible rock group of the highly visible '60s. More often than not, their recollection will be critical, remembering her as the *femme fatale* who broke up rock music's most famous quartet, or who bewitched and negatively influenced gentle John Lennon, or as the woman with the grating voice who keeps releasing bizarre CDs that slide off the charts with the speed of melting butter on a hot grill. And it's certainly true that history and circumstances have intractably linked Yoko Ono and John Lennon: their courtship, marriage, Bed-Ins, mutual projects and, finally, his murder in 1980 were followed by the media with a degree of attention normally reserved for developments within the British royal household. Nor has Yoko Ono done much to distance herself from her mega-famous husband; her maintenance of the relationship has to do with a range of things including family, memory and a need for public attention. And, of course, there's Strawberry Fields, the three-and-a-half-acre triangle in Central Park dedicated to Lennon's memory and cultivated with the help of a million-dollar donation from his widow in 1985. But in more recent years another concern has occupied Yoko Ono's mind. She has talked about having a "van Gogh complex," in which artists come to accept the fact that they will be under-appreciated when they are alive, only to be discovered as significant once touched by what Whitman called "Death's democratic finger." It will probably come as a surprise to most devotees of popular culture that Yoko Ono not only had a life before John Lennon, but that she was regarded as a serious avant-garde artist. By the time she and Lennon met she had already given over her Chamber Street loft to a series of now-famous concerts, had had a one-woman show at the AG Gallery in New York, had staged performances at the Carnegie Recital Hall, and had additional solo exhibitions at the Indica and Lisson galleries in London in 1966 and 1967. To be sure, it was their meeting at one of these openings and Lennon's witty response to her work that launched the thousand shifts of their relationship. Ono had an instinct for media attention—not all of it favourable—and had been nicknamed the "High Priestess of the Happening" by an English newspaper in 1967. The media would continue to both serve and attack her for the next twenty-five years. One of her most effective and disturbing films, shot in London in 1969, is called *Rape*. In the film Ono's crew picks out a woman and begins to follow her, documenting the transformation from being flattered to being harassed by the attention. The sense of violation is clearly evident in the film and it's difficult not to read it and the predicament the woman finds herself in as a chapter in Ono's surrogate autobiography.

Yoko Ono's artistic career begins at Sarah Lawrence College in the early '50s and proceeds through her friendship with John Cage and her involvement with the group of artists, musicians, performers and poets who were yanked together by George Maciunas under the name Fluxus. Cage was enormously influential on anyone making "radical" art in this period through his preoccupation with breaking down the barriers between art and life. For Cage the world itself was a work of art and it needed only a minimal amount of stewardship to achieve that recognition. In his most famous composition a musician walks on-stage, sits at the piano for exactly four minutes and thirty-three seconds and then walks offstage; indicating the end of the performance. The music is provided by audience members as they shift in their chairs, cough, look around and otherwise perform the repertoire of unrehearsed human reactions that constitute the act of waiting. Fluxus artists had a healthy disregard for the precious art object and preferred events that focussed on a simple gesture, or an insignificant phenomena; like sweeping a stage, releasing a butterfly into the air, or merely asking a single question. The simplicity of these events allowed them to be easily transcribed so that they often took the form of aphoristic performance directives or "instructional art." The roots of this art practice were in Dadaism and Surrealism, with a fair amount of adolescent hijinx thrown in for bad measure. George Maciunas, the group's name-picker and organizer, called Fluxus "a fusion of Spike Jones, vaudeville, gags, children's games and Duchamp." He was right.

Ono's early pieces shared in this improbable pedigree. She described the instructional pieces in her Indica exhibition in 1966 as work that "makes art come down from the pedestal." Sometimes the dismounting could be crude. One of her instructional pieces is imprinted with Surrealism's quirky sexuality: "Stir inside of your brains with a penis until things are mixed well. Take a walk." Or, in her questionnaire for *The Stone* which was performed at New York's Judson Gallery in 1966, she lists a series of bizarre statements to which the audience is encouraged to respond true or false. "Roaches are moving forms of flowers ..."; "Teeth and bones are solid forms of clouds"; "Plastic is a portion of sky cut out in solid form." The lines are quixotic, bizarre and often explosively delicate.

Among Ono's best pieces in the instructional art genre are those which deal with sky and the idea of limitless, unimpeded perception. *Painting to See the Skies* (1961) tells the audience/imaginer to "Drill two holes into a canvas / Hang it where you can see the sky." The installation of her *Painting to See the Evening Light Through* in the Walker Art Centre's In the Spirit of Fluxus exhibition in February of 1993 made people aware of how exquisitely simple her pieces could be. Ono's painting looked out onto Siah Armajani's luminous yellow and blue 375-foot-long pedestrian walkway that crosses sixteen lanes of Interstate highway ninety-four; the bridge itself is an inspiration and Ono's framing of it was doubly inspirational. "Sky people," as she tells us on her *Starpeace* album (1985), are those who've "got the blues in what they wear." No one can be unaware that the blues she's referring to are measured through her own experience.

Ono's objects and text pieces (eventually one hundred of the instructions were brought together and published under the title *Grapefruit* in 1964) are also a unique hybrid of haiku, Zen and Conceptualism; they often don't have to be realized except as ideas inside the audience's head. So in an unproduced film script from 1968 called *A Contemporary Sexual Manual (366 sexual positions)*, the physical gymnastics alluded to in the parenthetical description are experienced only in the viewer's imagination. Had the film been made, the only thing anyone would have seen would be a family scene showing a couple and their four-year-old daughter lying in bed for an entire night. Similarly, the instructions for *Concert Piece* (1963) indicate that the performance will be very spare indeed: "When the curtain rises / go hide and wait / until everybody leaves you. / Come out and play." So minimal is Ono's aesthetic that she is obliged to offer a warning caption on *Disappearing Piece* saying "the object in this box will evaporate when the lid is opened." This may be clever but it's not altogether benign. Occasionally in the works the element of required complicity turns on the audience: if you do this, then this will happen and you'll be responsible. But the works can also be disarmingly simple; in *A Box of Smile* whoever opens the lid sees their own reflection in a mirror and the inescapable result is that they fulfil the expectations of the box. "All my work is a form of wishing," Ono has said and the wish she holds in these deceptively simple works is that the viewer will be sensitive to their pure, uncynical innocence.

In 1966 Yoko Ono wrote that our natural state of mind and life is complex, so what art can offer "is an absence of complexity ... a complete relaxation of the mind." This is the reason she places such emphasis on daydreaming—which is simply a way of keeping her head clear for thinking. For Yoko Ono art is a paring down, a process of radical simplification. In her early years she thought of the sounds she was producing more as Zen practice than as music. "The only sound is the sound of my own mind," she said in 1966. "My works are only to induce music of the mind in people." The conceptual impulse had much to do with her work in film, as well. "Most of my films are film instructions," she has remarked, "they were never actually made." Even so, between 1966 and 1982 she did manage to complete sixteen of her never-mades. It's here that her major accomplishment as an avant-garde artist is located. It isn't simply that Ono's films were part of a larger assault on the conventions of filmmaking but more importantly they anticipated a number of issues that were to become central to feminist writing and thinking years later. *Film No. 4*, *Fly* and *Rape*—among others—remain powerful and controversial films for contemporary audiences. So it is with her best work in other media (her observation that her event performances were "vagabonds, drifting from one form to another" well describes the ease with which she moved across genre barriers). Pieces like *Painting to Hammer a Nail*, *Three Spoons*, *Half-a-Wind*, and *Cut Piece* walk a delicate line between being there and being almost nothing; between acting and being acted upon; between art and life. When Yoko Ono offers that "my events are mostly spent in wonderment" the work in all media persuades me to take her at her ingenuous word.

The following interview was conducted in August 1993.

ROBERT ENRIGHT: One of the things that John Cage did was to radically extend the idea and vocabulary of what music could be. You seemed to want to get beyond sound and silence to a sound that was only imagined.

YOKO ONO: Once you know Cage you have to either become totally Cagean or you have to go elsewhere.

RE: So you were aware of extending the possibilities of music, then?

YO: When I was at Sarah Lawrence taking music composition one of my teachers, Mr. Singer, said it probably would be better for me to meet a group of people in New York. He was giving me names like Pierre Boulez and Henry Cowell and then Cage. I wasn't really acquainted with their work and my attitude was, I don't need another composer, I am it.

RE: When you were at Sarah Lawrence were you innocent of what was going on in New York?

YO: I was very innocent about it, yes. I was mainly into Schoenberg, Anton von Webern and Alban Berg. But I wanted to go beyond that. In Japan there was a school called Jiyù-Gakuen, which you entered when you were kindergarten age. They gave you perfect pitch and they taught you harmony and composition. I composed my first song when I was around that age. It's very good training because they get you young. Actually, many famous Japanese composers came from this school.

RE: So there's a residue of influence that you carry with you from your upbringing in Japan?

YO: Naturally. If you're born in New Jersey, you're always going to be New Jersey, right?

RE: And Bruce Springsteen gets to sing about you. I'm just wondering how you measure the aesthetic influence of coming out of another culture into North American culture?

YO: When you're born in a third-world country—which Japan was considered at the time, especially by the West—it's slightly different because the culture is very mixed. First of all I went to a school that taught western harmony and composition and most kids grew up reading western books. I'm not talking about western books in English, I'm talking about translated western books. They grew up reading *Gulliver's Travels* or *Robinson Crusoe*, the whole gamut of Western literature, and then proceeded to Chekhov, Dostoevsky and Dickens. It's a very mixed culture. We read mostly French, Russian and German literature.

RE: You came out of a fairly privileged home, didn't you? I read the word "aristocrat" a fair amount. Is that an accurate description of the kind of world that you came from?

YO: I'm afraid so. But in one way it was an ideal thing for me to be comfortable with so that I could make it on my own. My mother's side of the family was as well known as the Kennedy's. So it was marvellous just to be bumming around in New York where nobody knew me.

RE: Was there an element of rebelliousness about you? Were you conscious of rejecting the values you had inherited through your family?

YO: I'm very thankful for the cultural influence of growing up in a environment like that. I was in the studio one day and I called my mother and thanked her for giving me training in music in my early childhood because it really helped me all my life. But the reason I mentioned this early training was because in that particular school it was normal that we be asked to translate all the sounds around us into musical notes. Every morning in Scarsdale at my parents' summer home when I woke up there were thousands of birds singing. It was so beautiful, so incredible, and I tried to translate it into musical notes. But it was too intricate; I couldn't do it. I thought there must be a way of creating music without using the limited musical notes that we know of.

RE: And what did that lead you to then?

YO: The first *Instruction* was made then. When I was telling my teacher about it, that's when he told me that there were many so-called avant-garde composers in New York and that maybe I'd feel more comfortable among that group of people. I didn't really make a move then. I wasn't thinking about that at all until I bumped into Cage. I thought he was very interesting.

RE: Sarah Lawrence had a reputation then for being the kind of school where you could flex your wings more than at other schools. How did that manifest itself in your activity? I know you wore black, had long hair and looked mysterious.

YO: That was in the beatnik days. I was leading a very simple life then. The wardrobe was also for practical reasons: you didn't have to match so many colours.

RE: What was John Cage's influence on you and the group of people around you who ended up performing in your loft on Chamber Street?

YO: Well, there was a group—people like Christian Wolff and Morton Feldman—whose compositions were directly influenced by Cage. And then there was the second crowd of people like La Monte Young and Jackson MacLow. But La Monte was not so much directly influenced by Cage as by Cage's spirit. I consider myself in that spirit too. I don't think I was composing à-la-Cage. As a friend he influenced me in emphasizing that it was all right to be unique.

RE: The performances that you staged at your loft are now part of New York avant-garde history. Were your plans at this time fairly ambitious?

YO: It was a very practical idea in a way. By then I knew all these interesting young composers, including myself, and we didn't have a place to present our work. At that time there were only a few places—like the Carnegie Recital Hall—that gave classical music concerts to avant-garde composers like us. We felt we didn't have a chance to get a concert. Later I found out the mechanics of it: you had to have money.

RE: Had you seen any of the things Jim Dine, Claes Oldenburg and that group were doing at the Judson and Reuben Galleries? Were you aware of the beginnings of what came to be described as Happenings?

YO: I went to one Happening that Claes Oldenburg did. But I wasn't even aware of the Gutai Group. I was watching this performance and somebody said, "Well, Gutai has done this sort of thing a long time ago." I was pretty naïve. And I think Jim Dine came a bit later. By 1962 I had already gone back to Japan. But the things we were doing on Chamber Street were mainly on the composers' side. The reason that all these people gathered in my loft at the time was not because they were necessarily Cage people. There were all kinds of people who had been doing things in other places. Most of them were from the West Coast. It wasn't like we gathered and decided to do something in a certain style. The reason they gathered was because they were kind of far out to begin with.

RE: So initially you weren't aware of being anything that could be labelled a movement. But by the time George Maciunas got involved and named the group Fluxus, I assume there was a general sense that the members of the group shared a similar aesthetic?

YO: That's not true. I'll tell you why. Fluxus was not twenty people getting together and saying, "Shall we give a name to our movement?" It wasn't to be a statement. I was doing the concert series with La Monte Young on Chamber Street and one night George Maciunas came down. By then we were popular enough that a lot of artists and intellectuals were coming. We'd give a concert and one hundred to two hundred people would show up. Then one day I got a call from someone who shall remain nameless because it was a mean call to make. He told me that all the artists were queueing up to do the concerts at a midtown gallery on Madison Avenue run by George Maciunas. And he said, "You've lost it. Nobody's going to do a concert in your place because you're in a loft and this is a midtown gallery." I was a bit hurt but I thought, so what. We've already made a statement. So I said, "Who's George Maciunas?"

RE: Was it something of a raid on your people?

YO: Call it whatever you like. But the artists were delighted that somebody was going to give them a concert in midtown. And then I got a call that George would like to do a show of mine, so I thought, that's not bad. I went to see him in this gallery and I think we kind of dug each other. We were kindred souls. So I did a one-woman show there in 1961. Anyway, while we were doing it George started saying we had to make a name for this movement and he should think of the name. I was against the idea because I thought that all of us were doing our own thing.

RE: I gather this unnamed movement was primarily artists working in America. Were Joseph Beuys and Nam June Paik involved?

YO: Beuys wasn't but Nam June Paik was through John Cage. He was doing incredible "happening" things independently. But all of us were independent, each one with a different background. There were a number of incredibly interesting artists and not just because Fluxus became very popular and famous.

RE: Did Maciunas explain to you that the name came out of "flux" as a constant sense of change?

YO: Yeah, he first brought out the dictionary and said, "See, there are so many different interpretations of Fluxus."

RE: I gather as far as he was concerned all of them were applicable?

YO: Well, he pointed out "flushing," as in toilet, because that's the kind of humour he was especially attracted to. I think he liked the word Fluxus. I was against the idea of a movement. I was a purist. But here's the point: Fluxus was George and George was Fluxus. He would list all these names sometimes without the permission of the artists and then sometimes he would drop a name or two because he'd had a personal fight with them. He was headstrong and so was I. I'm not criticizing him; it's just that he had his quirky side. You also have to remember that there was another person called Charlotte Moorman who was putting on an avant-garde festival every year. So Charlotte and George were both organizing concerts and because there were limited numbers of interesting avant-garde artists the same people would be asked to both festivals. All these arranged concerts were very good for us because they created a space where we could express our work. We went with Charlotte as well as George because we did not have a clear awareness of being Fluxus artists. So, if Norman Seaman asked us to do a concert in Carnegie Recital Hall, which he did, of course we would do a show there. I did one at the end of '61. George spent a whole day making a poster for it which I didn't use.

RE: You weren't keen on his poster design?

YO: When I think about it now, you know, I was very headstrong and sometimes I may have hurt George.

RE: Were you difficult back then?

YO: I was difficult but I refuse to think I'm a difficult person. I'm a very accommodating person but as far as my work is concerned I always want to do it my way. That's natural. Anyway, I was pretty uncompromising at the level of untalented posters. But this Carnegie Recital concert was a very big thing. All my avant-garde friends, La Monte Young, George Brecht—everybody performed in it. At the time Charlotte Moorman was not in the avant-garde at all. She was a cello student at The Julliard School of Music. Norman Seaman was her producer, and the reason we met was because Norman said, "I don't know anything about avant-garde and I don't want to do this show. I will give you the concert in Carnegie Recital Hall, but the condition is that I'm not willing to do the dirty work of mailing out announcements." He didn't want to use up his energy on this sort of concert. The other condition was to get Charlotte Moorman to do the actual production. I said, "Who's Charlotte?" I'd heard about her through Toshi [Ichiyanagi, Ono's first husband] because they were both in Julliard. So I said, "Okay," but I thought she was just doing the production end. And then the night before the opening (this was only a one-night concert) she said, "How are we going to play this thing? I want to perform too." She brought this cello out and said, "Tell me what to do." And that's how she got into the avant-garde. Of course, she was always very nice about including me in every one of her avant-garde festivals even when I had hard times and people were avoiding me.

RE: Was it a mistake going back to Japan because of all the activity that was going on in New York? If you could do it again, would you have stayed in New York?

YO: No. There were many things that I did that were inspired directly from the environment in Japan. Had I stayed in New York I would have become one of those grande dames of the avant-garde, repeating what I was doing. But in 1962 I did a concert in Japan which had a disastrous review. It got to me. That was in the early days and I was not used to disastrous comments about me in public.

RE: How vicious was it?

YO: Vicious enough that I had a nervous breakdown or something. I volunteered to go to a rest home. So most people say, "So you were in a mental hospital." But it wasn't like being an alcoholic and going to Betty Ford. I was totally normal but I needed a rest. They talked about me in Tokyo and the pressure from it was just too much. It was incredible. It was like a storm.

RE: I've read that you had a reputation for being a pretty tough broad in New York. What you're saying is that you were far more fragile and vulnerable than those reports would indicate. Do you sense you've been maligned in the way that you've been presented?

YO: I think it's a very normal thing in a male society. Women are depicted as being benign and naïve. And if they stand up for themselves, or for their work, then they're considered a bitch. Isn't that how it works?

RE: Were you sensitive to the fact that your work was coming out of a female sensibility and that it was different from what the male artists in Fluxus were doing? I'm thinking here of a work like *Cut Piece*, which seems a precursor of strong feminist performance.

YO: Yeah. *Cut Piece* was considered too dramatic or too theatrical by a number of the male artists in Fluxus. That's the way they put down the piece. They couldn't quite pinpoint it but something was disturbing them. There was a feminist sensibility that surfaced in that piece and I think it was hard for them to watch.

RE: I didn't see the piece but the documentation makes it look slightly terrifying. As you were performing it, was there an element, a sensation, of danger?

YO: Most definitely. I first performed it in Kyoto in 1964. At that time a guy came up on the stage with a pair of scissors. It seemed like he was going to stab me because he raised his hand. I just thought, oh dear. It turned out that he was simply being theatrical. He raised his hand and stood there like that for a long time.

RE: There's something frightening about a woman allowing herself to become the object of any kind of scissor activity.

YO: In a sense it was symbolic of what was happening to women. But it was also a kind of total giving; you're sitting there and asking people to cut wherever they want, which was very important.

RE: As if you were a sacrifice in some sense?

YO: Yeah. I felt very strongly about the piece. And around that time I had only three or four different sets of clothes. Even though that's all I had, I would always make a point of taking my best suit for the performance.

RE: Were people discreet about where and how much they cut, or were you almost unclothed by the end of the process?

YO: Well, it was always different. It was almost like I was going through a process of teaching myself because I'm a very shy person. When you see a videotape of the performance in Carnegie Recital Hall you can see that by the end I'm just holding my breath hoping they won't take off the bra. In Japan they were very discreet, as they were at Carnegie Hall.

RE: Did it seem a radical piece to you then?

YO: Oh, it was very radical. When I did it in London, it was like a massacre. There were all these cameras and they cut everything off me there.

RE: So the world had changed by then and I gather so had you?

YO: The world had changed but I didn't change very much. I thought, I have to go through with this and it's not going to be like Carnegie Hall. I was making a statement but it was very difficult.

RE: In *Film Number 8*, you trace a woman's pregnancy. What interests me about the film is that it depicts the experience of a woman's pregnancy without any mythology or sentimentality.

YO: We live in a world of illusion created through the mass media in which the family is always depicted as beautiful, in which having a child is a very beautiful event and so on. When you see a photo of a pregnant woman it's usually a model with some sort of pillow. The reality has always been hidden.

RE: Was it the desire to express concerns out of your own experience that led you to the performances or had you a larger political agenda in mind? I mean, do you think of yourself—did you think of yourself—as a proto-feminist?

YO: I was trying to show what women go through. I didn't have any notion of feminism. When I went to London and got together with John that was the biggest macho scene imaginable. That's when I made the statement that "woman is the nigger of the world."

RE: I want to talk about a show you did at the Lisson Gallery in London in 1967. All the objects that you would normally find in a bedroom are painted white and then cut in half. Where did the idea for that piece—which you called *Half-a-Wind*—come from?

YO: At the time I was having a very difficult time in my marriage. This was before John and I got together. I felt the emptiness of the other side of the bed and I thought, what if I cut all the things in half because I'm like a half now. So the actual inspiration came from my private life. There was another sense too, in that there are two sides to most people and I think that two-sidedness is especially prevalent in my pieces. I think it's also very interesting that when we see something we only see half of it. The other half is actually hidden.

RE: You said that all your work, in one sense or another, is autobiographical.

YO: Well, I don't see how an artist can really create anything other than from her own experience. I was inspired by what I was going through at the time, but then I realized it was interesting in another way.

RE: Why did you paint everything white? Did it have any symbolic value?

YO: It was probably something that was deep in my subconscious. In Japan when you get married, women wear white and men wear black. The reason for that is man has to stick to his principles and black can't be changed; whereas white is able to be any colour. In other words the woman has to be willing to be dyed any colour. That must have been in my subconscious. The other thing I was thinking about was conceptual: white is the colour before colour is put on. And it's the colour that also includes all colours.

RE: It's around this period when you first meet John, isn't it?

YO: I met him in 1966 when I did a show at the Indica Gallery. In '67 when I did the Lisson Gallery show we were already very good friends. We were both aware of the fact that our marriages were not going very well. I told him about the idea of the *Half-a-Wind* room and he came up with the idea of putting the other half in a glass bottle and exhibiting it on a shelf. But it was a two-sided thing. If I put John's name on the piece then I'd be using it because he was so famous. I didn't want to do that. But I also didn't want to put all these beautiful antique bottles and jars on the shelf with labels on them without his name.

RE: Was the idea that they would be ground up and reduced in size and put inside the bottles?

YO: No. Each bottle was empty. But it had a label which was a beautiful idea. So what I did was put the jar on a back shelf and put JL on it. But I did indicate in a brochure that it was his idea. I felt it was a more discreet thing to do.

RE: Is the story true about your meeting with John? Your *Painting to Hammer a Nail* was in the exhibition and when you offered him an opportunity to hammer a nail for five shillings, his response was, "Well, how about if I hammer an imaginary nail and give you an imaginary five shillings?"

YO: That's true.

RE: It's a fairly witty response.

YO: There was a practical side too. I didn't know it at the time but John didn't carry any money. He was like an aristocrat. So when I said five shillings he didn't have it.

RE: As I look at the collaborations that you did together, it looks like both of you gravitated towards each other's worlds. While you were trained in music, I assume that the avant-garde world of conceptual art was new to him?

YO: But you have to understand he was an artist before he became a rock star. He was an art student. So we were both very rounded artists in a sense.

RE: But he talked about the two of you moving into one another's spheres, and how the mixing that went on got very exciting for both of you.

YO: It got very exciting. But he was a very offbeat artist to begin with. He had that sense. It wasn't because he met me that suddenly he learned something. He would have wandered into New York City because he had that kind of sensibility. He always used to say, "If I were born in New York City or in the Village, I would have been a great avant-garde artist."

RE: You said in 1966 that the intention of your works was to induce music in the minds of people. You talk about the sound of the mind being the only sound that exists. Where were your notions coming from?

YO: I don't know. It might have been very Japanese.

RE: You mean because of its austerity and economy?

YO: Yes, but also as simple a thing as normal vocabulary. I don't know if they talk about this now because the young generation is so very Americanized but there was a word, *Kehai*. *Kehai* is when you're in a room, sitting, and you sense a person behind you.

RE: Is it like second sight, you mean, or just an apprehension?

YO: No, it's like you sense the vibration of the person. A certain vibration that is just beyond tangible, obvious reality. That's the kind of thing I was interested in bringing out.

RE: I want to shift for a moment to more of your films—specifically I want to talk about *Film Number 4*—its more colloquial title was *Bottoms*. You'll forgive me for saying it's your cheekiest piece.

YO: I was wondering what it would be like if I had something blocking the whole screen and moving. Would it look like the screen is moving? So it began as a visual concentration.

RE: These were shot full frame so that flesh filled the entire image area, then?

YO: Not only did flesh fill the entire image, but there were four lines in the centre that would create a different kind of movement. It was purely an aesthetic consideration. I thought it would be the first time anybody had done that. The sexual angle certainly did not come into my mind. As it turned out you sometimes saw a penis or whatever. But conceptually that was never in my mind. I just had four lines making the movement.

RE: Were you surprised by the reaction of the British censors to it and the fact that you weren't able to show it initially?

YO: Well, first of all, I had made a short of that film for Fluxus. George Maciunas helped because calling around and getting equipment was beyond me and George was very good at those things. He was very politically minded. When the film was made I saw that it was not the pure thing that I had been thinking about. It was not just four lines. So when I did the *Bottoms* film in London I was fully aware of the visual impact. I thought of it as an avant-garde statement to the world. And that part of it I liked. But I wasn't aware of the sexual impact. I realized there was a sexual dimension when I got quiet calls from English gentlemen asking if they could have a private viewing.

RE: But you were aware of playing with notions of sexuality. In a work like *Bag Piece*, which you had done as early as 1965, wasn't there a degree of sexuality implicit in the piece?

YO: No. The initial idea was just like *Half-a-Wind* room; the fact that you don't really see the thing in full. It's like you and I are talking and we are communicating at a certain level but you would never see how I really am on the inside. So it was a logical decision to show how we only see the movement of things or people in outline.

RE: Were you actually physically making love inside the bag? Is that what you expected would happen when people entered it?

YO: No. Call me a prude or whatever. But some people did and it kind of ruined my bag.

RE: So the audience would see the outline of the participants' activity and would have to imagine the actual event happening?

YO: It was an imaginary piece. When Tony Cox [Ono's second husband] and I went into the bag all we did was take off our clothes and then put them on again. But most people thought something sexual had happened. It was just in their minds and that's what I wanted to show.

RE: Very often your work demands a degree of audience involvement before it becomes complete. An audience member becomes a participant in the process, if not in thinking about the piece, then in actually undertaking an activity. Were you aware that you were doing work that anticipated notions of postmodern art practice—that the reader, the looker, the viewer becomes as important a part of the process as the maker?

YO: Yes. It had a lot to do with the fact that I was brought up in such an incredibly repressive environment. When you go to a museum the tendency is to just look at a painting. I thought that art was a verb rather than a noun and so I wanted an action quality to the experience.

RE: So that was there from the beginning? When you gathered together your instructions in *Grapefruit*, there was already a necessity for the reader to imagine themselves making the piece?

YO: This ties in with your earlier question about the wisdom of going back to Japan in the early '60s. It's when I was in this rest home that I first decided all my pieces would be imaginary.

RE: I find that oftentimes the imagined pieces have a poignant, lyric quality about them, almost as if they were haiku.

YO: Exactly. I used to write haiku a lot. That was parallel to making music. When I was young I used to write my dairies in haiku and I was quite good at it.

RE: I want to talk some more about your films. Tell me about *Fly*, which you did in 1970. What was the idea behind it?

YO: Well, it came from a newspaper cartoon in which a man was looking at a woman with a low-cut dress and when his wife asks him what he's looking at, he says, "I'm looking at a fly on her." But the film wasn't about a joke; it was about men's attitudes towards the reality of women's lives. It's like the fly's crawling on you and instead of seeing the reality—which is a fly crawling on a woman's life— they would see women simply as a sexual object.

RE: How did you get a model to do the piece?

YO: We advertised and we auditioned. Then we filmed each woman and screened the auditions. Strangely, I wanted the body not to have any movement, as a symbol of passiveness in women's lives. I wanted a body that didn't look interesting when seen alive on screen, one you didn't notice when you were filming. Everybody's body twitches once in a while, so I took the one who was not twitching at all. She was a marvellous subject or object or whatever.

RE: How did you get the flies to come to her body and then stay on?

YO: We actually had to put on a little honey. But then the honey would shine and I didn't like that. So we had to dilute the honey to the point where it didn't shine.

RE: You've said that after your partnership with John you "lost a little edge" in your work. What did you mean by that?

YO: I don't know if I said that or not. I think I lost more edge after John died because I made a conscious decision not to offend people. I had done enough of that and for Sean, my son's sake, I wanted to be more conservative in the sense of not wanting to create waves.

RE: So your life has got in the way of your art-making, then? It must be complicated—having been the wife of John Lennon. You're a public figure in a way that you probably never dreamt of.

YO: When I came to New York, Nixon was the president and I said to John, "I don't want to be Pat Nixon." It was getting to the point where I could not speak easily without feeling that my statement might hurt John's position. And so I was very careful about that. The truth is, together we hurt each other's career and position just by being with each other and just by being us.

RE: Did you resent the restrictions your relationship with John imposed on your life?

YO: Well, I resented the fact that I had to be Pat Nixon and shut up. I felt very sympathetic towards Mrs. Nixon because there was a point where she went to a psychiatrist and the things that she said somehow got out and people in the underground were laughing about it. I was thinking it's very, very sad when a women can't even say something to her psychiatrist.

RE: Prior to talking to you I read through a lot of material and much of it is not very flattering. You've been characterized as the black widow spider who destroyed rock music's greatest group. Were you hurt by a lot of what was written about your role, not just in the break-up of the Beatles, but about your ongoing relationship with John over the years?

YO: Of course. I think it had a lot to do with chauvinism and with racism as well. Even John said that if he were married to a blonde English woman there would not have been any problem. The fact that I was Oriental really turned people off. In hindsight I think that what I went through was good in some ways. I'm still a pretty vulnerable person, but I think that it might have been a good thing that the pain was transformed into many of the songs, and into many of my works.

RE: The reason I asked whether you had been hurt comes out of listening to a song like "Remember Raven," on the *Starpeace* album. There's a lot of—

YO: … Anger coming out.

RE: It's probably as angry a song as you've ever written. Is it about your sense of betrayal and anger over what happened subsequent to John's death?

YO: Well, yes. A lot of things came out after John died. Even the people around us whom we thought were okay turned out to be not really okay. A lot of terrible things were written about us.

RE: The obvious one being Albert Goldman's book, *The Lives of John Lennon*, which was published in 1988.

YO: "Remember Raven" was written when Goldman's book came out. It was very strange because after John died a lot of people closed off their acquaintances with me. What they couldn't say when John was alive they didn't mind saying when he was dead. It was really a very hurtful time.

RE: The *Double Fantasy* album was very revealing: in some ways courageous; in other ways, arrogant. You were laying the dilemma of your lives out on the line in lyric form, writing a narrative of dislocation and then one of coming together. What gave you the nerve to do it?

YO: Well, we were two very arrogant people. The combination of extreme vulnerability and extreme arrogance was just about the same in John and me. John was an extremely vulnerable person. I had a totally protective feeling for his vulnerability.

RE: And you also came up against his arrogance?

YO: He came up against my arrogance too. The thing is it was a very lucky combination. We intentionally decided that we would show our arrogance in our work. Which was probably a way to keep our relationship too. But I was like that from the beginning. Most people thought that I was being arrogant when I got together with John. They should have met me when I was alone in New York City.

RE: Was there a period when your involvement with John stopped you from making a lot of your own work? Since his death you've been much more visible.

Are you back in the art-making game?

YO: I never felt that I left it. I couldn't have done any more museum shows because when I did a show in Syracuse, everybody was queueing up waiting for the Beatles to show.

RE: The coat-tail phenomenon was just too much to overcome, then?

YO: Also the artwork literally disappeared from their minds. I think they were more interested in looking around in case John or Ringo might appear around the corner. I didn't like the idea of using that celebrity status as a draw to a show of mine.

RE: But you've been accused of exactly the opposite: of using the Beatles connection to further your career.

YO: I'm too proud to use that, too arrogant.

RE: One of the things I've always sensed about the Bed-In in Canada in 1969, was that it was largely misunderstood. No one recognized that, apart from its political motivation, it was also solidly within the frame of a Fluxus event.

YO: Since the art world per se didn't understand the performance, certainly the larger public would not have understood anything like that. At the same time we were totally naïve as well.

RE: How do you mean?

YO: We were very naïve about how much the public understood. John probably had more sense about it. I think that what he went through after his "Jesus Christ" statement made him a different person. Before that there was a conformity to the Beatles, but after the Beatles basically retired he changed. He always had a rebellious character but he wasn't expressing it. What he was saying was, I was honest and you've persecuted me. When I came into his life I allowed him to express those things.

RE: He said meeting you was like meeting Don Juan. It was an amazing thing to say because it reversed normal roles and cast you as the seducer.

YO: I think John was exaggerating because the world was so much against me. He was pretty aware that we were teaching one another.

RE: I'm very fond of *Play It by Trust*, your chess set in which all the pieces are white. It eliminates the possibility for the combative notion of chess. It's a kind of trickster piece; it sets people up.

YO: I think conning's okay as long as you're showing the con and the mechanics of the con at the same time.

RE: Because nobody is being taken advantage of then?

YO: No, it's just showing the slip as well.

RE: So you see the pea move but you're still intrigued by it?

YO: Yeah. Then it's funny.

Terry Winters

Fertile Regions

In November of 1987, I found myself angrily leaving the Sonnabend Gallery in New York, hitting the streets of SoHo in a perplexing rage, muttering under my breath about an exhibition of paintings I'd just encountered by an artist named Terry Winters. They were the most infuriating paintings I'd ever seen. I remember thinking they were ugly, maybe even repulsive; big, aggressive organic forms occupying wet, oozy-looking grounds of paint, although if anyone takes that word to mean these works were anchored I mean the opposite: everything in them seemed to be moving; shapes appeared to be penetrating or overlapping one another in some kind of slippery, chthonic, sexual dance. The paintings were mucking about.

Once on the street the only levity I allowed myself was a pun on the painter's name; he was most assuredly the Winters of our discontent. I can't remember what other exhibitions we saw that afternoon, mostly because we couldn't stop talking about the one we'd so summarily left. An hour later we were walking into the Sonnabend Gallery for the second time that day, peering at those maddening paintings one by one, and not leaving again until the gallery closed.

In October, 1991, I went to Los Angeles to see a major survey of Terry Winters's work at the Museum of Contemporary Art, a show that included 150 paintings, drawings and prints made between 1979 and 1991. I didn't stomp out this time. Instead I spent two days with the exhibition, attempting to understand what it was in the work of this enormously gifted New York painter that could drive a seasoned gallery-goer out into the streets. Today I think that Winters is among the most significant painters of his generation. He is in that cluster of American artists including Susan Rothenberg, Brice Marden and Eric Fischl who have, above all else, recommitted themselves to the art of painting. But even among this aesthetic pantheon, he is the painter's painter.

He still makes me uneasy but I like him for it. He is the only painter I know who can sit with the uncomfortable viral ooziness of William Burroughs and David Cronenberg, at the same time he rests comfortably with the exquisite scribblings and loose architectonics of Cy Twombly and Brice Marden. His biomorphic abstraction, though, is his own. The central stuff of Winters's world is a cellular shape that he has reproduced parthenogenically throughout the course of his career. For the catalogue cover accompanying his survey at the Museum of Contemporary Art, Winters designed an original lithograph; it's like a rough-edged, blackened and dripping cellular strip, tracing across a float of tan space—you can't quite tell if it's evolving or devolving. It led Winters to create his dangerous, gorgeous piece called *Event Horizon,* which registers as if it were a microscopic look at the aftermath of a shark attack. But his self-fertilizing doesn't only go forward; in the *Spine Series C* the painting's perfectly awkward grid is the prototype for what later became his blood garlands, while at the same time it seems to re-imagine an orderly Franz Kline.

Winters situates himself in an admirable tradition of gutsy picture-making that looks back to art history's past and forward to its future. I don't mean to suggest that he is a quotational artist and that his work is a closet of painterly clothes worn better by other and earlier artists. His *Dark Plant* drawings (especially number sixteen) use a black that Motherwell would have admired, breeding a *fleur du mal* that has the quality of impenetrable velvet. But as the poet Bill Bissett has written in another context, "nobody owns the earth," and, he might have added, nobody owns its dark, disturbing palette either. Winters has earned his own colours. As a painter, he's his own organic construction, having evolved into the self he'd always intended to be. In the back of the catalogue for the survey exhibition in Los Angeles, there is an unidentified and undated drawing of plant life—pods and leafy things scumbling about a finely worked surface. All the marks count. The drawing was made by Winters when he was seven years old and its inclusion verges on an act of hubris. It's a maddeningly precocious drawing (it's better than what Picasso was doing at the same age in his quickstart career) and it didn't take long to grow into a dark plant. Everything in his work is connected to everything else; the background of *Montogolfier* is a reprise in a rusty tone of the painting surface Winters scraped into life in *Untitled,* a work done eight years earlier. He just added party balloons to celebrate the continuity and the unpredictable interconnectedness of his painting life. He approvingly quotes Burroughs's notion that language is a virus; for him images function in the same way. Winters is entranced by aesthetic languages and the vehicles—paintings and books—that carry them.

The following interview was conducted on January 28, 1992 in Winters's Tribeca drawing studio.

ROBERT ENRIGHT: You're a frequenter of second-hand bookstores, presumably on the lookout for something. What do you learn when you go through books?

TERRY WINTERS: I don't know how much I actually learn, but I began collecting books about painting—formulas, recipes and methods. When I was a student in New York, there were a lot of used bookstores. It gave me a focus and satisfied my collecting habit. I enjoy looking through those books as a way to think about how paintings are made. I was very attached to the idea that painting was about structure, and that paintings themselves were laminated structures. It seemed like a narrow way into a very wide field, and it was a way to allude to things outside the paint itself, to know where the paints were coming from, what they were made of.

RE: So the things that feed you are not merely pictorial, they're also poetic and literary?

TW: Poetic, literary, yes. Also technical—I read a lot of non-fiction books about architecture, about science, computers, and science fiction.

RE: Is it all stuff for the appetite of art-making?

TW: Hopefully it all ends up in the paintings. I use it as a kind of fuel to drive the engine of making the pictures and give myself a context in which to imagine images.

RE: So you're not attracted to the abstract mode of American painting, where you get inspired and start throwing paint around? The process is a much more elaborate and conceptual one than that?

TW: I always begin with a source outside myself. I don't know if it's any more elaborate or conceptual than what any of the Abstract Expressionists did. I think the reality of Abstract Expressionism is very complicated. It's been simplified, and many of its aspects have been denied.

RE: There are some quotations in your work and I wonder if you find yourself part of an American tradition of painting.

TW: I think so. I'm from New York, and have always felt connected to the paintings which were made here. I say that with some qualification, because of my love for so much European painting, but it's true to the extent that I feel that the accomplishments of the New York School are still a way to measure contemporary work.

RE: No American painter, then, in the waning part of the twentieth century can avoid dealing with that inheritance?

TW: I don't think so. I don't think painters can anywhere, even in Europe. Despite regional or local differences, we're all operating out of their achievement.

RE: The reason that I ask is because Lisa Phillips argues in the Whitney catalogue that you're a breacher of sensibilities and even of generations. Clearly one of the bridges she thinks you cross is into the European tradition of painting. Is that a tradition of which you feel a part?

TW: I do and I don't. I don't feel the need to make the break with European painting that was important or perhaps necessary for that earlier generation. Maybe I don't feel the need because they already did it—Pollock had to discount Europe in order to create a space for himself. All the interest I had in paint—my sense about classical techniques—I wanted to know about them. I felt I could still embrace that tradition, and also acknowledge the innovations of those New York painters.

RE: Did you deliberately go out and attempt to subvert that tradition?

TW: I came at it with a sense of scale and energy that is very different from the refined way those classical techniques have been used.

RE: I think of a lot of your work as being elegant. Does that word sit happily on your palette?

TW: In a way yes, in a way no. I don't think I start out with that in mind, but if I end up with something that is also elegant, why not?

RE: Do you know so much pictorial language now and about how your materials work that elegance may be unavoidable?

TW: I don't think I know anything about it. I think I'm just developing a vocabulary of methods—the way I paint. I'm making images which are part myself, and part an expression of the material itself. Those two parts hopefully make a whole, which is a third or other part—the difficulty of reaching that other part tends to discourage any easy elegance.

RE: Is there a distinction between material and image?

TW: Hopefully not now. When the images first started to appear, I was just trying to look at them. I would put them into the paintings, just to see them. My relationship to them was perplexing to me. Now that relationship is more securely connected. Or I at least accept it. Now I'm interested in the varieties of pictorial space that the objects occupy.

RE: Did any of your paintings make you uneasy?

TW: Some of them, yes.

RE: Even the act of making them? Do you ask, "Who made this?" or is the question, "What is this thing being made?"

TW: Both, with different degrees of emphasis at different times. Right now it's about who's making them.

RE: Then I want to ask you Yeats's question, "How can you tell the dancer from the dance?"

TW: I think there was a period of time when people wanted to separate the person who made the object from the object itself. That seemed to be what Jasper Johns's early work was about, focusing on the literalness of the object. I don't think even he believes that now.

RE: It's as if Johns went out of his way to separate himself from the thing he made. He wanted to insist upon the neutrality of the personality in relationship to the object.

TW: It's an interesting stance to take, but I don't think it's possible. It's something you can't even do in quantum physics, so how can you do it in painting?

RE: Was there a point where you recognized in some kind of epiphanic way that "suddenly I've got it," that the self and the object were synonymous rather than one being a reflection or a meditation on the other?

TW: There were a series of realizations. Gradually it became clear that the pictures I was making were inevitably a reflection and a projection of myself. When I was first working on what became the *Schema* drawings, they seemed like a private record of what developed in the studio. When the opportunity to show them arose, I came to the realization that the things I did, and felt closest to privately were the things I was most convinced about showing publicly.

RE: What in your mind constitutes a body of work? What came together in your mind where you could say that together these pieces were about something rather than being separate objects?

TW: Well, after I had gotten almost halfway through them, it seemed they were introducing new imagery, as well as working over older imagery. Also, they included so many different kinds of drawing materials and techniques—which itself seemed to be a subject .

RE: Do you think of your work as being autobiographical?

TW: I think they track my relationship to myself in ways that might not be clear to anyone except myself. But that goes back to why I would find some things disturbing.

RE: Disturbing in what sense?

TW: In recognizing things about oneself. Like the disturbing distances of old photographs of yourself. You're able to see your own behaviour more clearly, or have it informed by the present. Looking at earlier work, mostly I'm pleasantly surprised that things aren't as bad as I've imagined.

RE: You like yourself more than you thought?

TW: I've accepted what I've done. There is an inevitable autobiographical quality. Hopefully there's also a text being written across the work—a pictorial narrative.

RE: What did seeing the exhibition at the Museum of Contemporary Art tell you? Was there a sense of completion, a sense that you no longer had to investigate certain aspects of yourself?

TW: Not that I no longer had to investigate them. It's overly simplistic, but there were ten years when I was becoming familiar with paint making. Then there were ten years of working with this kind of imagery. And now I think that both of those things are merging for me in the work, and I'm getting closer to the heart of what I'm after.

RE: Is part of that heart, to appropriate a line from literature again, a heart of darkness?

TW: Maybe, but then a heart of light also. I want a wide range of qualities.

RE: Is that something that you have to impose on the work or is it something that comes naturally out of you?

TW: I think it's something that occurs, something you recognize and decide not to obliterate. In one instance, something might seem elegant, and you accept it, at another time you reject it. I don't think elegance is a worthy destination. I could continue to make paintings that are familiar and get better and better at it. But my inclination is to change rhythms often enough so that there's always a quality of being off-balance with my own work.

RE: Is that deliberate?

TW: Yes, that's deliberate. Right now I'm working on very small pencil drawings. Later I'll need a change of scale or material, or I'll need to adjust the medium.

RE: Are those choices entirely capricious? A product of what appeals to you that week, or that day?

TW: It's all instinctual.

RE: What keys you off? What would have got you going on a painting like *Good Government*?

TW: It was a change of rhythm. Before I did that painting, I had worked on a group of ten smaller paintings—back and forth with a fairly wide colour range. When they were finished, I wanted to work on one big picture.

RE: And then limit the palette?

TW: Yeah.

RE: Do you think of your work as menacing?

TW: Do you think there's menace?

RE: I think they're unsettling. I think people find the work discomforting. It makes you nervous; it makes you edgy. You can't quite get at why, but you know that something's up. And I wonder if you sense that in the work?

TW: It's definitely there in the work for me. That's one reason why I continue to work on it. *Plane of Incidence* and even *Folio* seem to have a gothic quality. I painted them in a very programmatic way, building up the layers in the same way, and then at the end there was a picture with psychological characteristics. Images appeared out of purely structural elements. Once a flying saucer was sighted in the middle of one painting—that caused some discomfort on my part!

RE: And bewilderment?

TW: Sure, bewilderment, and embarrassment, fascination, and resolve. There were all those reactions, and I wanted to keep going at it in some way. The objects that appeared in the early paintings I thought of as occurring outside, in the world. But somehow I felt that they were also existing inside myself.

RE: So that directs the perspective in the paintings, the question of where I am as a viewer? In a single painting I can seem outside the cosmos and inside a cellular structure. That constant shifting is something you have a conviction about, not just in a painterly way, but in a physical and real way?

TW: Absolutely. That's the way I see the world, and that's the kind of space I want the paintings to have. The images are all one-to-one. They're all actual size, but the virtual place is the mental space of the viewer, and that's constantly shifting on a perceptual and metaphoric level.

RE: You've made a statement that I want to read …

TW: Am I contradicting myself?

RE: No you're not, but you make me think of Walt Whitman. He asks, "Do I contradict myself?" and answers, "Well, then I contradict myself." In *Song of Myself* he would have beetles rolling balls of dung as well as a sort of cosmic, otherworldly consciousness. There's something American about that stretch: from the smallest piece of shit to another solar system. Is there an affinity in your background that allows you to make those kinds of shifts? Have you come out of a tradition and a culture for which there are only frontiers?

TW: I don't see that as a particularly American sense. Don't you think it's true in a Tantric diagram or an African folktale? It has been a driving force through all art making. I think things have particularly opened up now because of information technologies. So many aspects of other cultures are now available to us.

RE: Yes, I think our scientific and technological knowledge allows us to make those movements more easily. I'm just suggesting that Americans have a natural predisposition to shifts in scale and kind.

TW: Maybe that's true in a way I'm not aware of. But I'm sympathetic to it, even though I haven't read that much Whitman. Maybe I've read Whitman through Ginsberg.

RE: The reason I decided to quote you back to yourself isn't because you contradicted yourself, but because you raised the question of audience. You say you "start with these configurations and then you re-specify the painting through shifts in scale and juxtaposition"—all of which is true. Then you add, "there's the physical clarification of paint, and then the inevitable emotional effects that accrue from these procedures." It seems to me that you can control all the factors except the final one: the emotional effects. How do you know what happens with the viewer, or does what happens to the viewer, once you've organized this incredibly tense visual world, matter to you?

TW: I can only hope that the viewer would be as engaged with looking at the painting as I am. Some of what you've said implies that we don't have that much control over what we intend, because there's such a huge, invisible force that drives everybody. And I think that painting is a particular place where that is very apparent. One of its qualities is that it can register, like a seismographic reading, unintended images, unintended marks. You can start out with a whole set of intentions, but what you end up with is a picture you couldn't predict, and a picture whose meanings are constantly shifting, even for the person who painted it.

RE: Do you know where the work's going, or does its own self-generating language take over? Are the shapes, the scale or the textures carrying you as well?

TW: I've been drawing quite a bit in the last few months, so I've been thinking about the visualization process. What is it? I don't start out to draw a specific object, then draw it—once in a while I'll make a drawing like that, but generally it's about discovering the image and working with it, amplifying it, or toning it down. It's a process of improvisational development.

RE: Is that what you set out to do in *Early Animals* or *Fungus*, those early paintings? They seem more literal.

TW: I think that's true. At that point I was taken with the actuality of physical facts and their presentation. I was interested in looking at those structures.

RE: And rather excited by their sudden appearance?

TW: Absolutely. That still is an aspect of what I'm doing.

RE: Look at the difference between those works and later paintings, where a number of shapes bleed in and out of the background. I wonder if "bleed" is the right word. It's difficult to find the language to describe what happens inside one of your paintings. Put simply, the later paintings seem more complex.

TW: I think they are more complex and more direct. Their complexity is a consequence and build-up of very direct actions. They're openly episodic.

RE: Do you mean you think a number of episodes occur within a single painting?

TW: Yes. I think each time I make a mark, it's an event within the history of that painting. I'm now more willing to let those episodes accumulate to become an image.

RE: So much of the painting seems constructed, in a sense. Think of the cellular, soccer ball shape. It becomes a metonym for the overall painting itself. The paintings, then, are a series of these constructed things.

TW: I think that's true.

RE: What do you call these structures?

TW: I don't necessarily call them anything. They occupy different positions in different paintings. I've been a big Buckminster Fuller fan for a long period of time. I'm seeing now that I'm really designing and engineering each one of the objects.

RE: A new kind of architecture of images then. You have this interest in architecture?

TW: Yes, I think that's the approach I've always tried to take, something akin to engineering. I like images that aren't only about aesthetics—I want the paintings to have a sense of function and purpose.

RE: I look at a lot of your paintings and think they're about the time before things happen, like the time before sex, or when things were just beginning to move together, when things were just shapes. They have a strange timelessness about them.

TW: Or the time during sex?

RE: You bet. So you think of the paintings as being sexual?

TW: Sure. But everything's sexual. You know, *eros, c'est la vie.* It's the condition.

RE: You mean that the world is a confluence, things meeting and penetrating all the time?

TW: Of course.

RE: Paintings like *Good Government* and *Dystopia* have titles that indicate the meaning of the painting goes outside the work itself. They argue some relationship to society, maybe in a larger way to human nature. I want a sense of what the paintings mean and how far their meaning extends beyond their painterliness for you.

TW: I hope as far as anybody's imagination can carry it.

RE: But the titles argue a relationship to society. And it's not a utopian one but rather, one that's breaking down. Is it your sense that disintegration is also a process of reformation?

TW: Actually, I was working on *Dystopia* when I saw a documentary film about a colony of insects that inhabited a certain tree. For these insects, the environment inside the tree was a utopia. There were seemingly endless things to eat, but it was a complete dystopia for the tree, and ultimately for the insects as well. I'm interested in ideas about social relations and boundaries. J. G. Ballard said that the ultimate dystopia was the inside of one's own head.

RE: Is the painting a metaphor for the way society can and does operate?

TW: It's not an illustration, it's an analog world. It's as if the picture were a postulate, a model of how the world might work.

RE: You seem to have no interest in hierarchy, in the ranking of things and any relative moral value ascribed to them—animal less than man, man lower than the angelic realm.

TW: I'm not interested in ranking them, but differences exist. In my own work, there are no hierarchies of media—the categories just describe different things. A small etching and a big painting for me are equal, although they necessarily describe different situations, and come at that description in different ways.

RE: Where did the idea for *Fourteen Etchings* come from?

TW: It started initially as a project to illustrate a story of Edgar Allan Poe. I was approached by someone to do a book, and I suggested using "Eureka." I always liked that essay, because it combined scientific observation with total fiction—all presented as fact. Years before, I had collected a set of X-ray images, and I always wanted to use them for something. Poe seemed like a good excuse. And then for one reason of another the book never happened, and I was left with the idea of juxtaposing the X-rays with my own images.

RE: What is the relationship between the X-ray image and what you add to it? Is it this dialogue of equivalence that you mentioned earlier?

TW: I think so. All the images used have a diagrammatic quality. They seem to be describing something almost mechanical. My pictures allude to things in the world that are abstract, while the X-rays are very specific.

RE: Like what particular bone you're looking at, for example?

TW: Right, but the X-rays have an abstract quality for me also. They reveal something that's invisible to the eye, except through the use of a special instrument.

RE: Where did the series called *One to Twelve* originate? They're big, biomorphic sexy drawings.

TW: They came out of wanting to work with one material in a single group of drawings.

RE: So when you do a single lithograph, does that provoke you to do a series of lithographs which are more complex?

TW: Right. Once again, it has to do with changing the pace. I got into that series of twelve drawings because I wanted to use one material on a larger scale, and really just draw more directly with my arm. Before that I had been working on smaller drawings.

RE: And you wanted the gesture?

TW: Yes, I wanted a bigger gesture, and a more direct relationship between the image created and my body. I think I started out wanting to make one large charcoal drawing and instead ended up with twelve. Those weren't the images I had in my head, that's for sure. They were found. I did the first one and then put it aside, and didn't know what to make of it—it really looked like a big face. Some of that's inevitable—if you're going to deal with ideas about symmetry, which that series dealt with, then you're going to end up with things that seem anthropomorphic. That becomes the psychological link to the imagery.

RE: The most recent piece in the Museum of Contemporary Art survey is a dangerous-looking painting. It looks to me like a shark feed with this beautiful, terrifying suspension of red in the water.

TW: It came from the cover of the exhibition catalogue. I had done a lithograph for the cover composed from drawings on separate plates. It bridged all the different breaks in the cover, and I wanted to make a painting where the image bridged the canvas from side to side.

RE: A kind of memory necklace?

TW: Right. *Event Horizon* also looks towards the new paintings. I see something implied about colour in it, too. That strange purple thing coming out of the top.

RE: It's such an unusual painting. It seems cervical or internal somehow. What is the new work—the work we haven't seen, the work that goes beyond?

TW: I think it has more to do with designing and engineering pictures—with the realization that I'm fabricating the biologies. They're less something outside myself than something I might have previously thought. I always *start* from a point outside myself, but I'm very clear now that the pictures are driven by something much more internal and invented. I think that conviction has made me feel more connected to the work.

RE: What about this connectedness? Is it a question of ownership, of you taking over these things, like keeping your Poe images to yourself?

TW: I think it's about me describing the forces I see at work in the images. Those forces are filtered through my sensibility. I process information, which is then projected as a picture. I function as a lens in some way. I'm much more confident in the image I project. I'm excited about it. Before I wasn't clear where I saw the subject, and where the painting was located. Now they occupy the same space. Picasso describes this problem in that series of paintings of the painter and the model.

RE: About situating the object?

TW: Yes, the subject and the painter and the painting. Those very classical ideas. He dealt with it as depicted narrative. It's a fantastic story about where the artist locates himself in terms of his subject.

RE: I'm intrigued by the metaphor of the lens. Do you know what the thing left out is?

TW: Hopefully nothing is left out. I mean I'm not trying to leave anything out. This is something I'm just trying to articulate to myself—an idea of equivalence between inside and outside, where existing information is rearranged and re-pictured. I'd like the paintings to be as open and inclusive as possible.

RE: The paintings seem improbable sometimes. It's as if the viewer has to catch up to the painting somehow. Is that the way you feel in the making too? I go back to these paintings and try to figure out what you're getting at that's getting at me. But it's me behind the paintings, rather than there with the paintings. It's an uneasy feeling, but one that I'm paradoxically comforted by. Maybe I'm just saying that the excitement of the work is that it remains uneasy.

TW: I think that's true for me, too, that I have to become aware of what the pictures describe, that part beyond my initial intentions. It's an uneasy process. To have the pictures stand for themselves, as an artifact of this culture. I'm interested in tribal art, but I wouldn't claim a connection to Maori tattooing patterns, for example.

RE: Any more than you want to say it's connected to African art by way of Picasso's Cubism?

TW: Right, and hopefully it's all connected. Those are the things that I look at and care about, the things that contain trans-cultural truths.

RE: Do you have a sense of a tradition of art-making and of perception that may come from Maori tribesman and from African art and now comes through you? Is it continuous or fragmented? How does the language work?

TW: I don't know. That's such a loaded question, in terms of how we might perceive art in other cultures, under circumstances we don't understand, and what their function was within a particular culture. I feel connections, but it would be presumptuous for me to say that I share a shamanistic intent. But the tradition of western painting is a conversation that takes place over time, and that's part of its appeal to me.

RE: One of the other consistent things in your work is a respect for, and love of, material.

TW: The material is the access or aperture to these imaginative domains. The knowledge of material is about technology.

RE: It's about technology but it's also about the technology of the hand that can make the mark. Your mark-making is like Twombly's. I mean that small curl of graphite below the surface really matters to you.

TW: Yes, absolutely. I'm a true believer. What the paintings look like is what they mean. They're a product of gesture and material.

RE: It occurs to me one of the things that's happened because of your growing confidence is your language has become less private. Or is it that the language has been around long enough that now you're comfortable with the way in which the rest of society interprets it?

TW: It's not comfort. It's more like sending out radar and seeing what gets bounced back.

RE: Does it matter what gets bounced back?

TW: Well that's what's interesting about finally deciding to show. The experience of seeing what other people think, both the acceptance and resistance, helps you to locate yourself. The same thing is true when you look at other people's work—right now I'm looking at a lot of late Picasso.

RE: Why late Picasso? What's interesting about that work?

TW: The license and the incredibly direct pictorial way they were put together. The space is so complicated, there's so much projection of his imagination. The quality of how he draws, especially in the etchings, and then the directness of the way the paintings get put together is fabulous.

RE: The late works were thoroughly disparaged and dismissed by the generation that stopped with the Modernist experiment. Art history is always a process of re-engaging the past, but there are certain periods of the past that become more interesting to painters of one generation than another. It makes perfect sense, because Picasso's late work seems so chaotic.

TW: Yes, that's the other aspect about the space we were describing before. It doesn't seem to have any structure at all. That was always something not to do. The grid was always such a major structuring device.

RE: Ginsberg appropriates the idea from Kerouac that mind is shapely, that things are shaped in the process of coming to be. All things ultimately end up connecting in a way. The Beats were accused of being chaotic, and Ginsberg was just pointing out that this criticism lacked the long view. If you wait, things will take shape.

TW: Right. Kerouac was willing to believe that to the point of never editing. I'm more sympathetic to Burroughs—however much he might have experimented doing cut-ups and fold-ins, he didn't believe in unedited stream-of-consciousness work. I don't either. I think I have a certain aversion to it. I'm interested in using expressionistic devices and certain aspects of spontaneous mark-making. But the final result is not spontaneous. I tend to be interested in paintings that have an almost geological sense of time, so that in looking at the picture, you're deciphering how the image evolved. If the structure is too simplistic, it doesn't hold for me as a viewing experience.

Tony Cragg
Necessary Appetites

Tony Cragg moves it around. In the last twenty years he has been the most radical and restless sculptor of a remarkable generation of British artists who came to prominence in the late '70s. Rather unimaginatively called the New British Sculptors, there was nothing unimaginative about their work or the range of materials they used to make it. Edward Allington, Richard Deacon, Antony Gormley, Richard Long, Anish Kapoor and Bill Woodrow transformed sculpture in Britain from a-running-out-of-steam Modernist practice to a dynamic engagement with an unprecedented range of objects, subjects and aesthetic processes. British sculpture was suddenly contemporary.

Cragg was at the core of that sense of newness. Without being entirely aware of what was happening in Europe, he went through his own versions of Body Art and *Arte Povera*, making objects and documenting activities that were an early indication of his protean creativity. He has always been a prodigious worker who believes in activity, even if that activity is the simple act of throwing mud at a wall until something happens. He has made himself familiar with all materials, working with crushed brick and cement, string, sandstone, found plastic, cast aluminum, glass, wood, rubber, granite, cast iron, styrofoam, bronze and marble. Anyone aware of the history of sculpture will recognize in that list the complete material history of an aesthetic medium, from Classicism to Romanticism and from Pop to the postmodern. And it's along that aesthetic stretch that so much of Cragg's activity occurs. He is engaged in an ongoing dialogue with the ghosts of sculpture past. It isn't simply a dialogue that sits in summary and uncompromising opposition to the formalism of Henry Moore and Tony Caro, but one that also uses classical materials to make decidedly unclassical subjects. Cragg has undergone something of a sea change in his own work: from being the fabricator-king of sculptures put together out of synthetic plastic fragments, he has emerged as the newest, old master of bronze, creating quotidian objects of monumental beauty. Consider his use of the detergent bottle—its various incarnations trace the range of his visual and material activity. In 1980 they are simply *Five Plastic Bottles*, commercial containers sitting on a gallery floor, nominated to the status of art (in this elevation of the commonplace you can see how much Duchamp and Warhol have shaped the conceptual side of his imagination). In 1982 they are *Five Bottles on a Shelf*—green, yellow, red, blue and orange bottles in various shapes sitting on a white wooden shelf which has been screwed to a gallery wall. In the same year a piece called *Green, Yellow, Red, Orange and Blue Bottles II* places the five containers in front of massive bottle re-constructions, made from hundreds of pieces of found plastic assembled on yet another gallery wall. By 1987–88 in *Bestüchung*, two of the bottles are cast in iron versions that are seven feet tall. In that same year, three different bottles are installed in a church, standing below religious statues silhouetted in ecclesiastical windows. The largest is eleven feet tall. This last incarnation indicates that Cragg's work is less about the vengeance of discard culture on Classicism than about a radical extension of what we have come to regard as classical. His bronze statuesque bottles are so elegant and moving that I wouldn't be surprised to find penitents praying to their giant hieratic presence.

Equally impressive are Cragg's less traditional objects. One part of *Untitled (Large Bronze, 1990)* looks like a huge version of a vacuum cleaner attachment; another looks like a partial replication of a Trojan warrior's helmet. I find myself continually using "like" in writing about Cragg because his pieces—or pieces of his pieces—often evoke comparisons with other objects. At the same time his work is full of examples of a thing transforming into something else, or into a new thing made up from two or three other components. One section of a two-part piece called *Untitled, 1988* looks like the leftovers from the visit of a giant plumber with a penchant for classical materials, while the other section is an amazing approximation of a bottle, a contour that looks like a bronzed turtle back and a lyric, expansive line with an aerodynamic character. What makes it amazing is the slippage the eyes experience as they negotiate and depart from the various original shapes. It is a tribute to Cragg's skill and thorough absorption of an entire sculptural vocabulary, running from classicism to postmodernism, that these hybrids look so good and make their transitions so effortlessly. You think you have seen these unique pieces before but you haven't; what you've seen are the traditions out of which they have evolved. *Incubation*, a three-part granite piece from 1990, includes a spoon shape which seems to have been generated out of the piece of granite with the scalloped indentation on its surface. It may also be a variation on the bronze mortar and pestle from 1987–1988, the place where things get metaphorically pulverized before they can begin their imperceptible process of shape-changing. It is a process that moves from mashing up to making miraculous.

The following interview was conducted in the fall of 1991 by telephone when Tony Cragg was in New York to install an exhibition at the Marian Goodman Gallery.

TONY CRAGG: When I was young I wanted very much to study science. After doing the school qualification my parents moved away from where we lived, which was a town about twenty miles north of London. They moved to Bristol, leaving me on my own for the first time. I had a job as a laboratory assistant in a place called the Natural Producers Rubber Research Association, which was financed by the Malaysian Government. I was about eighteen then and this was going to be my way of doing a degree. I was there for about two years. I had romantic ideas but the job just wasn't what I thought science was. My father used to design bits of aircraft, originally for the military and then later on he worked on the Comet, the Trident, then on the Concorde. They were his projects. My grandfather had been a farmer but my father belonged to the generation that believed science and technology were going to save the world. I believed in it as well until I found myself sitting in that laboratory, bored out of my brain. I completely lost interest.

ROBERT ENRIGHT: It was pretty disillusioning for you?

TC: Well, sitting in this laboratory all day and sometimes into the evenings, was kind of a numbskull activity for an eighteen year old. It was probably the worst job I ever had. But because I had a lot of time waiting for things to happen and for results to come up, I started to draw. They were really the first things I drew. Also this was 1968 and there was so much going on outside—student demonstrations, a lot of good rock music—and there I was stuck in this laboratory.

RE: What kind of experiments were you waiting to see resolved when you worked in the laboratory?

TC: We worked on a product called polyisoprene, which is the chemical name for natural rubber as opposed to artificial rubber. It has a weak double bond and can be oxidized very easily, especially by ozone. We were looking for an antioxident to make it as commercially viable as the artificial rubbers, which were then very cheap. I worked with a professor who decided what to do and I had to do it. I was very unhappy there and felt isolated. So my dream about science became a big disappointment.

RE: What was the nature of the drawing you did in the laboratory?

TC: Scribbles. It was very unconscious at the time. They were really just doodles.

RE: But you'd had no art training, so you were entirely on your own?

TC: Yeah. It was coming from my general discontent with what I was doing and with my indecision about whether I was going to continue with science. I even thought for a short time about studying philosophy. Then I had the opportunity to go to art school. I met a very nice guy there, the first artist I ever met. He showed me how he made paintings. This was at a low level, so the first thing I had to do was to leave the area north of London, where I was living, in order to get money. I tried to avoid taking it from my parents. I went to live in the country near Bristol and attended the Gloucestershire School of Art in Cheltenham. In Britain you do an obligatory foundation year where you simply draw and paint and make sculptures and ceramics. You have this much wider course and you're encouraged after to go into one of fourteen different disciplines. It varies from making jewellery, films, video or fashion to industrial design. Somewhere in that range you could also go and be a painter or a sculptor. So after having done that I went on to a painting course at the Wimbledon School of Art.

RE: Was it painting, then, that you gravitated towards in these early years?

TC: Not really. But making sculpture is very difficult for a twenty-year-old. I still think it's one of the most difficult things in the world.

RE: Did you know what sculpture was at the time?

TC: No. In our society there's very little practise. Children don't do it at home. They do drawings and the times they actually make something three-dimensional are relatively rare. And when you get into art school it isn't considerably different. The first sort of bumblings are how to mix up plaster and how to get it to stick together. I wouldn't regard that as sculpture, it's just that painting comes together a little faster. Other than that, I enjoyed drawing very much. It's actually what I mainly did.

RE: By this time had you decided you were going to be an artist?

TC: Yeah, this was a fantastic part of my life. I did this foundation year and then I had to earn money again, so I worked in a steel-casting foundry in a place called Yate, which is north of Bristol. It was a night job, half-past seven in the evening until half-past seven in the morning. There were mainly West Indians and Pakistanis working in the building and they were very, very nice people. Our relationship was quite vital because I'm a slight, red-headed person and I didn't know it at the time but, when I first started there, they took a bet on how long I would last and some said, "He won't manage the night." After I'd been there a month this big guy said, "I'm going to take you out for a meal on the weekend." And I said "Why is that," and he said, "Because I said you'd last the month."

RE: This was rigorous work, then?

TC: It was very tough work and badly paid but it didn't matter because I felt the place was beautiful: this incredibly huge dark hall, four hundred metres long, immensely high. It was sweaty, dirty work and you seemed to be always hurting yourself on something, but it was also dynamic. Things like the way the casting sand ended up in a ten to fifteen-foot-high cone after it had been sieved out. When you see things being made in front of you, you understand better the energy and the reason for them.

RE: This experience must have planted the seeds of your fascination with cast pieces.

TC: I never actually thought much about that. More important for me was this appreciation of a physical world and how things can be made. When you ask about making sculpture: that's when I decided. I simply couldn't stand in a room with thirty people and paint something; it was out of the question. I'd just had a year of working and I was too muscled up, too energetic.

RE: So you actually had been radicalized by the work force?

TC: That's how I felt anyway.

RE: And what about your art education?

TC: I stayed at the Wimbledon School of Art. Rather than paint, the first thing I did there was to make sculptures, things that I could somehow put together or squeeze in my pocket.

RE: This is even before your string pieces?

TC: Yes. They were made with a kind of plasticine, just squooshing them around in my pocket, more like playing with your balls than anything else. These were more or less raw responses to the situation of life. Then I made the string pieces and after that a whole series of different things which were based on combinations and permutations, sometimes with found material, sometimes with material I made myself. Then I made another series of things and I showed photographs of them outside and somebody said to me, "This is *Arte Povera*" and I thought, "Great, *Arte Povera*, what the heck is that?"

RE: So suddenly you connected to a European tradition you knew nothing about?

TC: No idea. But it was really fantastic when I found out. I looked at these black and white catalogues and I said, "Right, it means I'm not completely on the wrong track here." Suddenly I saw a whole generation of people already out there who, probably for different reasons than the ones I had, wanted to make work on a level I understood. An everyday, related-to-existence kind of art.

RE: There's certainly nothing more commonplace than string. Was there any philosophical basis for what you were doing or was it just activity?

TC: It was really just activity and it's something I still believe in doing when I get caught in a hole and don't want to go for a formal solution. It took me two weeks just to get the string together and to tie the stupid knots. I'm a very nervous and energetic person, and sometimes these bouts of senseless activity are very good for me. Even now, I'll just start throwing handfuls of clay at the wall for days until it sticks together and falls off. The odds are high at having some success with it. It's just a response.

RE: Did you need the validation that came from *Arte Povera*? Was that outside support important to you?

TC: I didn't know anything about art. I'm not trying to play the naïve one. Pop Art I could have just about got together. I remember Warhol and Oldenburg but I don't think I would have been able to tell you the names of any other artists. I wouldn't have known what Abstract Expressionism was.

RE: You were that much of an art historical innocent?

TC: In a way, that's right. I didn't ever expect to end up where I was. Anyway, I thought art school was just for fun.

RE: And art wasn't going to be something you'd do for a living?

TC: Well, that was another thing. People at that time didn't go to art school because it was a career option. I work in the Academy in Düsseldorf today and the kids come in and they're already so well educated. In the late '60s and early '70s the people who went to art school were painting the tackiest, shoddiest things. But somehow it didn't matter because there was still some kind of idealism. You weren't going to get a job, you weren't going to get paid and you weren't going to become famous. Everybody was very clear about it at the time.

RE: When you did a piece like *Stack* in 1976, were you aware that your work could be read as an homage to Kounellis?

TC: What happened is that after I'd actually discovered these things—which was fantastic—I very quickly said, "Wait a minute, these bastards have already done it."

RE: You hate to find a wheel when you've just made one, don't you?

TC: Yes. That was a funny, two-way experience. That's when I did these things using my own body. I also used quite pretentious language just trying to find a way of actually describing what I was doing.

RE: Did you also use your body because it was there? One of the advantages of having a body is that it's a tool which is always available to you.

TC: It's a support system. I think the work was a little about just trying it on, trying to look for new solutions. There was no great content in it, other than what comes out because it's not an uninteresting thing to have done.

RE: There seems already to be evidence of a lot of ideas operating. I'm thinking of the precariously stacked bricks. It's a very simple piece, but amazingly mature at the same time. You were also putting small objects on your leg or upper arms; you were photographing yourself on a beach. You were involved in a wide range of art activities.

TC: That's my whole attitude. I don't feel like eating the same thing for break-fast as I do for lunch. Tomorrow I'm going to eat something else. It has to do with appetites and what's necessary.

RE: Tell me, then, about your sense of the importance of the *Crushed Rubble* piece. There are critics who have argued that it was the first significant piece you did.

TC: It was just good work. I was one of two students accepted at the Royal College out of something like a thousand applicants. They took me into a very traditional, boring situation, which was dominated by a generation of young bloods. British would-be sculptors I didn't even know, people like Nigel Hall and Martin Naylor. By the time 1972 came 'round they had a complex that things were hap-pening in Europe and that they were very dowdy. It never happened again that they took somebody with my interests into the college.

RE: By this time had you recognized there was what could loosely be called a British tradition of sculpture, one that included people like Henry Moore, Barbara Hepworth and Tony Caro?

TC: No, I've never been interested in Moore, I've never even considered his work. And other than the few formal conventions of the late '40s which I think are interesting, I think I've considered it as much as is warranted. You have to realize that Brancusi and Picasso and Hepworth and a whole bunch of others worked at the beginning of the century. They really did do something about chang-ing sculpture. Moore didn't.

RE: What about Caro's position?

TC: Caro is a carbon copy. He makes the same sculpture as Henry Moore and as he's getting older he looks more and more like Henry Moore's assistant. He had the clever idea of using those constructed materials to somehow find a little place for himself. That's legitimate. The works that came out of it—like *Splash, Early in the Morning, Prairie*, half a dozen to a dozen works—were fine. Then he did something terrible: he made the whole thing into a dogma, so that in Britain, at least, you have endless generations of brainless metal-welders. Dogma is a very, very dangerous thing. It's terrible. Creative young people actually get stopped. I've had friends and associates who lost the whole thing because they got sucked up in dogma.

RE: You've described yourself as an "extreme materialist." I assume you don't mean that to be dogmatic. Is it meant to be descriptive?

TC: The word comes from *matea*, from mother, something which in its origin is a spiritual word. But that's very difficult for people living at the end of the twentieth century to actually appreciate. For us, materialism is equated, through the Renaissance and through the whole process of the industrial revolution, with the production of things.

RE: In 1988 you made that wonderful bronze piece called *Mother's Milk II*. Did you mean to comment on your root notion of material as well as on bronze—one of the most traditional sculptural materials?

TC: That work was made because my wife was having our first child. It was the time of Chernobyl and she was neurotic about her baby, which was still in her stomach, and about how to get food that wasn't contaminated. We couldn't drink milk because there were all these things going on. So the origin of that piece had much more to do with mother's milk.

RE: Since we're talking about specific pieces, I want to return briefly to *Crushed Rubble*. It seemed to be a deconstruction of the notion of sculpture, rather than a making.

TC: I've never really looked at the term "deconstruction." Deconstruction is a way to describe cultural venom; it's not something I accept very easily. I accept changing processes.

RE: It must be wonderful to take something that exists as a solid object, crush it and then bring it back in its component parts. On the surface that process would seem destructive but the actual result resembled a beautiful floor painting.

TC: It was very, very beautiful, that's true.

RE: You know that, don't you?

TC: I do indeed. Sometimes I very much like the difference between hitting something abruptly, in a sense destroying it, and then having it reveal itself in a different kind of way. I like looking at things for their internal qualities as well. The same time I made the *Crushed Rubble* piece, I also made a lot of work by slicing things up. It was my idea that we should try to find at least one function for a sculpture: one that attracted me was to find symbols or ways of describing a state—like either the microscopic or macroscopic—that we can't perceive normally. Something we don't actually pick up—like radio waves—or something that happens to be out of our ear pitch, or happens to be darker than light. It's very necessary just to look for images. Then the freedoms that remain are the freedoms to dream, to have fantasies, to make the things that are already around us more interesting, in the way that everyday objects and other materials can be carriers of information. To work on that very concentratedly, making sure that the bubble of information around any object or material gets filled in, in as interesting and significant a way as you can manage, that's all it's about.

RE: Peter Schjeldahl had that lovely phrase in his essay about your sculptures; he talked about their being in "the fraternity of the republic of existence, where no object is a second class citizen." Is there a democracy of components that you've consistently used and held as an attitude?

TC: I think it's from a slightly different position. In Britain you cope with the tradition of Romantic sculpture. This Romanticism, this ignoring of the man-made world, is something that disturbed me greatly. Having found a generation of people who came out around the end of the 1960s—people like Richard Long—I tried to get a hand-hold on the problems of that generation. Obviously, one tends to go for the weakest point. So apparent democracy really starts with putting natural materials and man-made materials on a parity with one another.

RE: The piece called *Leaf*, for instance, where you have that radiant big green thing that's basically made out of plastic—is that an unavoidable comment about the close relationship you see between nature and culture?

TC: Put like that, it's sort of abrupt. But it's like that on one level. The terrible thing is the greenness of it. We only see the greenness and the translucency of the plastic. I mean, the problem we have when we walk up and look at a plant is to determine whether it's plastic or not.

RE: It's a bit disconcerting for anyone who is wary of technology to see the detritus of consumer culture thrown up on a wall in such a beautiful way.

TC: Well, it's not so beautiful. I keep looking at it and I go backwards and forwards. I think there's a nice edge there. I think it also looks a little tacky and a little bit disgusting. For instance, there are no beautiful or ugly stones. There's real democracy in nature and we're forced into accepting it all. Also, we bring criteria to man-made objects which are incredible. If you're picking material for a suit you go through these agonies: the more sophisticated the culture is, the bigger the choices and courses of action about how to make things. They're very complicated. I don't know if it is a real democracy. I think it's really more a question of respect. First of all, parity between the man-made and the natural world is never possible. But I'm not doing it faint-heartedly; it's just a device for me to say we have to find this borderline between the two things, which has always been an absolute. Nature is an absolute, which is why we see and think about the world in the way we do.

RE: Is that an ethical position that you hold? Would you be willing to push it from aesthetics to ethics?

TC: No. I really prefer somebody else to decide that. Let me just say that you have to have other values behind what you're doing, otherwise there's no point in doing it at all.

RE: That leads me inevitably to ask you about the material you use. Obviously, there are a number of people who look at your work as being a reclamation of discard culture. They see you making a comment about consumer culture. You easily get locked into being perceived as a kind of ecological moralist.

TC: I've never attempted to address the problem of ecology. There's nothing interesting in recycling materials to make art. I mean, there is something interesting about it, but it's something that has been done and done very well—by Arman and people like that. They really established something. I think there are two things here. One is that I wouldn't like to approach just the question of ecology. What I try is to make a description of the way things are. It's almost like there's something inventorial about it.

RE: Inventory rather than taxonomy? Some of the early work seems like the kind of classifying that I would call taxonomical.

TC: Yeah, taxonomy. You have to go through it anyway. Sometimes I think it's just a tool. I don't attach too much importance to structure. You just need *some* structure. Sometimes it can be just the formal carrier. For example, in *Newton's Tones*, the work was about my revelling in something grotty or neglected. But when you look at it you know it is also incredibly beautiful. I do revel in that. I made *Newton's Tones* very quickly and I was annoyed that—as a formal device— I only managed to get it down into this quadrangle. You just have to have a formal device and the quadrangle was the best I could do at the time. The quadrangle is also good because it retained a sincerely felt respect for Richard Long, but also the warning that I wouldn't accept the argument his work makes. The work that came after was when I started to break away.

RE: What accounts for your prodigious output, by most accounts some seven hundred works? That's a remarkable number. What compels you?

TC: I'm just a nervous, very tense person and I don't have anything better to do in my life. If I'm not playing with my children, I'm usually making something. That's all there is to it. Also I sometimes get into a nice sweaty kind of working process. It rejuvenates you sometimes; kills you off at others. But I don't find it so difficult. The difficult thing is to look at what you've done and be really honest about it.

RE: Your work seems to be the product of someone who looks very intently. Has that been a significant way of informing your sense of art-making?

TC: I've come to make my work by looking at things. That's why there are relatively few cultural references or sources in the work. I'm not going to start quoting mythologies.

RE: So you're obviously not going to be the proprietor of the junkyard with a thousand faces. But it seems to me that when people look at your work, they also apprehend what it is you've thought about the act of looking.

TC: I'll just say something because it's central to what I believe in. You're obviously a writer and there's an arrogance in philosophers and writers. They think in terms of written language, but when I dream and think, I do it in images. I've never thought that two people looked the same. You just have to look at three centimetres of skin or look at somebody's face and you see their age, their sex, their mental state, whether they're excited or slightly ill, whether they're muscular or fat. A tiny little bit of skin gives you all this information. It's incredible how we read it. It's like a book already. We have the potential for understanding and using a much more complicated syntax than we do with traditional writing and the spoken word. I feel the syntax of looking provides a whole difference.

RE: There are pieces of yours that seem very simple on the surface, like *Boat* or *Bird* or even *Landscape on a Wall*. It's as if they're the record of having been able to get down the gesture of sculpture. They're reduced and their power comes out of a sense of your having seen the thing, thought about the seeing and then being able to get it up there on the wall.

TC: I hate to admit I don't think about it for very long. I think about it afterwards and then I worry about how to make the next piece. In the actual making it makes itself.

RE: They have that quality. What about a piece like *Riot*? The large, fragmentary murals seem to be a different order of work.

TC: No, because that's a simple decision. What I'm scared of initially is whether it's going to work as a thing in a space or in a room. I was more or less in the death-throes of the plastic works with that piece because I realized that I didn't want to have to make a signature piece out of the plastic work. I haven't done one for five or six years but I'd make another if there was a real reason for doing it. I had an assistant at the time who was an ex-coal miner and there was this terrible strike going on. So the piece reflected a bit of human sympathy for him. He was very much involved in the trade union movement and felt very bitter about the whole thing. Also, it was an opportunity for me to exhibit in Great Britain after a couple of years of not having been there. And it was simply what I can loosely call the artistic challenge of trying to get a theme in that material. I just pick out the images and put the whole thing together, which doesn't really take a great deal of time. I think the idea world is more complicated and I fight more often with it than I do with actually making something. Making something is a great relief.

RE: Your exhibition at the Whitechapel Gallery in 1987 had *Crown Jewels* in it, a piece that seemed to deal explicitly with political and social concerns. Am I right in assuming that it was a piece that spoke to British culture at that time?

TC: They were very direct. I'd been offered this exhibition at the Whitechapel but I'd forgotten how big the gallery was. I'd only been there a couple of times before and they used to have the offices up there, so the building was half the size that it is today. I was quite shocked to find out the space had doubled and I had only ten days to make a work. I went into top gear. I didn't know what I was going to do and I didn't know what my materials would be: I was more or less shooting from the hip. We got in a van and drove day and night to get the materials together.

RE: Were you frightened or intimidated by the prospect of the show?

TC: No. If you're scared I think you've lost it. I'm not someone who's going to get scared about that kind of thing—that's all art voodoo. It's only making things. What I want in the work is a quality of self-understanding. Why this holiness-of-holies attitude in looking at objects? There's so much physical material around us and there's a hell of a lot of work to be done in looking, reassessing and thinking about it. And you're not going to do that if you make voodoo and make it into some stupid nineteenth-century cultural game.

RE: So *Self Portrait with Bottle and Bricks*, where it looks as if you're about to be rained upon by the objects of your own making, I can take to be a piece that has a degree of self-deprecation involved in its motivation?

TC: Yeah, that's how you feel sometimes. When I grew up exhibiting in the late '70s and early '80s, the scene really was dominated by painters. I was fascinated because these people very quickly got to become personalities. People are always disappointed in meeting me. They think I'm this six-foot giant with foot-wide forearms or something and they find out I'm just this skinny, red-headed, balding person. So I'm not going to get into a personality cult thing. It's just about making objects.

RE: You said that *Riot* was a farewell to the plastic works. What was it that made you gravitate towards a wider range of things, especially the cast bronze pieces?

TC: Lots of things, but two essential ones. One was a push and one was a pull, if I can put it like that.

RE: That's dangerous Modernist talk.

TC: I'll tell you what I mean by push and pull. I described to you the time where I was running around everywhere making work: it was a very exciting, energetic period. The positive thing you learn when your energy is low is that you start resorting to certain things. You actually get together a vocabulary of responses. At that point I found things had become less interesting. The gains became less and less. I was someone who really never had any money in his life but after the first few years of exhibiting I got into a very strange state where I actually bought a house and rented a studio. So you get stuck halfway between existential needs and your own reasons for doing something. I think this is a Faustian moment. I see this with every young artist who suddenly comes on to the market. Two or three years later you wonder which way he's going to go. But I did this unconsciously. On one level I feel I was very lucky. It was about the time my parents died and I was going down the motorway to do another show somewhere and suddenly my energy level said to me, "This is stupid to continue." So I stopped and went back to the studio. That was around 1983. There was a real dip in activity. Then a little later on I became aware for the first time of a generation of new sculptors coming up, partly out of Britain—including Richard Deacon and David Mack—and also in Germany and Holland. So suddenly I didn't feel quite so alone. The thing that gave me energy was that I didn't have to fight against the painters anymore. It sounds like a strange thing, but at that time I was formulating an argument against their dominance. Then I realized that this new generation of sculptors dealt with the object in a very different way than I did. I had been included in a large survey exhibition in Holland and I was shocked to realize that the way I used material and thought about objects, and the way they did things— this glorifying of industrial and man-made objects—was so different. I thought, "Wait a minute, that's not what I'm interested in doing." So that was the push. The pull was another thing. As a student I'd used materials with absolute democracy and I realized I had to start assuming more responsibility for making the parts of the thing. There were also some materials—like bronze, plaster, clay and wood— that I hadn't been using and I had to think about that, too. It's very difficult for an English sculptor to use bronze today because Henry Moore has fucked it over so badly. It's occupied. So it took a long, long time for me to get used to it. I just wasn't prepared to give up a certain freedom. It's not a matter of chance that people use bronze. For a lot of jobs it really is the best material. I said, "Damn it, I can't afford to give up this freedom." But I cringed at the first few bronzes. I hated the patina; I still hate it. At the same time I can't stop myself because I know I have to make it. That's something that you can't get away from. So that's the push and pull thing I'm describing. First of all the necessity of responding again to what other artists were doing around me, and then being forced to concentrate more on the studio. I'm eternally grateful for that because my understanding of my work in the last five or six years has increased greatly.

RE: Those large cast bottle pieces are pretty cheeky. To take bronze and a monumental scale and make something as commonplace as a detergent bottle is a fairly irreverent thing to do.

TC: Yeah, but the advantage that artists of the late '60s had was that they could still nominate things. It was still a big non-art world and they could nominate a material and make it into art. Think of Warhol. After the late '60s, everything from shit to gold could be an art material. You could make art any way you wanted. And the content you were dealing with was experimental as well. The vocabulary available to artists has been immense. Younger students today don't stop to think about using something like fat. They don't thank Joseph Beuys because he said they can do it, they just do it. So the question, "Is it art" doesn't interest me anymore. It was the basic question for the late '60s generation of artists—whether Richard Long or Lawrence Weiner—but it's more or less irrelevant now.

Donald Baechler

The Incidental Tourist

Donald Baechler made a painting in 1989 that contains everything you need to know about why he is among the most compelling painters of his generation. *Balzac* is bizarre, cranky, improbable and irresistible. It shows a figure—the artist's version of Rodin's naked Balzac—sitting on a scabrous looking mound of something dark, his distended belly more like a ledge than a physiological feature. A stubby arm appears to be reaching out to catch or juggle the smallest and least colourful of three hovering beachballs. Surrounding him on a scumbled white ground are objects and shapes—a spool of thread, a patch of paper, smudges and drips of colour—all reminders of a haunting pentimento. Always, the work shows the memory and the mechanics of its own making.

Baechler's painting is about making strange. None of the components have anything to do with one another and yet the more you look at his work, the more sensible it becomes. Balzac himself appears to have made an accommodation with the curious situation in which he finds himself and, as a viewer, it seems vexatious not to respond in kind.

Baechler's paintings, drawings and collages are never without interest. His special skill is to take commonplace things and place them together in improbable relationships. What do crocodiles and cucumbers have in common; Abe Lincoln and okras; flowers and subway tickets; dinosaurs and basketballs; owls and squares of colour? If you answer nothing to any of these combinations, then you've never seen a work by this peripatetic New York artist.

Baechler himself is wary of reading the content of his work as significant. "I'm interested in a sort of suspension of meaning in the pictures" he told Joseph Kosuth in an interview, and you can see his point. His concerns are formal and strategic; he is interested in what shapes, colours and surfaces work for him personally and he is committed to a way of making art that encourages a radical degree of defamiliarization with his own processes. He wants to unlearn everything he knows. His method is a kind of willed forgetfulness and his materials are wayward and unconventional. He has used the technique of left-handed drawing, the art of the insane, drawings made by drunks and prostitutes, children's school work, graffiti on toilet walls, prison forms, linguistic tables from encyclopedias and Arabic script. All of these can be combined to build "resistance into the surface," in the artist's knowing phrase. A Baechler surface is a cobble of textures, marks and materials that places him in the painterly tribe of Twombly and Ryman and Schwitters. It's in this sense that his art departs from Surrealism. While his work shares with that movement an attachment to startling and illogical combinations, you comprehend those combinations in entirely different ways. In Surrealism the sense of surprise must persist for the piece to work; with Baechler the initial impression of being startled goes through a gradual accommodation, until, after repeated scrutiny his combinations seem congenial, even inevitable. This may account for the self-consciousness of his figures who often awkwardly dramatize their own sense of surprise at where they find themselves. In *Forest* you can hear the vaudevillian drum roll behind the gesture of Abe Lincoln's extended arm, as he experiences a close encounter with a fir tree. There are occasions—as in *Yankee Pieces*—where the same figure in a stove-pipe hat finds himself surrounded by a vegetable suspension of potatoes and onions and okras. They hang around him in a sort of *trompe-l'oeil* intensity. I have the sense that a devilish impresario has thrown the figure the wrong objects to juggle and that the whole enterprise is about to come tumbling down, a humpty-dumptied world of organic confusion. Worse still, the figure looks about to be impaled on a particularly pointed okra. While he may be nervous, the young boy in *Potato Painting* is shedding tears over the dream (or maybe over the presence) of four floating spudniks. You don't know whether to laugh at him or weep with him. "People have nightmares about my paintings sometimes," Baechler said in 1987. "It pleases me enormously." It's precisely this uncompromising and unrepentant attitude that characterizes Baechler's art and personality.

The following interview took place in Baechler's New York studio in December of 1994.

ROBERT ENRIGHT: This may seem a funny place to start, but now you're famous enough to be the subject of a Gap ad, I want to know what's going on in that image. You're cradling a gourd as if it were a musical instrument and you look positively divine doing it.

DONALD BAECHLER: It was actually inspired by a Robert Mapplethorpe portrait of Louise Bourgeois where she's holding one of her phalluses. I had done sculptures that were three-dimensional versions of the vegetables I used to paint. It seemed a nice idea to be holding a sculpture. And I wanted to avoid the self-advertisement involved in standing in front of a painting.

RE: I want to ask you about paintings in which you put together in the same work outlined figures and almost *tromp-l'oeil* fruit and vegetables. Give me a sense of how those compositions operate?

DB: I was after a very simple, formal tension in those paintings. There's a black and white image painted very flat—and then almost another language operating in a colourful ball or colourful abstract device, or there were these three-dimensional vegetables which grew out of playing with abstract biomorphic forms. I decided they should have a more specific nature, so I turned them into vegetables. A big part of my project has always been learning how to do things I don't know how to do. I set myself the task of learning how to paint these things because I couldn't paint them. I'm not sure how important that is to anyone else's reading of the paintings, but it's important to my own procedures.

RE: It's your own way of keeping interested in the work?

DB: Yes, exactly.

RE: I want to know about how you proceed. I assume you work the ground first and then overlay the images?

DB: Yes. I began using patches and things as an editing process. I've never liked very thick paint so if I made a mistake, instead of painting over it I would glue something on top. It was a way of getting back to that fresher surface but it ended up becoming a device. I have since tried to abandon it but it provides a very useful way of breaking up the line. I was always afraid of things becoming too perfect, so I built all this resistance into the surface. The Australian art critic Paul Taylor once said that my line "had the quality of chewed string," which I liked a lot.

RE: One of the things that struck me about the ground in some of that earlier work—work from the mid 1980s—is how elegant and beautiful it is. Other critics have commented about your membership in the Twombly painterly tradition. Does it bother you when people say that about the work?

DB: No, but I think it's incidental. I've rarely been after that. Well, that's not entirely true but I'm *often* not after that. It's just a way my hand moves, the way I make marks. I usually try pretty hard not to make a beautiful white field. It's a very methodical process—things are glued down, white paint is applied, something black is painted. It doesn't look good, so I paint over it and the erasure makes a certain hazy wash.

RE: I guess I'm getting at the notion of left-handed paintings—that you consciously set about to frustrate any beauty you may be getting in the composition. Is that the strategy?

DB: That's what I always thought I was doing.

RE: And maybe it isn't working?

DB: Maybe not.

RE: The other artist who comes to mind—especially in the way you compose—is Kurt Schwitters. A lot of his collages seem to be less about composition than just about putting things up there and not worrying about any sense of cohesion. Even in your current show at the Paul Kasmin Gallery certain sections of the works on paper look a little bit like Schwitters. Is he someone who interests you at all?

DB: He is. And also Rauschenberg. I certainly am much more familiar with Rauschenberg than with Schwitters.

RE: I was thinking specifically of someone like Brice Marden who tries to frustrate his notion of beauty by painting with twigs and ends up making beautiful paintings anyway. It's as if the gesture just won't go away.

DB: I don't know what you can do about that.

RE: I want to talk a little bit about other artists you may look at. You gave me a clue when you advised me to go and look at the children's art exhibition around the corner. Do you spend a lot of time looking at other art for ideas?

DB: Hardly ever. I look at the art of my colleagues out of professional curiosity. And I look at, for instance, ancient art and art that's a bit outside my experience, but I've never been interested in the kind of career that only exists in dialogue with other artists. It's actually quite common for a twentieth-century artist to look outside of art history for inspiration or ideas. But in American art especially there's a very academic, self-reflexive strain going on, where artists are commenting on other artists. This doesn't interest me at all.

RE: I've read that you have a huge correspondence with people who keep sending you images from all over the world. Is that how a lot of the images come to you?

DB: What comes to me is a lot of the things that end up in my collage backgrounds. They either arrive or I find them when I'm travelling. And a lot of types of drawings that I have sometimes used as models for my own drawings. But it's not a big part of my activity to just appropriate things, if that's what you mean.

RE: So if someone sends you a child's drawing you may work it into the composition?

DB: I'm actually not at all interested in children's art and never have been. But people keep sending it to me anyway. I am interested in children's written school work which finds its way into my work. I also manufacture things in the studio now. I had a series of works I wanted to complete that needed certain elements and I didn't have enough of them, so instead of Xeroxing I hired someone to make fake vocabulary lessons and fake maps which come from geography lessons. Originally I found the models for them in the street. But the images came from all over. I was looking into the art of the insane and the art of schizophrenics as well as at drawings on toilet walls. I used to have a project where I'd go to bars and drink with people who weren't artists and have them do drawings for me. I'd be sitting at the bar with my pad and paper and talk to somebody and say, "Listen, why don't you do a drawing for me." What I was after was different ways of putting lines together. My impulse in drawing a face is to start with your nose, and when I'd ask someone else to draw a face they'd start at the ear. I'd think, well that's an interesting way to start; I'll start with the ear next time. So I was looking for models on how to change my own drawing, how to reinvigorate it by taking it away from things I knew too much about.

RE: So why do people keep sending you things?

DB: The whole project started in 1981. In 1980 I had started to copy illustrations from magazines onto abstract grounds. I stopped drawing, lost all touch with my hand and wanted to get back into it. I learned about Dubuffet's collection in Lausanne and I went to visit that and went to visit hospitals in Austria and Brazil. I also started talking with drunks in bars. The whole investigation was to relearn how to draw. That's how the collecting started. When people would come to my studio they'd see these piles of drawings I'd brought from the hospital, or piles of drawings I'd found in the red light district in Hamburg, or had prostitutes draw for me. Then they'd start sending me things. Most of them are sitting in boxes in the storage room and I've never even looked at them.

RE: Did you consciously go to what in the nineteenth century would have been called the *demi-monde*? Were you trying to find an energy in the experience coming out of this world that wasn't art experience?

DB: It had nothing to do with experience. I enjoyed going to these places and I knew I would find people there who weren't artists and who were friendly to talk to and have a little collaboration with.

RE: So your life and your art were inseparable. You liked going to those places and you were there because you'd be able to, as you say, steal ideas for your art out of it?

DB: Steal ideas for my art?

RE: That's a quote from one of the early artist's books you did with Ajax Press. You talk about stealing ideas from Guillermo Kuitca.

DB: That was a joke. I have no use for anyone else's ideas. I have too many ideas of my own.

RE: The life you seem to be leading has a certain quality of being outside the mainstream.

DB: There's nothing unusual about that, I mean I'm not William Burroughs; I'm not an outlaw junkie. It's just that I get bored in art bars so I go somewhere else.

RE: Do you believe in beauty? Is that a notion that makes any sense to you at all? Does it matter to you whether what you get is beautiful or not?

DB: I don't think about it. I think about processes a lot. I suppose the end result inevitably ends up being beautiful or not beautiful. I suppose that the decisions I make are all formed by a search for some kind of beauty but I don't know how I would define it. Some people think the things I do are awfully ugly, you know.

RE: That work called *Balzac*, do you remember why you made it?

DB: I was at the Rhode Island School of Design as a visiting artist, and they have this Rodin sculpture of Balzac in the museum there.

RE: The naked or the clothed one?

DB: The naked one. So I just did some drawings. Actually, I bought the postcard and I still have it. I went back to the hotel. I tried to work in the museum but there were a bunch of students drawing there, so that was a kind of deflating experience. Drawing in a museum is depressing. Anyway, it turned into a series of paintings. It was the first beach ball painting and so the title is a kind of joke.

RE: You like drawing and working in hotel rooms?

DB: Well, there's nothing else to do. You can watch TV or you can draw.

RE: Are you obsessed with work?

DB: Well, there are several aspects to my work; a lot of what I do when I travel is research. If I'm not sitting in hotel rooms drawing, I'm going around aggressively collecting the things that end up in the collages, and aggressively looking for all sorts of different books that become source material. At the moment I'm interested in bad advertising. I've lost interest in so-called outsider art for various reasons. So I'm looking a lot at the sources Pop artists sometimes used—like very bad illustrations from the Yellow Pages and back pages of magazines, hand-painted signs from Africa and Asia. I do a lot of photography for source material when I'm travelling, and I do a lot of collecting of things which either find their way into my art or into my closets.

RE: Do you pick places because you have some notion that you may find things useful to you there? Or does it really matter where you go when you travel?

DB: Usually I have some idea what I'll find based on friends telling me or on something I've seen in a magazine, or just an idea of the visual culture. I knew India would be a really rich place to visit and it was.

RE: There's an early painting that interests me a lot. Its subtitle is *Potato Painting*.

DB: That was the first painting where I used vegetables. There's an earlier version of that painting in Brazil that has the same figure with three brown balls floating in front of him. It was a surrealistic device that I used in several paintings. There were often little girls playing with balls and I suddenly realized they ought to be potatoes instead of balls.

RE: So, it has nothing to do with van Gogh and his potato-eaters? There's no art history being played with; it's simply what looked and felt right to you at the time?

DB: Yeah. Also I had a desire to learn how to paint potatoes.

RE: Do you sometimes ransack art history?

DB: I find some good titles. Like the first painting I put balls in. There's a great Jasper Johns called *Painting with Two Balls* and I wanted to do a painting with the same name so I did one of a girl with two balls. And that led to many other paintings with balls. So the balls acted as an art historical reference, partly.

RE: And that wonderful painting *Joy of Life*. Two naked figures are running—it's hard to tell the gender actually. Where did that painting come from?

DB: It was based on a drawing I had done several years before. I go back to old drawings an awful lot. Everything is photographed. I have about forty-five slide binders full of images. I'm usually working only with a current set of themes, but I'll often go back to something from the past that I haven't used.

RE: You could be one of the most self-referential contemporary painters working. You continually reuse your own work in new and interesting ways. A single image will pop up again with seven or eight years separation between your initial and subsequent use of it.

DB: That can happen, yeah, but not very often. In fact I don't think my work is at all self-referential.

RE: In the paintings from the '80s are there specific people that you have in mind?

DB: Well the drawings were usually based on some model. They don't have to end up looking like them. All the paintings were based on particular people. I was just using whoever was handy as a model; I wasn't trying at all for likeness. I needed a certain type of figure for a certain composition.

RE: You're currently interested in birds and flowers. I mean you have a wonderful series of owls and various and sundry birds.

DB: A friend of mine found a taxidermy book for me in New Orleans with wonderful photographs and diagrams on how to stuff dead birds. Then I rented a house in a very lovely spot in the summer of '92 and I was completely surrounded by birds. They kept flying into the windows. It was kind of a Japanese glass house and the birds could see through the house to the ocean. And they'd end up flying into the windows and killing themselves, so there'd always be dead birds lying around outside the house. Well, a dead bird is not really a pretty sight to draw, but I had this bird idea on my mind, so I got out this taxidermy book and started drawing birds from it. That series of work lasted for the next year and a half. I started working on them that summer. Actually, the bird collages were done quite recently.

RE: Does that often happen, that you'll develop a series of collages out of a larger body of paintings? Does the reverse also happen: are there preliminary drawings?

DB: There's always a preliminary drawing, which is usually a magic marker or an ink drawing, about eight by ten inches. That can extend into both a series of paintings and collages. I never exhibit the preparatory drawings.

RE: Does a single preparatory drawing dictate to you that it needs something else; is that where the compositional energy comes from?

DB: They're abstract and formal, not narrative choices at all. There are all kinds of abstract choices, if that answers your question.

RE: Yes, it does. They're formal questions then; about arrangement and what seems right to you? I'm trying to get at what provokes you to combine the things you do. Because what critics comment on are the unusual juxtapositions in the work, or the contrariness of the way a figure is rendered in comparison to another object in the composition. People wonder why things turn up in the same composition.

DB: I don't know.

RE: I've asked you about the birds. What about the flowers?

DB: Well I spent almost ten years painting human figures and I just lost interest in them. Around the same time I started the flowers, I started drawing hands, which are mostly a species of self-portrait, and then fingertips. The flowers function compositionally very much like the human figures I was painting before. I don't know why flowers; flowers are nice. For me a flower is an object, like a light bulb. It's something you buy in a Korean deli, along with the cat food.

RE: In a show at Sperone Westwater there were four pieces, including a tree, a leafless tree and a musical instrument. I think the word the *New Yorker* used to describe the images was "sublime." With your sense of wanting to avoid beauty, you get pretty close to beautiful painting in those four don't you?

DB: Well, if you saw me painting you wouldn't think I was trying for beauty.

RE: Does it bother you that they look so good?

DB: No, it doesn't bother me. Doesn't anything you put under glass and in a frame become beautiful?

RE: Okay. Let's let beauty loose. When did you start doing the sculpture?

DB: The first one was cast in bronze in '88 or '89.

RE: What made you decide to move into three dimensions?

DB: Well, I'd been wanting to for a long time and I had been going to the art supply store and buying papier mâché and art sculpture materials and never quite figuring out what to do with it. Then I was invited to be in a sculpture show and I said, "Okay, sure I'll do that." And at the last minute the truck was coming to pick up the work and I had no idea what to do. So I thought well, I had been painting balls, so I'll make some balls. I scrunched up some newspaper and wrapped it in the same kind of layers of cloth that my paintings have and painted them white. They were very lumpy, crude objects. I thought they were great. It started with the same learning process with which I approached my drawings in the early '80s. Trying to learn how to do something in the simplest way possible and trying to learn it from scratch without remembering what I knew from my sculpture class in art school.

RE: You knew how to make sculpture so you had to unlearn what you knew?

DB: I'd never made sculpture extensively but there was a conscious effort *not* to do things, not to build wire armatures and do the kind of thing that you're supposed to do. I wanted to respond just to the material and forms. I was really trying to do a sculpture with a blank mind about what sculpture was.

RE: How do you unlearn what you already know?

DB: It's a process of will. You just hold a pencil and you try. I used to draw with my left hand. That was futile because I became ambidextrous very quickly. So there was no point in that anymore. It's just a process of awareness and recognizing that a certain kind of mark is not satisfying because it's too familiar or it's too conventional. I suppose every mark eventually becomes conventional. I'm terrified of the kind of complacency I see in so many mid-career artists who just go on very comfortably painting the same painting. I would hate to run into such a dead end.

RE: Do you have nightmares that you're going to run out of ways to forget?

DB: The only terrifying thing is that over the years I've presented myself with so many options, that when I finish a body of work I have thirty or forty different choices about what to investigate next or what body of images to draw on. That's difficult. Too much choice can be paralyzing sometimes.

RE: Where did the idea come from for stacking the figures in your large totemic sculpture?

DB: It was done improvisationally in the bronze foundry. We had done a series of reclining figures and we had some extra figures left over from the casting. There was a spot welder there, so I said, "let's see what they look like standing on top of each other."

RE: Maybe there's a clearer way to ask you about the material you use. Are the source materials essentially neutral for you then? Does it matter to you what they look like?

DB: I'm not sure what you mean by source material, because there are two very distinct and totally separate bodies of material that enter the work. There's the collage material, which can be both drawings and found receipts and things from newspapers. That's one source. Then there are the images that become the primary image painted on top. More often than not those are my own drawings.

RE: Right. So is that background material essentially neutral? Are they just compositional elements for you?

DB: I used to be pretty strict about what they had to be, actually. Like if they were receipts, they had to be receipts for something I had actually paid. But that finally became restrictive because I just ran out of them. How many times can you go back to Egypt to get receipts if you want to do ten more collages. So I started manufacturing them and I started accepting other people's receipts.

RE: So everything is just fodder for the composition then. It doesn't matter what it is?

DB: It doesn't mean anything. There's a sort of vague autobiography operating, very non-specific.

RE: In the paintings at the Sperone Westwater show the grounds are worked more, there seems to be more going on? Why is that?

DB: I don't know why—fear of empty spaces.

RE: They look like drop cloths. I mean they actually look like they come out of a studio.

DB: They are drop cloths.

RE: Did you work them even more?

DB: No, they're exactly as they came off the floor. The only thing I did was to send them to a commercial laundry to get the actual dirt out of them. And then whatever paint was still left was painted on top of. But I didn't touch them after they came off the floor.

RE: You rely on accident a lot then. It's as much a compositional element for you as are notions of deliberate mark-making?

DB: The funny thing was that I realized I had sent these off to the laundry because they were dirty, and when they came back clean and nice and fresh, I just looked at one and recognized that it had the same range of incidents, the same density of colour as my collage backgrounds. I thought, well, here's an idea, let's just paint on these. But that was a complete coincidence. The problem is that those are my *only* drop cloths, so I can't do any more of those paintings. But that's okay, I'll just do something else. I'm not going to spend my life making fake drop cloths.

Martha Clarke

Dark Rainbow

Martha Clarke, the American choreographer and director, is very generously disposed towards animals. But when she says that "the best choreography in the world is the way animals arrange and rearrange themselves," she unfairly separates herself from her own kinetic hierarchy. In works like *The Garden of Earthly Delights* (1984), *Vienna: Lusthaus* (1986) and *The Hunger Artist* (1987) her personal arrangements and rearrangements of dancers has created a moveable feast of surpassing visual intensity. *The Garden of Earthly Delights* remains the most successful borrowing of a visual source I've ever seen: Clarke took Hieronymus Bosch's nightmarish and beatific painting and re-envisioned it as a moving parable telling the range of human emotion and action from the transcendent to the demonic. Her transformations—turning humans into boats, musical instruments into prisons and the long hair of a woman into a seductive snake—all take their inspiration from Bosch's bewildering masterpiece and then go off in a direction that makes her realization of them parallel and not parenthetical. Clarke performs a similar feat by re-imagining the enticing world of the Viennese painter, Egon Schiele. Schiele's figures are among the most disturbingly eroticized in modern art and the heavy aroma of sexuality that surrounds them seems to have flared right into Clarke's nostrils. All of the images and movements of *Vienna: Lusthaus* enact a slow decadence, as if everything were happening inside the imaginative space of an erotic dream. Men groom women like horses; they become the horses they ride; a woman narrates her amorous reminiscences, then places her sex firmly on the face of a soldier; an officer recites an inventory of his seductions while discreetly lifting the skirts of a supine woman using his riding crop; another gentleman wears shoes on his hands and then autoeroticizes his transformed arms. It is a world, like the Danube so lovingly described by a professor who appears in the piece, that "overflows with the very essence of life." It should be clear that the life moving throughout her work has its blacker contours. "I've always been drawn to what's seamy and dark," she says candidly, "I see everything with a shadow." Not surprisingly, the look of *Vienna: Lusthaus* is uniformly sustained: the black stockings, the mannequin soldiers and the puppets, the provocative angularity of the movement all take their lead from Schiele. But Clarke never directly appropriates images or ideas from the artists or works to which she's initially attracted: instead her pieces are surrounded by the visceral residue of those encounters. "I go in like a painter," is how she describes a creative process that is essentially intuitive, "with empty white paper or a room full of people." So far what she has been able to come out with are works of astonishing directness, beauty and visual intelligence. Martha Clarke continues to run amazing risks with her art by using the natural body—whether animal or human—in unpredictable ways. She seems perennially on the lookout for any dark edge into which she can lean her irresistible, incorruptible bodies.

This interview was conducted in Martha Clarke's home in Sherman, Connecticut in May of 1994.

ROBERT ENRIGHT: What was it about Bosch's *The Garden of Earthly Delights* that made you think you could turn it into something danceable?

MARTHA CLARKE: I was asked for an idea for a National Endowment for the Arts grant. I said to my producer, "Call me back in twenty minutes," and I got a flash that an interesting way to spend the winter might be trying to put on stage the feeling of these figures in the painting. I read a wonderful quote from Jean Cocteau, who said that he didn't think he was an intellectual, but that he got his ideas through flashes and instinct. I hardly approach anything intellectually and I've always responded to visual things: the movement of animals, clouds in the sky, garbage on the street.

RE: But Bosch's painting remains an enigma to most people. Was doing the piece a way of trying to figure out the painting or a way of trying to capture the essential mystery the painting seems to sustain?

MC: That *Garden* isn't easy. But the idea of doing the Creation and Adam and Eve and Hell and the Seven Deadly Sins in a succinct theatrical form with only ten people seemed a terrific challenge. It touches all the emotions. There's such wonderful generosity, something so grand in the gesture of that painting. You've got people popping out of birds' mouths and musical instruments as instruments of torture; you have people lying on strawberries and dancing with crab shells on their heads. Nobody's ever beat Bosch when it comes to fantasy. I suppose he was the first Surrealist. Not much is known about his life, but he was rumoured to have been an Adamite and was considered by some people to be a heretic. My recollection is that they were encouraged to do a lot of sinning to become pure. It's a kind of Siddhartha story. Or *The Garden of Earthly Delights* was about potential damnation and death through sin. I was having a very difficult relationship at the time. My work is always involved with where I am emotionally.

RE: So the work is autobiographical?

MC: Emotionally, yes. Not strictly speaking because nobody would know which parts are me.

RE: Or which parts are Bosch?

MC: Exactly. Or if I'm the victim or the victimizer.

RE: That's a nice confusion, because it would be hard to figure out whether it is a piece about salvation, or a piece that restates the utter confusion of our lives. It doesn't end with any sense of resolution, it seems not to be about simple answers.

MC: I don't think there are any simple answers. I agree with you that it's hard to know what it's about. It's kind of yin-yang. I hope my work will evoke responses that have to do with people's lives and the baggage they carry. I hope that the vision can be approached subjectively. I'm not didactic; I don't have any great messages for anybody. And although I've done a lot of work about things that degenerate and that are harsh, I also think there's some hope and some humour. I want to cover a rainbow of feelings. If you live a good life, you get all of it don't you think? I mean a rich life, one that's not too self-protective. There's a big territory to live through in a lifetime.

RE: One of the most striking things about the piece was that you actually took images from the painting. It never would have occurred to me that anyone could visualize the painting so completely in dance.

MC: I used only two specific images. What I did was I looked at the picture and read about Bosch and about his times and then forgot it all when I began to work. Once I'm in rehearsal I don't ever go back to the source, because by then I hope it's digested. For any good dancer, singer, musician or writer—you learn everything you can and then you have to forget it to find your voice.

RE: But some residue of that experience is clearly there?

MC: Certainly. I've been affected by all of it, but I don't want to do anything that's a literal reference. My new rendition in London is much nastier. I've tightened things. There's a wonderful dancer in it and I just let her go hog wild. She's added terrific bits of her own to the part where the woman with potatoes in her stomach gets stabbed with a spoon. When I recreate my work on other companies, I give them some freedom to improvise and make the works their own. It's important to give the performers the chance to leave their scent on the work, to make it about them. Otherwise they're just recreating somebody else's work. If they're learning it and I suddenly see they're doing something else, I often like it better. I love a really good mistake.

RE: What was it about Egon Schiele that interested you enough for his work to so thoroughly inform *Vienna: Lusthaus*?

MC: I think I feel like a Schiele. You know, you have body types that you respond to; I look at those women and I know their bodies are like my body. And emotionally I feel like them. There's something animal-like about the women.

RE: Had you always been attracted to his work?

MC: It just felt familiar. I was travelling in Italy in 1985 and there was a retrospective in Venice. It was a complete revelation. Actually, I had been commissioned to do a piece about Hiroshima and my composer, Richard Peaslee, came out for a meeting in the fall, and he dropped his head and said, "I don't know how to write music about Hiroshima." So I said, "Let's do Vienna at the turn of the century." It was another of those illogical flashes based on just seeing Schiele's work and being floored by it. I find Schiele coming back in a piece like *Dämmerung* and he was in *Endangered Species* as well. There's something about the physicality of his women. They're very tall and they have a natural sense, a kind of angular dance.

RE: They look like dancer's bodies actually. They can splay like dancers.

MC: And there's a lack of self-consciousness. They feel voyeuristic in a way. It just seemed to be the right look. The piece is very poetic and isn't particularly linear. I order these pieces in a completely intuitive way. I don't have a ground plan going into rehearsal. I go in like a painter with empty white paper or a room full of people and I say I want the feel of something and we begin to talk about the subject matter. I sometimes bring in books of paintings. If it's good, it's spontaneous combustion. If it isn't, it's like having the stomach flu. It can be a very long process. What's been nice about working in opera is that it's forced me to do work in four weeks. I said to many of my friends after *Endangered Species*, I will never do a piece from scratch again; I want a libretto, I want a story, I want a text. Like those insects who make hills out of little bits of mud, I was squeezing out my own intestines—my life, my dreams, my hopes and my disappointments. I just couldn't take the mental abuse of making these evenings the cloth of my own skin. I couldn't do it anymore. And here I am doing it again with the ballet, called *Dämmerung*—actually the title might change. I'll have German lieder, but other than that I don't know what the hell I'm doing with it. I'll know what it's about when it opens.

RE: Is there something about the circus that you really like?

MC: Yeah, I love it. It seems like a microcosm for life. I mean in the familial sense. In the twentieth century we've all been shattered in terms of family, and the circus is a place where you get very strong connections without being related by blood. I love the nomadic quality and the fact that the circus is always the same no matter where it is. It lives within its own house like a turtle. If it goes to a city they're still sleeping in their trailers. There's something about it I find timeless. I think it's a very poetic idea about continuity.

RE: It's tribal in a way, isn't it?

MC: It is tribal and I find it very moving. At the same time, the people I've known who live in the circus are myopic.

RE: Some people would consider them freakish.

MC: They don't fit in and they're not chameleons; they don't change themselves to talk to interviewers, then go to audition performers, then go to the opera and talk with producers. They don't pick up *Scientific American*. There's something about the compulsion to balance on eleven chairs that seems like a metaphor for life. Do you know what I mean about the chameleon thing that we all do? We're constantly adjusting as contemporary people. Circus people are never asked to do that. There's something quite touching about the simplicity. It's like a whole world in a little world. It's like looking down at the grass and watching the movement of insects. I don't mean that in a demeaning way, but you see a whole culture, a whole way of living and dying, of dealing with death and with animals. I find the people are extremely vulnerable. They're tough *and* soft. They have to understand animals, they have to work as a unit, they have to understand each other. They live on top of each other.

RE: Do you think of carnival in the same way?

MC: That's another area, isn't it. I think displaying freaks is really awful. And morally I'm not even sure any more about performing animals. It was a romantic notion of mine about the idea of a company. Having toured with a dance company for many years on the road, I think I saw a romance in the idea of being on trains and one night stands and new audiences and new places to see. So the company becomes a family. I used to call it life in the bubble. When I was younger I loved Colette's writing and she has a novel called The *Vagabond*, which is very much about vaudeville. I saw that as being close to my life. I saw the circus as a way of identifying, even as a performer, and I danced until I was forty-three. I often felt like I was meat on a hook. I felt something tragic about being a performer. I loved performing, but sometimes I found it humiliating to go out and try to please people. I felt whore-like about it, and yet I work with performers all the time and love performance. But again it's the way I see the world: in the light I see the dark, in the dark I see the light.

RE: You've been very open in your work when it comes to investigating sexual identities that could be described as whore-like as well?

MC: It doesn't frighten me to think about or explore it in my work. Ultimately, artists' work is a permissible journey of self-discovery. It's a cliché, but I think that's what my life is about. It's certainly not about making money. I enjoy the process of doing it but I've never been commercial. I guess I feel quite lucky because I actually make enough of a living to sustain my curiosities. I'm just about ready to take on anything. If I can find a spark of reason I'll do it at this point. My son is twenty-five, I'm not attached and in a way I feel like I did right after college. I have a home, so I've got somewhere to come back to and nurse my wounds. But I'll do just about anything that I feel will open my head to a new experience.

RE: One of the dangers with art is that it tends to aestheticize violence. Is there an ethical question involved in this process?

MC: I don't know. I did a work called *Fromage Dangereux* and there was a lot of violence towards women. At the time I was in a wonderful relationship which tended to get a bit violent emotionally. I put it on stage and there was a famous dancer at the American Dance Festival who stood up and booed and hissed and wrote me a hate letter. Now the interesting thing about showing violence is I'm not condoning it, I'm saying that it's a fact of life that people kill for love. I have felt desperate enough to jump out of a moving car myself. So having experienced near-deadly emotions, I don't condone it. I accept that it's a chord all of us have and we're lucky if it's not plucked like a harp string. But sometimes you're not that lucky. I saw *Medea* in New York a few weeks ago, because a friend of mine directed it, and the day before I read about a woman whose child peed in her pants and the mother put the child in boiling water and she died. What's the difference between that and *Medea*? This is a woman who was on welfare and was at the end of her tether. I think it's the most hideous thing I've ever heard; I think *Medea* is hideous. But is it wrong to put it out there, to recognize that it exists, like Bosnia exists? We're not talking about the Trojan War are we? By ignoring it we make the world like the Good Ship Lollipop. The world isn't like that. I think that darkness and violence are here to stay.

RE: Tell me how you got involved in doing *Endangered Species* in the first place.

MC: It had to do with a monkey. His name was Tony, he moved so nice, he had such a good body and such a beautiful tail. He was so agile.

RE: You better stop while you're behind.

MC: I was in Charleston for the Spoleto Festival where *Miracolo d'Amore* was being performed. I was living in a hotel and feeling quite unhappy because my work had incited such controversy. I'm a nice middle-class girl and I like to be approved of and I was not being approved of. I sought refuge in the circus that was in the town square. Joe Papp introduced me to the director, David Balding, who had this abused monkey from St. Louis who they were trying to tame to be able to play in his circus. I babysat for him. He'd been abused as an organ grinder's monkey. His teeth had been pulled and if he picked up any coin smaller than a quarter he'd be burned by cigarettes. I loved taking care of him and playing with him and seeing him begin to recognize me and get over his terrible fear of people. It was very rewarding. There's always been a side of me that felt "Peace Corp"— I really mean this. Sometimes I wonder if work in the arts really is important. There's a little bit of a Mother Teresa in me that wants to contribute something and I feel the arts are an ivory tower. It's like candied violets—only the *chi chi* and the well-informed go. I was in Holland recently working on this ballet and I hadn't had an easy week rehearsing because I wasn't sure what direction I wanted to take the work. I went to see *In the Name of the Father* and I felt it said something terribly concrete. I worry sometimes that what I do, even if I'm fairly capable at it, is not significant. I'm not sure art is significant any more. I have this dialogue with myself. I keep doing it because I like the people I work with. I like having the license to be a kindergarten person. Being an artist is like an approved way of staying a child. But I feel a certain guilt and a certain irresponsibility in making images for wealthy people. I haven't resolved it.

RE: Was your work with the abused monkey a way of salvaging something for yourself?

MC: I think it must mean something to me. You know, I've often thought about actresses who have had connections with animals—Jeanne Moreau, Brigitte Bardot, even Sandy Duncan had a home for cats. I'm going to be fifty and I think there is some small humanitarian voice that is expressed in an event as little as working with an injured monkey. So David Balding and I became friends and decided it would be fun to see if we couldn't do something with the circus. And it was a fabulous experience. Maybe being a vet would have been my other life; maybe just taking care of animals would have been fine.

RE: You certainly know how they move. In *The Garden of Earthly Delights* there's a moment when the humans bend at the waist and become animals. They walk on all fours and the movement is breathtaking.

MC: Yeah, the humans become animals again. I took it out this time. I'm left now with a very different image because of this amazing actress-dancer. She's so wonderfully innocent at the same time that she has the appetite of an animal. I've dovetailed and cut frames so that things jut across each other. There's more overlay and dissolves, nearly like real life dissolves. I find I'm much more into that in my work now, having these overlays so that just as you're losing the scent of one thing, another is beginning to pull over it.

RE: *Garden* was like a circus in that it had seperate areas of activity going on simultaneously.

MC: I don't know why, I just find it a very interesting form. It wasn't so conscious when I did the Hieronymous Bosch piece. I wanted to fly and my first idea for a flying piece was to do a Chagall bride with a huge armload of fresh lilacs. I didn't do it. I did Bosch instead.

RE: You seem to find in animals a grace and dignity that you don't find in the activity of human beings.

MC: Yes, they never have motives. I like their purity and I love the way they move. They have the most perfect sense of timing. You know you can't repeat the look. If a great actor is really lucky he'll have the spontaneity of an animal. It's something about timing. It's a thrill to see a swan take off from a pond. I had a farm, I had cows and goats and peacocks and horses, and I used to sit in my hen house and the hens would forget I was in there and begin to treat me like another hen. I'd get right down to their eye level.

RE: Didn't you scare the hell out of them?

MC: Not if I sat there for two or three hours. I'd watch the incredible interaction and pecking order. Now, they knew that I fed them, but they forgot I was there. I can watch animals for hours and hours. They're beautiful, better than dancers.

RE: I didn't ask you if you actually went to circuses when you were young?

MC: I used to go to Barnum and Bailey and buy those little chameleons in boxes that had strings with a safety pin. And I would put them in hat boxes with cut grass. That's where the circus started for me. Do you remember those? They were ghastly. And they'd always die. They'd get out of the hat box and be found under a radiator six months later.

RE: Was your attraction to the darker, seamier side of the circus?

MC: I'm a nice Jewish girl from Baltimore and to tell you the truth, I've always been drawn to what's seamy and dark. My background is German, French, Alsatian and Polish. All my work—and I find this interesting because my family's been in this country for a rather long time—but everything I do is pulled toward Eastern Europe. I've done two shows on Kafka, one on Vienna, I look at *Dämmerung*, mention Anselm Kiefer. August Sander has been a big influence in the way I costume. Actually, August Sander is major in my life.

RE: Are you saying there's something in the blood that attracts you to the darker side?

MC: I think it's in our Eastern European blood, don't you? I mean I was raised Chippendale, totally, in the Maryland countryside. My mother has a collection of English china. But I've gone on a diverted route. I"ve got stuff that is so dark you can't believe it. I don't know where it comes from but I think it has to do with my father. He was an extraordinary man and he was as dark as could be. He had a wild sense of humour, but he was also absolutely quiet. I'm very drawn to dark things and to outrageous, dark people and I also love to play. I'm not drawn to things in the middle. It's always dark or immensely silly. Middle audiences don't like my work. You either have to be totally ignorant or terribly sophisticated, but the whole middle bunch doesn't get it. A pendulum swing is where I am.

RE: So the fevered heat of *fin-de-siècle* Vienna must have appealed to you?

MC: I always felt that piece was like a cake with beautiful icing and flowers with maggots.

RE: In *Vienna: Lusthaus* you have a character who talks about the colours of death. The palette goes from light pink to red, from light blue to dark blue and to purple red. That's the bruised palette of Schiele. It's also a way of transforming the grotesque into art. Is that the compulsion: to turn the palette of death into something lyric and beautiful and light?

MC: I hate to be a disappointment but I wasn't conscious of any of it. I really don't know what I'm doing when I'm making things. Often I've felt like a blindfolded child in an attic. I might put my hand into a mousetrap at one moment and into a down pillow at another. I don't know why those colours are there. I only accept them and try to work out of them. I occasionally wake up from a dream and jot down a note. And if I'm in a receptive mood, everything I see will turn me on, from a photograph in a newspaper, to somebody getting off the bus, to a crowd of people waiting in a movie line. If my eyes are with me and if I'm on, then everything will move me. I watch everything. For years I watched horses in a pasture and crows landing on a corn field, and thought that the best choreography in the world is the way animals arrange and rearrange themselves.

RE: Are there things that you feel are taboo, that you won't put on stage?

MC: I'd do anything. I feel we should be able to see just about anything. I'm just wary of having shows close down.

RE: But there's no ethical compulsion to do or not to do something?

MC: I wouldn't kill a rooster on stage. I don't want to do anything that's physically harmful.

RE: You certainly call up some of the darker aspects of sexuality. I suspect the link between violence and sexuality in much of your work would make a lot of people pretty uncomfortable.

MC: I think a lot of people like it, they just don't admit it. I'm not talking about whips and being tied to bedposts. But I think real passion is a violent thing. Watch animals. Watch a swan mating, when he takes the neck of the female and steps on her. It's not always lyric. Violent, passionate emotion can be extraordinarily exhilarating. And I don't mean fighting violence.

RE: Do you know John Berger's great essay on Caravaggio? He says the facial expression of the boy in *Boy Being Bitten by a Lizard* is an expression he's seen only on the face of animals—"before mating and before a kill."

MC: I understand that. When we were doing *Endangered Species*, Mike Nichols let us work at his place for six months. In the spring he had champion horses mating: Arabs, a Lipizzaner and a pure white Andalusian stud. We would stop rehearsals and watch the stud mate because it was one minute of the most thrilling physicality. It's terrifying, but also extraordinarily beautiful and very erotic because you have these things that are meeting nearly like combustion, like gasoline and fire. I guess I'm drawn to things that ignite each other. It's not easy and you can't sustain it with an audience. You don't want to exhaust people so when you're using those elements in theatre they've got to be done very discreetly. You've got to lead people and build for them. One of the most wonderful theatrical experiences I've had was at the Zingaro Circus. It's a horse circus from France which has gotten a little bit *chi chi*. But when it was first done in Avignon in a stone quarry it was two hours of extraordinary horse work. The last scene is a light beaming on two horses mating and you're sitting in the summer night with shooting stars in a quarry lit by candles. It was phenomenal. It's a circus that is borderline. It's supposed to be all Gypsies. One year I went and they used music from Russia—men from the Balkans singing without accompaniment on one hill and on the other hill were women from Turkey doing Arabic singing. The director, Bartadas, brought the two cultures together with these horse acts. Then he saw Pina Bausch's work and suddenly started getting self-conscious about something that had been so raw. I myself am attracted to things that are extremely raw. But by the time you get into a theatre you've rehearsed everything so thoroughly and you've done this enormous refinement. How do you keep the rawness and be able to do it over and over again? It's a problem as a performer. One of the things I love about the circus is that, ultimately, animals aren't controllable.

RE: So they carry with them an implicit rawness.

MC: You cannot predict completely. I mean one night doing *Endangered Species* the elephant dumped next to Mike who's three feet six inches, and the mound was as tall as he was. It was a cold night in the circus tent and it was steaming. And the audience was out of control with laughter because he had to do this poem standing next to this steaming pile of dung. It was a great evening of theatre actually. I love the spontaneous and I love accidents. The rehearsal process is such a wonderful time to have things like that happen. Hopefully I'll learn to recreate that moment. And it may never be as good as the first time, and it may have to be cut or changed. But there's nothing more wonderful than real life.

RE: Do you tend to think dialectically? There's a line in one of the pieces that goes "every blessing is tethered to a little bit of hell."

MC: I feel very fortunate in my own life but unfortunately I see everything with a shadow. Or fortunately, because it does develop a sense of humour and humour is the thing you get by on, isn't it? I love really silly humour. I'm supposed to be this artsy-fartsy person. But the truth is I like real down-and-dirty. Or really funny and irreverent.

RE: You took a certain delight in the whole scatological sequence in *The Garden of Earthly Delights*, didn't you?

MC: It's a little embarrassing now. It reminds me of my Pilobolus days. When I was first teaching it I said, "Look, I must apologize, this is utterly sophomoric but it is funny."

RE: Your imagination works by way of biting off about as much as anybody could chew, doesn't it?

MC: Yeah, I like big ideas. I admire Wendy Wasserstein, but I'm not about to do *Sisters Rosenzweig*. Eventually I'd like to try directing Chekhov. But not Shakespeare. I wouldn't touch him. Maybe *A Midsummer Night's Dream*, but I don't have the ear for language.

RE: What you do have is this incredible instinct for movement. You would do a Flamenco *Carmen* instead of a traditional one.

MC: I'd love to do *Carmen*, I want to do *Lulu* and *Wozzeck*. I'm doing *The Cunning Little Vixen* at Glimmerglass in 1996, and I may do a new opera by a wonderful Chinese composer named Tan Dun on the journey of Marco Polo. He's taking me to the Orient and that will be a new world for me. I consider work like going to school, and every new subject allows me to go back to books and learning and travel, and gives me a chance to reinvent. Like Madonna, I feel like a different person with each piece because I have a chance to rummage around in a whole new world.

Robert Wilson

A Clean, Well-Lighted Grace

"I'm known primarily as a visual artist working in the theatre" is the characteristically succinct way that Robert Wilson sums up a twenty-year career that has changed fundamentally the way we look at and hear plays and operas. I can think of no other director—other than perhaps Peter Brook—whose effect has been as profound. There is something unmistakable about a Wilson piece; its look, its sense of time and its radical precision all seem to be unique to this artist who, while born and raised in America, has been nurtured and mythologized in Europe. Even a partial list of Wilson's activity—from the 1970 production of *Deafman Glance* to the American remount in 1993 of *The Black Rider*, a collaboration with Tom Waits and William Burroughs—gives a sense of the unparalleled range of his imagination: *The Life and Times of Sigmund Freud* (1969), *The Life and Times of Joseph Stalin* (1973), *Einstein on the Beach* (1976), *The Golden Windows* (1982), *Medea* (1984), *Alcestis* (1986), *Salome* (1987), *Cosmopolitan Greetings* (1988), *Orlando* (1989), *King Lear* (1990) and *the CIVIL warS*, his most ambitious project which was scheduled for the 1984 Olympics in Los Angeles but which has never been performed in its entirety.

Wilson seems inexhaustible and his art is a chameleon practice—changing from directing to drawing, from making videos to curating exhibitions, without any regard for what are the traditional distinctions between these forms of art. "Listen to the pictures," he has said on another occasion. It's the same spirit of resisting categories that Tom Waits draws our attention to when he says Wilson used his actors in The Black Rider "... like clay. They'd melt themselves down, pour themselves into any mold." There is nothing lazy about this shifting of language in either its articulation or in what it produces in time and space. Wilson's art is extremely formal. I mean formal in every sense; the drawings he did for *Cosmopolitan Greetings* in 1988 look as if Barnett Newman could have made them. It's an association Wilson himself would likely encourage: one of the few things on the clean, white walls of Wilson' offices, the Byrd Hoffman Foundation in New York, is a honeymoon photograph of Newman and his wife taken in September of 1936.

Newman's greatness as a painter comes out of the way he addressed the "cross of time and space" that Wilson perceives operating everywhere in man and nature. It's this dialectic that informs the structure of Wilson's work in all media. And structure is insistent; in his chair portraits, which end up being surrogates for the actual figures appearing in his productions, and in the way he uses light as an almost three-dimensional presence. In the recent New York production of *The Black Rider* you'd swear you could bounce off the intense plinths of coloured light that Wilson cast about the stage. This dark tale which transforms romance into necromancy was audacious and startlingly beautiful, and is only the most recent example of his theatrical inventiveness. The effect of Wilson's movement across genres is to produce a species of visual poetry that is almost intolerably pure. I mean in the way we see it, not the way it comes to mean inside our heads. "I think that theatre has to be about one thing first," Wilson says in the following interview, "then it can be about many things." With Wilson what we see is only a small measure of what we get.

The following interview was recorded in a meeting room at the Byrd Hoffman Foundation, in New York, in December 1993. During the conversation Mr. Wilson constantly made points by drawing on a piece of paper he had in front of him. It was a telling example of what he means when he advises us to listen to the pictures.

ROBERT ENRIGHT: Where did the idea first come from for *The Black Rider*?

ROBERT WILSON: About six years ago Tom Waits asked me to do a work with him. At that time he had written a piece called "Frank's Wild Years," and I thought about doing that. It turned out I didn't but Tom and I still wanted to do a work together. So I began to look for a piece that would be right for us. About a year later in a friend's library, here in New York, I saw the original ghost story that *The Black Rider* is based on. It's a German ghost story from the seventeenth century. I thought it might be something that would be appropriate for the two of us. I made a little outline, did some drawings, and sent Tom a copy of my notes and he responded favourably. I had the idea that he would write the text, the libretto and the music, but he said he didn't feel comfortable writing the text and that he would like me to do it. I didn't really feel comfortable doing it, either. But I studied it further and continued to diagram the work. I usually make drawings of my plays so I can readily see them.

BC: Do you mean that you work out a storyboard as you go?

RW: I work out a storyboard—the timing and the structure, how different scenes can relate to one another, whether there might be recitatives or something spoken, a duet, or some song. I do it with drawings to see the construction, to see how the story is told visually, how the architecture of the piece looks in time and space. I met with Tom again and he was still insistent that he didn't want to write the text. So I came up with the idea of William Burroughs. I had just finished a piece called *Cosmopolitan Greetings* with Allen Ginsberg for which Allen had written the text. It was an opera that we had done with the Hamburg Opera and Allen kept saying, "I think you should work with Burroughs, he would be a good collaborator for you." I mentioned it to Tom and he liked the idea, so I contacted Burroughs and he responded immediately. Then I went to Lawrence, Kansas, and spent some time with him going over my outline and got additional ideas from him.

BC: Was it a true collaboration or were you primarily working on your own?

RW: It's a real collaboration. It depends on which artist I'm working with—but what I usually do is to put together a structure, a form which people then fill in. I'm not the best one to write a text and I can't write music, but I can put together a synopsis with a visual book. In my theatre the visual book is different than in other theatres in that it can stand alone. In fact, in the first rehearsals of this piece we had almost no music and no text, so I staged the whole work as a silent piece.

BC: Do you mean that it was like dance?

RW: Yes, it is like dance, but all my work is dance. So the movements are choreographed, staged, blocked, including what the scenery looks like and what the stage looks like as a room full of furniture. For example, the furniture can be very large and through the course of the play it can be reduced until it's sometimes very small. There's some kind of structure. I work with original props and scenery, rehearsal lights, which are then videotaped, and based on that videotape the music and text can be written. Much the way you would score a film. But in this workshop both William and Tom were present and we wrote during that time. So yes, it was a true collaboration. Tom and William were both very visual, so we could talk about the visual book, and I could talk to them about text and about music.

BC: Was it the Gothic nature of *The Black Rider* that initially convinced you Waits would be a perfect collaborator? What was it you two had in common with respect to this material that made it seem so compelling?

RW: It's something I can't explain. It's just something I felt would be right. I liked the fact that it is a very simple story. It's a story that's still current—a man who makes a pact with the devil—you see it in the paper every day. It's a subject matter that's universal. I think theatre has to be about one thing first, then it can be about many things. I think this piece can be about one thing, a very simple story, and then it can be about many stories after that.

BC: A number of critics have remarked that even though they hadn't heard the songs before, the music seemed disconcertingly familiar. Why would that be?

RW: Often artists are rediscovering what we already know. Socrates said that the baby is born knowing everything, and that it's just the uncovering of that knowledge that's important. In a sense I believe the same thing—that the work is there, you just have to uncover it.

BC: How do you decide who you should go to in order to help that process of uncovering? You use people like Stalin and Einstein—larger-than-life figures—as characters around whom you frame the structure of your narrative. What makes you choose someone?

RW: Well, often people who have written for the theatre have made characters who are commonly known by the man in the street. Look at the Greek playwrights, writing about the gods of their time; or Racine, considering the situations of our time. Stalin is a man who is a part of the twentieth century; a man who is known by the man on the street. Or Einstein or Queen Victoria or Sigmund Freud or Marilyn Monroe or Mickey Mouse. And what appealed to me was that this story of *The Black Rider* is still current and still popular; it's still part of our unconscious mind, our psyche. So in that sense it has a certain appeal to everyone whether they live in China, Germany, New York, Africa or Brazil.

BC: Do you feel an obligation to respect the nature of either the narrative that you borrow, or the biography of the character you use? What's your attitude towards the flexibility of personal history?

RW: Well, my theatre is a formal theatre where ideas are presented. You have a certain responsibility to present an idea to the public and in this case you try not to interpret it for them. You may have your own interpretations, your own emotions, ideas or feelings about it, but there's a certain distance that you maintain. That's so the public can fulfill the action and the emotion of the work. We are only there to help, to guide, or to present situations at hand.

BC: That sounds like Brecht to me. It sounds like you're prepared to leave a lot up to the viewer. Are you relatively flexible when it comes to how I might read *The Black Rider*?

RW: I'm very flexible that way. I don't want to dictate the response of the public. That's not my job as an author, director, designer or actor. We make theatre to ask questions and not to give answers. If you know why you're doing something then there's no need to do it.

BC: You don't have the answers, either?

RW: No, of course not. I don't have the answers in the beginning and I don't have them in the end. It's something that remains open. A great work has no answers, or if it has an answer, it doesn't have an interpretation. You can read *King Lear* one night one way and the next night another, and the third night still a different way. There are many different ways of reading it. If we *fix* an interpretation to it we only limit or narrow the work.

BC: Are you saying that great works of literature, theatre or dance are amenable to that degree of multiple reading? Or can you read a bad work in the same way and still make great art out of it?

RW: I think we have to do that as responsible people, because art is making work. Regardless of what the work is, we have to approach it with an idea of asking what is it, instead of saying what it is. If you can say what it is, don't do it.

BC: Why would you choose Virginia Woolf's *Orlando* to do something with?

RW: I was interested in Virginia Woolf as a person, and in a sense this text is autobiographical. I was also interested in it for a selfish reason; I didn't know very much about England because I hadn't been there very much. I performed more in France and Germany and Italy, and I was interested in learning more about England. Also, *Orlando* is really about four centuries of English history. I liked it, too, because of the visual imagery. As you know, I'm known primarily as a visual artist working in the theatre, and what I did in presenting *Orlando* was to have a very neutral abstract background with blank canvasses so that the colours or the pictures of the text could be in the foreground. In terms of the architecture of the stage I simply put a formal frame around these blank canvasses which lent themselves to pictures from the text.

BC: I'm intrigued by Woolf's involvement in spatial time. In a novel like *To the Lighthouse* she amplifies a single moment of consciousness and makes it the whole space of the novel. You seem inclined to do that as well. I wonder if you feel an affinity with the way she deals with the coordinates of space and time?

RW: It's in the nature of my work too. Although, one could see this piece as starting with the time of Queen Elizabeth I, going through four hundred years of time and then entering the twentieth century. It's not a piece that is rooted in a fixed time, it's a piece that's full of time. I often hear, "Well, in your plays people move slow." But if you have that idea in mind and you move slow on stage it will never work, because the concept has nothing to do with it. It's not something intellectual, it's something that has to be experienced, then it becomes full of time. Something that's full of time can have no concept.

BC: How did you direct Sheryl Sutton in the 1970 version of *Deafman Glance*? How do you get an actor to move in a way that's almost not moving, to slow activity down so that a whole different visual relationship seems to be set in place?

RW: Well it depends on the piece. I did plays that were seven days long; I did plays that were twenty-four hours long; I did plays that were twelve hours long; I did works that were thirty seconds long. Depending on the length of time, you make certain decisions as to what to do. You don't make the same decisions in a play lasting an hour and a half that you do in a play that is seven days long. One of the basic principles in my work is to think of time and space, and the tension that exists between these two lines. Space for me is something that's horizontal and time is something that's vertical, something that goes into the cosmos and goes to the centre of the earth. And it exists in all works. It's in the construction of this table or that chair or this building. If you want to conduct *Lohengrin*; if you want to stand on the stage and sing; if you want to sit in a chair—to me it all has to do with these two lines and the tension that exists between them. Sometimes they can be more relaxed and at other times they can be more tense, but it is the architecture. Often a work falls down for me simply because it lacks this tension. I went recently to the Metropolitan Opera and there was no structure—the movement and the standing of the singers, the placement of the scenery on stage, the way the conductor stood—to me they were all wrong. How the violinist sat was all wrong.

BC: So when you say that Marlene Dietrich was great because she could sing three songs without moving what you are admiring is her mastery of the dialogue between the horizontal and the vertical. Is that what gets to you?

RW: Well, the lady simply knew how to stand on a stage. And she could walk on one, too. Maybe the most difficult thing to do is simply to stand or to walk on a stage. You have to learn it, you have to start from the beginning. Kids are getting out of acting and music schools with no training in basic techniques—how to pick up a fountain pen, how to pick up a glass of water, how to sit in a chair, how to stand, how to walk on a stage. It's all become so intellectual. They're thinking too much. Ideas can happen later, but you've got to first have your roots in fundamentals. Then you can do naturalism or formalism, then you can have expressionistic theatre or psychological theatre, or whatever kind of theatre you want. You see an actress coming out of Yale, or singers coming out of Julliard and there's never been one hour spent working with their bodies. No one even talked to them about a gesture, about the line of their head or shoulder, the length of a finger, or the movement of an eye. Western theatre has been bound by literature and we see today that we have really failed to adequately develop a visual book for the theatre. Shakespeare, Goethe, Schiller, Molière, Racine, Tennessee Williams are men who wrote words, who wrote literature for the theatre—which is great—but nothing was written or thought about that considered the visual book. If we look at Balinese theatre you see that from the age of three a child is learning how to move its eyes, so that by the time they're thirteen years old they have a vocabulary of three to four hundred movements of the eyes alone. If you talk to an opera singer about having a vocabulary of twenty movements of an eye they look at you like you're crazy. We just haven't developed a language. If you look at the classical theatre in Japan—Noh or kabuki or whatever—as much time is spent on learning a gesture as on the sound they produce or the poem that's being spoken or the story that's being told. How do you stand in a Noh play? It's training from childhood and you learn it all your life. How do you pick up a fan, how do you hold it, how do you turn it, where is the placement of the fingers, what is the line of the finger in space? What are the lines of the eyes in the back of your head, to the corner of your head, to the left, to the right? How do you place a motion? They have a theatrical language developed through the body that is simply lacking in our theatre. We've developed it in dance.

BC: So are you asking for less dramaturgy and more movement in Western theatrical training?

RW: What I'm asking for is that we be aware that theatre is a forum in which we want to have an exchange with the public. It's something we see and something we hear. These are the primary ways in which we relate to one another, through our eyes and our ears. And in the theatre that we have in North America, the United States and Europe, the visual book is, by and large, simply there to support the literary book. Something we call scenic decoration is always there to second what we're hearing. So it's often superfluous. What I've tried to do in my theatre is to make something that we see be structurally sound, to make something that can reinforce what we hear without always having to be decoration.

BC: I want to get at how you perceive narrative operating in your work, because I sense that the structure is more poetic than linear—a kind of visual poetry. Is movement one element in the larger strategy of how you present something to an audience?

RW: I'm not sure I know what you mean. In some of my early works there were spoken texts but no stories. They were more like the weather in the room, they had to be spoken with a kind of transparency; they were like concrete poems. They were something that you heard but didn't necessarily want to think about much, just something you experienced. I've also presented works—Chekhov, Heiner Müller, or Shakespeare—in which there are texts that you want to think about. So you deliver them in a different way than you deliver a text by Christopher Knowles or a text from my early plays, which were more like sound poems. But in all my works I tend to look at each of the elements as something that on its own can be structural and tell a kind of story. Yes, I guess you'd say it's poetic. I look at a chair, I see it outside of the context of the play and hopefully it can stand alone as a piece of sculpture. So it's a piece of sculpture and it's like an actor.

BC: A surrogate for an actor? Are the chairs that you've done *for* characters meant to be displacements *of* the character? Do you want them to have a life of their own in the formal language of space?

RW: Right. It's like a giant hero sandwich, where you have a piece of bread and some lettuce and you can have some cheese and you can have a tomato and you can have some ham and you can have some pickles and you can have some mustard. You've got all these textures and structures, and each one on its own can be very different, but together they offer something else. And it's how they can counterpoint one another; how they can be put together structurally so that we can taste and smell and experience them. Each element, whether it's light or a gesture or an object, is thought about as something that has its own validity. Light in my work is something special. To me, the most important element in theatre is light because it's the element that helps us to hear and to see. Without light there's no space.

BC: Without darkness there is no light, either. Is that how the argument goes?

RW: Yes. Light functions like an actor, too. It's structural, it's something that's done in the last three days of rehearsals. In *Einstein on the Beach*—a work which was drawn in storyboard from the beginning—there's one scene with only a bar of light moving for sixteen minutes on stage. There's no one else on stage, so in a sense it's like an actor. You see a horizontal bar, and then it rises to a vertical line and flies away. This vertical bar appears three times: in the first scene of the first act and in the beginning of the second scene. We have a third interlude scene with lights flashing on a small panel on the lower right-hand side of the stage. Then by the last scene of the last act the entire back wall of lights is flashing. So what's been introduced is that visual theme in light and then later on it becomes a major visual theme. It's structured like music.

BC: You have no hierarchy then. An actor is no more or less important than light, or a chair. An object on stage is no more or less important than an actor. So the way your theatre works is that these things have equivalent value which you'll emphasize at one time or another during any single production?

RW: Yes. Sometimes one is stronger or more prominent than the other. I have a respect for the integrity of each object on its own and I see them all as a part of an architectural whole. Marcel Breuer said, "You can find all of my aesthetics in this chair, they are the same aesthetics you see in the building that I've designed, or in the plan of a city."

BC: Would you say the same thing about your chairs?

RW: Yes, I would say the same thing.

BC: A couple of questions about space. There's a Margaret Atwood poem called "The Progressive Insanities of a Pioneer," that tells of a character standing in the middle of wide open Canadian space, screaming, "Help, let me out." It occurs to me that one of the things American artists are compelled to deal with is space.

RW: I was born in Texas, and the landscape of Texas is in my head and in all my work. I think one of the dilemmas we have in the United States is that we've never been invaded. We are a country that's boundless. We know no borders. If Saddam Hussein or Gadaffi were to drop a bomb in the middle of New York City we might know where those countries are, but I think until then we're really never going to know where the borders are. And it's about that realization we want to scream.

BC: Is space for you just something that is animated by light? Charles Olson said, "Space is the whale that's going to swallow the Jonah of the American character." So he composes poetry by field. In this office you have a photograph of Barnett Newman, a painter who recognized that space was the thing he had to attack. He had to make painting its equivalent.

RW: The reason Barney is a great painter takes us back to this cross of time and space. He could put a stripe down the middle of a page and that construction— a vertical line hitting a horizontal—made him for me one of the great artists of our time.

BC: You sound like a Modernist when you talk about the vertical/horizontal cross. Are you talking about symmetry, about a way of finding a coherent aesthetic that comes out of a sense of balance?

RW: Well, I've always been interested in classical architecture, music and design. When I first came to New York I went to Broadway, and I hated it and I still do. I went to the Opera, and I didn't like it and I still don't like it. Then I went to see the work of George Balanchine, and I liked it and I still like it. And I saw the work of Merce Cunningham and John Cage, and I liked that and I still like it. I think the reason I'm attracted to the work they've done—and they've been very influential—is because of the mental space they created. I liked their formality and the fact that they were primarily interested in classical patterns.

BC: When I look at the way you composed the rooms for the show you curated at the Boymans-van Beuningen museum in Rotterdam, you seem to be operating out of a pretty formal dialectic. You'll have a Chantilly lace shawl obscuring the hard edges of a series of squares by Donald Judd. That strikes me as being an essentially Modernist strategy.

RW: Yeah. That's a very difficult thing to do, to put a piece of Chantilly lace in front of a Donald Judd. It's too easy to say that it's simply a counterpoint.

BC: But counterpoint is the word you use in describing your strategy.

RW: I think that's what artists have always done. We hold a vocabulary with the public. If we want to be pretentious, we can say we invent a new language. And once the language becomes discernible we can destroy it. And in these deconstructed parts, we reconstruct another language. But take the show in Rotterdam; it's a very classical presentation. You have a room that has a very wide opening. The walls are painted white. You have light from exposed light-bulbs that's rather harsh and aggressive, there's aluminum shelving. It looks like a warehouse. You can walk through this labyrinth and see things up close. You come to a second space that's a series of twelve rooms with a less wide entrance, openings that keep you at a certain distance from the objects. Here the objects are very carefully lit. The room's grey so it's a middle field of seeing something. In the last room you had four or five thousand objects; here you have one hundred or less. And then the last space has the narrowest door. It's very tall and narrow, and the room is dark. When you enter you don't see the edges of the space. And you just have two or three objects. You sit and you have light changing for seven minutes.

BC: That's the nocturnal blue room with the Degas dancer and the monitor lizards.

RW: Yes. So you again have this big, wide, horizontal opening here and this space that's actually vertical.

BC: What you've done looks like a drawing for a cathedral floor plan.

RW: It is a little bit like a cathedral. There are these vertical stacks here with a horizontal opening. I can see three traditional ways of looking at a painting: you see an object up close, even if it's a landscape painting, as a way of measuring space, I can consider that a portrait. The twelve middle rooms—the grey ones—are like still lifes, so that I see them at a middle range. And the last room with the tall vertical door is something that's darker and more formal with fewer objects.

BC: And more personal for you?

RW: More emotional. The first room with the portraits is less formal. It's something you can freely walk around in—here you sit down and watch something. So this is a construction, a cathedral like you said.

BC: The juxtaposition of the Degas dancer with these lizards, which are ostensibly crawling towards her, creates a tension of an evolutionary kind. You must have been aware of the play between Nature and Culture. I can't imagine you weren't conscious of those ideas.

RW: Well, you play with many ideas. And as you said, the work is poetic, so one can see it in many different ways.

BC: When you first attended the Pratt Institute you studied with Sybil Moholy-Nagy. You said that her method of lecturing on the history of architecture was simply to have a bombardment of images coming at you all the time, and that you had to make the connections. It strikes me that part of your initial choices in the "portrait" section of the Rotterdam show follows that same strategy.

RW: That's true. I mean if you have a hundred seventeenth-century porcelain figures, it's one thing to put a taller one in the centre, but if you take that taller one away and put a 1950s, red radio there, then it's something else. Maybe the red radio helps you see the other porcelain figures simply because the two objects are so different in their nature. If I take a baroque candelabra and place it on a baroque table then that's one thing, but if I take that candelabra off and I put a computer on the table, then that's another. And perhaps I can see those two objects more clearly together.

BC: Is it intuition that you rely on?

RW: Well, I tried many things. I worked on the exhibition for nearly three years. I would collect different things and put them together. People would suggest things. But I had a piece of architecture and I had a structure, the way an architect does if he designs a city. He has a mega-structure and then people can fill it in. But it was very difficult to put one object next to another. It was how one thing—in form or in colour or in line or in motion or texture—could help me see the next thing. That's what I was hoping to do, to set up a situation so that we could see the vast collection of the Boymans museum in a new way. How can we actually see the objects? How can we see this bronze Degas woman? I don't particularly like the figure myself, but how can I see her in a different way. One of the curators at the museum said, "You know I've grown up with that figure and I never really looked at it." Suddenly we could see the eyes or the hands, the shape of the dress, the attitude of the head.

BC: So your role as an artist is to reframe. You can take *King Lear*, you can take *Orlando*, you can take the image of St. Sebastian and recontextualize them.

RW: What's dangerous are the frames. I mean, one of the problems we have today is that the boundaries have been limited, especially in theatre and in film. What I try to do is to remove the frames. Think of radio drama; you were free to imagine pictures because you didn't have pictures.

BC: Did you grow up with radio drama in Texas? The Canadian Broadcasting Corporation has a great tradition of radio drama.

RW: I did. I often think of silent movies because we were free to imagine an audio score, a text, a sound or whatever. The edges for the audio and visual screens in those media are boundless. But what's happened in theatre and film is that the edges have become bound, so that I have a text and then I illustrate it with a picture. In that sense they have become limited. If we can set up a situation where we have the kind of freedom—the mental state—I was talking about with

Balanchine and Merce Cunningham, then there'd be time for interior reflection. I think that often we don't allow this kind of reflection to be a part of the experience of a work. We simply don't allow enough time to think.

BC: In the part of Canada where I was raised, we have a thing called tractor time. That's when farmers get in their tractors to summerfallow. And while they're doing it what they fill their heads with is whatever comes into their heads. It has very little connection with the activity they're doing. Tractor time sounds pretty close to the condition you want to create.

RW: Well, I think in this age of technology that our only chance of beating the machine is to become mechanical, to become automatic. That's why in my theatre-works you can't rehearse anything too much. And the more mechanical you become, the freer you become. It's like learning to type or to ride a bicycle. The first time it may be awkward or difficult, like learning to play Mozart on the piano, and in a sense we never learn. But the more we do it, the freer we become.

Rebecca Horn
Fierce Vulnerabilities

Continental. Olympia. Royal. Fortuna. Optima. Imperial. Mercedes. Triumph. These are among the names of thirty-six typewriters suspended upside-down from the ceiling in a former tax office converted into a gallery, situated in a very good section of Berlin. Their keys are quiveringly pressed by invisible hands and the carriages on some move as if by magic. The sound is so persistent that you feel a secretarial pool was on a work binge. Also suspended from the ceiling is a motorized white cane that feels its way along as if it were a miniature space arm, or a surrogate for a blind man. Its movement is tentative and vaguely menacing. Diagonally across from the room with the *machines à écrire* (the French name better carries the sense of functional technology) is another room, its floor entirely covered by a raised platform consisting of wooden slats on which sit four thousand wine glasses. Alternately, the slats tilt and as a result the wine glasses bump together, creating a constant tinkling. Every so often—from a number of locations on the floor—a blue flame leaps up like a gas explosion from this fragile glass landscape. The sound in the room is inescapable and, while it seems irritating at first, after a short time it becomes less bothersome and even appealing.

The pieces are called *Chorus of the Locusts I and II* and they are among the many sculpture installations by Rebecca Horn, the German artist whose mechanomorphic machines have made her work among the most desirable in contemporary art. In October 1990, *High Moon* was on exhibition at New York's Marian Goodman Gallery; another piece was exhibited in Paris the same year she opened a large exhibition at the Museum of Contemporary Art in Los Angeles, which coincided with the release of her feature film, *Buster's Bedroom*. The film, which stars Donald Sutherland and Geraldine Chaplin along with a superb cast of eccentric character actors, is the result of Horn's long-standing fascination with the multi-talented Buster Keaton. It wouldn't be unfair to call it a love story, although very little that happens on the screen would seem to support that conclusion. But *Buster's Bedroom* is, certainly, an *hommage* and it's something of an exorcism too; Horn now feels she can be free of an obsession with someone who is her double—enigmatic, uncanny and a kind of escape artist. In an exquisitely written essay from 1983 called "The Inner Strait-Jacket within the Outer" (an essay written for Keaton), Horn imagines the filmmaker "as unperturbed as a fallen angel," a being whose "escape schemes are a ballet in defense of gentle violence." At the centre of his art of survival is Keaton's ability "to master the dangers with daredevil precision," and it's easy enough to read Horn's admiration of him as an understandable degree of narcissism. Both she and Keaton come from the same family of artists; both are able to breathe soul into machines and to use them to ward off "unleashed ener- gies." In fact, most of what she says about Keaton describes what she herself has been able to effect in her astonishing career. "Gentle violence" perfectly captures the subtle paradox that is at the core of her own expression. Horn is excruciat- ingly subtle, and all you need to do to measure this quality is listen to the intense presence of sound in her films—eggs being cracked on the edge of a bowl, or the whisper of a cloth on the bow of a cello in *La Ferdinanda: A Sonata for a Medici Villa*, another feature-length movie made in 1981. This same quality is present in her art: *Peck of Glory* is a small kinetic sculpture in which two mechanical arms mark a gallery wall, and all the viewer hears is the dull thud of the steel brushes and the soft purring of the motor. Horn's art involves the spectator in a kind of sensory overload; the aural and the oral, visual epiphanies and the radiance of looking are all an explicit part of the experience. In the exhibition at the Museum of Contemporary Art, which was called *Diving Through Buster's Bedroom*, the de- scription of activity in one room will give you an idea of the (occasionally discon- certing) aliveness of the installation. The *Snake Piano* is a long black container which lies on the floor with a thin line of mercury running its entire length. Sud- denly a roar comes from inside the box—a sound that moves up the piece and back down, and which causes the mercury to become agitated and toss about as if it were alive and angry. At the same time, two shoes suspended from a small motor on the wall do a heart-breaking tap-dance; you hear the electrical buzz of the copper horns in another piece and above all, there is the persistent measure of a metronome. Similarly in *Der Eintänzer*, a blind man, whose white cane has been reprised in numerous Horn sculptures, describes the deeply exotic aroma of a shaved peach in a way that is undeniably sensual.

In looking at Rebecca Horn's films, sculptures or assemblages, you are never able to forget their artfulness and their sensuality; in one of the rooms of *La Ferdinanda* a Man Ray photograph hangs on the wall—it's the image where Kiki's naked back is turned into a cello. Horn is enamoured of sleights of imagination in which qualities normally attributed to humans or animals are grafted onto machines. And what a techno-menagerie she has developed: mechanical peacocks and butterflies; an array of painting machines that make gorgeous, chaotic messes on gallery walls and floors; dancing tables; a gigantic, magical fork—all these are characters that have inhabited Horn's movies and exhibitions. Their interventions are not always easy to take. Horn investigates the tension that exists along a spectrum of wonder and aggression. "It has to do," she says, "with my getting together in one piece a balance between the cut of a knife and a caress."

There is no doubt that Horn's eroticism is unconventional and disquieting. There is an astonishing scene in *Buster's Bedroom* between Dr. O'Connor, the dangerous snake-lover played by Sutherland, and Micha, the filmophile who is searching out Buster Keaton; they maintain their human forms, by and large, but their instincts become reptilian as they lick and turn on themselves like a pair of snakes in heat. In scenes like this Horn's work has an edge that is unequalled by her contemporaries in Europe or in the United States. They also can't equal her splendour. As early as 1976 in *The Chinese Fiancée*, Horn was seeking the apocalyptic, the moment when menace and vulnerability, when brutality and wonder meet. In *The Chinese Fiancée* the viewer is trapped inside a black, hexagonal mini-temple, what the artist calls "submission to the darkness." What follows is pure, unadulterated Horn: "Then so suddenly, the doors all open to release you once again; out into the most dazzlingly alarming brightness." In *Buster's Bedroom* Geraldine Chaplin plays a woman named Diana Daniels who has confined herself to a wheelchair and is in thrall to Dr. O'Connor and his serpentine science. "There's drama in my body," she tells him. "But if I stay still long enough I will shoot from this wheelchair." This, as the film says, is the problem of the snakes' energy. It's an expectant tension between a condition of stasis and then being startled. Sometimes, encountering her work, you feel as if you've just been released from a dark, psychic confinement and suddenly you are tossed into an almost unbearable light. Rebecca Horn is the most thoroughly electrifying artist of her generation.

The following interview was conducted in the artist's Berlin apartment in May, 1991.

REBECCA HORN: I was born at the end of the war, and I was brought up by a governess and an old aunt in my grandparents' house in the countryside. I had a quite beautiful childhood in a tiny village in the mountains, not far from the Black Forest. At one point my parents thought it was time for me to have another education—I was speaking a heavy dialect—and so they suggested I go to a boarding school. I made a strange deal with my mother. In the village we always played around caressing ourselves—at this age you begin to be interested in sex and so you have these games you play—and I said, I would love to have a blanket made of butterfly wings that caresses my whole body. My mother said, Okay, you go to boarding school and we'll make one for you. I was eight and a half, I think. My father wasn't around much. He was a fashion designer and he lived in Milan and Paris, and I visited him everywhere, living in hotels with him. Anyway, my mother gave me a big package and put me into the car with her chauffeur and I was taken to the boarding school. It was an idiotic big castle in a park. The chauffeur dropped me off and there I was sitting with my package and my suitcase. I saw all these crying children arriving and I thought how strange this place is. Right there I decided that I would stay for only one day. At some point I opened my package.

In it was just an ordinary blanket with printed butterflies on it. I was so furious I took the blanket and I climbed up on the high wall surrounding the park where they couldn't find me, and I sat there all night crying, waiting till the chauffeur came back so I could throw the blanket at my mother and go home. But no one came back for a year. I became this wild, individual kid from the country. I ran away all the time and did very strange things—I lived in train stations—but they always brought me back.

ROBERT ENRIGHT: Had you decided to be an artist when you were very young?

RH: Yes, and that also had to do with my Romanian governess. She taught me to draw. And I decided that's what I could do best, to become an artist and have a free life and not have to get up early in the morning.

RE: So you associated being an artist with some kind of freedom?

RH: Yes. I had an uncle who was a painter and he lived quite a wise life, a life which I loved. And some people in my family were in creative professions—architects and painters—so it was not so foreign.

RE: You were a gypsy in some ways?

RH: In a way, yes. My way of working on projects contributes to this, as well. It's not like a painter who works in a studio and then the work travels by itself to the museum. When I work, I go to the place, I try to understand the atmosphere, the space and everything connected with it, and then from there I create the work. You take the measurements, the proportions of the room. Also you have to find the right people to work with. So it's a tremendous effort, different from when you create everything at home.

RE: I'd like to return to the butterfly story. Has much of your career been a way of regaining that sensuous contact with butterflies that you initially desired as a child? One of the pieces in your exhibition at the Museum of Contemporary Art in Los Angeles was called *The Lover's Bed*. It had mechanical butterflies flexing their metal wings. It's as if you went after the butterflies on your own after having been denied them at boarding school.

RH: Yes. The first time I talked about them was in *Buster's Bedroom*. I created this story for Valentina Cortese. She is a fantastic Italian diva, the kind of person who doesn't age and nearly doesn't exist any more. I mean she *is* like this in real life, not just in the film. I had worked with her before in Tuscany where we were shooting *La Ferdinanda: A Sonata for a Medici Villa*. I created this monologue about her dead lovers and these souls transformed into butterflies and waiting in her refrigerator to come back to life. I had this great idea of bringing cocoons to Portugal where we were filming, and in a few days I would have the most beautiful butterflies. I wanted big blue Amazonian butterflies, which we found in this English catalogue. It was quite expensive, and then these two crazy men flew to Portugal with snakes and cocoons. But it was so cold there that we had to have special heaters in the hotel rooms. And when the butterflies slowly came out they were tiny, stupid lemon butterflies. I was shocked, but the summer before I had already had an intuition that something could go wrong so I said to my technician, We'll develop a tiny butterfly machine. We had hoped to have two thousand in the film. On the film set we had the whole crew on chairs standing up with these fishing rods on which were hanging the mechanical butterflies. It was crazy with all these men asking how long they would have to hold them. In the end it looked pretty good in the film. My idea was really to have clouds of Monarch butterflies because I had seen a television program where they travel from Canada through America and down to Mexico to a special valley. When they go there in winter and breed you can't see the trees: the whole forest valley is a red, vibrating, trembling cloud.

RE: How did you go about realizing your early goal to be an artist?

RH: I always liked literature and art in school, and everything I did there had to do with my wanting to be an artist. I finished my baccalaureate and studied Art History. I went to an academy in Hamburg where the professor I studied with— and admired a lot—was a relative of Thomas Mann. He was quite crazy because he lived after the war with Hans Bellmer in Paris and with Michel Simon, the old actor. The first day of school he gave me the diary of Jean Genet. I had also taken a little studio near the red-light district, and I just walked around and looked at everything and everybody. After two weeks I came back and he said, Now we'll start to work. It was a very free and beautiful way of studying. The good thing in Hamburg was also that we had a lot of guest professors like Allen Jones and Peter Phillips and Richard Lindner. It was an international group that came just for a few months but you still had a real connection to artists who worked and not just to professors who taught. Richard Lindner talked about New York in such an exciting way that I immediately dreamed of getting out of Germany. I had started doing big sculptures using polyester. We had no masks because nobody thought about how poisonous this whole process was. I suddenly got tuberculosis. I became very skinny and they sent me to a public hospital for one year. It was not an elegant place and I had a really terrible time. It was a frightening and strange atmosphere. It took me two years to finally recover. But because I was so isolated from everyone I started to make sculptures for friends. I started using soft materials as a consequence of working in bed. And I started writing and making drawings that were dedicated to the people I created the sculpture for. That was the origin of my performance pieces.

RE: Has art always been a way of communicating directly with your friends? Has it always been very personal for you—the making and the message?

RH: Yes. Some of these people I knew, others I had seen somewhere and something about them fascinated me. It was like an initiation and it's the same now. When I first saw Donald Sutherland I said, I like you as an actor so much, if I write something especially for you, will you do it? It's the same thing I've done for Valentina Cortese. So with *Buster's Bedroom* the cast developed a very close relationship and very often after the shooting was finished at four o'clock, we'd say, Okay, now we rehearse.

RE: You'd rehearse the scenes for the next day as you went along?

RH: For the next day, even for the next few days. Geraldine Chaplin was the only cast member I had never met before. In the film she's paralysed from love. She had this beautiful long hair. One morning she came and said, I had this strange dream in which Donald was brushing my hair. I understood she was much more female and beautiful with this loose long hair. Then I asked Donald how he liked the idea of having a scene that should be very soft and very personal—something that they might share every day—and it starts this volcanic explosion inside her. But Donald used two brushes simultaneously in a nearly mechanical rhythm. Things like this were developed during the filming.

RE: The process is so flexible that a major scene could be added that easily?

RH: Always. This is the way I like to work and the actors like it because it's creative.

RE: Do you think of it as collaboration, or would you not go that far?

RH: It was. It was a lot of fun too. I mean, I wouldn't do anything I didn't believe, but it was like we all had a little fever there in Portugal. We were seventy people on the crew, totally isolated in two hotels for seven weeks and the weather was crazy. I mean, in the film it looks like Los Angeles in the California sun. And for the first ten days we had beautiful weather and then we had to create this illusion while we were in the worst rainy season. We had big mud streams under us while upstairs Sven Nykvist created the magic of California light.

RE: How could you afford to get Sven Nykvist? He must be among the most expensive cinematographers in the world.

RH: I met Sven in Paris a few years ago when he was shooting *The Unbearable Lightness of Being*. We talked and I told him about Buster Keaton but I wasn't able to get the money together in Hollywood. They would say, Oh, brilliant idea, but you need another writer and you need this actor to get this box office, and you end up with nothing left of your ideas. So I went through that horror for one year with an English producer and then I just stopped and went back to my old script and decided to raise money through the art scene. After all this I sent my old/new script to Sven and two days later he called me and said, Your film is so visual that I would love to do it. Sven loves to do small productions in Europe between big films—now he's doing the life of Charlie Chaplin with Richard Attenborough. It was fantastic to work with him because he's such an old pro—my film was his 111th. He was always telling stories about other actors and the whole crew would sit around like a family and listen.

RE: Earlier you mentioned your love of music. It's an activity that comes up repeatedly in your films and it leads me to ask whether your art is autobiographical. How much of what goes on in the film comes out of your own interests, obsessions and seductions?

RH: Let me put it this way. Before *Berlin Exercises* my films were just documentations of my performances. But *Berlin Exercises* was different. Once a year I came from New York to Europe to work. I had to be in Berlin and yet somehow I was homesick because all my friends were in New York. I was isolated living in one room. I invented these exercises in order to become part of this world in Berlin. But I transformed a lot of my longings and my fantasy. I started a diary for each day with another exercise to finally arrive in this place as my own.

RE: So *Berlin Exercises* was a process of personal accommodation?

RH: Yes. To become my own space. I constructed these extensions of my fingers and I scratched and touched the room until it became part of my body. In New York I really had no money so I had to rent my studio each year in the summer. After I left, everything got out of order. It was a permanent horror; when you came back everything was rotten and destroyed. I had nightmares about what would happen in my studio in New York when I was gone and I wrote them down and that became the script for *Der Eintänzer*.

RE: I want to talk about one of the *Berlin Exercises*. In the one I'm thinking about you cut your hair and it's actually terrifying to watch. Did you know it would have an effect on the audience?

RH: It had an effect on me, I was crying after like hell.

RE: It's so incredibly vulnerable and it looks so dangerous.

RH: But you only can do it once.

RE: I realize that. So you're a good actor, then. But what I'm getting at is the combined sense of menace and vulnerability in that scene, a combination I find often in your work. The haircutting settles on different sides of experience. I mean, it's a sequence that terrifies the viewer, and not only because they're worried about danger to you. The danger moves out and becomes threatening for the audience as well.

RH: Yes, but the danger moves also towards me, you see. It's a destructive moment. That's always what interests me the most: how can you find together the most vulnerable and the most aggressive moment?

RE: Is isolation something that you actively choose?

RH: Yes. Jannis Kounellis and I talk about this monk-like life where the artist very often has to isolate himself to create something, to find through his own experience certain images and fantasies, to dream of finding a line to utopia. And for that reason very often you have to isolate yourself, to live in your own little cage.

RE: So how do you replenish yourself? Is it by going inside again, dreaming your dreams and then externalizing them?

RH: Yes. I must tell you that because of this film and my recent exhibitions I'm tremendously tired. I just want to disappear and not see anyone, not give any interviews. I want to write in the summer. For me the most complicated step is to start to write and draw a new scenario again.

RE: Do you draw all the pieces before they're actually made?

RH: Yes. But these are sketches. I have a totally other world of doing drawings. I never go to a psychiatrist, I just do drawings.

RE: Do you mean they're therapeutic?

RH: I don't know. But they're very special. I have these periods where I'll do a lot of drawings for two or three months. It's the most healthy thing.

RE: There is one other of the *Berlin Exercises* I want to ask about: the conversation with the parrot. It's an amazing thing to watch because first of all you seem to seduce that parrot and then you frighten it. How did you manage to get the bird to perform?

RH: First of all, I found out I can imitate bird sounds very well. You learn it as a kid in the country. And then I've always liked zoos. I went to the Berlin Zoo where there were these cockatoos. They have a certain way of communicating with each other and they get very excited or irritated with certain sounds. I learned the sounds. Then we hired this innocent cockatoo and left him alone in my room. We had a video camera and a monitor in the kitchen so I could watch him for a day. Through these sounds I made, he became so aggressive that he tried to attack his own image in the mirror.

RE: Did you know what was going to happen?

RH: I had no idea what would happen. But again, as with the haircut, you shoot once because you can't do it again.

RE: How did you feel about the exhibition *Diving Through Buster's Bedroom*, in which all the objects from the film and from elsewhere were brought together?

RH: I liked it. I mean, the most complicated thing in the exhibition—because everybody warned me—was how to deal with this enormous room. I had an idea that came out of my first trip to California in 1973. John Baldessari had organized these teaching courses in colleges around the Mexican border and California. I showed my early movies and tried to make a little money so I could sit on the beach in the winter. I came by plane from New York and there were all these blue squares below me. I thought to myself, Oh my God, a country of swimming pools. Water is a very important thing in *Buster's Bedroom* too, as the two young people end up in the ocean. I said Okay, why not have the whole show underwater?, which I couldn't do without destroying the museum, so I decided to do it with lights. I constructed this mirror bath with waves projected onto the walls and the ceiling, and painted the skylights a turquoise transparent green.

RE: I don't think I've ever been to an exhibition in which sound was so present, as well. There were sounds all over.

RH: Yes. *The Chorus of the Locusts* installation in Berlin this spring is even more of a sound piece. It's two rooms where the nightmares really switch—the sky is on the earth and the earth is on the sky—and all this is balanced through sound. It's like the apocalypse, a situation which may reflect the next decade because of Uranus.

RE: Do you come up with the sounds on your own? My first encounter with the snake piano piece was amazing because I looked around, thinking something was coming.

RH: Like a train.

RE: It did sound like a train, now that you mention it.

RH: Inside the sculpture is a miniature version of one of those little wagons, a coalminer's wagon which is going back and forth.

RE: Is the sound recorded?

RH: No, it's not recorded. Underneath the sculpture is an incredible scene, as beautiful as on top.

RE: Why wouldn't you have wanted to make it visible so that the viewer could see what was happening?

RH: Because then you destroy the movement of the snake. The force that makes this thing move is a balance between two different energies—above and below. This is why I think it's fascinating, because you can't figure it out right away. It's the same thing in movies where you have this total illusion; it's flat on the screen, and if you see all the layers behind, the illusion is broken.

RE: Did you study engineering or anything similar while in university?

RH: No, but I'm very aware of how things have to function.

RE: So I shouldn't be surprised by the quality of your pieces? I mean, their machining is quite remarkable. They work so well.

RH: I work with two or three very good technicians to develop these things. I say, "It should look like this," and then I'm not interested in what motor he finds. I make all the drawings. *The Kiss of the Rhinoceros*, for example, was a pure love piece because it was so complicated. In the end, it took three years to construct.

RE: Is it dangerous, that mesmerizing triple charge?

RH: Sixty thousand volts.

RE: While I know you're not involved in realistic sculpture, there is something about the weight of the base and the way the legs collapse that actually looks like the wrinkled skin of a rhinoceros.

RH: I know. I said it had to have these strange little animal feet down there. And they're simply done, they're just iron tubes that had a kick here and a kick there. It's a very specific piece.

RE: Do you know the W. B. Yeats poem that has in it the line "a shudder in the loins"? When the two long arms of the piece first meet, they settle into one another in a way that is inescapably sexual. Did you intend that association?

RH: Sure.

RE: The rhythm is also exactly right. There's something about the inexorable upward movement of the arms that's just so; it couldn't move any faster or any slower.

RH: Yes, it needs to build up this enormous tension for the kiss. And that makes you gasp. It has to do with my interest in this balance between the cut of a knife and a caress. Another piece which is like this is the one in the collection of the Art Gallery of Ontario—an early piece—where a goose egg is nearly caressed by a sharp-pointed pendulum.

RE: There's a similar segment in *Der Eintänzer* when that Japanese man comes to prepare sushi for the twins. At one point doesn't he think to himself that he could separate them from their skins exactly the way he does the fish? His ritual activity is seductive, but it also frightens the audience.

RH: Yes. There are steps along the way to being frightened. When the girl falls out the window, it's more of a shock because of all these scenes of tiny terror that came before. And of course there's the irony of David Warrilow, as a blind person, dancing with the Russian ballerina, the most beautiful Argentinean tango immediately after the girl's death.

RE: And the sushi expert? He introduces a high level of anxiety and potential violence to the film.

RH: But this is New York for me. It's such an aggressive, frightening place where I always have the feeling things like this are happening, or can happen very easily.

RE: I want to ask about *The Prussian Bride Machine*.

RH: It's a crazy little machine with a brush which jumps around and splashes paint about.

RE: I'm reminded of Duchamp somehow, the notion of the bride splashed bare. And because umbrellas occur very often in your work, I can't help but make surrealist associations. Are you taking some kind of fanciful revenge on previous art? Is that part of the dialogue that you're involved in or is it merely an accident that objects with an art-historical pedigree appear in your work?

RH: I refer to these other works. I collect a lot of things and somehow these objects end up in my work. *The Chorus of the Locusts* has thirty-six typewriters hanging from the ceiling, typewriters of all different nationalities. Last summer I went with my two assistants to the flea market here and we bought these old typewriters from East Berlin and from Poland. And I had no idea what I'd do with them.

RE: They have bizarre and wonderful names. Back in 1972 I had a typewriter in Paris that was called Hermes Baby.

RH: They do have beautiful names. I have used shoes in several pieces too. The first time was when I had to work on this exhibition in New York. I go to Canal Street where there are certain shops filled with junk. I just hang around all day and then I buy these things. Then I go back to the gallery and I lie everything down and think, What will I do with it? A few years ago I found a beautiful pair of very large brown and white mafia shoes. I took them home to my hotel room and when people came to visit they saw these strange, large shoes and they wondered, Does she have such a tall lover? Everyday I would come back and contemplate who could be the owner of these shoes. I figured out it was three men— somebody very elegant in the '30s or '40s, somebody he gave them to, and then the last person was a little black man. He was so small but he loved the shoes and had to put paper in the toes because his feet were too small. The toes of the shoes were facing the sky. They were like little boats. I took these shoes back to my studio in Germany and I named them Moses. And now it's like an opera piece for three men. All three men died, but their energy went through these shoes and changed them to a new form and that's what's left. What exists are a lot of drawings about Moses, about the energy of these three people.

RE: That transformative impulse is one that you're naturally attracted to, isn't it? It comes to you naturally as an artist working within a European tradition.

RH: Yes. But it's not because Duchamp had done this machine that I refer to him. I mean, Duchamp knew Raymond Roussel and in the end Roussel interests me much more than Duchamp. And Dostoyevsky interests me, so does Kafka. And then from Kafka you go to Beckett. But these are always energies you understand and know about. They're part of you, like different skins.

RE: Ideas are visceral for you, aren't they? They're gut things with which you work within a rigorous intellectual tradition.

RH: You transfer part of your own fantasy to something. Because everything starts out with a story or an idea. I've used *The Divine Comedy* as a source in which Dante looks from Paradise through binoculars to find Beatrice, who is a dragonfly in the third ring of the Inferno.

RE: And the binoculars have stayed with you?

RH: Yes. It has to do with all the years of using a camera, catching things in a frame.

RE: So is it about framing devices as well as about voyeurism?

RH: Voyeurism, framing devices, yes. Also about a person who looks at you when you are not yourself. It's like when you came into the first room at MOCA [Museum of Contemporary Art]. There were these binoculars watching you and that's so American. If you go in a bank, you are watched from all different sides. Other things in the room watch you.

RE: Michael Brenson wrote a piece for the *New York Times* in which he referred to the wit and sense of humour in your work.

RH: Some pieces are light and amusing, some are tragic.

RE: Is that why Buster Keaton appeals to you so much, because he embodies this tragi-comic vision of the world?

RH: Yes. I mean, this little man who, at the beginning of the film, tries to fall in love or to be a hero, but the whole world starts to be against him—he has to develop a strategy using his fantasy to survive. The ideas he develops are so absurd, so fantastic that you just have to fall in love with him. I remember when I first saw films like *The General* and *The Cameraman* at a festival in New York in 1974—and there were also his early films with Arbuckle—I was so touched by his loneliness that I fell totally in love.

RE: You fell in love with Buster Keaton?

RH: Why not? As an artist you live in a world of fantasies, why not turn the world upside down?

RE: But as I read "The Inner Strait-Jacket within the Outer," it seemed as much a self-description as it did a description of Buster Keaton's methodology and intent.

RH: I wrote it as a kind of love letter. I started suddenly to see the world also in this absurd way.

RE: Keaton actually constructed machines, didn't he?

RH: Yes. Crafty mechanics. I found out all this after I'd seen the films. I was quite often in Los Angeles and wanted to know more about him. I met his last wife and some friends of his who knew him very well. After his tremendous success as a kid and as a young man, everything switched. It was when he was thirty-three. Part of it was the end of the silent movie era. Chaplin left and went to Europe. You see, Keaton worked with a very small crew, with technicians who knew him, and he had one idea that they developed on the set. He had fantastic people for technical things and then he edited his films himself. It was his film, his sculpture, it was his work.

RE: Have you been able to exorcise Buster Keaton now that you've paid homage to him in the film?

RH: Now it's finished. I will not have another boyfriend looking like Buster Keaton. It's over.

RE: I'm glad to hear it. You've put that one to bed, so to speak.

RH: It's done, the magic carpet is in the clouds.

RE: Let's go back to the film for a minute. It seems to me Sutherland is a villain in *Buster's Bedroom*.

RH: On the other side he's very fragile and sensitive. I mean, you see him with his snakes and then this young girl, who is like a butterfly, comes and kisses him and he is so afraid that he nearly faints. I love him for the way he managed to do this. It's perfect, because everybody in this sanatorium is so isolated in their own world, that the moment something comes from outside they are totally helpless. Everything is fluttering and they get in this total turbulence of love which they don't know how to handle and suddenly—for one night—everything gets out of order. The next day they are all shocked by what happened. So Serafina says to her young lover, "Who are you? Get dressed and get out of here." That scene was the worst shock for Americans—especially men. They couldn't stand the idea that this young man who had spent the night with this seventy-year-old lady and made love to her is thrown out. For American men, it was the worst insult.

RE: How did you direct the scene with the snakes?

RH: You mean the erotic scene?

RE: Yes. It's quite extraordinary. Did you have to do much directing, or did you just give them an idea of what you wanted and then let them go at it? It's pretty charged and pretty curious at the same time.

RH: It is. As with all the rehearsals, I talked and deliberately developed a lot of tension between the actors. I talked to Amanda differently than I talked to Donald.

RE: You encouraged that tension between them?

RH: Yes. Love scenes are the most complicated. We had a very small crew and I had different fantasies about what could happen in this snake cellar. I thought the more absurd the better it would be, because normally in love scenes you have all this banality, the same things happening in bed between men and women. All my life I've wanted to move in the direction of unusual sensuality.

RE: Do you think of machines as being sensual? I'm thinking specifically of the piece in the Vancouver Art Gallery collection, the one where the long pointed tip ever so delicately splits the water. It's very subtle and yet it has a visceral intensity. It's like making love to a woman with your mouth.

RH: But you see it more sensually than I do; I see it as wounding the black surface of the silent water. That's what I wanted with the goose egg. It's the same pendulum and each time it goes over the goose egg there is the tension of it possibly being destroyed. But it's not destroyed. It still exists. And this has to do with timing and millimetres. That's what it is about. In *Chorus of the Locusts* there's a double floor which is moving and there are four thousand glasses moving on top of it, making a nervous tinking sound. And every once in a while comes this little flash of lightning in certain parts—aggressions—and a glass falls off the floor and crashes.

RE: Tell me about the source for your peacock pieces.

RH: The most fragile bird, or animal, is the white peacock. They are so nervous that sometimes when shocking things happen around them they break their own neck and die. I wanted the marriage scene in the film to coincide with the mating season of the peacocks. But we didn't have the money to shoot in summer which is the time—for only three or four weeks a year—when the males have their fan-tails. Afterwards the feathers fall out the male looks the same as the female. So we couldn't shoot before September. I was disappointed because I had written in all these scenes with the birds and the marriage. So I had to develop a machine; that was the first mating peacock machine. Then the next year I was invited to *Documenta* and they had this Peacock Island and I realized I could finally do a real machine without feathers. Then I discovered this little temple on the island and I constructed a machine to fit exactly in the space. When the doors were open and the metal fan was fully extended, like in a Chinese temple, nobody could walk in. Outside, the peacocks with their real fans were walking around and having a provocative dialogue with the sculpture.

RE: You've referred to yourself as being on the outer edge of feeling. Now you talk about white peacocks being bred so sensitively that movement is an act of suicide. Do you personally like that edge?

RH: Yes, but you always go from the most security to the most dangerous point.

RE: Why?

RH: I don't know. Why did Buster Keaton do it, why do certain people live on the edge? Maybe for certain people it's the only way to transcend.

RE: So do you feel vulnerable in the process of making art?

RH: Yes, totally.

John Berger

The Intimate Idealogue

John Berger is a polymath; he seems to know everything. And he has so thoroughly considered what he knows that it comes to his readers as gospel, as infallible, as having been hammered out on the anvil of his own labouring with language and living. He is the author of some twenty books, including seven novels, eleven collections of essays, a major book on Picasso, a pair of collaborations with photographer Jean Mohr, and an influential television series for the BBC called "Ways of Seeing." He has won the Booker Prize (in 1972 for *G*), has written screenplays, dramatic plays, published poetry, written hundreds of essays and articles for magazines in Europe and North America, and has even acted in films. And throughout a good portion of his writing career he has also made drawings.

It would be difficult to overestimate the influence of Berger's art criticism. From his earliest years as the art critic for *The New Statesman* beginning in 1952, Berger has brought to the act of criticism an uncompromising conscience, a wholeness of vision and a spiky artfullness that is without parallel among contemporary writers. While it's possible not to agree with Berger's assessments of artists and their art, it is impossible to ignore the precision and rigour of his arguments, and the language which transports them through the sea of discourse. If you'll forgive the conceit, the body into which Berger has floated his bark of ideas is more accurately rendered as the "see" of discourse. Sight is his most informing sense and through his eyes come observations of remarkable intelligence and feeling. For him the declaration goes: I see, therefore I am. He is a writer who thoroughly banishes the divided self of Cartesian thinking. In this sense, he is one of the most complete writers I know.

Berger is always in the process of retrieving those people and ideas that have been dispossessed, marginalized or under-appreciated. These categories include everything from the poor to van Gogh's chair, from toast crumbs to the ways in which Caravaggio inhabits space. His deliberations are often visceral; in an essay published in *Harper's* in 1989 called "Muck and its Entanglements," Berger describes in learned detail the spring ritual of cleaning out the shithouse. Emptying his wheelbarrow provokes the observation that excrement carries with it the "smell of mortality." Then the essay picks up a tone of indignation and lyricism that is characteristic of his best writing. This smell he tells us, "has nothing to do—as Puritanism with its loathing for the body has consistently taught—with shame or sin or evil. Its colours are burnished gold, dark brown, black: the colours of Rembrandt's painting of Alexander the Great in His Helmet." What an alchemy he performs! The linguistic equivalent of transubstantiation (a mystery that fundamentally changes the nature of a thing), it is an act that takes the quotidian and nominates it to a state of glory. What is evident from his voyage through the eschatology of muck is that Berger's great strength is his ability to write personally, to speak, as he says, what we know in our hearts. The book in which he brings together most successfully all the marks of his personal and critical selves is *And our faces, my heart, brief as photos*. A small book (only a touch over one hundred pages), it is a meditation on time and space that uses every genre and literary form Berger knows: prose fiction, memoir, poem, critical essay, philosophical inquiry and manifesto. It is as emotionally and structurally coherent as any of his books and as Berger himself comments in the following interview, there is something about it which encourages people to respond in an inexplicably personal way. I've read it over and over and it never fails to humble me as a writer and make me hopeful as a human being. There are two sections I especially wish were mine; his estimation of the work of Caravaggio is the finest piece ever written about that difficult and seductive painter. It makes me think there is nothing left to say. And the other section comes at the end of the book. "What reconciles me to my own death more than anything else," he writes to his wife,

> is the image of a place: a place where your bones and mine are buried, thrown, uncovered, together. They are strewn there pell-mell. One of your ribs leans against my skull. A metacarpal of my left hand lies inside your pelvis. (Against my broken ribs your breast like a flower.) The hundred bones of our feet are scattered like gravel. It is strange that this image of our proximity, concerning as it does mere phosphate of calcium, should bestow a sense of peace. Yet it does. With you I can imagine a place where to be phosphate of calcium is enough.

This image of lucid and fearless commingling is the wish of all true lovers. It draws me to the quality of Berger for which I am perhaps most grateful. His ability to flesh out rhapsodic moments from the remorseless movements of history confirms him as one of the most indispensably elegiac writers in the English language. The capacity to memorialize our loss at the same time that everything in him resists its causes is the source of his inexhaustible passion for life and his unmoving distrust of power. John Berger is aware that he is a conservative man. His compulsion—and certainly his achievement—has been to cherish the exquisite intimacies of the body and to embrace the rhythms of its recalcitrant heart.

This interview with John Berger was conducted by telephone with the artist from his home in the French Alps in the spring of 1995.

ROBERT ENRIGHT: I want to start with the subject of drawing. My motivation is selfish because drawing is the medium that I love as much as any. So in a general way, tell me what drawing means to you?

JOHN BERGER: What do drawings mean to me? I really don't know. The activity absorbs me. I forget everything else in a way that I don't think happens with any other activity. The act banishes everything else. When I'm drawing I'm looking and trying to put together things I've found a little differently from what they always are.

RE: Is the act of drawing an obsessive activity for you?

JB: As soon as I've begun it is. But I can go for weeks or months, or if I look back at my life, even years, without drawing. I'm not addicted in that way. But after a certain moment it does become obsessive. And then one drawing leads to another and it leads to another. To begin with they're usually shit.

RE: Does it become an obsessive activity because of the pressure of looking? You've talked about the subject of the drawing meeting the aim of the drawer, intimating that when a drawing is really working there's some kind of integral relationship between the thing being made and the maker.

JB: That's in a piece called "Drawing of a Young Woman with Hand to Her Chin," about a woman named Anyishka. I had news of her from Odessa three weeks ago. She's having a very hard time.

RE: I was fascinated by that work because you create the drawing in words. Which leads me to ask whether you actually see the act of drawing and making the drawing in words as parallel?

JB: That's a bit complicated. It belongs to a series of short pieces that I have written over the last three or four years which will eventually be published as a book. I call them Photocopies. Each one is really a photocopy of an instant, or an encounter, or even just a story that somebody tells me. Of course I very deliberately set out to give them something of that graphic quality. But it wasn't really to do with drawing. I work more through my eyes than any other sense. Only a couple of weeks ago I did a portrait. This was a portrait of a Polish woman who is a friend, and she and her husband and brother-in-law came and spent the evening. Mostly they were talking Polish or Russian. So I started drawing. Maybe one of the reasons that I draw is that I'm often with Russians and I don't speak their language.

RE: And Anyishka was playing the piano which gave you an excuse to draw her. As long as someone is engaged in some other activity then you can draw them?

JB: That's right. I drew her all evening and it was really very bad. There was one that she quite liked so I gave it to her, but I was rather ashamed of it. And then at about midnight I was by myself and I decided to try another one—one in colour with acrylic, the others were charcoal and ink. Then something began to happen. I was no longer looking at her and I wasn't even trying to remember what she looked like. I was now drawing completely from something which was inside me. All I had to do was be intimately tuned to that. So I did this drawing very quickly, roughly. In one place I made a hole in the paper. But at the end there was a real likeness because her likeness had entered me.

RE: You say something of the same thing when you talk about Picasso and his drawings of Marie-Thérèse Walter. Your sense was that because such an intimacy existed he becomes her and that the act of drawing becomes an act of self-recognition.

JB: If we're talking about important art there's the artist's intimacy and truthfulness to himself, but an equal intimacy to the Other. I think those Picasso drawings are like that; I think the Rembrandts are like that. I think the artist who most often did that was probably van Gogh.

RE: But with van Gogh the relationship is rarely with a woman, is it?

JB: No, it's not with a woman at all. But equally, it seems to me, what we're talking about can be a chair. If you are the kind of person who watches and looks passionately you can be passionate about the chair's intimacy to itself.

RE: Is there a sense in which drawing ultimately disappoints you? When you talk about the drawing of Anyishka you say that you fall in love with her and then something is lost because no drawing can ever be more than a trace of that relationship. Is there a built-in limitation in the act of drawing when it becomes that intimate?

JB: No more in drawing than in taking photographs or in writing. It's very strange because the whole impulse, the whole urge to make art, in a certain sense, is to save life. But at the same time you're aware that compared to life it's only art.

RE: Yes. Why would Picasso want to paint a young girl when he could make love to her? It seems to me a very telling observation about the way in which art can never replace the intensity of life.

JB: Yes, but drawing doesn't disappoint me. On the contrary, I think when I succeed in doing a good drawing, it satisfies me more than anything else. More than writing. Another thing I can say about the way I draw is that I use charcoal a lot. Partly because it has such a fantastic range but also because it is very easy to erase. For me, drawing is a lot to do with taking out, with returning to the white of the paper.

RE: Ironically it's Matisse, the great bourgeois painter, who taught us that drawing is erasure.

JB: Yes, indeed. I love Matisse because he had such incredible skill. He didn't have to erase. It's more in what he left out. When you are writing, the point of the story, and finally I think even its truthfulness, depends upon the unsaid. So it's a process of elimination. I think the same is true in drawing.

RE: Does your sense of perception come out of the very specific, and then go on from there to grow into something larger?

JB: Yes, I think so. I don't ever really begin with general ideas. I guess it has to do with an eye. Anything you see in nature, because it's a manifestation of life, has something sacred about it.

RE: I want to ask you about a book that has had a tremendous influence on a number of writers in Canada, *And our faces, my heart, brief as photos*. It's a hybrid that includes everything from personal essays to art criticism, from meditations to poetry. How did the form of the book evolve?

JB: It was written as a series of letters going one way to one person. Then afterwards I didn't want it to appear in that form. Anyway, there are some things to be said about this book which are quite interesting. First of all none of my publishers—and I have good publishers so I'm not beefing—wanted really to publish it. They didn't see it as a viable book. But it's a book that has led a strange subterranean life. Obviously people have discovered it, they've talked about it to other people and have handed it on. It's happened like that in countries as different as Turkey and Spain. The reason I'm telling you all this is not to boast, but because I think most living books are books where there are two things operating; the intuition that this book addressed a need, often an unarticulated need, out there in the world. And I had this feeling very strongly about *Faces*. It was a hunch. Now what were the needs it addressed? I suppose it was the need in our contemporary times—our dark times, and our very timid and blind times—to place the experience of love and the kind of hopes and feelings that love evokes. How to place this, and how to be able to talk about it, how to have confidence in those feelings in a world that seems to offer very little confirmation. I had the feeling that this need was perhaps quite keen amongst the young.

RE: Yesterday when we spoke briefly you said something similar about *To the Wedding*, your new novel. What's your hunch there? What is it in that book that the world needs?

JB: The three books where I felt that very strongly were *The Seventh Man*, the book about migrants, *Faces* and *To the Wedding*. For this last book I find it very hard to talk about it because I'm much too close.

RE: Then let me try and articulate what I sense is significant in the novel. It brings me to the question of love, which is something that seems always to be circulating in your writing. In *To the Wedding* you really test the limits of love because of the nature of the relationship between Gino and Ninon. She's HIV positive and clearly she's going to die. In one sense Gino teaches her not only to love him but to love herself and her condition, without sentimentality. That strikes me as being a significant recognition. Does that make any sense of what the book is after?

JB: Yes, I think so. It's happening in the context of this illness today. In hundreds of thousands or more cases, love is being tested in that way.

RE: You're always populating your books with couples. In the criticism there's Jackson Pollock and Lee Krasner; I've already mentioned Picasso and Marie-Thérèse; there's Rembrandt and his beloved. You even raise it to the cosmological level when you talk about the sky and the earth loving one another. It seems to me that coupling is central to your sense of how the world operates, or at least ought to operate.

JB: Yes. I think that's true, but it's very old, isn't it? It's there in the yin and yang; it's there in the writings of Novalis, and one could go on and on. So I don't think there's anything very special about that, except maybe I insist upon it more than some writers today.

RE: I think it is insistent. I would say it's almost prescriptive in your writing.

JB: Perhaps it has to do with something which I now recognize about myself politically. As you know, I was, and in a sense remain, rather unfashionable and revolutionary because I find the state of the world intolerable. Not life. Not at all, but the way life is run. This is one aspect of my visceral being, and that probably determines to quite a large degree the choice of figures I write about—migrant workers and poor peasants or lovers, to whom the world is not often very welcoming. On the other hand, I'm deeply traditional in my imagination. The text which means so much to me is the Bible, particularly the New Testament and the Greeks. To some degree I'm interested in Buddhism and in Zen and above all in the real mystical writers. Perhaps the answer to your question about my insistence on searching for lost unity through the couple is a reminder of that for us.

RE: At the end of an essay on your mother she uses the word "love" and she makes the noun active. She verbalizes love and makes it sound as much like a thing you must do, as an observation about a condition that exists in the world. Was this notion of love something that was passed on from your mother?

JB: That's very complicated to answer. I think that essay, written just after she died, is a recognition and celebration of something she gave me. Why it's complicated is that actually I didn't have very much obvious and evident love from her—especially when I was a child. Not because she was unloving but because of a whole variety of reasons. I was sent away to school, I saw her very little, and she was very humbly trying, along with my father, to earn the money that could send me to this school. And so I didn't have a childhood in the ordinary sense of the term in which I was surrounded by caresses and love. So that's why it's quite a complicated question. Like so much in life, it's very paradoxical.

RE: There's a kind of searing honesty in it. I admit to being both moved and saddened by the section where you rub her hand and she thanks you for it, but lets you know it's irritating. The reader wants the gesture to be more significant than it was, as I suspect you did. Her reaction is almost heartbreaking.

JB: Yes, but for me it's far more a tribute to her stoicism—and you can't be stoic without being a realist—than a complaint from my part.

RE: You haven't talked much about your past and so I have little sense of what your life was like. You don't give much of that away.

JB: I think it's quite true. I'm exactly the opposite of autobiographical. I don't really know why, but it is something that I recognize as being quite strong in myself. I think I even talk about that in the essay.

RE: You say that autobiography is an orphan form. Is it because autobiographical writing is too self-indulgent? Is it too much about self and not enough about larger and more significant issues?

JB: You can talk here about the nature of talent because I think very often talent is a compensation for a weakness.

RE: Are you talking personally?

JB: I'm talking generally, but I'm also talking personally. I think it would be interesting, for example, to look at the biographies of really great athletes. I'd guess that quite often they had some physical difficulty early on, or thought they had. I think that when I was a kid I had a very weak sense of my own identity. I think I still have, actually. Maybe some demon in me has a sense of my identity, but I don't. As a result of this weakness, I was able spontaneously and impulsively to identify myself with other people, obviously people with whom I'm intimate, but even just somebody I pass in the street. Maybe that began my impulse to tell and to write stories. As you can see, that is the opposite of an autobiographical impulse.

RE: Is it an escape from autobiography?

JB: If you need to escape from autobiography you can. But to be honest I don't have the feeling that I'm running away from something.

RE: Tomas, the taxi driver in *To the Wedding*, is accused of using his encyclopedic knowledge as a way of not having to face the pain and the cruelty of life. Is there something of Tomas in you in this regard?

JB: I don't feel I have much to do with Tomas. When I was writing that section, I felt I was much more Zdena.

RE: Yes, she's a fabulous character. In the beginning when the two of them meet I shared her irritation with him. But by the end of their encounter I've grown to care for him a great deal. Was that a difficult thing to pull off? Were you nervous about being able to achieve such deft manoeuvrings?

JB: No, because when Zdena and Tomas were first there I didn't really know what was going to happen. I certainly didn't have a plan. In fact, that part of the book came relatively easily. Somewhere behind that—at an intellectual level which has nothing to do with the level at which one tries to tell stories—was my awareness of AIDS. With AIDS many hopes and dreams were destroyed or scattered. And this was true politically in the world as well, particularly in eastern Europe. So it seemed to me that their encounter brought together these two developments of our time. One of the things which was planned in the writing of that book was that, as we know, people who are viral positive and then suffer AIDS are placed—physically and mentally—in a kind of ghetto. That is one of the most terrible consequences of this anyway terrible disease.

RE: Which is what Ninon wants to do to herself in the beginning?

JB: Of course it is, because it's natural. Unfortunately that is confirmed by a lot of the world. In writing the book, I said two things to myself. One was to try to tell this story so that their destiny is not in a ghetto and is connected with many other things happening in our time. And the other was not to flinch from what had actually been. Of course, I wouldn't have been able to write the book in the way that I have if I hadn't been close to people who have suffered.

RE: I suppose you have your mother's stoicism? You don't flinch at the consequences of this disease. There's nothing sentimental about Ninon being able to dance so triumphantly at the end.

JB: Yes. If one wasn't unflinching towards that there would be no triumph.

RE: Let me ask this very directly. Do you ever get depressed?

JB: The first thing is that I believe, and I think have always done so, in the force of evil. I think evil exists and is in and around us all. But first of all *in* us all. So if I have a great attachment to what is alive and its beauty, it isn't a result of ignoring the existence of evil. I think evil begins with lies and with people pretending about the consequences of what they do, or what somebody else is. Evil begins with the liberty of man and with the creation of that liberty which is intrinsic to man.

RE: I was raised Roman Catholic and, of course, I believe in evil. The way you're talking sounds familiar.

JB: Yes, I think that's true. I haven't said anything about my father. I had some arguments with him, sometimes rather bitter conflicts, but I loved him very much. He was in the infantry in World War I and he survived four years on the Western Front as a lieutenant. He was completely marked for life by that. But before he joined as a volunteer, he was training to become an Anglican priest. Then after the war he was not able to continue and so he did something completely different. But that's just a footnote. You asked me if sometimes I'm depressed. Yes, of course. Sometimes I get very depressed. It's always very violent and I become impotent in every sense of the word. But with the incredible luck that I have, it never lasts for very long, I don't know why. I always forget that it's happened before, and I always think it's going to go on forever, but in fact it passes fairly quickly.

RE: So what's the source of that resilience? Hope?

JB: Yes, I think so. But with hope one has to be very lucid. I don't see hope as a sky full of light, I see it as a candle in the dark.

RE: You've written about Ernst Fisher and his high quotient of belief. Then you go on to quote him saying that we're forced back to offering visions only. Is that a recognition of a certain defeat? Not for him personally, but for all human beings who have to live in the relentless movements of history? I guess I'm asking if history invariably dooms us to being utopian. Is that the best we can hope for?

JB: I don't think so. The point about Utopia is that it imagines resolution whereas the nature of life is a constant struggle. I'm going to reply in terms that again will be familiar to you. It seems to me that there is the law of necessity and then there is also the nature of man's freedom. This is already, by absolute definition, a conflictual situation. All attempts at Utopia really are a denial of those two principles of existence. That's precisely why Utopianism is so dangerous.

RE: Is it a question of tendering our hope with vigilance? Is your strong sense of the need for ethical and political vigilance because the gains we've made are so small and their hold on society so precarious?

JB: Yes, but one has first of all to be vigilant, not only about what is happening, but about oneself. I mean one's own capacities for evil, one's own systems of cheating, and one's own egoism.

RE: Are you very self-critical? I don't have a sense of that from the writing. In fact, oftentimes the writing seems thoroughly assured, rather than in any way hesitant.

JB: Yes, I think that is true. But immediately after having written a page or a paragraph or maybe just a line, I am very critical. In fact most things—not only stories, but even essays—I write many times. Anything between four and ten drafts. It will perhaps surprise you, but I'm not a very verbal person. Writing for me is a continual struggle with words. They do not come very easily or naturally, and almost never do they lead me. But somewhere in my imagination there is something which is like a melody in music, or maybe like a drawing. And then begins the long effort of trying to find words which will not do violence to that melody or that drawing, which will—as far as possible—be faithful to it. So when I'm finished, if I have the feeling that they are reasonably faithful, then I forget them. And that faithfulness is not a question of accuracy in the automatic sense; it's not a question of naturalism; and it's not a question of making a copy. It's a question of tact. I think the real gift of the imagination is that of tact.

RE: You mean discretion?

JB: No, not discretion and not politeness. But respect for what is. Tact is tactile, it's to do with touching. When people write not so well, it seems to me that it is always a form of tactlessness. We haven't talked one single moment about other writers of our time. Why I so much admire Raymond Carver, for example?

RE: Because he's the most tactful writer you can think of?

JB: Yes, like Chekhov in the last century.

RE: I've never heard the word tact used in that way. It goes beyond a sense of aesthetics?

JB: Completely. It seems to me to do with faith and ethics.

RE: Although in some ways the making of art, the attempt to try and get our experience into some form that makes sense of what we do, to write stories that, as you say, speak to what we know in our hearts, is ultimately an ethical act, no matter the subject with which it deals.

JB: Yes, I think so. And it's to do with what one can always see more simply long ago. It's there so incontrovertibly in Homer, in his absolutely infinite respect for what is.

RE: You must be one of the most complete combinations of the elegiac and the hopeful of any writer I know. You quote approvingly that beautiful phrase from Rembrandt about tenderness experiencing itself as the end of the world. That strikes me as being the essence of the elegiac.

JB: I don't know because I don't see myself very clearly. When you say that, I immediately think of Ahkmatova, a poet for whom I have enormous respect and love. I think she was that: with all of the harshness around her and even in herself, because she was quite a harsh woman. So I can recognize it in others.

RE: But you have written that "it's on the site of loss that hopes are born."

JB: I believe that. Everybody knows that. But another artist today whom I admire enormously is Tom Waits.

RE: Now what is it in Waits that so attracts you?

JB: Well, I thought of him because of what you just said about the elegiac and the hopeful. *Waltzing Matilda* is about that. Every old man in his wheelchair knows it. I think that's why I love Waits so much.

RE: Do you believe in mystery?

JB: We're surrounded by it. At the same time, I hate mystification. But that's quite different.

RE: Is the act of making art—in any of the areas you work—an attempt to demystify, or to enhance the nature of the mystery all around us? Which direction does it move?

JB: I don't know, it's too big a question. I only know that in my own particular case, when I try to write something, whether it is an essay or a story or a play, for me to summon the energy to do it, I have to believe—and it may be an illusion—but I have to believe that what I am trying to say has two qualities. One, that it is actually something quite common and has been lived by millions of people. And the second quality is that it hasn't yet been said or said enough so that, in very modest terms, it represents a breakthrough.

RE: In one sense you see your role as being a witness?

JB: Witness, yes, but maybe one has then to add that the witnessing we're talking about is not just a question of recording. If we go back to what I was saying about the drawing of the Polish woman. I had been observing her and suddenly she was inside me, and then I could bring out at least an aspect of her. So I use the word witness in that sense. There's nothing objective in the usual sense of the term, nothing documentary about witnessing. Witnessing is a form of being, of trying to make oneself open, not of observing.

RE: You have no sense of the hierarchies of genre do you? In *Faces* the parts which are meditation or personal essay or poem or criticism seem to occupy an equal place of value for you.

JB: That's completely right. For me there is no hierarchy at all. Also, insofar as I can observe myself, if I'm writing a poem or if I am writing about a book that somebody else has written, I don't feel another part of myself being used. It seems to me they're always the same parts.

RE: One of the things that I find most remarkable about your criticism is that it's never formal. What really brought that home to me was the essay on Caravaggio in *Faces*. Your explanation of his claustrophobic use of space was that it was a function of his being poor and crowded and your sense that the poor fear distance and solitude. So his space is a reflection of what he knows and his comfort within it. That's a very different analysis than a formalist would make. You always tie your criticism to something real in the life of the painter. Is that a necessary strategy for you?

JB: I don't know that it's a strategy. It's just a way of working and a habit. But maybe it begins the other way around. In the case of Caravaggio maybe it has nothing to do with museums, or with even looking at Caravaggio. It is to do with being in the back streets or the bars of Rome, or somewhere else in Italy.

RE: Or your memories of the paintings you did in Livorno?

JB: Not only my memories of the paintings, but of being in Livorno. Then when I see Caravaggio, that comes back to me. If my criticism is not formal, it's because of this distinction between art and life.

RE: You don't buy it at all, do you?

JB: Exactly. I don't buy it. And when I'm writing about painting, I'm always aware of or trying to write about life.

RE: Your writing is both visceral and rational. The only writing I can think of that's like it, oddly enough, is Metaphysical poetry. It strikes me as being simultaneously locked into the mind and the body without any separation.

JB: Yes, I recognize that when you say it. And like I said, I owe a lot to the metaphysical and mystical poets. But I would say that I owe much more to a writer like Camus, where one might perhaps find the same thing.

RE: Doesn't Camus defines glory "as the right to love without limits?"

JB: Yes, yes. He was an enormous influence on me when I was young. I now have lived for thirty years in France, and people ask why did you choose to come to France. I wouldn't exactly say I came to France because it was the country of Albert Camus, but the fact that he was alive and writing was a consideration.

RE: Did you also leave England because you had grown to dislike London?

JB: I hadn't grown to dislike London, I always disliked London.

RE: There has been speculation about your choice—about whether you left to run away from a world rather than to go to one? It's a cruel question in a sense, because it implies you weren't able to handle English society?

JB: That's very curious. It's also more complicated because I left London in 1960 and I spent almost fifteen years living on the Continent writing books, like the book about Picasso or *G* or *Corker's Freedom*. But then in the mid '70s, I did come to live here in this village and I started writing about peasants. And at that moment a lot of people—including friends—said, "You're just retiring, you're running away from something." Now I didn't feel like that at all because I had a sense that the lives of peasants were actually quite central, even to the modern period. I think I was guided in a slightly prophetic way because now everybody is becoming aware that the disappearance of peasants and their way of cultivation, their relation to the land and to the planet system, is an incredibly important world question. Even the toughest politicians in Russia, after having destroyed millions, would be happy if they could reinvent peasants. So it was not as marginal a choice as it appears.

RE: I remember fondly a piece you wrote, published years ago in *Harper's*. I think it had a much more sanctified title, but it was basically about the necessity of cleaning out the shithouse in the spring. While I recognized the activity I thought it might be a prescription for the imagination as well. You talk about demons and about the darker side. Is it necessary to go down to the place of excrement to use Yeats's phrase?

JB: I don't know. I wrote it spontaneously because it's something I do—and have done many times—in the spring. I suddenly thought maybe I should write about it. But behind it—and I may sound sort of folksy and primitive—but it seems to me that the avalanche of information and images that we have about the world have become increasingly bodiless, disembodied—especially in the media. And the screen on which we see them actually becomes an opaque screen between people and physical life. That also means that it becomes an opaque screen between things that are done and the consequences of those things. One of the most monstrous and terrible examples, of course, is the Gulf War. But if one becomes much more modest, it is also to do with the fact that we all shit, and we shouldn't forget that or deny it. In the same way—but not in any kind of sadistical way—there is a deep crisis caused by the fact that people eat meat and refuse to picture abattoirs. The whole notion is lost that the eating of meat is a sacrifice. The crisis is there because without the notion of sacrifice life becomes both much more solitary and, in a way which I can't quite explain, much more despairing.

RE: In one sense what you're recognizing is the need for ritual, that we have to find ways to contain our experiences and to structure our emotions, which is what ritual does.

JB: Exactly, exactly. And it seems to me that the best stories, without ever falling into symbolism or anything with a capital letter, actually describe what happens as a certain aspect of ritual.

Peter Greenaway
The Rational Extremist

Peter Greenaway makes exquisite, horrifying films. The characters in them are possessed by monstrous devotions and, as a consequence, they religiously perform acts of intolerable strangeness and cruelty—acts, as the language of ritual would have it, even unto death. These occurrences are offered in such a casual way that they begin to make the ordinary seem suspect, unreal. Greenaway's most controversial film is the rule that proves exceptional. *The Cook, the Thief, His Wife and Her Lover* is a ripe, gorgeously corrupt film that was deemed "unsuitable" by the Venice Film Festival and that, in turn, attracted the attention of America's neo-conservatives who see it as a full-frontal assault on everything good, decent and motherly.

They are not alone in their condemnation. I can think of no film, perhaps since Bertolucci's *Last Tango in Paris*, that has provoked such intense reactions from intelligent, seasoned film-goers. I work with a television producer whose brother-in-law is a filmophile when he's not a teacher. "If you like this film," he told my colleague, "I'll never speak to you again." His extreme reaction is not uncharacteristic. People regularly walk out of the film, unable to stomach its unrelieved program of psychological and physical violence.

The opening scene will give you an idea of what they're reacting to: a man is dragged into a greenish-blue, wet loading area, alive with threatening echoes and packs of marauding dogs. He is roughed up, stripped, thrown on the back of a car and systematically smeared with dog shit that is brought out on delicate squares of paper, as if they were hamburger patties. After he falls to the ground in this place where love, ironically, is about to pitch his mansion, the thief from the film's title who has actively participated in the humiliation, unzips his fly and urinates all over the wretched victim. The film goes on to elaborately document a menu of repugnant acts including torture, sexual perversion, grotesque murder and cannibalism.

The Cook, the Thief, His Wife and Her Lover doesn't lend itself to reductive categorizing—it is a film with meanings as various as its assaults. But one of the things it is about is Mrs. Thatcher's England, a country Greenaway describes borrowing Wilde's phrase, whose citizens are taught "the price of everything and the value of nothing." In Albert Spica, the thief of the title, Greenaway has created one of the most thoroughly despicable characters in contemporary cinema, a man capable of any barbarism, most of which he supervises in the Hollandais, a London restaurant which he and his henchmen use as a finishing school for terrorism.

His brutalized wife is among his party, but not of it, and the love affair she conducts in the bathroom, kitchen and pantry of the restaurant with a bookish gentleman is an attempt to counterbalance her husband's malevolent world. The affair takes place under the benevolent witness of the cook who, by the end of the film, will prepare the dead lover for a meal that I can only describe as unconventional.

The Cook, the Thief, His Wife and Her Lover, like Greenaway's other films, investigates states of almost unbearable anxiety. These films are intelligent, scrupulously constructed and elegant and are often shaped by an overlay of systems—alphabets, numbers, games, repetitive narratives and naming devices—that contain the terror of what it is we're anticipating or actually seeing. Ritual and pattern have the effect of structuring emotion and in Greenaway's film world the most insistent rituals contain the most voluptuous emotions.

The artfulness of the films has a similar effect; Greenaway studied painting—and continues to exhibit in galleries—and his films look like no one else's, partially because of his art training. They are loaded with references to art history and to specific paintings—a Frans Hal is the visual centrepiece for *The Cook, the Thief, His Wife and Her Lover* and painters as different as Vermeer, Samuel Palmer, Ford Maddox Brown and Stanley Spencer turn up throughout his body of work in some form or another. His training as a painter taught him to value every frame; if you were to stop a Greenaway film and blow up the image you would invariably be confronted with a stunning composition. Art mediates horror for him and no less frequently, art *is* horror as well.

Greenaway is among a handful of indispensable filmmakers who asks us to witness our worst possible selves operating in the world, and then further asks us to consider what we would put in place to control that ominous operation. The machinations of the world he makes are unsettling and wonderful. In the following interview he states his admiration for encyclopedic works of art—poems, novels and paintings—which aspire to contain everything. William Faulkner once said he wanted to get the entire world into one sentence; Greenaway's intentions are no less ambitious. He wants to make a film that becomes the whole world, a world which then plays itself out according to his willful, astonishingly beautiful and utterly necessary plan.

Peter Greenaway's films include *The Falls* (1980), *The Draughtsman's Contract* (1982), *A Zed and Two Noughts* (1986), *The Belly of an Architect* (1987), *Drowning by Numbers* (1988), *Prospero's Books* (1991) and *The Pillow Book* (1996). The following interview took place in July of 1990.

PETER GREENAWAY: Mine was a very conventional English art education. They'd hardly heard about the Bauhaus. It was in the early stages of English Pop Art and I was certainly thrown into all that flux. But I felt a personal antipathy to the sheer pop culture of it all. I think that's why I was attracted to the work and activities of two painters, one an ex-patriot American, R.B. Kitaj, and the other an English painter, Tom Phillips. Their particular brand of Pop Art had a high intellectual content. Kitaj was especially interesting because he managed this very heady combination of politics and sex and was quite happy to use all sorts of arcane and political references. As a student I was always described as being very very literary and there was a way in which Tom Phillips and also Kitaj legitimized my interest in text, in literary allusion and so on. And I suppose for several years my paintings did rather look like early Kitaj's.

ROBERT ENRIGHT: British painters are often accused—and I think that's the right word—of being too literary. I gather you don't have any sense that there are limitations in layering the painting with references to literature or myth or narrative?

PG: I think its been the curse of English painting ever since Nicholas Hilliard in the late Jacobean period. It certainly was a curse of salon paintings of the eighteenth and nineteenth centuries. After all, the Pre-Raphaelites needed about eight pages of text underneath each painting in order to explain it. I think that has gone on right through. No surprise really, we're not basically a painterly nation. I think our forte has to be in terms of the novel and certainly the theatre. But if you are a painter in England you are confronted with this tradition. It has to do with temperament as well.

RE: You began exhibiting in 1964 at the Lords Gallery. Were you successful as a painter?

PG: I think if I persisted that I could have carved myself out a career—a minor career certainly—as a painter. I had a whole series of exhibitions—both mixed and solo—of which that one you mention was the first. But I think my general interest in cinema began to predominate and I spent much more time, energy and indeed funds to make a series of very short films. I started with a movie which is never seen now called *Death—The Sentiment*. And there must have been twenty or thirty of these short movies leading up to *The Falls*, which came about ten years later.

RE: You've called *The Falls* "the trash bin" for all of your other films.

PG: Well, maybe that was a slightly pejorative term. But it's certainly a receptacle, an encyclopedia in which to slot many, many articles.

RE: A number of critics have called you a filmic painter. Is that an accurate description of what you do?

PG: I think there are all sorts of paradoxes and contradictions about using painterly language to explain film and vice versa. I always find abhorrent filmic criticism which describes an image as being painterly, as though somehow what is allowed for painting is not being allowed for film. It's a peculiar backtracking, that wretched persistence we have of using out-moded critical jargon in the confrontation of something new. And the sooner we can get rid of that the better. I think in that respect cinema is its own worst enemy. But to go back to the beginning of your question, I do as much painting now as I do film-making. There's a way in which I still think that painting is the supreme visual art because of its composite, experimental nature and because of the relationship of the painter to one single uninterrupted space in front of him, a space which doesn't need so much compromise and so much collaboration. And I sincerely believe that the ideas and experimentation that have gone on in the twentieth century have left cinema a long, long way behind.

RE: But you've gone a fair distance in trying to make those languages have more in common than they do in mainstream filmmaking. What I'm getting at is that I know of no filmmaker who spends as much time as you do composing individual scenes. I'm thinking of the use of Vermeer in *A Zed and Two Noughts*, of the Frans Hals painting, *The Banquet of the Officers of the Saint George Civic Guard Company*, which is the centre piece for the *The Cook, the Thief, His Wife and Her Lover*.

PG: Well, it used to be said that cinema was a combination of literature, theatre and painting, and I've always felt that painting was the poor cousin of the other two. Not enough was ever used in terms of heritage and background and reference, whereas the other two were constantly raided, as it were, for information and reference. And I still basically think that dominant cinema, certainly dominant American cinema, is a form of illustrated novel. I think that was true right at the beginning and it's still true now. If I can put it another way, my cinema is best considered in terms of the critical language you use in the discussion of painting aesthetics. For example, I'm quite happy to talk about content, form and surface. I don't know of any other filmmakers who talk about surface. And I'm sure you'd agree that the predominant concern of twentieth century painting has been a fully-fledged understanding of what surface means in the painterly context.

RE: How do you talk about surface in film language?

PG: Well, I have a great concern and demand for what might be described as the abstract values of filmmaking, which have to do with related forms in painting: organization of space, not only in three dimensions, but in two dimensions; and the use of the frame. The frame is omnipotent. My concerns for symmetry and asymmetry, the idea of centre points and golden sections and the geometrical division of the composition in the way that perhaps Piero della Francesca would have done it. I can't imagine any other filmmaker playing with those sorts of ideas? And also an actual concern with the sheer matter—if I can use that word—of what film is. After all, it's total artifice. Only look above your head when you sit in any cinema and you can see the attributes of the artifice in the beam shining over your head. And although I'm not particularly interested in what might be described as totally abstract picture-making, I do want people to constantly realize that when they're watching a piece of my cinema, that they're watching cinema and nothing else. This is not a window on the world; it's not a slice of life; it's not an attempt at reality or naturalism. Whatever those chimera are, I don't think they're even worth pursuing, because they're unobtainable. And I'm determined all the time to indicate this artificiality. Nonetheless, I want to use the whole gamut and range of expression that cinema has invented in its ninety-five years. So I'm conscious of the screen as a flat surface and I'm concerned with the organization of space and light. And these, of course, are largely painterly concerns. I'm interested in the colour coding; in relationships of texture, flesh against cloth against matter; I'm interested in the sculptural, choreographic spacing between people—so when Albert Spica walks across a room it's important to examine the negative and positive areas of his passing. The language—the syntax and the grammar—that I'm using is probably a very unfamiliar one to film-goers.

RE: I want to ask what may be a naïve question. How do you keep all that in your mind at one time? Because while these formal aspects are being investigated, you're also highly conscious of narrative. At some level viewers are looking at a story in which they are willing to suspend their disbelief—to use a phrase from literary criticism—and become involved with some of those characters.

PG: Well, I think it's entirely an equivocal situation. It's said that nobody ever consciously listens to every single note of music; it's a process in which you drift away and come back. I like to use that continual shifting of perception. Sometimes you are deliberately dragged inside a narrative and sometimes you are deliberately repelled from it. There's a two way activity going on. I think basically it's to do with my anathema towards a cinema which is predominantly about two things: one is psychodrama, which again is the basic American model of cinema, and the other is the use of actors and acting in the star system. In those early days from the late '50s to the early '70s, I was very much a part of the Structuralist, non-narrative cinema that was happening in North America, Europe, and to a certain extent, in Great Britain. I think a lot of my early ideas, which still persist in the game-playing and the use of universal systems, like alphabets and number counts and so on, stem from those times.

RE: I want to shift from form to talk about what the references or illusions add up to in your films. How do they make the narrative clearer?

PG: Let me answer your question a little more elliptically. The perfect film I would aim for—and who knows, one day possibly make—would be an equivalent of James Joyce's *Ulysses*. There is a magnificent novel which is totally self-reflexive but which also works extremely well as a drama. It is interested in the language of its own making; it is very innovative and experimental, but it still has tremendous power to synthesize and organize whole masses of information. I think there's evidence in all my films of a sneaking admiration for the encyclopedic point of view. All the great artifacts, certainly of Western art, have somehow been encyclopedic in their concept. Now there's no way one can put all the world's information in one place, but every now and again there are extraordinary landmarks. I just spent nearly eighteen months doing a television version of Dante's *Divine Comedy*. We've just finished the first eight Cantos of "The Inferno." There's an extraordinary and encyclopedic work. Or we could talk about Rabelais, or another famous English early novel, like Laurence Sterne's *Tristram Shandy*. I've also done a filmscript version of Flaubert's last novel, *Bouvard et Pécuchet*, which again is a novel of extraordinary range. I'm constantly attracted to these things, and I suppose the contemporary hero for me has to be Borges who manages to encapsulate this same phenomenology of being able to somehow put all the world's language in one place. Now, this is an arrogant ambition. It's an ambition which constantly mocks even the attempt to describe it. But it's this total synthesis of many, many layers of meaning into some sort of cohesive whole which I'm constantly entertained by. Tom Phillips and I have attempted to try and find a contemporary television equivalent for Dante's "Inferno." There's no way that it would make any sense to recreate the poem in its period, so we've made it very much in the twentieth century. I've learned a great deal from that and I've realized that every man's hell is completely different, though curiously most people's heaven is the same. Somehow that's been brought out to me in the examination, metaphor by metaphor, of the poem. And I found that it gave me permission, or a licence, to continue to think and behave and make films in the way I'm still doing.

RE: Are you arrogant?

PG: That's for you as viewer and, at this present moment, conversationalist to decide. I think I have the arrogance of a rather self-centred obsessional filmmaker, which tends to be a bit exclusive. I would suggest that the majority of the cinema that is being perpetrated at the moment is not of great interest, but I think that's the normal arrogance of a primary creator.

RE: Is it fair to describe you as obsessive? And if you are, how much of that obsession comes out of your own thinking about order and chaos in the world?

PG: I suppose however hard one would try to hide one's identity, I'm sure that all these films in some ways are autobiographical. I mean I could point out to you close associations, but I don't know whether that would be of any particular benefit to either you or myself. I suspect people who know me and know the films can see much more. I live a very even-keeled domestic life. I spend a great deal of my day working and I'm not particularly gregarious or extrovert. I thoroughly enjoy the whole process of examination of aesthetics in both painting and filmmaking and find it totally and absolutely absorbing.

RE: There's a character in *The Falls* who invents fictitious languages and then adds a camera so that he can record his enthusiasm for the written word. I can't help but think that you're somewhere in that character.

PG: Right. Many years ago when I first started filmmaking, I invented this character Tulse Luper. He was a sort of alter ego for whom I could arrogantly, maybe even flippantly, invent all sorts of ideas and structures, and then be able to talk about them endlessly. He was also a composite figure of all the people I admired at that time, Buckminster Fuller, John Cage, certainly Marcel Duchamp, these great world cultural figures who have an endless store of anecdotes and who were great raconteurs. On a much more personal level, he was based upon my father who was an ornithologist. It was some sort of homage to him.

RE: You said earlier that you're totally absorbed by the aesthetics of film and painting. I want to look at some specific areas of that inquiry and ask you about your special interest in Dutch painting.

PG: I have a great enthusiasm for all periods of European painting, but I have a sneaking feeling that the most successful painting, in a social, political and aesthetic sense, was done during the golden age of Dutch painting. It was painting at its most democratic, at its most social. Before that time the activity was the preserve of either the state or the church. It was largely distant from what even might be described as middle-class man. And ever since the late seventeenth century I feel that the attitude of painters towards a more personal vision has taken them further and further away from people's appreciation. But there seemed to be that happy period between 1590 and 1670 in what was then Holland, when painter and client, subject and content, metaphor and narrative, came together to create a language of painting which seemed to be comprehensible to great numbers of people. I also like the way both public and private metaphor and the highly accomplished literal appreciation of the world were all bound together in these years. I find that marriage very, very satisfactory.

RE: How do you use that satisfaction, though? The surgeon in *A Zed and Two Noughts*, is obsessed by Vermeer but he's not a particularly attractive character.

PG: Indeed not. What I tried very hard to do in that film was to go beyond recreating the tableaux of the period and to try and investigate from lots of different angles the whole phenomenon of Dutch painting and most particularly of Vermeer. People sometimes describe my films as being a thesis about a given subject wrapped up in a narrative form. Despite the flaws and the infelicities of that film, it's one that I feel most endearing towards because of its attempt to consider all manner of different activities. Some European critics suggested that *A Zed and Two Noughts* was really five films struggling to become one film.

RE: Aren't the runners who pull Hardy, one of the endangered husbands, out of the water in *Drowning by Numbers*, called the Van Dyke brothers? Is that just a bit of fun you're having, an artful pun?

PG: No, that was part of another structure. If you examine all the characters in *Drowning by Numbers*, you'll notice they all have some connection with famous people's last words. For example, the English painter Gainsborough's last words are supposed to be, "We are now all off to heaven and Van Dyke is of the company." Edward VI's last words were supposed to be "Bugger Bognor," so you have the Bognor brothers. Nelson's last words are "Kiss me Hardy," so you have a character called Hardy, and so it goes through all the characters. I suppose on one level this is rather recondite, but it's also a consideration of the cyclic phenomenon of death which is one of the preoccupations of that film.

RE: All of those allusions are worked out ahead of time. Are there any accidents in your films?

PG: Well, I don't think you can ever prevent accidents from happening. It would also be very stupid of me to try and eradicate any serendipitous activity. These things *are* extremely well-planned and there's a very practical reason for that: our budgets are extremely small. I think each movie is made for about a million pounds, which is extraordinarily cheap. Also, we have to shoot them in about eight weeks, so there's no opportunity for me ever to re-shoot anything.

RE: Let me ask you about a particular scene in *A Zed and Two Noughts*. It's the one in which Venus de Milo and Phillipe Arc-en-ciel talk in front of a cage which contains a zebra. The animal moves in and out of frame in a wild and almost erotic way.

PG: I'm very glad that you appreciate that scene because its certainly very high on my list of excitements too. The Zebra basically is one of the horse forms that man has never been able satisfactorily to harness and use for his own power, which I think in itself is an emblem. There are a number of ramifications in that scene: the prostitute who's dressed in black, meets the cripple who's dressed in white; the Zebra is a moral or equivocal animal halfway between black and white. It's the one animal that carries its own bars on it, so it's already caged within its own skin. And the two characters are talking about hybrids and obviously bestiality is a sub-text of the film. So all these connotations come together in that image.

RE: I can see why you would mention Joyce because as you talk I think of his notion of layering. There are no simple images for you.

PG: You're absolutely right. But we're really desperately trying to explain the power and the extraordinary excitement of visual images and we're using words to do that. That's one of the sad and paradoxical things about being a filmmaker.

RE: You've said that all of your films are "violent and cruel and misanthropic at their centre." Does love play into that world at all?

PG: Probably in all my films there is an attitude which is not exactly anti-romantic, but which tries very hard to reduce all the conventional romanticisms to a negative. It seems to me that cultural life, certainly cinematic life, is concerned with sentimentality and with romance, in what I would regard as rather a cheapening way. There is the concept of deep, emotional identification between an audience and the screen in the ideal model of American cinema. And I constantly query that, because it seems to me that ultimately what cinema offers is some debasing of human cultural spirit. I suspect that my antagonism is very apparent in the films. I try and reduce what I regard as superficial romance to a basic level. For example, in *The Draughtsman's Contract*, the contract is to try and eradicate a concept like love and take it back down to the basics of sex. And I think probably the same attitudes are held towards death. It's a process of demystification, of de-romanticizing. I think this has got to do with my education, my culture and also with my own temperament.

RE: In *The Cook and the Thief* there was something very moving when Georgina lies down beside Michael's dead body and tells him the real horror of her life. I found that a very poignant scene. It seemed to me a scene that was about romance.

PG: Yes, it's possibly true. I think there are things in that film which hadn't happened before. I think the changes have come out of my antagonism, anger and concern with the wretched Thatcherite years in England which have told us about the price of everything and the value of nothing. I suppose there is a lot more concern for passion in all of its forms seeping up through that movie. But when people say that my movies are cold, calculated and intellectual, I would like to remind them that the subject matter indeed is grossly violent, is extraordinarily passionate. If you consider the grief that motivates those animal behaviourists in *A Zed and Two Noughts*, if you consider the terrible anguish that's behind the architect in *The Belly of an Architect*, and the unutterable sense of loneliness and isolation that the coroner feels in *Drowning by Numbers*, then you'll recognize the great anguish and passion at the centre of all these film scenarios. I have this hope to express these extraordinary emotional extremes, but to do it in the most rational way possible. Now a lot of people find that these two ideas are contradictory. But I think if my cinema has any characteristic, it's this peculiar stretchmark between the passion—some people describe it as the cruelty of the human predicament—and the rationality with which I'm determined to try and express it.

RE: In *Drowning by Numbers* one of the male characters says that women have a lot to answer for. And I can't remember a more loathsome character in his attitude towards women than Albert Spica. Where does all the loathing and misogyny come from?

PG: I break down *The Cook and the Thief* into seven large areas, which I'm sure we could talk about for a great deal. One of those areas started off as a technical exercise in which I deliberately considered personifications of evil in Western Culture.

RE: Do you mean like Satan in Milton's *Paradise Lost*?

PG: Well, yes, Satan turns out to be the most entertaining and exciting character in the whole of the poem. Take, for example, Shakespeare's Richard III, an appallingly ugly man with whom Albert Spica has lots in common. But there's a man, certainly when played by Laurence Olivier, who somehow has great charisma and charm.

RE: But when Richard III woos Anne, the widow of the man he's just killed, as she accompanies her father-in-law's funeral bier, as improbable as it sounds, we go with him. I can't imagine Spica wooing Georgina, even under normal circumstances.

PG: Exactly. What I wanted to create was a character you could not possibly have this attraction for. I deliberately tried to make this man so appalling—this bully, this tormentor, this man with a foul mouth, foul behaviour, and appalling ethnic morality—but of course he became much more interesting in the end than just a cypher or a solution to a technical problem. And when the character got into the hands of the actor Michael Gambon it took off again in other directions.

My male characters, like Stourley Kracklite in *The Belly of an Architect* and Richard Neville in *The Draughtsman's Contract*, are all mediocre men. And perhaps Albert Spica is the most mediocre of them all. There's a way that the germs and ashes of all the films are present in all the others. And my attempts at this character probably started with Kracklite who is a weak man, a mediocre architect whose ambitions will never be fulfilled, and in some sense Albert Spica has taken that character a stage further.

RE: Let me confess something. In *Drowning by Numbers* I can't believe that those three extraordinary women would be with those three unextraordinary men. The only male character of much interest, other than Smut, is his father, Madgett.

PG: I wonder why the men get such a poor deal in this situation. That distresses me. I don't find them so unattractive. Okay, I've given them attributes which may be unappealing but one of the points of the film is that these women really don't have motives to get rid of their husbands. Their motives are ephemeral. The first woman says that it's because his nose is too red, or he doesn't wash his feet. I mean it's not as though he committed terrifying crimes. So there's a deliberate waywardness about the female activity in that film.

RE: At points in the film they look like benign witches, witches whose beneficence can very suddenly turn.

PG: Do men ever come in threes? Why do women always come in threes—the three Fates, the three Furies, the three witches in *Macbeth*? Or again you have Titian's Vanities as a *memento mori*: the young woman, the middle-aged woman and the old hag. I deliberately subverted those genres. After all, the young virgin in *Drowning by Numbers* is anything but a virgin; she's always talking about screwing. The middle-aged woman, who's represented in the painting by Titian as very fecund and probably pregnant, is apparently sterile, and the old hag who's supposed to remind you of death is a very attractive elderly woman. So I've tried to subvert that particular genre as well.

RE: The traditional role that sexuality plays is to frustrate order and become subversive. How does sexuality operate in your films?

PG: Well, perhaps it's best for the onlooker to see that. It's certainly a preoccupation most of my characters have, as indeed I have myself. It's not often seen to be a very satisfactory solution to problems, but there's always the anxiety with sex in all its various forms.

RE: Healthy sex seems to be the way that Georgina is able to escape the situation in which she finds herself in *The Cook and the Thief*. Does it play that role for her in the film?

PG: I think that's true. There's also a great deal of complexity in her attraction to Spica. In some perverse sense his attraction is that of evil itself. I mean the very unsatisfactoriness of their sexuality could be conceived as positive as well as negative. And there's also the sub-text of maternity and the homosexual relationship that seems to exist between Albert Spica and his young protégé. And there's the whole peculiar anti-machismo twist of this rather bookish bookworm to whom she's attracted. All these layers of traditional stereotyping are being played with in *The Cook and the Thief*.

RE: Are there layers of traditional Christianity being referred to as well? In the book depository, Michael puts a large cross-beam to hold the door secure and when he's finally found by Georgina he looks very much like Christ in a deposition painting, with a foreshortened perspective?

PG: Yes. The centre of the movie has two characters who are finally united in their love, and then they are put into the dark van which goes down into the underworld all covered in decay. They are then washed down by a man called Eden, who is supposed to be Noah's first son. Then, in the book depository, which is obviously associated with the Tree of Knowledge, they are cleansed, both physically and metaphorically, in order to prepare themselves for the sacrifice to the ultimate lover of all time, who is Christ. What did Christ say, in the *Beatitudes*? "Take this and eat, this is my body which is given to you," which becomes the illogical explanation for cannibalism. Another more recondite area is the question of the small boy who sings in a high falsetto voice. He's always accompanied by an orange light behind his white hair and he is obviously the manifestation of innocence. And what does Albert Spica, the satanic figure do? He makes the kitchen boy into an angel by taking his navel away.

RE: That torture scene is one among many in the film that seems almost unbearable. So is the murder of Michael—the way he's killed—and the eating of his elegantly cooked body. Did you have a sense in the film that you were really pushing the limits of what the audience could tolerate?

PG: Well, there is this tradition in which I've always had a great interest. I suppose it goes back to Jacobean Drama, through Webster's *The Duchess of Malfi* on through de Sade, Bataille and Genet, it surfaces again in Peter Brook's Theatre of Cruelty and the Theatre of the Absurd, and then again in Pier Paolo Pasolini and Luis Buñuel. There is a tradition of provocation, of taboo-breaking, of finding sensitive areas for examination, on the grounds that examining the extremes helps us to understand the commonplace.

RE: Are there taboos for you? Are there things you won't make films about?

PG: Theoretically no. When it comes to the crunch though, I don't know. *The Cook and the Thief* is the beginning of a trilogy; the other two parts are about different subject matter and different people. The second film is called *Love of Ruins*, and examines the rights of a woman over her child, not only her embryo but also of the child. It's based very much on the Medea myth. I think my task might be to try and convince an audience to be sympathetic to a woman who murders her own child, a terrifying and somewhat unbelievable proposition. That might raise all sorts of incredibly sensitive areas. The third part of the trilogy is called *The Man Who Met Himself*, which takes the ideas of twinship and cloning much further than *A Zed and Two Noughts* and actually presents the situation of a man meeting himself and considers what his reactions would be. It's based very largely on the myths of Apollo and Marsyas and the tension of the Apollonian versus the Dionysian. As we know from Titian and indeed Ovid, at the end of that story Apollo has Marsyas flayed. I actually want to take that proposition to its limit in contemporary terms, and to examine the edges of that state of desperation. Maybe there are barriers which I might force myself up against when I come to finalize the script.

RE: What drives you to do it? I'm not asking out of a sense of outrage or horror, but who do you do it for?

PG: This is really a perfectly innocent answer. I really make these films for myself, as I suspect everybody who is a primary creator does. I mean, it's so arrogant to do the opposite. How could I possibly make films for you, how could I possibly make films for audiences, because every single person has a different requirement. But I know that in the pursuit of these interests other people are also entertained and intrigued, so I feel my search is not entirely isolated. I suppose it's a cathartic situation. I'm very curious to find out how far my imagination goes, to see what I can dredge up, to see what's lurking down there, to turn over the stones. But also to fit them into a tradition. My cinema is classical and based on the two grand narratives that exist in the western world, the Judeo-Christian and the Hellenic-Roman tradition. I suppose it's the background to our Western painting traditions, too. So I feel in key to that long line of investigation which has been going on both in literature and in painting. In that sense, I don't feel isolationist.

RE: In the United States *The Cook and the Thief* has been controversial. Are you concerned at all about the kind of reaction that it has provoked?

PG: The film has been seen now in probably all the major cities of the world. And the only problems I've ever had have been in America, which probably says more about Americans than it does about the film.

RE: You're not surprised then? It seems that Americans don't like the naughty bits and the dirty bits being mixed up.

PG: I'm not so sure it's just that. I must be very careful here not to become xenophobic, but there is a way in which American culture at large—and certainly American cinema—now pervades the whole world to disastrous effects. It's a very nursery-like attitude towards the human condition. It's simplistic, without metaphor and it demands a satisfactory moral ending. I think *The Cook and the Thief* confronts those issues in a way which obviously makes the average American very uncomfortable indeed. American movies are often full of blood and thunder—tomato ketchup from corner to corner and reactionary behaviour—but it's done in such a gleeful, ephemeral way that it creates no problems for them. But *The Cook and the Thief* is determined to examine the proposition that if you cause some predicament, then you must take the consequences. There's a great sense of cause and effect in this film. While I know it may be very difficult for some people to disassociate one from the other, I'm using this violence and this appalling behaviour to deliberately point up these effects, and not simply to engage in them for a quick *frisson*, a quick giggle, and then forget about it the next moment. I think that moral attitude is more of a problem to the average American audience than the overt descriptions of violence in the film.

RE: Are you concerned about aestheticizing violence?

PG: That is always a danger. Some people in England have found my concern for baroque imagery to be dangerous, as though I were supporting the world of advertising and the world of superficiality. And there is a way in which those things are very important for me. It would have been very easy to set *The Cook and the Thief* in a greasy café somewhere, but that would have missed half the point. What I'm trying to say in the film is that here is respectable society, a society that spends its money on clothes and fashion and high food, which is behaving abominably. It's like the Holbein corpse, which is dressed in a beautiful uniform with a flowered hat but inside it's rancid and rotten.

RE: Let me ask you a reverse question: is there also a danger that you might in a sense brutalize aesthetics? You take these exquisite things and the context that they are realized in is pretty terrifying much of the time.

PG: I think the very fact that you're asking that question is really providing its own answer. You yourself are provoked to pose the question because the film is disturbing you. In a peculiar way, I've therefore been successful. It's provoked you to reconsider what violence means in terms of aesthetics. It's very interesting that French audiences—who have very largely been my best audiences for a long time—have had great problems with this film. French intellectuals find it very difficult when the sex of the gutter permeates intellectual argument. And that stretchmark is very interesting to me because it shows the ghettoizing of their intellectual activities. I think that's one of the good things this film has provoked.

RE: Helen Mirren, the actress who played Georgina, called you courageous for doing this film. Do you think of yourself in that way?

PG: No. I'm a bit surprised by people's reactions afterwards. This was the film that I wanted to make and I sat down and wrote it. It wasn't until myself and the producer began to try and gather money together that we realized what I'd written and the power it had. For the first time Channel Four Television, which had backed me so rigorously and courageously in the past, drew the line and said there was no way they were going to support this film. But it was only after the film was first shown and I got some sense of how people were reacting, only then did I begin to realize exactly what we'd made. So I hope you believe I'm being honest when I say there was no sense of *épater le bourgeois*, there was no sense of mischievous manipulation in the production of this film.

Attila Richard Lukacs

Regendering the Garden

There is a photograph of Attila Richard Lukacs, taken in his Berlin studio in 1990, that goes some distance in summing up his art and life. He is standing among a number of military paintings that would end up in his exhibition at Vancouver's Diane Farris Gallery in September of that year. He holds a panel with the word "discipline" printed on it and he is wearing his characteristic bad boy smile. The single panel became part of a twelve-part painting called *We care a lot*; the smile just becomes him.

Hard work and impishness are two attitudes he holds in abundance. Lukacs's ambition is commensurate with the scale of his largest paintings, like the spectacular *This Town* (1990) from his E-Work series, in which a group of well-built skinheads construct, with equal attentiveness, a road and a sense of unease. It is an impressive work: over six metres long by four metres high, a huge, anxious mural that is part fetish arena, part history painting and part personal elegy.

The complications of its inspiration and intent are often present in Lukacs's work; he is the most significant and ambitious painter to have emerged in Canada in the last five years. Only in his thirties at the time of this writing, he is also the youngest. The fact that his multi-functional tea house installation took Documenta (the international mega-art exhibition staged in Kassel, Germany every four years) by storm in 1992 seems almost unsurprising now. The "tea-house" is an elegant pissoir where gay men can go, to repeat Lukacs's wishful thinking in the candid interview that follows, "for their Documenta quickie."

His career has had about it a hurried quality. His early exhibitions in Vancouver—Prime Cuts at the Unit Pitt Gallery in 1983 and Young Romantics at the Vancouver Art Gallery two years later—were the closest thing Canada has come to a *succès de scandale*, out of which Lukacs emerged as a painter to watch. In 1986 he moved to Berlin, the city where he lived for ten years before moving to New York. Berlin gave him the freedom to make work that is fascinating and problematic.

Lukacs's skinhead and monkey paintings represent the marginal made epic and they hint at a wide range of interpretive possibilities. They are not easy paintings, nor are they meant to be. The troubling ambiguity of the skinheads—are they neo-nazis, proletarian heroes, gay-bashers or available homosexuals?—makes the numerous works in which they appear difficult to decipher. We're encouraged to ask similar questions about the monkeys—are they rude representatives of mindless humanity, symbols for the imprisoned imagination, or surrogates for the painter himself, a species of anthropomorphic voluptuary, chained to the excesses of his own personality?

Lukacs creates a similar uncertainty around his uses of art history. His method is to take familiar images which we're inclined to read through the rose-coloured glasses of received wisdom, and to undermine any security we feel in that recognition. By randomly picking images from his constant, unsystematic ransacking of high art and popular culture, he is able to rehistoricize art history. In this process he gets by with a little help from cannibalizing his friends: artists as different as Breughel, Hans Baldung-Grien, Caravaggio, Delacroix, Manet and Degas (not to mention Roman fresco painting) have all been swallowed up and put to radically different uses in his work. Lukacs's own phrase to describe what he's about locates both the intention and the scope of his project: "I'm rewriting 'paradise.'" Thomas W. Sokolowski, the director of the Grey Art Gallery and Study Centre in New York, has observed that Lukacs "has given us a lot to think about and it's frightening as hell."

When Lukacs talks about his art and life his conversation is direct and undiluted. What may not come through on the page is the playful tone of a number of his observations and responses. He is like a contemporary version of Edgar Allan Poe's "imp of the perverse," overflowing with the self-delighting wickedness of his own being.

The following interview took place in Lukacs's Berlin studio in May 1992. He was working on his installation for Documenta IX in Kassel, the opening of which was less than a month away.

ROBERT ENRIGHT: I read somewhere that you actually went to art classes with your father.

ATTILA RICHARD LUKACS: My father used to take evening art classes when I was very young. He always wanted to be an artist and, like every kid, I just mimicked him. He'd be home painting and I'd set up beside him and paint too. Eventually I got better than he did and so he gave me his paints.

RE: That's the Picasso story. It might be apocryphal, but the story goes that when Pablo was fourteen his father ceremoniously turned over his paints because his son was already light-years ahead.

ARL: I wasn't that much better. I'd be dabbling in still life, painting things for my grade three teacher, and my father would fix them up in the middle of the night because I never got that far with them.

RE: Did you want to be an artist from an early age? Did you like messing around as a young child?

ARL: Yeah, but I don't know if I wanted to be an artist from an early age. I wanted to be a doctor. My father played a role in this too. His basic stance was that it's fine and noble to do art—and he always encouraged me—but you've got to be realistic and you can't make a living by painting. So it was off to medical school and then you can do your thing.

RE: Did you ever have any intention of studying medicine?

ARL: I wanted to, eventually, but my father preferred that I go to university right after graduation. I'd had it with exams and couldn't do any more schooling but he insisted. He bought a condominium in Victoria and basically shipped me off. So I said, Okay, I'm going to take Fine Arts. I went to the University of Victoria, enrolled in painting, print-making, drawing, and then I had to take all these additional academic courses. I'll start with the painting course: I dropped it on the first day because they told us to mix black, and I said, Why the hell should I mix black when I can buy it in a tube? Then, as soon as an exam came up in the academic courses, I stopped going. By mid-semester I had five Fs.

RE: It wasn't a terribly auspicious beginning.

ARL: No, but I kept on with drawing and with print-making. Anyway, after that year at the University of Victoria my father saw it was hopeless, so I went back to Calgary, mucked around for a few weeks trying to find a job, and finally got one at The Bay doing displays. I did that for one-and-a-half years and then certain things happened that made it better for me to leave again. This time I went to the Emily Carr College of Art in Vancouver because my best friend was going there. My father always said that as long as I went to school he'd support me, so I said, Great, I don't want to work any more, I want to get the support. I was about twenty and I went to art school on the premise of fucking around.

RE: Did you do interesting things when you were dressing windows for The Bay?

ARL: Actually, I did some really nice things. I loved it. I worked my way up to being the head of Ladies Fashions and Cosmetics in the display department.

RE: This was when you were nineteen years old and had no experience in window dressing?

ARL: Yeah. The very day I went in to apply for the job they had just fired half the department. I went in and when the woman supervisor asked me what magazines I read, I told her *GQ, Vogue, Architectural Digest*, and she said, "You're hired, can you start this afternoon?" Unfortunately, it ended in disaster when they told me to do an ethnic set of windows. I was thinking Ukrainian dolls, big pompoms and layered skirts. I didn't have the clothes I needed so I cut up three-hundred-dollar dresses and glued them together. I destroyed thousands of dollars worth of merchandise for that one set of windows. On the Friday the windows were supposed to open, my supervisors came down and freaked out because their idea of ethnic was Inuit. They freaked out, I freaked out about them freaking out, and I went around the store destroying things.

RE: You literally went on a rampage?

ARL: Yeah, I spent the whole afternoon clearing the place out before security got me.

RE: So you were summarily dismissed from your position?

ARL: Fired.

RE: And charged?

ARL: Well, we made an agreement and I paid back a certain amount of money and they didn't press charges.

RE: So this ended what could have been a fairly auspicious career as a serious ...

ARL: Window-dresser? Are you teasing? Anyway, my life in Calgary was ruined because my best friends were also working at The Bay and as a result of what I'd done they all got fired as well. So no one was talking to me any more and there wasn't very much happening in Calgary, so I thought I might as well go to Vancouver.

RE: Did you go to Emily Carr with the intention of doing serious work and actually graduating or was it just to pass the time?

ARL: Just to pass the time.

RE: But wasn't the atmosphere conducive to doing what you wanted to do?

ARL: Well, I don't know. I was lucky I didn't have to do my foundation year; on the basis of what I'd done in Banff and at the University of Victoria they let me in half-way through second-year painting. So in January at the beginning of the second semester, I walk in with a pot of acrylic paint and a tweed suit, put down a piece of paper and start painting from the model. Everyone's going, "This kid's going to last three days, right?" "Hopeless," the instructors were saying.

Then I did this one really horrible Keith Haring-inspired painting—Mickey Mouse with a hard-on—and my instructors just flipped out. I was working on it one night—this is my first big piece on canvas—and they came and just pulled this thing apart. They were going on about what a piece of crap it was. I couldn't believe my ears. The next day they talked to me and said, You can't do something like this. Go out and sketch. So I went out to Granville Island with a pad of paper and black felt pen, and I started drawing these meat counters. I came back and they loved them.

RE: So Mickey Mouse with a hard-on was unacceptable but raw meat was okay?

ARL: Well, Mickey was a horrible painting, so derivative—it was just like flipping through an art magazine and going, "I'll use that and that and that ..."

RE: But lots of painters—from Rembrandt to Soutine—have done raw meat. Did you have historical models in mind or was it just that you saw the shops on Granville Island and figured here was something to paint?

ARL: Well, I knew Rembrandt had done carcasses. In high school I painted some water-colours of carcasses because my dad was a hobby rancher and we used to butcher our own beef. In the winter time we'd have them hanging in our garage. For a school assignment I went out to the ranch and did some watercolours of these things. My art teacher was beside herself. She thought it was great because she said Rembrandt had done the same thing. So I did have an example but I didn't have any models for the Meat series.

RE: You developed a reputation quite fast. Were you already ambitious?

ARL: Yeah, I got to like the notoriety as the Prime Cuts thing came about. I really liked painting and I wanted to be a painter but I also knew how I liked living. I'd never be able to live on an artist's budget. I'd been fairly spoiled and so I said, Okay, if I'm going to do this thing I'm going to have to make money at it. So I decided I was going to make my million at painting.

RE: Are you serious?

ARL: I literally said I want to have my first million before I'm twenty-five. But that didn't work. Then I said before thirty. Well, I'm going to be thirty in ten days, so maybe it'll work out by forty. A friend of mine asked me to design a hotel and oyster bar and I'm very seriously considering doing it because of the money involved. He wants me design the interiors and everything. I want to make my million but I want to do it painting, mostly because I couldn't imagine doing anything else. So I said, Okay, I'm going to be good enough so that I can reach that goal. That's why I work so much because the only way you're going to get anywhere is by working really hard. Maybe that's why I've gotten so far in so little time. That's one thing I did learn from my father: anything you're going to do you're going to have to work at. I was never into hanging around cafés and saying I was an artist. I've seen so many people do that. I'm in Berlin because no one knows who I am here. I've had friends for five years and they still don't know what the hell I do. I really shocked someone the other day when I told them I was an artist.

RE: How do you feel about being asked to be in Documenta? If you're going to be a millionaire in a decade do you need it?

ARL: Almost. It would be immodest of me to say that I'm not really happy with it. Sure Documenta is very important in someone's career. I'm not going to say I don't really care because it does matter to me.

RE: Let's talk about the scale of your work. Is it related to your ambition?

ARL: Yeah, I always worked big, It's just the size that I'm comfortable with. It's easier for me to start a six-metre long by four-metre high painting than it is for me to start a small still life. If I have a small canvas in front of me, I immediately get a block because it's got these really present borders. If it's something big those borders don't really exist.

RE: You seem to have an inexhaustible variety of ideas. Are you inventive in that way?

ARL: That's my big problem: I have too many ideas. I'm about two years behind my mind. It seems as if I'm always trying to catch up. You don't really do justice to an idea in one painting because it changes and evolves even as you're working on it. When it's finished, it has created a whole new set of problems and ideas in relationship to the original idea. So now I categorize my ideas; I tend to weed them down and look at them in terms of bodies of work. That really started with the monkeys.

RE: Tell me about the Young Romantics and their quick rise to fame. Was it a graduating show for you and three of your fellow students?

ARL: The four of us who happened to be working very closely together at school—Angela Grossmann, Derek Root, Graham Gillmore and me—were all involved in that show and much of the attention shifted on to us because we were so young. It was described in the press as a graduating show but it wasn't that at all; it was just a survey of young Vancouver artists. There were four other very good artists involved, so by no means was it our show. We dominated it because we were an entity within ourselves.

RE: Were you all fairly canny? The way you describe things, it seems as if you all understood what the game was about.

ARL: I look at it now and I think we were fairly canny. It was that time in the early '80s when being a painter also meant you had to have a major presence or be a personality, so Clemente was in *Vogue*. You looked through the magazines and the work wasn't enough. All these artists were cultivating their images as much as their work and we thought, That's cool, we can do it too. We were also very manipulative.

RE: What do you mean?

ARL: Just in terms of getting what we wanted at the school. I mean, we were four very strong people and we put our energies together and said, We want this and we want this; Angela, you go out and work on this side of things and Derek will take care of that; Graham's got his charm, and so on.

RE: And what was your role in the foursome?

ARL: My role? I don't really know. Usually, I was able to get financing. My father was very generous. It was like, Dad, we need to make some money, and he'd come up with a big plan where we'd do some work for him and we'd get paid very generously for doing basically nothing.

RE: Your father was supportive throughout?

ARL: Yeah, but he was still looking at it as a phase I was going through. Actually, he was quite horrified when I finally graduated and said I wanted to be a painter.

RE: What does he think now?

ARL: Well, now I earn as much as he does, maybe even more. But he's my biggest fan. I've managed to do what he always wanted to do. He had the responsibilities of being a young immigrant and having a large family to support. I'm sure if he looks back on his life he would have been much happier doing something else but he couldn't. So he respects that I've been able to and be successful doing what I wanted.

RE: What made you come to Berlin?

ARL: Well, I had to leave Vancouver, just like I had to leave Calgary and Victoria. It always seems that a city grows very tired of me after one or two or three years.

RE: Do you actually do something to encourage that? Do you push the limits as much as you can and make yourself unpopular?

ARL: No, I never consciously push the limits, it's just that I get myself into trouble.

RE: What did you do in Vancouver?

ARL: Oh, it's a long story that involves a messy court case. After it was over my lawyer and my dad suggested I leave the city. I had just received my first Canada Council grant and I said, Okay, I'm going to New York. Every young painter at that time dreamt of going to New York because there was so much attention being paid to painting. And the art world and the art market were booming so New York seemed like Babylon. I had a one-way ticket, but a few days before I left I had second thoughts. I loved New York, but I knew I wouldn't be able to survive because I'd been there before. I knew how expensive it was and I knew I couldn't live without having to work. And I had decided much earlier on that I was never going to work again because basically I'm unemployable. I can't work for someone else, I can't serve people. I was playing with the idea of going to Europe and some friends said it would be a good thing for me. So I made the decision on the plane, actually circling over O'Hare Airport. I had my two double Scotches and got all romantic and teary-eyed and homesick for my friends. I knew Germany was the hot spot for the art scene and Berlin was the only German city that I knew. So I landed in New York and the next day I got the first plane I could to Amsterdam, stayed overnight and caught the first train to Berlin.

RE: Just like that? Once you decided there was no hesitation at all? Did you know anybody here?

ARL: Well, I had met Michael Morris in Vancouver. He came to our studio and we had dinner and he said, If you're ever in Berlin, look me up. Actually the other three had fucked off already to Europe. Graham had been in Berlin and Michael had set something up for him. I was left alone in Vancouver, feeling sour grapes, so I said, Okay, it's my turn. Michael was able to help Graham, so I phoned Michael up and said, Hi, I'm here. He was tremendous, he got me used to the city and he really helped me get my first studio.

RE: Did you know any German at all when you first came?

ARL: Not a word. Everything I knew I'd learned from *Hogan's Heroes*. That's about it.

RE: Did you start painting seriously when you first arrived?

ARL: No, there wasn't any pressure on me at all because I took it as a new start. I got here in the middle of October and I didn't start painting until about March when I got my studio. Between that time I was a couch-potato, two days on one bed, a week at somebody else's, carrying my luggage around the whole time. It was the coldest winter Germany had had in fifty years; I had no place to live and already the money was getting pretty low. It was literally hell and I hated it, but I was determined not to go back. I'd seen it happen to so many other people from Vancouver. They have some degree of success and they decide to go somewhere else—usually Toronto or Montreal—and they all end up coming back within half a year with their tail tucked between their legs. They couldn't make it work so it was back to safe and comfortable Vancouver. I didn't want to go back to what was safe and comfortable.

RE: Where did this sense of pride come from? Were you proving this to yourself or to the community you came out of?

ARL: To myself and I think to the others as well. Because I'm sure when I left everyone was saying, He'll be back in half a year. I just wanted to spare myself the embarrassment of going back.

RE: When you finally got your studio, did you know what you wanted to do right away?

ARL: No, because I hadn't really been thinking about painting for five or six months. I just basically carried on what I had left off doing in Vancouver. I spent a couple of months doing some really horrible work. I realized it wasn't working and then at some point I loosened up and said, Okay, I'm not going to put pressure on myself, I don't have to produce the kind of things I did in Vancouver.

RE: Partially because no one was watching?

ARL: Exactly. I didn't have studio visits and it didn't matter if I had a flop. There were other things too. I had a sense of being somewhere, which you don't really have in Vancouver or, for that matter, in Canada. Here you have a sense of history around you, going to a museum and seeing all the works that you've seen in magazines and books. When I finally saw some of these paintings I said to myself, Hey, I could do that. I know I could do that.

RE: So you recognized what tradition meant in painting and that you could easily imagine yourself as part of it?

ARL: Just in terms of technique. I was able to see how that background was done because it was not how I had imagined it. It was like, Okay, that's not so difficult. He cheated, I could do that.

RE: The other thing about Berlin is that it's dense with art history. In looking back, have you realized that you were naïve in Vancouver and that this was the first time you were coming up against the real thing?

ARL: Sure. But I'm still naïve. I don't know if I've learned so much. I haven't really set out to learn that much. Art history has never really interested me more than being a place to find something I could use or steal. I have favourite old artists from certain periods for certain things but I couldn't say who my favourite artist is, or, say, my five favourite artists. Now, there are certain artists whom I really respect or appreciate but my approach is really no different from the way I get my other source materials—just flipping through magazines. I buy about ten magazines a week and just image-search.

RE: Do the magazines run a range from art publications to weekly news magazines?

ARL: I never buy art magazines, I never even look at them. No, I buy trash magazines like *People*. I don't read them either. I go through a magazine in five minutes, just looking for images. I'll know if there's something interesting. Usually I read the horoscope.

RE: But you're not saying that you don't look at other art? There are all kinds of direct quotations from other painters in your work.

ARL: Sure, I look at other art but not that seriously or intensely.

RE: What about other media? Do television and cinema interest you?

ARL: Oh yeah. Television is really important to me. Cinema too, but I hardly go any more. Mind you, when I go to a movie I want to see *Robocop* or *Terminator 2*. I want to see a million bucks flash by my eyes every five minutes.

RE: Are you the perfect consumer?

ARL: No, I just want value for my money. I'm in my studio all day and I want to go to the cinema and erase that. The last thing I want to do is sit and try to interpret a Derek Jarman movie.

RE: You don't have any interest in the kind of thing he did in *Caravaggio*?

ARL: There were parts of it I liked and some parts that were really stupid, like when they showed him painting. I just went, No way. But then they did the whole thing on a contemporary theme. I hate to go to the movies and think. I just want to sit there and be blown away, just go, Wow. It can be *Nightmare on Elm Street* or *Terminator*, it doesn't matter to me.

RE: What keeps you painting so compulsively?

ARL: Well, it's possible I've become a workaholic in the process of trying to make my million. I love to work and I can't imagine not working. I can't go on vacation any more because I go away for three days and I feel guilty. It's really horrible. The same thing happens if I take an afternoon off. When Michael Morris or someone invites me to dinner, I can't justify taking those three hours when I could be getting something done here. But sometimes I really hate painting. Sometimes I just sit here and think, God, I wish I could make money at something else. So I'm ambiguous about it. I wouldn't say I'd give up painting entirely but I don't look out through the prism of the romantic artist, either. I don't live for painting but I also couldn't imagine living without it. It's become so much a part of my life. It's my job basically and I take that very seriously. I'm not going to allow my vision to be compromised. I won't allow myself or anyone else to compromise just for the sake of earning some of those hallowed bucks. So I stick to my guns. And if the work gets tougher, fine. That's what I'm going to do.

RE: When did you first use the monkey, a figure that's become a significant presence in the work?

ARL: I first saw a black and white postage-stamp-size reproduction in a book Graham had in my studio in Vancouver. I thought, What a curious painting. I found out it was by Breughel and I started to read something about it. I got into the Flemish tradition of the monkey representing the artist, chained to his own world but imitating the real world outside. Then the monkey started appearing in the corner as a spectator in some of my large paintings.

RE: As a kind of commentator on the content of the painting as well?

ARL: Yeah, and then I saw that painting here in the Gemaldegalerie and I was blown away. It was such a small work and it was so powerful. It's one of my favourite pieces. That's when I started doing monkey paintings where the monkey wasn't just an observer in the grand tableau.

RE: He was quite literally centre stage?

ARL: He became the subject of the work.

RE: Was the monkey a surrogate figure for yourself? Did your identification become more immediate and more thorough?

ARL: Yeah, that's basically what it was. They dealt with being an artist. They were sometimes very humorous works.

RE: They also seemed to represent a whole range of human activity. They were pretty frisky a lot of the time, pretty outrageous and aggressive.

ARL: I wasn't concerned about the human condition at all. I was really thinking about my own self, my own psyche. I have enough worries about myself, I can't be expected to deal with the rest of the human race.

RE: One particularly lyric painting called *The Allegory of Water*, shows a stream of water pouring down on a monkey. Where did that painting come from?

ARL: It came from a magazine in which there was a photograph of a boy showering.

RE: So there was no direct influence of David Hockney's shower paintings?

ARL: No, it was like a *National Geographic* photograph from India or something and I copied it verbatim—just the water and the figure. I simply used my background and suddenly this boy became a monkey.

RE: It's very poignant too. Some of the monkey paintings are not so obviously beautiful, some are irreverent and cheeky, some are priapic. But *The Allegory of Water* has a lot of emotional clout. Is that what you wanted; is that what you recognized in the source photo?

ARL: Not really. That kind of thing usually comes about after the work is done. It turned out really well because the image held so much of its own on the canvas. It just happens to be what I consider my best painting.

RE: You've stuck with the monkey for a number of years. Does it continue to play the same role, or has its role evolved in the work?

ARL: I have stuck with him but I don't know why. He's something that I've been trying to get away from for a long time. It's almost starting to become like Freddie. He keeps haunting me, keeps popping back.

RE: Monkey the thirteenth, part twenty-eight?

ARL: That's what it's becoming, like a bad serial. But the monkey's still important to me. He really defines that whole part of the human psyche that I can't really get into with the other works. There's always that animal and human behavioural aspect to him, his disrespect and the whole thing.

RE: He can do things that you won't let your human figures do?

ARL: Yeah. It's just that so many more things can be read into him than into the skinheads, for example. And it's nice because I don't like to define the painting. It's one reason why I don't explain any of my works, because I don't think an explanation from me is either necessary or warranted.

RE: Other painters have used the monkey in the same combination of mimicry and reflection. Picasso in some of his early brothel works and Oskar Kokoschka did some pretty menacing mandrills too. When you use the monkey, do you intend to plug into art history? Does that complicate your use of the figure at all?

ARL: I don't plug into art history in terms of nineteenth- or twentieth-century art. Artistic value for me in the monkey lies in a seventeenth-century sensibility or in earlier fresco paintings. You do see the monkey popping up everywhere, but I don't use those as references. I use them as a place to start.

RE: You mention fresco painting. I want to talk about your use of it—the gold leaf, the heroic patterning, the flatness. What initially attracted you to that technique?

ARL: It didn't have anything to do with the technique. I guess at the same time I saw that monkey painting, I also came across an image of a Roman fresco. I just liked the way it looked. The background was very abstract, very contemporary. It had all the elements that make contemporary painting what it is today—the use of colour, brushstroke, imagery. I just thought I'd like to look in that direction.

RE: You like paint, don't you? The feel and the smell of it? You said earlier you like mucking about in oil paint.

ARL: I used to really like thick paint but I don't know whether that's very important to me now. A lot of the work that I'm currently doing has none of that thick, impasto business at all. It's very much putting down a field of colour where there's no room for mistakes. It's just one application and it's there to stay.

RE: Do you feel confident enough about your painterly abilities that you can get away with that?

ARL: There's a lot of things I can't do or am afraid to do. I know what I can do and I'm comfortable in dealing with that. But then again what you can do becomes very boring so you're always looking for something new. And when a new style evolves, that involves a different process of painting. As you get on with it you become more adept and more competent in dealing with the paint, in what the painting requires in application and handling. The first ones might be a tougher battle. They're just basically a learning process and one painting leads to another. So the more I work on one body the more I accumulate skills and technique. But then it gets to the point where it's boring and I can't think of painting like that anymore. Like with the Military paintings. I'd never done a painting like that before so the first ones were interesting. But I got as good at it as I want to be. You can always carry on and make a painting better; the thing is knowing when to stop.

RE: What do you do, then, to keep yourself interested? Do you have to put pressure on yourself and your own technique? How do you know when it's time to move on and do something different?

ARL: When I feel that I've settled what I want to deal with in a body of work, when it doesn't matter any more if there's another painting or another five paintings. When it becomes superfluous.

RE: Is that when the series ends?

ARL: That's basically when the series ends. I never really finish a series because there are always more ideas in my head. It just comes to the point where I realize that one painting or five more paintings isn't going to help things. So instead of painting the same thing I'd rather go on and deal with some of the other ideas I have. That's what's happening to me now; I mean, it's happening with painting itself. That's why I'm trying sculpture, because there are things I want to do now that are exciting to me precisely because they don't involve painting.

RE: Were the Military paintings misinterpreted? People looked at them and saw you approving of that way of life?

ARL: I do approve of that life. I was dead set on entering Military College. I don't think the paintings were misinterpreted in any way. The beauty of it was when I conceived of the idea and had done most of the paintings, the ninety-day war in the Gulf wasn't an issue. When I exhibited the paintings in the middle of the Gulf War they took on a meaning that wasn't even in the back of my head at that time.

RE: But was your initial attraction to the good-looking guy in the uniform? Was it a kind of visceral attraction that you had to the whole idea of military cadets?

ARL: Those magazines were jerk-off material.

RE: Do the paintings carry the residue of that sexual attraction?

ARL: For me they did.

RE: I want to deal with the homoeroticism in your work. Do you view it as a means of talking about a way of life or about a pattern of obsession? Is that important to you as you make these paintings?

ARL: I don't think about it because it's my world.

RE: But you think about how to stage it, whether to present it through a quotation from *The Young Spartans* or whether through a series of sexual activities?

ARL: I never really think of applying—or implying—sexuality, or what the male figure means in a painting. It's simply there. It's so much a part of my world that it's just my vocabulary. It's the way I put together a sentence and those are the verbs, nouns and metaphors that I use to say what I want to say.

RE: Let's talk about what is probably your best-known painting, *The Young Spartans Challenge the Boys to Fight*. I remember being overwhelmed the first time I saw it at Harbourfront in Toronto. I know the two sources, Degas and Caravaggio. I guess I'm getting into treacherous ground here because I'm going to ask you what the painting means and I know that you tend not to respond to that line of inquiry.

ARL: All those things that the painting means come through the process of developing the painting itself. I didn't sit down and plan out the painting and say, Okay, I want this and this because this gaze is going to imply that, or this group against that is going to have these implications. I didn't think about that. I just had those two groups.

RE: But you're not an *idiot savant*. You know that you're taking art historical sources and remaking them, that you're rehistoricizing sexuality by having, not a group of young boys and girls looking at one another, but rather, two groups of men from different social contexts. Surely you were aware of that?

ARL: Yeah.

RE: I guess I'm asking what was the dynamic that made you decide to pit those groups one against the other inside the painting?

ARL: I don't really know. It's hard to talk about that painting now because it's so long ago, it's really out of my mind. But I know what you mean. Sure those things were in my mind. I omitted the female figures and instead of having the female group and the male group I chose two male groupings. Sure the dynamics of that were clear to me at the time. I'm not sure if I can go on fast rewind right now and dig them all out. But it was also on a very basic level. My world is very male so that a grouping of female figures held nothing that interested me. It's natural that I omitted them and substituted the male grouping.

RE: Do you have a program where you're doing something that goes beyond your own personal obsessions? Is there a larger project in your mind?

ARL: Yeah, sure, but I couldn't for the life of me try to define it. There's a body of work I'm dealing with right now that has to do with the whole thing of regendering. It's my Garden series. You think of the classic garden as the Garden of Eden. Western civilization's whole set of law and morality is based upon a concept of what original sin is and what took place in the Garden. In my Garden paintings I've taken out the female.

RE: So Eve gets moved out.

ARL: Eve never existed.

RE: Is that a hostile notion or merely a reflection of the nature of your own sexuality?

ARL: I don't think it's a hostile notion. Maybe some people could read it that way but that's really digging down deep. It's probably more romantic than anything else.

RE: In a sense, then, you've undertaken a "What if" project. What if the garden were two men and original sin was based on something that happened between them rather than what happened in a heterosexual world?

ARL: Maybe original sin would never have happened. What would our society be today? I'm just rewriting paradise.

RE: Is the Devil in your rewrite?

ARL: Sure, he's there. He's popped up in whatever form he takes—a snake, or half-beast, half-human, or just within the figures themselves. There's nothing to say those figures are not evil in themselves.

RE: So notions of good and evil are part of your moral framework?

ARL: How could they not be? I'm living in a world where everything, especially in the last few years, is being defined in terms of good and evil and black and white.

RE: But is gay bad and non-gay good in a mainstream world?

ARL: I'm not trying to say what's good or evil. I'm just trying to suggest that people look for themselves, that they question their notions of good and evil. And also to accept what they don't know. So much ignorance is not only being tolerated but cultivated right now. That's what's evil.

RE: And you feel a lot of that ignorance is directed at gay culture?

ARL: Yeah. We were at the point some years ago where being homosexual was almost considered to be a norm. Then everything took this nasty, Draconian, right-wing bend backwards. People started thinking in a very Victorian manner and now they're having a hard time dealing with homosexuality in art.

RE: What I read from what you say is that in one way you've become a more serious painter with respect to your role within gay culture. Has this attempt to reinterpret paradise now become an issue?

ARL: I've never really tried to play an important role in gay culture. As a matter of fact, I always used to steer people away from interpreting the paintings as homoerotic because they were just normal to me. I expected people to see that. But in a funny way it's gotten important to me now. I still don't think that I'm going to go out and affirm my position as a spokesman in gay culture. I don't know if I'm so comfortable dragging politics into my work. I might do it later when I feel more comfortable.

RE: We're talking about painterly language, not about someone who is on the barricades?

ARL: Yeah, but today if you're a painter of gay subjects then you're going to end up on the barricades.

RE: Are the paintings still a turn-on for you?

ARL: If they weren't I probably wouldn't do them.

RE: What was it that made you decide to use more distanced and objective pictorial devices? Sometimes the rendering seems to run an elegant gamut from Roman classicism to Christian references?

ARL: In *True North* that's exactly what I was looking for and I searched those references out very specifically. In a more general sense it was probably because my art historical knowledge was fairly limited, so I was using what I knew and was comfortable with. Today I'm not using the art historical thing so much. It gets to be a crutch, not for me, but for other people when they look at the work. They get hung up on the appropriation and they can't handle work that doesn't deal with it. It's fine if a fuck painting refers back to Caravaggio, but if you have a fuck painting that they can't immediately link back to something three hundred years old, then they have a problem.

RE: So that displacement was a strategy? By dressing up the male body—either through art history or back through history—you've got more room for transgression? Does it allow you to get away with more?

ARL: I don't think I was conscious of trying to get away with more. I used it because I was comfortable with it and I liked that link to the past and what artists were dealing with back then. Caravaggio keeps popping up so let's talk about him. When I looked at a lot of his paintings my immediate reaction was how sexual they were. I thought, Are people too blind to be able to read the sexuality that Caravaggio had written into them? In some of my earlier works I was bringing in contemporary sexuality or just trying to use an historical reference that had sexuality already implicit in it.

RE: You're attracted to sources that have an implicit—if not explicit—sense of sexuality in them? Is that what you want to exploit?

ARL: A lot of times when I use a reference I do.

RE: You mentioned *True North*. I take it to be an ironic title. The "true north, strong and free" from the Canadian national anthem is very different from the true north that you imagine?

ARL: Actually, it didn't come from the anthem at all. It's really stupid where I got the title. A friend of mine designed these T-shirts for another friend and I saw them in his shop. I read "True North Strong and Free" and said, Oh, that's great. I was doing this body of work and I thought it needed that kind of title. I realized later that it was from *O Canada*.

RE: The painting called *This Town* has the birth and death dates of the art critic Peter Day on it. Was it meant to be an act of homage?

ARL: It's from a body of work that I started about two years ago and will probably finish in another three years. It's only about seven paintings but I do them for my own entertainment in my spare time. They're six metres long—the one I'm doing now is going to be twelve metres long. The series is about labour and industry. There's a coal mining one; there's a steel mill; there's one with people who build roads. The one I'm doing now deals with agriculture.

RE: Is this a large-scale visual essay on the dignity of work?

ARL: Sort of like that. But getting back to Peter Day, I had that banner in the painting and I didn't know what to do with it. I knew I had to put some text on it and I certainly didn't want to put up Frank Stella or Robert Rauschenberg. Suddenly one day it struck me: I wanted to put Peter's name in there and the year he was born and died. After the painting had been exhibited, Vincent Trasov told me those years—1949 to 1990—are also the years of the D.D.R.

RE: So a very personal reference, that would perhaps mean very little to someone outside of Toronto, ends up having an historical resonance inside the painting?

ARL: Yeah. More often than not people ask me who Peter Day is. But it's a personal reference that means a lot to me.

RE: Let's talk about the pissoir you're doing for Documenta. The opening is only a little over three weeks away.

ARL: The pissoir, which I call the *Tea House*, is a funny story. First of all Kassel thinks it's a tea house because we had to call it something to get permits. So they think it's a tea house where you go to drink tea, but the British word for a public toilet where homosexuals go and have sex is also tea-house.

RE: So what does Kassel know for sure?

ARL: They don't know it's a pissoir. It's based on the old pissoirs in Berlin which are really beautiful structures. It's where everyone went cruising. Sex is probably the only thing they're ever really used for and they're in danger because the city is actually taking them down and replacing them with these horrible toilets like you have in Paris. You put in a coin and you have fifteen minutes to get out, otherwise you're going to be drowned. So my Documenta work is a place where people can drag someone off for a quickie in a nice atmosphere.

RE: Do you actually think that will happen?

ARL: I'm going to do it. Why not? It's a place for sex. That's why I built it. It's a place for your Documenta quickie. I'd be really happy if I came in one day and saw sperm on the gold leaf. Then I'd know it was worth it. There's nothing to stop anyone from pissing in it, either.

RE: So there's a sense of fun in this piece, apart from its irreverence?

ARL: Sure there's a sense of fun. With Documenta you have a situation which is like a cathedral for art, right? You go in there and you have to view these works with a certain amount of reverence—don't get too close, don't touch. I'd like people to be able to go in there and piss without a guard coming up and saying they can't do that, because they *can* do that. I was even trying to figure out how to get the smell of piss inside.

RE: What are the sources for *The Four Seasons*, the four figurative panels for the tea house? Tell me about the process of coming up with the completed installation.

ARL: *The Four Seasons* are just my four seasons. As for the figures, there was a magazine that reproduced paintings by Hans Baldung-Grien and I knew I wanted to use them for something. So I've based my Polaroids on that source but I've contemporized them. I took three to four hundred Polaroids for just those four panels because I'm changing the pose.

RE: Have you used a different model for each season?

ARL: No, the same model for each one. They come out looking different when you paint them.

RE: But the model you found is physically beautiful. When you work from a model, do you also attempt to make him perfect? Is it a process of literal transcription rather than invention?

ARL: It's transcription, but it takes a long time for me to find the right model. I go down the street or to the train station and I just have to look through the clothes and figure, Does he have the chest, does he have the ass, does he have the arms that I want? If he does, I take him home, check him out and say, Okay I can use you. I don't like to embellish, I just like to work from what the model has.

RE: Do you have notions about what's beautiful or is it simply about what appeals to you physically?

ARL: No, I would say the cult of beauty has very much to do with it. I go for a very specific type in the models I choose. That's why it's actually hard for me to find them.

RE: You're accused sometimes of misogyny. Feminist critics have trouble with the fact that you depict a very exclusive world that seems hostile towards women.

ARL: My answer is tough luck. It's not hostile at all. I mean, my sexual world is men. I don't want to sound patronizing by saying things like some of my best friends are women. It just has nothing to do with my work, really. When Desmond Tutu was accused of being a racist he said, tough luck. I'm not going to start defending myself because it's just the way it is. Either they accept it or they don't.

RE: Do you live a pretty wild life?

ARL: Yes I do. Not as much as I used to. My wild life now is pretty much on the weekends. I work till about two or three in the morning and then I'm on my wild hours.

RE: Then you cruise?

ARL: For sex? Oh, I do that in between. That usually comes before work.

RE: You really push the limit?

ARL: I didn't use to. After about half a year in Berlin I found a boyfriend and I lived the most blissful married life with him. He owned a bar and so when he was working I would go out there, and when he wasn't working we'd just sit and watch TV or go out to dinner. But since we broke up I've really gotten into the club scene. At the beginning of the year it was getting pretty messy.

RE: Are you self-destructive?

ARL: Oh yeah, very.

RE: Will you or can you do anything about it?

ARL: I can always pull myself out of it. Now I'm controlling it to the degree that allows me to get the Documenta piece done but I'm not giving it up. I've got my four hits of Ecstasy waiting for tonight. Come three o'clock I'm off. Sunday I sleep all day.

RE: You're a Presbyterian when you work and a profligate when you're not working. It's as if you live two lives.

ARL: I don't live two lives. It's all part of one thing.

RE: You just have a very professional and thorough approach to working?

ARL: Well, it's something I learned from my friends in Vancouver. It doesn't matter how many drugs or how much drinking you've done. If you have an appointment at eight o'clock in the morning, you get up and make that appointment. So I'll go out tonight and be whacked out of my brain for eight hours and thinking about sleep tomorrow evening at nine o'clock, but come hell or high water, I'll be in here painting Monday morning.

RE: Is there anything you won't paint? Do you have any personal sense of what's taboo?

ARL: No, I couldn't say there's anything I wouldn't paint. Sure there's things that I don't want to paint or that don't interest me but I don't know what's unmentionable to me. There are certain kinds of physical or sexual violence that I'm not sure I would be happy painting. I haven't had to draw the line yet. I haven't had an idea and said, No, I can't do that. What wouldn't I paint? What I wouldn't paint is something that would outright glorify Fascism. I know my work deals with elements of Fascism but I think if anyone with a two-bit mind looks at the work, he would see that it's more of a comment against it. I'm not interested in being used to profit that kind of propaganda.

RE: Why do you flirt with it, then? Are you a kind of rough sociologist?

ARL: Well, that's part of it. It's out there and it has to be dealt with. Skinhead sex is in. You'd be pretty hard set to find a fag who wouldn't drop to his knees for some skinhead. First of all, not all skinheads are Fascist. But they're the same people who would beat the living shit out of fags on the subway. It's that fascination with violence and power and evil. That's why those elements are in there.

RE: But do you feel any moral responsibility not to appear to be in favour of all its manifestations?

ARL: I don't think I appear to be in favour of it. If you read that into the work, then it's a very shallow interpretation. But whether I'm accused of that or not, I can't do anything about it. One of the risks of not commenting on my own work is that it's left open to misinterpretation.

RE: But as a gay male you share a fascination with violence and power. It's something that attracts you.

ARL: Sure, I share a fascination with it.

RE: Is painting a way of dealing with it?

ARL: Sometimes I think I'm just airing my dirty laundry, but then again, who has the guts to do that? I don't have to worry about running for public office. It's a way of getting it out there. There's lots of things that interest me about sexuality that I might find hard to talk about with somebody. I guess my way of talking about it is to put it in the painting. Once I've done that it tends to lose its fascination.

RE: You are a romantic in a lot of ways, aren't you? You're pushing the limits all the time, you sense there's very little that's taboo, you don't feel you owe society anything, your responsibilities are largely self-generated?

ARL: I have myself to answer to. As long as I can do that, I'll be happy. It's when I start having to answer to other people that I won't be happy. And that's where I draw the line. The reaction of most people who first meet me is that I'm an arrogant son of a bitch. It's hard to be an artist without being arrogant. How can you be an artist and expect success if you don't believe you're the best? If I didn't believe I was the best, then I'd let the best do it. But I'm doing it because I believe that what I'm doing is so much better than everything else out there.

Maria Fernanda Cardoso

Making a World From Scratch

Even in a period when the range of material from which artists make art has expanded and stretched in unpredictable ways, the Colombian-born, San Francisco-based artist Maria Fernanda Cardoso is something of a radical soloist. "I devote myself to working with animals," she says in the following interview, "most of the time I work with them dead." The objects of her devotion have been dried frogs and snakes, cow bones, fish scales and marine animals like starfish and sea snails. What is most amazing about them—and this quality she shares with the best contemporary sculptors and installation artists working world-wide—is that she has been able to arrange these dead, dried-out and disconnected materials into objects of unusual beauty. Her sculpture called *Pirarcu* is a three-foot tall column of garlanded fish scales deftly held together by wire. The scales look like flower petals or like the delicate parts of a woman's sex, while the whole object looks like some kind of basket. As is so often the case with Cardoso's art, the combination of fragility and insistent form makes the work irresistible. *American Marble* operates in a similar way. She has taken hundreds of tibia from cattle and arranged them on the floor in geometric and decorative patterns which make reference to Moorish and Pre-Columbian visual design, as well as to minimalist sculpture. But Cardoso is no innocent folk artist; she was raised in an artistic family and she has an advanced degree in sculpture from Yale. Much of the appeal of her work comes out of the way she is able to use minimal means to get maximal effects. This is, in part, a product of the content carried by her materials. Both in her tradition and in our own the display of dead animals or animal parts in a context other than museums of natural history has disorienting implications. (A number of people would argue that even in museums the display of natural artifacts is problematic but that is a debate Cardoso is not party to: she saw her first preserved animals in just such a museum in Bogota and the experience had a shaping influence on her.) The dead animals make an inescapable reference to the category of *memento mori* but Cardoso's art, through its sheer beauty, is able to transcend the more pessimistic aspects of this medieval idea. So in *Woven Water*, a series of green starfish joined tip to tip to create a pattern of alternating presence and absence, Cardoso is simultaneously able to suggest both object and idea. The piece is equally insistent in its conceptual subtlety and its material presence. *Scribble*, an onomatopoeic linkage of sea snail shells is a perfect metaphor for Cardoso's art practice: what she is engaged in is nothing less than the process of writing her own aesthetic language.

At the centre of her work has been the rich web of associations—symbolic, cultural, transformative, emotional and even political—that exists between animals and people. Those myriad associations in her work with non-living animals have now been transferred to her more recent, and most demanding, project: The Cardoso Flea Circus. Since 1992 she has concentrated on making a flea circus from scratch—buying, raising and training fleas, then getting them to perform a series of traditional tricks (including swordfighting, being shot from a cannon, and trapeze work), as well as some refinements of her own (cheerleading and golf). Working with fleas has been a lifelong desire and she is intensely serious about her part in reviving what in her studied estimation is "almost a dead art." (One aspect of her project is to produce a film of the flea circus which promises to make her the Cecil B. De Mille of the appropriately named pulex irritans: she could call the film *Chariots of Fur*.)

In this interview you will discover everything you've always wanted to know about fleas but didn't know to ask: which of the sexes is dominant, are fleas good dancers; when does flea copulation turn into flea pornography; why do they swordfight; and how do you feed them? "Fleas are not pretty," Cardoso admits, "but they can make you laugh." So can the artist. I have conducted hundreds of interviews during my career and there were occasions when the artists were funny or when they incorporated aspects of humour into their work. But this interview (which was conducted by telephone in November 1994 with Ms. Cardoso from her San Francisco studio) is the first time I found myself playing straight-man to a consummate humourist. As Maria Fernanda Cardoso, ringmaster to the fleas, says: "Every aspect is bizarre and every conversation I have about it is hilarious." I'll scratch to that.

ROBERT ENRIGHT: I know nothing about flea circuses and to tell you the truth, I didn't know that they actually existed.

MARIA FERNANDA CARDOSO: Well, they are almost like a lost art, so nobody believes anymore that they exist.

RE: Have you done research on the history of the flea circus?

MFC: There are some skills which are passed from trainer to trainer. The story goes that there was a prisoner in Siberia who was many, many years in prison and he took to training fleas. Then he went to Paris and became a success.

RE: So the first flea circus came out of duress, imprisonment and boredom?

MFC: That's part of the story but I don't believe it. I have some flea circus posters from around 1830 featuring Bertolotto. He was the most famous flea impresario and his performances were very elaborate.

RE: How elaborate could they get? First of all, how large an audience can you have for a flea circus? It's not like the "big top."

MFC: Maybe ten or fifteen people at a time. Because you don't use magnifying glasses, you see them with your plain eyes.

RE: So what would constitute an elaborate flea circus?

MFC: He would do flea ballrooms, in which two fleas are dressed as ladies and two as gentlemen and they dance a waltz. Here I'm reading from his circus poster: "Twelve fleas at the orchestra playing different instruments of proportionable size. The music is audible and the room, one inch square, is eloquently fitted up with a glass chandelier."

RE: This is even more picayune than miniature painting. A room that is one inch square is an amazing idea.

MFC: I know. So too are costumed fleas. I have made some costumes, I have a Batman and Robin costume and I have a wedding.

RE: Batman and Robin?

MFC: It's just two black capes that move. And I have a wedding costume for a flea—it has a big hat and a veil for the bride.

RE: What interested you in doing a flea circus in the first place?

MFC: One of my uncles mentioned there was a flea circus in New York and I just had this picture in my mind. Since I hadn't seen any I decided to make my own. It's my lifetime desire since I was a child. I did homework in my science class about the flea. I drew a giant, enlarged flea by looking through a magnifying glass and I wrote a description about its hairy legs and stuff.

RE: When did you start this particular project?

MFC: Over two years ago and its going to take more years.

RE: Are these cat fleas you're using?

MFC: The ones that I'm using right now are cat fleas. But the traditional flea for the flea circus is the human flea. It's called *pulex irritans*.

RE: Probably for good reason.

MFC: They are not available in this country. They have been almost extinct and that's a problem for flea trainers all over the world. They anguish about not finding enough and not finding the right kind of fleas.

RE: Are there characteristics that the human flea has that make it more desirable as a performer than cat fleas?

MFC: Some say they're easier to feed. Some say they might be stronger. I believe that. But they're not larger. I ordered one from a biological supply house to compare. I put it on a slide and they look exactly the same size. You can also feed them yourself. That's part of the training. You have to feed them yourself because you have to establish a relationship with them.

RE: Do fleas have individual characteristics?

MFC: They do have different personalities. I didn't believe it until I started to test them. I have maybe three hundred fleas, and I would take the little ones and put them in this big plexi box, one in one, and one in another box. One would be very passive and the other would just be jumping everywhere. I could command it to jump in certain directions with a lamp. That's my trick; I can direct the heat of the lamp in a spot and then I can make it jump where I put the light. You can sometimes make them jump with your own breath because they like carbon dioxide. They think it's an animal walking around, so they jump to try to get on. They're also very sensitive to vibrations and to darkness. They want to go to dark areas to hide. It's a survival thing.

RE: So you have a whole series of provocations that you use to make them move in the direction you want?

MFC: Yes, but there are talented fleas and there are fleas that are good for nothing.

RE: Just like people. Among your three hundred fleas have you been able to determine what percentage look like they're going to be first-rank performers?

MFC: I think there's probably ten or fifteen. Also, the males are no good.

RE: This is circus imitating life is it?

MFC: It's true.

RE: So the females are the performers?

MFC: Yeah. But you can name them with male names. The females are larger; they have these big round bellies, they're much stronger and they live longer.

RE: What are you training them to do now?

MFC: Right now I'm trying to train a flea to wave a flag. And I'm doing a flea golf game. I'm trying to make a flea wave the little flag that marks where the hole is.

RE: Do fleas have a memory track? I mean once you teach this flea how to wave a flag, will it wave a flag forever, or does it retire?

MFC: You can only train them for one trick. One flea, one trick. You have to go over and over and over. Once you've chosen them, you have to keep them separate.

RE: I gather there's a strong sense of playfulness and humour in what you're doing with the flea circus?

MFC: Yes, definitely.

RE: But it's also a thoroughly serious pursuit?

MFC: Yeah. I want to be remembered as a flea trainer.

RE: Is it gratifying?

MFC: To me it is very gratifying. I have a great time even though, at the same time, it's very boring. It takes hours and hours and you need a lot of patience. So it doesn't seem fun sometimes. But every aspect is so bizarre and every conversation I have about it is hilarious. Still, it's very difficult because I don't have a master.

RE: There's no mentor system for you, then? No apprentice system?

MFC: No, so I have to figure things out just by observation, by trial and error and by calling people. I call scientists and I call people who have seen flea circuses. I have spoken with two flea trainers, including a retired flea trainer who was also self-taught. He did it just for fun. I asked them their secrets but they don't tell you because it's their livelihood.

RE: Do you use tweezers to handle the fleas?

MFC: I got tweezers but I ended up using my own fingers. It's hard to calculate the pressure and you can kill them.

RE: Have you ever killed one accidentally?

MFC: Yes.

RE: I'm sorry, I shouldn't have asked.

MFC: It's terrible. In one way they're very strong because they are made to survive a dog or cat scratching itself, but you also have to be really delicate about how you handle them.

RE: Do they really sword fight?

MFC: They do.

RE: What would compel them to fight? Why wouldn't they just move in opposite directions and stage a spontaneous retreat on both sides?

MFC: Well, they're attached to the stage. So they cannot go away.

RE: So they're obliged to fight. It's either that or just hang there, limply?

MFC: Yeah. You attach the swords to their arms. They try to get rid of the swords and that's what makes their moves so desperate. It looks like they're fighting. You know, I want to make a movie where the stars are the fleas and they have flea voices and speak in different languages and they perform all the acts.

RE: Would you move in very close as if it were *Ben Hur* except that in your film fleas would be pulling around this little chariot?

MFC: Yeah. I want it to be a projection of these gigantic fleas. So the skill is not much about human skill, but about flea circus skill.

RE: There's a danger of it being like a B-movie: *The Invasion of the Fifty-Foot Flea*. Has anyone ever made a film of a flea circus?

MFC: There is a film in which there are three seconds of fleas performing. They're pulling a chariot and some are dancing—moving in little circles.

RE: I don't want to sound too politically incorrect, but do they have rhythm?

MFC: They do.

RE: What kind of dances do they do? Are they Latino dancers?

MFC: In Europe in the old times they made them waltz. And in New York they made them dance early jazz.

RE: So these fleas can really get down and get dirty?

MFC: Yeah. I'm sure they can dance mambo.

RE: That's perfect. Exactly, *The Mambo Fleas*. You can get Arnold Glimcher to do a movie.

MFC: I need a music box with a tray that spins. The vibrations help them move and I want this to be a mechanical device, not a recording or something like that.

But the only problem with the music box is that it has such silly songs. So probably I have to have one made with my music. There is flea music from the early circuses.

RE: What do you mean by flea music? Do they actually make musical sounds?

MFC: No, I have to make it. It's music especially written for fleas. There's a book on the history of fleas by Giovanni Berlinguer and in it are songs for fleas. I went to the theatre library at Harvard and they told me they would try and find scores for me. So the historical research is fascinating because it's such an obscure subject and there is so little documentation. I have been researching for two years. Sometimes I think I'm not going to find anything else, then I do.

RE: So you're a flea scholar, or a flea archaeologist. In making a world from scratch there is a sense in which you're playing god.

MFC: But on the other hand, I'm their slave. I work with them, I feed them, I take care of them. They have control over me because I devote my life to them. This domination is very complex. I think there's some satisfaction for the trainer but I'm starting to think that they dominate you more. It's like a pet. You take care of them and they end up taking advantage of you. In North America people have eighty million dogs and cats—half of them even worse than babies. I think that's pretty advantageous from the animal's point of view.

RE: You have a small drawing of two prisoner fleas with balls and chains on their legs. You've also got escape artists, fleas escaping from a kind of minimalist cube. What is that a reference to?

MFC: Basically it's a struggle to escape and that's part of their instinctual behaviour. If you put them in a white area, they need to go quickly to a dark place, so you take advantage of that. They pull chariots because they're just trying to get away. I don't know if this is cruel or not.

RE: Is this a metaphor for something that goes beyond the relationship between you as the trainer and your fleas as performers?

MFC: I think it changes in different stages; different acts are different. At times they are certainly anthropomorphic. But sometimes not. I have some more abstract ones. I have these little threads of silk for my flea clowns. When they jump there is this pretty little colourful thread just moving up and down.

RE: Are they like the cheerleader flea? Or is the cheerleader flea a variation on the clown?

MFC: It's more a variation of the flag waving. You can make them sweep the floor too.

RE: That makes perfect sense to me. Somebody's got to clean up after the circus. How big will the circus be when you get it done?

MFC: My circus is really big. Right now the largest stage is over one metre in diameter. I have another one that is more like an oval—maybe 150 by 70 centimetres—and it's for the trapezes and stuff. It's totally walled so they can be free but not escape. And I have a big cage for them. Right now I have three main sets.

I also have a small arena for the sign that says "Cardoso Flea Circus" and it's activated by fleas.

RE: How far along are you on the training? Have you got separate training programs for a number of fleas?

MFC: Before I was trying different things at the same time. Right now I'm picking one at a time. I'm trying to make one juggle a ball and to pull chariots, which is a classic. I can already make them walk the tightrope. I have the prisoners; I have the cannon-balls. And I'm playing with different versions of the flea clown. When you want to perform they have to work perfectly and smoothly.

RE: How would the audience know when it's *not* going perfectly and smoothly?

MFC: Well, if you're trying to make them jump into a little pond of water and they jump elsewhere, that would not be perfect.

RE: I see. Well, you could just say that it's the clown flea. There must be room for some degree of postmodern radicalism.

MFC: I'm not a performance artist and I'm totally, totally nervous about this. I don't want to perform. That's why I want to make a movie. I'm not comfortable with my own body and the attention that will be paid to it.

RE: You mean because of the difference in scale between you and the fleas?

MFC: No, it's just because I am shy, I don't want to be in the spotlight. I'm looking at what the fleas do. But when the audience looks they take in me and the fleas. I'm not very comfortable with that. You also have to announce the different acts. So I have to train myself to be a ringmaster which is even more difficult. But my boyfriend is really good at improvising the narratives. So, for example, if the flea in the cannon-ball jumps in the opposite direction, he says he's inspecting to see that the security systems are in place so there is safety in the jump. You have to improvise all of these things.

RE: Are the fleas expensive?

MFC: They are. They are seven cents a flea.

RE: So you've got twenty-one dollars worth of fleas.

MFC: They told me there were five hundred, but I think there were around 350. I think they cheated me.

RE: That's terrible. They cheated you out of forty percent of your order.

MFC: I bought fifty dollars worth of fleas and I got less than that. In the beginning I thought I would order one thousand fleas but I'm glad I didn't.

RE: I want to ask you about the names of your fleas. Why did you pick the name Cochice Rodriquez?

MFC: Cochice was a famous cyclist when I was a kid. So I thought I would have my Colombian cyclist. I'm playing with different names. I like Pepita and Pepon.

RE: Is that a two flea act?

MFC: It's man and woman.

RE: I don't want to ask what they do.

MFC: They're the jugglers.

RE: Ah, perfect. By the way, do fleas mate?

MFC: Of course.

RE: I guess they have to. But that's not part of the act?

MFC: No, but my research says that flea copulation is the most fascinating thing. Let me read you a description from an article in a magazine: "Flea copulation has been hailed as one of the wonders of the insect world. The male, normally much smaller than his mate, lies beneath her from behind, embraces her back-to-belly with his antennae and softly caresses her genitalia. Then his tail curves up like a scorpion, and he penetrates her with the most elaborate genital armature yet known." I have an Asian drawing from 1749 of flea copulation. What they did was they made them copulate and then they froze them. Then they were able to study the genitalia.

RE: Obviously you can't ask if the earth moved or anything, but I gather this kind of event must be mutually satisfying?

MFC: Also, for the flea researcher this is flea pornography.

RE: There's another film you could make. You could become the Russ Meyer of flea films. But we can't talk like this any more, we have to get back to the art. So here's a change of pace. How far are you willing to push the idea that your construction and training of a flea circus is a metaphor for relationships of power? Or is that irrelevant to your current project?

MFC: I don't really think much about power because there is so much to this.

RE: This seems to be a project that a woman artist would take on more than a male artist, because it seems *not* to be about power. Am I falling into the trap of believing that feminist discourse has opened things up?

MFC: Maybe it's a rebellion against these discourses because it's so humorous and so much about entertainment. We get pleasure out of other animals and I'm very intrigued by that kind of pleasure. So it is a power relationship I'm not critical of because it's all part of humanity. There was the Roman circus, there are horse races and dog races and there is the zoo and Sea World. There are incredible, elaborate spectacles. I think this fascination with animals is a very powerful force.

RE: There's a line from *King Lear* that goes, "As flies to wanton boys are we to the gods. They kill us for their sport." We use the animal world as well, and certainly the insect world.

MFC: But you know I'm not really sure that we are more than animals or that we have power over them. That's why I said maybe they found me. Maybe they are using me. We forget that we have been here with animals for millions of years. We are animals and there is not much difference between them and us.

RE: So implicit in what you do is your respect for the flea?

MFC: Well, I'm fascinated with them. I sit and look and try to understand.

RE: Is it a fascination with something that you can comprehend all at once? Levi-Strauss argues there's pleasure in that perception alone.

MFC: Yeah, except that you can't. That's impossible. It really takes a lifetime. The most famous flea researcher in the world is named Miriam Rothschild. She lives in England and her father was a flea entomologist. He had the largest selection of fleas in the world, hundreds of thousands of them. So you can devote your life just to that and still not understand.

RE: I can see that. So they remain a source of fascination because they ultimately remain mysterious?

MFC: Definitely. They're like creatures from another world; you just try to communicate. And every aspect is fascinating, I file every little piece of paper, every quote, every tiny question I get, every laugh somebody has.

RE: I want to ask a practical question here. How can you make a living from your flea circus?

MFC: Well, I really want to make a living out of it and that's part of the humour of this whole thing. But I don't want to do anything boring to make money. I'm just doing this on my own, but my goal is to make money. Right now I'm living from my art. It's also involved with animals. I devote myself to working with animals. Most of the time I work with them dead.

RE: That's what's interesting. Your installations with starfish are remarkable but they aren't living things. They're remnants of life and you transform those unliving things into works of art that have an extraordinary beauty. Why have you made the shift to living things?

MFC: I made a fly piece a couple of years ago and in order to get the flies I had to breed them myself.

RE: You did a housefly piece?

MFC: It was like a Styrofoam ball and I had hundreds and hundreds of flies glued to it. I glued them with one wing sidewards and up so I'd have a halo of these translucent wings. In this country you can buy anything. The starfish and seahorses I bought from a supplier in Oakland who supplies the souvenir industries. And a whole selection of other animals I found in biological supply houses. I bought preserved snakes and frogs and lizards. I even bought the pupae for the house flies. You have to feed them with a mixture of milk and tissue paper and a little bit of liver so they lay their eggs. And it becomes this gooky thing. Their eggs grow so fast they start to make a constant chewing sound. The smells were intense, the sounds were intense and I had to take care of them three hours a day. They basically became babies. In a way that's how I feel about the fleas. They are my babies.

RE: You have carousels of fleas too, don't you?

MFC: I'm making one. I think it's too heavy.

RE: You mean it's too heavy for them to turn?

MFC: Yeah. So I'm making it from watch parts. That's a classic prop. But my circus is not going to be so traditional. I'm also making some weird and different things.

RE: What's your biggest achievement so far as a trainer? What are you most proud of at this stage?

MFC: It's hard to say. I like my "Cardoso Flea Circus" sign. But I think that what I like most is the research. I'm having so much fun digging in, and finding more and more. You know I want to be buried in a flea coffin.

RE: What did you just say?

MFC: I recently saw this show on African fantasy coffins and there is a tradition to have a coffin carved in whatever shape and colour you want. It depends upon your profession. I saw one that was a big lobster for a fisherman; I saw a big pumpkin for somebody who had a pumpkin plantation. So, I want to have a flea coffin made and I want to be buried in it.

RE: Are you serious?

MFC: They are the most fantastic sculptures.

RE: The more I hear you talk the more I realize how serious this business is for you. The flea coffin is the real kicker. Why are you so obsessed by these things?

MFC: I don't know, it has no explanation.

RE: One of the things that's always struck me about your work is how beautifully it works in installations. You pay a lot of attention to aesthetics. How can you aesthetize the flea circus? It may be a fascinating process but how can it become a beautiful object?

MFC: The beauty is the pleasure you feel. It's an aesthetic pleasure. Fleas are not pretty insects but they can make you laugh.

RE: But they're also feeding on you and that relationship doesn't seem so pleasant?

MFC: But the pleasure happens inside you.

RE: You take some pleasure from them feeding on your arm?

MFC: Yes. I enjoy it.

RE: But you're not going to leave your boyfriend and run off with a flea or anything? There's no danger of your having a relationship with a flea?

MFC: No, but he's my flea mate.

RE: What do you mean? Does he share your obsession with fleas?

MFC: He's my flea valentine. He gets a kick out of it.

Guy Maddin
The Laureate of Futurepast

If fate arranges itself in some happy configuration with talent, Winnipeg film-maker Guy Maddin may well go on to become one of the best filmmakers in North America. By best I don't mean the most polished, the most coherent or the most profound. I mean the artist capable of making the most strangely compelling and disorienting films, characteristics shared by *The Dead Father*, *Tales from the Gimli Hospital*, *Archangel*, *Careful* and *Twilight of the Ice Nymphs*. These five films centre on loss, jealousy, amnesia and a collection of similarly disquieting conditions, all of which create an irresistibly elegiac tone. Still, an unmistakable cushion of innocence surrounds Maddin's films. It's a balloon that hasn't yet burst around him.

Maddin's narratives are often confused in the telling but gorgeous in the seeing. Watching his films is an exercise in frustration because you constantly want to stop them in order to savour single images. Maddin admits to no particular gift for photography but his shots are wonderfully composed. They look out of time in that they seem to prophecize a future that has already gone by. He is the laureate of futurepast.

Maddin would no doubt appreciate the absurdity of this timelessness; his sense of humour is witty, self-deprecating and unconsciously wicked. So are his films: their self-consciousness is a strength, their weirdness comforting. There's no question that Guy Maddin still has a lot to learn about filmmaking but in a way that I accept—and can't explain—he has already shown me the workings of an alchemy that transforms the strange, the curious and even the disgusting into a world of beautiful bewilderment.

Maddin's films include *The Dead Father* (1985), *Tales from the Gimli Hospital* (1988), *Archangel* (1990), *Careful* (1992), *Twilight of the Ice Nymphs* (1997), and a four-minute-long film appreciation of Odilon Redon's "The Eye Like a Strange Balloon Mounts Towards Infinity" made in 1995. Along with Britain's Brothers Quay in that same year, Maddin received a Telluride Medal "as a master of postmodern expressionism." The following interview was conducted in the offices of the Winnipeg Film Group in December, 1989.

GUY MADDIN: I was born at the Old Grace Hospital on Portage and Arlington in Winnipeg, delivered by Dr. Kufburg Hanford and named by my twelve-year-old brother after Guy Madison, the B-movie western star.

ROBERT ENRIGHT: Is that true?

GM: Believe me, it's true. It's a stupid pun my brother came up with. I never really gave movies another thought, other than all the crummy horror movies I loved going to at the Lyceum Theatre. Then I just watched a lot of television.

RE: So you went to a lot of movies as a kid?

GM: Mostly horror movies. They had to have some sort of macabre bent. Then I went on a long movie hiatus. I don't think I watched a movie for about ten or fifteen years. I remember in 1978 the only one I saw was *Saturday Night Fever*. I caught up with it about the eleventh month of it's run.

RE: But you indiscriminately watched television?

GM: Yes, I memorized the TV schedule. There were only seven stations, so you couldn't watch that much. Then I grew out of television and by the age of sixteen or so I think I'd watched too much. And I haven't really watched it since.

RE: What was life like at home? I know your father was a sometime manager of Canada's National hockey team.

GM: He was and my mother was a hairdresser. I grew up in a beauty salon on Ellice Avenue. It was one of those store-front homes. My mom and my aunt ran it together and when they retired I turned the beauty salon into the studio where I made *Tales from the Gimli Hospital*. Then my mom sold that place so I had to rent another studio, also coincidentally on Ellice Avenue, in which I filmed *Archangel*.

RE: Did you hang around your mom's hairdressing business a lot?

GM: I was a fixture. If someone spilled a bottle of peroxide or something, I'd be called in to mop it up. The kids at school would make fun of me because I smelled like perm lotion all the time. It was a smell in the house that I didn't even notice. And there was always the hum of hairdryers, about twenty of them in a row.

RE: Was this an anxious childhood for you?

GM: No, I loved my childhood. It was great. Just the other day a kid I haven't seen since grade one came up to me and said, "Hi, Guy, I'm Jeff from grade one. Remember me?" Of course I remembered him, even though it was twenty-six years since I'd last seen him. I used to spend years looking at my grade one photo and pining for those days.

RE: Would you describe yourself as nostalgic?

GM: I'm getting less so now. I don't lie on my bed any more wishing I was in the first grade. But I really thought for the longest time that my goal as a film-maker was to create in the viewer the feeling that I used to get when thinking of my childhood. I know a lot of filmmakers try to do that but I thought maybe I could intensify those feelings, make them not seem second-hand. I guess I wanted to do the work of poetry and actually create inexplicable feelings in the viewer that were equivalent to the myth-making feelings that you get as a child. Unfortunately, I've felt myself maturing a little bit lately and I don't know if I have those feelings any more. It's kind of sad.

RE: A couple of interesting things come out of what you've just said about childhood. Are the bogeymen Huns in *Archangel* committing the consummate sin in your moral universe when they attack children?

GM: In a way the idea of a child being that frightened is a joke. That a bogeymen would actually come in, put a sack on a child's head and chew on its nipples, just the idea of that kind of terror, even though it works out in the end, fascinated me. I hope it's nervously funny. Like in the movie *Poltergeist*—movie quality aside—there's a pretty good scene where a tree just shoots through a window and takes this already terrified kid in its grasp and pulls him out. Now it's one thing to be scared of a tree—and that fear is real for most children—but when the tree actually grabs you and takes you away it's so ridiculously terrifying that its pretty funny. I remember laughing like a lunatic during that scene.

RE: Let's let humour go for the moment. I have a feeling we'll get back to it. Do you have an informing mythology that is recognizable in your films?

GM: Mythology? I don't know. At times I'm a little vague on what it is. I guess when I think of myth I think of taking the first few things that happen in one's childhood and trying to create a cause and effect relationship out of them. Spring comes because you hang your laundry out—that sort of thing. So quite often it's the myths of early childhood that are most intriguing because they're not in the common parlance. The myths are wrong.

RE: Wrong because the cause and effect sequence is misread? Spring doesn't come because you put the laundry out; you put the laundry out because spring has come?

GM: Yes. But what intrigues me most are the early myths where you're really trying to make sense of something through trial and error. So I'm more interested in the rejected myths. I call them rotten myths. They're models of the universe that are constructed and then have to be disposed of because they don't work. The rotten myths are more intriguing because they tell you more about the way your mind works.

RE: Is myth-making and story-telling the same thing for you?

GM: I'm more interested in myth-making. Story-telling is something that if its told well then it keeps people awake while you're throwing these rotten myths at them. When you're forced to reject them they may recreate the feelings of childhood. Because that's what you're doing as a child, rejecting and sorting. That's my strategy for creating feelings.

RE: But feelings are treacherous. I don't know how to react to a film like *Tales from the Gimli Hospital*. At times it's hilarious and absurd; at other times it's upsetting. The viewer never knows quite how he or she should be responding.

GM: That's the feeling I was hoping to get because I feel it's not just children who are constructing myths. As you encounter new phenomena you have to somehow make sense of them. When you get older there's sex and death and all that stuff. I've never been very good at making sense of anything so for me that's where the real joy of storytelling is. As an example, the protagonists in my first two movies attempted to sort out events by just sitting there and receiving them. The narrative was a bit passive, so I tried to design a story where people were actively trying to sort out their worlds. Even total slugs try to do something now and then.

RE: What made you start making films?

GM: I had nothing else to do. I had worked at a bank for a little while as a Branch Administration Manager and it wasn't great. So I quit and started watching movies. At the university [of Manitoba] I dropped in on George Tole's class and then I saw a John Paiz movie. I was totally thrilled that somebody from Winnipeg could make a great movie at an affordable price. I guess I first saw *The Obsession of Billie Botski* and it was a moment of inspiration. I think his films are really good. John told me it cost five thousand dollars and I immediately thought if I had the same amount I'd spend it on a movie. At the time I only had three hundred dollars but it was enough to start. I ran out after two days and then submitted what I had shot to the Manitoba Arts Council and received the money I needed to make *The Dead Father*, which I guess cost about five thousand dollars.

RE: Did you have any idea what you were doing? Other than being a filmophile did you have any filmmaking experience?

GM: No. I got someone who agreed to be the cameraman and then he didn't show up for the second shoot. I went over to his house and he showed me how to work the camera from his bed. I left him there, never saw him again and was my own cameraman after that.

RE: Tell me about your camera work.

GM: I'm not an accomplished cameraman. I don't have the ability to plan everything and quite often I don't actually know what I want someone to do until I've looked through the camera. They'll be doing something, just kibbitzing around while I'm trying to adjust the focus and I'll see what they've done accidentally and I'll like it better. I wish I could be better organized but I just never get around to planning things well enough. So I realized rather early that I would have to be behind the camera. When you're editing you can get mad at yourself for taking bad shots and then it's far easier to forgive yourself. I didn't want to spend a month cursing a cameraman for screwing up my idea of what the movie should look like. Still, I have to admit every now and then I look at a shot and I wonder why I positioned people that way.

RE: Are you good at explaining what it is you want?

GM: I just didn't want to spend all my time explaining. Movie-making is incredibly boring and slow and when there's too much debate within the crew it's even more boring. I knew it would take a lot of energy to make this movie and I certainly didn't want to expend seven-eighths of it talking to my crew. So I got two of the most efficient and quiet crew members—Terry Reimer and Gerry Turcheon. And I don't think I heard them say more than three words in six weeks. Now and then I'd catch Gerry wiping vaseline off the lens because he's a technical purist so I'd have to scold him and put some vaseline back on.

RE: Do you buy the notion that there is a Winnipeg or prairie sensibility in a number of the films that have been made here?

GM: I have no idea about it. People talked about isolation here and I never really got a sense of it. What did they mean I was isolated? I knew what it looked like in Hawaii without ever having gone there. But then I started travelling and I realized we *are* isolated. So maybe there is something geographical and demographic that makes people from Winnipeg make the same kind of film. I have another theory, though. When you attend film festivals worldwide you realize there's a type of film that comes from an age group. There are films from Sweden and Denmark that remind you of films from Winnipeg. So this undercurrent is less geographical or cultural than chronological.

RE: You use a lot of appropriated images in your films, images that pay homage to earlier filmmakers.

GM: I'm just putting what I like in the films. It's just fun. I guess those old movies are my favourite worlds to be in.

RE: Let's talk about your first production, *The Dead Father*, the film that started with inspiration from John Paiz and three hundred dollars from your pocketbook.

GM: I'm half proud of that movie. I think it's a bit too slow—or a lot too slow—but there's nothing phoney about it. Everything I put in there I put in for a reason.

RE: Where did the idea come from?

GM: It came out of the most persistent of all the stories I had bouncing around in my head. It was this recurring dream where my dead father kept revisiting me; I also remembered my dog died when I was little and it used to make cute little dream visits back to my lap. It left me with really strong residual feelings. I thought my only chance of making a short movie with any impact as a total beginner would be to zero in on one poetic feeling and try to recreate that in the viewer.

RE: What about with *Gimli Hospital*? What was your informing idea in it?

GM: There wasn't as legitimate a source for that story. I wanted to make a second film and there was a grant deadline coming up at one o'clock that afternoon. I was painting houses for the summer with a friend and one rainy day we were writing little sketches about the pathetically tragic history of the Icelandic settlers in Gimli. The accumulation of tragedies was bizarre. They arrived with nets which were meant for ocean fish and it was years before they caught anything. I think Lord Dufferin offered five dollars to the first Icelander to catch a fish and he died with the coin. Some hunting expedition went out on October 21st and returned on Christmas Eve with nothing. Then the poor souls got smallpox. It was just awful. I got all this information from a book called *Gimli Saga* which was put out in the '60s by a local women's guild. So, anyway, Kyle McCullough and I each wrote little skits which were goofy and uncontrolled. They were more like Rowan and Martin's *Laugh-In* skits. But for some reason one of them which got jotted down on a match-book cover stuck in my head and I submitted that.

RE: So you met the deadline?

GM: Yeah, but I didn't win the competition. It was a Winnipeg Film Group script competition with a twenty-thousand-dollar prize. But at least the deadline made me type up the match-book cover proposal and I submitted it to the Manitoba Arts Council. I got the money from them.

RE: Do you know photography very well? I always want to stop your films because single images are so exquisitely composed.

GM: I am concerned about the way my films look. In the '70s I watched a lot of made-for-TV things on CBC and noticed that the images just weren't very interesting. So I made a pledge to give a little extra effort in each shot. Actually, the look of my films is something I take pride in because I'm not a visual person. I didn't even own a camera until after I'd finished my second movie and I still can't take a snapshot for the life of me.

RE: Do you spend a lot of time planning a film; do you story-board it and work out each shot ahead of time?

GM: No, the whole spirit of film-making for me, possibly because I'm lazy, is to do it. I never spend more than a couple of seconds on any decision.

RE: But now that you have dialogue and a more complicated plot …

GM: I know, there's way more ways to go bad. That's why I over-write now. But I still try not to spend too much time on it. The script for *Archangel* was written with my friend George Toles in three sessions and we just blitzed through it.

RE: Do you still have a suspicion that dialogue is optional?

GM: No, unfortunately it's a little more essential.

RE: Why unfortunately?

GM: Because I like to make movies where the dialogue is just trimming but in *Archangel* the dialogue has an expository duty to perform. I have a narrator who reads ominous requiem type things from cenotaphs. He's like someone reading *In Flander's Fields* at a Memorial Day Service.

RE: Is Archangel a real place?

GM: It is. A friend of mine—who is a World War I old movie and music buff—told me quite excitedly about this place where all the soldiers of the world gathered after World War I just to continue the fun of fighting. People quit fighting the Germans and started fighting the Russians. Everyone was sort of forgetful and after a while people were quite confused. Most of the countries were pretty tired of fighting at this point, so they would send special troops—elderly soldiers, with one leg and missing eyes. I've seen footage of the original Archangel and the Americans were still wearing their civil war uniforms. They look like Union Soldiers with red caps fighting beneath onion domes in Russia. It was really odd.

RE: Do you mean original footage from the town of Archangel actually exists?

GM: Yes, I have some on videotape at home but it doesn't look anything like my movie.

RE: Does the film take its inspiration from this polyglot of loon bags who were there or does it stick to some historical narrative?

GM: I had absorbed the setting over a period of months by reading about these things and through discovering pictures from World War I. Unfortunately, all those story fragments just didn't add up to anything. They were really just a mish-mash of things and so George Toles and I tried to pinpoint the difference between a script and a pile of garbage, a distinction I hadn't bothered making before. I had to ask myself what really mattered to me and I realized that forgetfulness was the dominant tenor of my life; I forget the most painfully embarrassing things, important things about myself. I don't know if I should be very specific because you'd blush. Let's put it this way, I've noticed in other people tendencies to forget they're married or forget they have children or forget they have any responsibilities. I could fit rather snugly into all of those categories.

RE: By forget do you mean that people choose not to act upon responsibility.

GM: No, I honestly forget.

RE: Is it important to you to make films that are correct, politically or otherwise. I guess what I'm asking is do you feel any restraints on what you do?

GM: I don't want to do anything that's absurd just for the sake of being an asshole but I'm also not interested in saying anything that isn't true just to make it correct. I'm not interested in propagandizing or proselytizing. A lot of times I get the feeling that I'm being propagandized, that I'm not being allowed to make conclusions for myself. Isn't it kind of insulting to have things given to you all sugar-coated?

RE: So *Archangel* isn't an answer to *Triumph of the Will*? It's not a deliberately non-propaganda film in any way?

GM: Propaganda can be humourous. Like in those great Edward D. Wood anti-pornography movies—you know, show me a clam and I'll show you a dirty picture that caused it. They're so ludicrously unsophisticated in their attempts at manipulation that they're hilarious. To a lesser degree a lot of overly correct movies strike me as just as ludicrous. I like the idea of propaganda as humour so *Archangel* has propaganda in it. It's stupid.

RE: The critic and poet Terrence Heath has argued that it's not realism that characterizes the prairie sensibility as much as surrealism.

GM: Well, there's an evolutionary aspect involved. When you're a novice filmmaker you can't make realist films. First films are often quite odd because that's what you can do best. You end up maturing into realism. But because I have this theory about novice filmmakers having to make surrealist films I thought I stood a chance of making a slightly watchable film if I kept in mind where a novice might most likely make errors—continuity, lapses in plausibility, things like that. You just keep adapting as you work along.

RE: Did *The Dead Father* matter to you emotionally?

GM: By the time it was in the final editing stages there was nothing emotional to it, but when I jotted down the story idea there was something there. It wasn't about my actual father, it was more about the dreams I had that he was coming back. I wanted to recreate that feeling for viewers and I think it failed in that. As a matter of fact a lot of the feelings people have reported are a tingling of the buttocks, a sort of a numbness of the thighs. I honestly try to make these movies in the spirit of prose poetry. The prose part comes in the story but I really want the feeling. I'll just keep trying.

RE: I like the prose poet idea because you must recognize there are moments of astonishing visual lyricism in your films.

GM: I'd like them to be there. I don't quite have the hubris to admit I've succeeded to the degree that I want yet. Little moments, yeah. But I'd like the whole thing to blow people out of the water.

RE: Have you been influenced by *film noir*?

GM: I don't like police movies that much for some reason, although there's some Fritz Lang movies that I like quite a bit. And I'm fond of wet asphalt movies like *The Sweet Smell of Success*.

RE: But you go back to the earlier sources of that tradition in German and Russian film rather than through the American variation of it?

GM: That's right, I guess I've seen so much of it now. It doesn't give me goose bumps like it used to. I just like what shadows can do in those German Expressionist films. If you're a low budget filmmaker then shadows are the cheapest prop you can lay your hands on; if you can't afford real sets you can start unplugging lights and adding sound effects. I think of it as Darwinian: I had to have sets and lighting like that because I couldn't afford real ones.

RE: I think *Archangel* is going to be a successful follow-up to *Gimli Hospital*. Are you worried about moving too fast?

GM: I have to watch out. A couple of people—one from Toronto and one from L.A.—have offered to hire me as a film director and I had to say no. I wouldn't know what I was doing with a real film and a real budget. The money was really tempting but I felt quite noble turning them down. Anyway, they would have found me out within three hours on the set. I'd yell into the wrong end of the megaphone or something. What I have to watch out for is never going too far beyond my meagre—instead of meagre, we'll call them nascent—abilities. So even with *Archangel* I fear sometimes that by going to a talkie I've already gone too far.

RE: You used the term "cannibalizing" the last time we talked to describe the way you borrow from other filmmakers. How much of that do you do?

GM: I guess first of all I have to say I'm not against cannibalism. The reason I have a clear conscience is I use it as part of my vocabulary the way other people use words. If people initially find it quirky and then ultimately derivative, then that's too bad. I'm not using it for those effects; I'm using it for my storytelling style.

RE: You said that you were proud of *The Dead Father* because there was nothing in it that was phoney, that everything you included you wanted there. When you use film references are they there to both take advantage of their previous meaning and the meaning in the context of your film, or are they included for more playful reasons. How much latitude do you give yourself in the way the images work?

GM: Ultimately I just put in what I feel like. Sometimes they're included to surprise a friend who might see it.

RE: Filmmaking is still extremely personal for you then.

GM: I've noticed around the Winnipeg Film Group that when a lot of people start making films they immediately speak in terms of winning Oscars. I think I was realistic in knowing that I'd be lucky if a hundred people saw my first film before it disintegrated totally. I thought if I can't even please two or three close friends who enjoy movies then there's no point in even making a film. So in that regard it was pretty personal. I made the second film that way too. Because I fully intended it to be seen only by the same number of people who saw *The Dead Father*—which was pretty small. I feel it's only by a miraculous stroke of luck that anyone outside Winnipeg has seen any of my films because I certainly didn't make them with any distribution in mind.

RE: Were you surprised by the success of *Gimli Hospital*?

GM: I'm not surprised because there's evidently no ceiling to my inner arrogance. Pleased though. It's funny, even though I made it fully intending it to be seen by only a handful of people, I guess like all the other dreamers I was secretly hoping it would win an Oscar. But I was also making sure that the top priority was getting it right for the people who mattered. I wasn't trying to fool the public or anything like that. Actually, I'm not so sure my few close personal friends did like it, so maybe that's why it found some success outside of town.

RE: "How Sweet to Die For One's Country" is the epitaph for *Archangel*. Is this film overflowing with irony or is it a pro-war movie?

GM: Not pro war, let's just say it's about standing up and fighting about things that really matter.

RE: I want to come back to the question of forgetfulness. Do you want to talk a little bit more about memory disorders in *Archangel*? How much of a comment is that on your personal life and how much is it a reflection on contemporary life?

GM: Forgetfulness is something I'm good at but it makes little comment on anything out there. I'm not a social commentator or anything like that; I go straight to the sports page when I get the paper.

RE: But cultural amnesia is very much a condition of contemporary life. Your personal interest in forgetfulness happens to be a cultural metaphor as well.

GM: One reason I'm not a social commentator is I can never get past the first assumption on theories. I always assume that society hasn't changed in a thousand years, or maybe in thirty thousand years. I take it for granted that there's an analogue in prehistoric civilizations for every social action today. I know that things I'm doing in my sleazy life have been done by cave men, maybe exactly the same things as a matter of fact.

RE: You've said that you want to keep a lot of things submerged in your films. What do you mean?

GM: I hate it when after you've watched a film for the first time you think it's really good and then after the second time it just doesn't feel like there's anything underneath. So I try to take a basic story and then pile on stuff to make it unrecognizable. That's my strategy for submersion.

RE: So viewing your films is an act of witnessing the emergence of the layers that you've put into the work.

GM: If you don't do it correctly you obviously just bore people. If no one's paying attention, nothing's going to emerge. I'm aware of that risk.

RE: Let me ask you about some of the layers in *The Dead Father*. You have the scene where the deceased father is laid out on the breakfast table while the kids eat peanut butter and jam sandwiches around him. It's an hilarious scene at the same time that it's positively macabre, even disrespectful.

GM: I was worried that my mom would be offended by the movie. Unfortunately she didn't understand any of it. But I was also worried that it was more generally disrespectful, and ultimately, it really is. I think most people are now pretty inured to any kind of disrespect when you think of the kind of images that are bandied around. It's like jokes in a court room or a church; they're not as lewd as you really think. I thought these issues were really quite volatile when I was handling them but even eating from the dead father's stomach didn't seem to bother people that much.

RE: It's a weird scene though. Did it come out of the sensibility of horror films? It's a scene that is more horrific than any other except maybe the wrestling scene in *Gimli Hospital* where the two men *glíma* wrestle and tear holes in each other's buttocks.

GM: I guess I figured if you're covered with pox and fissures you'd probably draw a little bit of blood in a fight like that. As far as the stomach eating goes, the movie needed a climax. It needed a crisis to come to a head.

RE: So that after he eats the "dead father" their relationship changes dramatically.

GM: I think the narrator says, "I admit it was a night of great excess." He maybe felt he'd gone too far. So it was time to settle on an even keel.

RE: I read the whole relationship as a parody of vampirism. You eat of the father and at the end of the film he's put in a trunk which is not unlike a coffin. I couldn't help but make associations with the whole Dracula story.

GM: I'm not really close to vampirism, other than those great *décolleté* shots in the Hammer films with that wonderful red blood. But in their purest Bram Stoker forms, vampire movies bore me for some reason.

RE: *Nosferatu* doesn't interest you?

GM: I watched it recently. It's my least favourite Murneau movie. Maybe because I watched a lot of horror movies as a kid I've just seen too many of them. So it doesn't have any mythological resonance for me because I've just assimilated it as a fact. In the same way I've noticed, much to my horror, some Walt Disney cartoons don't work on me anymore either. It's disappointing because that was always a given. But I have to admit that Bambi worked on me. I saw it two years ago at the Gimli Theatre.

RE: There's an aspect of horror in *Gimli Hospital*, too. The central tension in the movie comes out of an act of necrophilia. Did you have any reservations about including this incident, even at the level of comic suggestion?

GM: I keep forgetting it's in there, actually. It doesn't really have much to do with the movie. But necrophilia isn't common in films. I know there's a Nicolas Roeg film called *Bad Timing* in which we see Art Garfunkel's naked bum mounting what he thinks is a dead lover, but I didn't care for that. Maybe it's just Art Garfunkel's bum I don't care for. But I honestly keep forgetting that's in there; it doesn't even seem that significant to me. I just had to come up with an act that would really irk the former lover.

RE: How much of the film was shot with the full cast involved?

GM: Almost all of it was shot with two people at a time, me and one other person.

RE: So there were very few scenes where you actually had both participants in a dialogue in the same location at the same time?

GM: That's right. There'd be scenes with five or six people and they would never have met one another. It was just easier. Anyway, I wasn't ready to orchestrate twelve people together and do crowd scenes and things. I had to have a few of those but I usually tried to get rid of them after an hour because I knew I wasn't emotionally strong enough to deal with people grumbling about how boring it was.

RE: The film has some unforgetable visual moments, too. The nurses seemed to move almost as if they were joined together.

GM: Yes, the nurses' scenes I shot all in one day. It was originally going to be about three days but the mother of two of the nurses was such a pain that we got things done quickly.

RE: You've got a lot of death in your films so far. Are you going to start dealing with sex more?

GM: I like suggested sex. I can't compete with Jean-Jacques Beinex and his ten-minute-long single-shot copulation scenes. Jeez, ten minutes!

RE: You don't want to, or you can't?

GM: I don't want to. Just getting more and more explicit is a dead-end. I go in the opposite direction.

RE: The little shadow play where the nurse undresses is quite nicely done. It's a tasteful invitation to voyeurism.

GM: That part is autobiographical. I've always been totally passive. My entire social life has consisted of sitting in a corner of a restaurant looking at people having fun.

RE: You've said that you use storytelling as a way of personally clarifying things.

GM: They're as clear as they'll ever get before I've made the film. Making the film then just becomes work and any therapeutic considerations disappear. If there's any therapy it's the great feelings you get when the movie plays out of town. That's probably pretty bad for me.

RE: Why do you think that?

GM: It's a self-indulgent, ego thing. Every now and then I just stare at my poster and sigh.

RE: Were you raised funny or something? Why would you worry about success?

GM: I don't worry about it. I'd love to have success but I want to be my own most critical judge. That way by the time I pronounce myself successful I'll be successful. That won't happen for a long time; I'm just trying to avoid smugness which I haven't successfully done. Believe me, I want everyone to love me.

RE: What do you do when you're not editing?

GM: I sit around with a nervous stomach and I play a lot of ping-pong with John Kozak, another filmmaker here. He beat me eighty-nine games in a row and Dave Barber, who runs the Cinematheque, beat me something like ninety-two games in a row. But I've started to win. I actually beat Kozak two games in a row. As a matter of fact ping-pong has supplanted editing for quite a while.

RE: Do you have your next film in mind?

GM: No, I was thinking of doing a biblical epic or Guy Maddin's version of Gustave Flaubert's *Salammbo*, a book I enjoyed because it's so overripe. I took it to the laundromat one night and got to page five and had to re-read page five four times because I was sleepy. I thought if I could even get through chapter one of the book then maybe I could adapt it. So I put it aside for awhile. Maybe I just wasn't in the mood for it at the time. Then I started thinking of doing something smaller, maybe human movies with a room and one person in it. But that would drive me batty too. I have no idea what to do right now.

RE: Has Gimli been a place that really matters to you?

GM: Yes, it's a place I dream of constantly. At least once a week I dream of swimming in lake Winnipeg in the winter. I've been having that dream since I was four. I have ritualized the place to the extent that the act of swimming there is my church. I've swum in Lake Winnipeg ten out of the twelve months of the year now. Kyle and I went swimming on December 9th last year. It was pretty mild weather the day before when Kyle and I were sitting in the city and there was no snow. We said we're going to have to bring snow by swimming in Lake Winnipeg. So the next day a bunch of us drove to the lake. By the time we got there it was night time and we expected the water to be open because it hadn't been that cold. Greg Klymkiw was the first person to see the lake and he didn't have his glasses on. He remarked how calm the lake looked. It wasn't calm, it was frozen. But we'd all pledged that we were going to swim and we'd ritualized it in the ninety minutes it took us to drive out. We'd sung songs about swimming and how four went down and four went in. Of course none of us let on that we were absolutely convinced our hearts were going to stop. We drove by Gimli Hospital on the way all silently knowing one of us would soon be lying in there. So we stripped down and walked through the hoar-frosty grass. There was no snow, but the lake was frozen and there was this one open area. We took our shoes off at the last second and Greg Klymkiw took pictures to prove that we went in. Unfortunately, he took his shoes off before he had a chance to get in and he froze his feet. Then he walked over a bunch of piled ice shards about three or four feet high and because he had no feeling the ice punched holes in the bottom of his feet and blood was pouring out. He didn't know. But we all felt good. Kyle earned his nickname "Two Swims McCullough" by going in twice. It always seem to me that a trip to the lake isn't complete unless I've touched the water. Actually the night the movie premièred on April 16th we decided to seal the première by all going swimming. The lake had already started thawing but at night it froze over again, just a razor thin layer of ice and when all five of us ran in we slowly realized it was cutting all the skin off our shins. So everyone was wearing little crimson socks of their own blood. I think seven of us crammed into a car and only Angela Heck, the actress, didn't go in. She was the only one who wimped out. I have since learned that you can ice swim without any trouble. Snow baths are a Gimli tradition too. I was at a party last January in Gimli in a really cold caboose and I suddenly stripped to my boxer shorts and hoping to impress everyone, I made a big snow angel outside. Instead, it just terrified them; they thought they were with a madman. It really wasn't the social gambit I thought it might be. I felt like Einar in *Gimli Hospital*.

RE: Are you interested in power?

GM: I don't think so. If I am it's in a way that no one can figure out because I'm constantly trying to diffuse power. When I sense I have it over people I notice I always try to undercut it, just so. I'm uncomfortable with the feeling of having any power over people. If I'm beating someone at ping-pong I try to get the game a little closer. I'll even lose. It's odd, but then I suspect it's probably some sort of reverse psychology I'm using on myself to gain even more power over people. I don't trust my motives totally. I'm sure I would like nothing better than to control the entire world but do it with meekness.

Collaborations

David Salle
& John Hawkes
Complicities

In 1985 novelist John Hawkes made an "offering" to David Salle in the form of a brief catalogue introduction for his exhibition at the Mary Boone Gallery in New York. Three years later I interviewed Hawkes about his just published novel, *Whistlejacket*, and when Jack—the name he goes by—mentioned that Salle had inspired the novel, my interest was aroused. The seed of their brief connection stayed with me and in the summer of 1990, in the sage and wild landscape of Colorado, it took root and flowered. Hawkes flew from his home in Providence, Rhode Island to Crested Butte, where David Salle maintains a summer studio that allows him to escape the distractions of New York. Over two days in early August both of these artists responded to my badgering questions with generosity and, sometimes, impatience. The resulting conversation was an intelligent, passionate and occasionally indignant commentary on why and how each of these artists makes his art.

Both Salle and Hawkes have had their share of detractors. One critic has remarked that "there is something about Salle's work that brings out the worst in people" and Hawkes has been accused of having "a contemptible imagination." Critical responses to their work are never lukewarm, even when they're meant to be favourable. One night at dinner a young woman working in the restaurant where we were eating came up and asked if Jack was the same Hawkes who had written *The Lime Twig*? Jack was visibly pleased and said he was honoured to be acknowledged. The woman was quick to say that she was *more* honoured and then added, her brightness turning quizzical, "It was the most bizarre book I've ever read."

If making a place for the bizarre in the world is a good thing—and I happen to think it's a necessary thing—then these two artists are at the heart of contemporary culture. As Salle puts it, "You want to be able to see what you see in your mind's eye." And then Hawkes chimes in, tolling the bell for the eye-land inhabited by his artful companion. "I don't want to live in a nightmare but I want to create them." It's this uncompromising insistence on the operations of the unfettered imagination that makes both David Salle and John Hawkes, whatever their differences, more the same than different kinds of artists.

The following conversation took place around the dining-room table of David Salle's summer house in August of 1990.

ROBERT ENRIGHT: Why would John Hawkes have been your ideal writer, your ideal commingler?

DAVID SALLE: Well, the first of Jack's novels I read was *The Blood Oranges* and then I began to find the others. The work is so intensely committed to, and focused on, the creation of purely imaginative images and the symbolic and metaphoric realm of the imagination that I just can't think of a better parallel, written in English, to what I am trying to get at in painting. The kind of imagination that's necessary to create those images in fiction is the same non-programmatic intuitive, independent world of the imagination that I find valuable in life.

ROBERT ENRIGHT: Jack, what was it that made David the first painter you wanted to write about, since art criticism was a kind of writing you hadn't entertained doing before?

JOHN HAWKES: It was an immediate experience. It was the constant juxtaposition of elements and the amazing mutedness in the colours. His painting is like looking at a glass of red wine in total darkness: the ruby colour that you see but don't see would be what's in his work. So I included an excerpt about dead passion from *Travesty* in the catalogue for the Mary Boone Gallery. I was initially interested in David's work because of the idea of dead passion, because the entire sexual, erotic and imaginative life was somehow held at bay or denied, but in some strange way was also present and possible.

RE: The image of the red wine led you in your introduction to talk about "eroticism with its European tones." What was the recognition that you sensed?

JH: Since our first meeting, I'd read bits and pieces in these catalogues and I'd picked up some of the important subjects. Pornography is surely one, eroticism in general, and the whole question of narrative versus image. What's really happening in these paintings and in my fiction is not just an assemblage of images. What fascinates me is the amazing confluence of order, if not actual constraint, conceived against the possibility of looseness, or of an effulgence breaking out.

RE: Jack mentioned a whole series of things that argue for a kind of logic in the act of composing paintings.

DS: As a general principle, if the viewer doesn't sense that there's some internal logic holding those disparate images together then the picture is a total flop. It's very simple. And I don't want to make this sound sycophantic, or search out false parallels but I was very intensely involved with Jack's writing just prior to when I really started to make the work that's mine, probably in the late seventies. The thing that Jack did, for example, in *Second Skin*, was to locate a whole world of sensibility and meaning in a visual symbol. In European literature that symbol would more likely be musical, like a leitmotif. It's invoked and then it's periodically invoked again. The way I perceived Jack using a visual symbol was that it sprang from the imagination in a galvanic, creative way. It hung there in the air and the fiction kept spinning it around and extending it in an unbroken passage that would sometimes go on for twenty pages. Then it would come down from exhaustion or just terminate because it was time to go on to something else.

RE: Did it lead you to anything directly, or was it this overall sensibility that was catalytic for you?

DS: I don't think there's any direct references to anything in the books, although the painting *Black Bra* is a direct quotation from *Second Skin*. A little footnote is that I did enjoy the conundrum that *Black Bra* posed for almost all art critics, none of whom had any idea which book the image had come from. They assumed that it had something to do with Cézanne—an unbelievably off-the-mark association. It was really very simple—all anyone had to do was read the novel. It's not that one is copying the other, it's just that there's a parallel track that exists in the artistic world. Now we have blocked all that off because of specialization and professionalism. Opening it up again wasn't a deliberate goal; it just came naturally to me.

RE: Jack sees your work as dealing with pornography. Do you feel that it walks that edge between what we consider pornographic and what we consider erotic or sexual? Do you try and locate yourself somewhere along that spectrum?

DS: I don't know where the work is in that context because that spectrum is entirely subjective. For a long time I worried—is my work pornography and if so is that bad? After quite a few years of worrying about it I came to the conclusion that I didn't know the answer because it was always in the mind of the viewer, but more importantly, it didn't matter. If it is pornography, so what? I don't have any moral compunction about pornography. Any feelings I have about it are purely stylistic and like everything else in life there's good pornography and bad pornography. I mean well done and less well done examples of the genre. I don't see why it should be excluded as a serious subject. Certainly one of the primary drives in Picasso's work, and one of the reasons it remains fascinating, is because of its still untangled web of eroticism and blatant pornography. At the same time, if it were only that without the other formal gifts, then it would be as banal as André Masson whose work is pornographic and utterly uninteresting. To say that something is or is not pornographic is only the beginning of discretion about art. I never like to talk about art in terms of making points. Art doesn't make points; art is itself. But if you could talk about it in those terms one of the points I've been willing to make all my life is that subject matter is really a sucker's game and that the real subject is something in-between the thing depicted. It's unbelievably retrograde that sophisticated people in the visual arts would find themselves unable to cross the threshold of subject matter. In twenty years' time that inability will appear as one of the weirdest subcurrents that we lived through in the last ten or fifteen years.

RE: Jack, I want to get you to respond to the notion of pornography in both David's and your own work. How prevalent is it?

JH: It's a subject that I certainly care greatly about as a person and as a writer. I think we ought to keep in mind that my work begins forty years ago with *The Cannibal* and it begins in the antithesis of luminous eroticism. Certainly behind *The Cannibal* was the desire for fulfillment, for something whole and shimmering. In *Virginie* I was trying to write something pornographic and I couldn't do it. I wrote a little headnote referring to Nabokov and I said something about the line between pornography and great Provençal poetry being a very fine one indeed and I used a clichéd image, something about a shell. I was really talking about vaginal shape, its mystery and its colour.

RE: Why couldn't you write a pornographic book? Weren't you capable or were you disinclined?

JH: What I wrote was what I wrote. It turned out not to be pornographic. It may have been the absence of a scene that built up to sexual arousal that kept it from being pornographic. It has everything else. Bit in fact, it's a comic novel. It portrays the terror of a sexual act, the terror of experience in a brothel, but it has a marvelous scene at the end which includes this rather sad figure and all the women that he's turned into art objects. In a way I think we're all art objects, so I like to talk about it. Because I'm a voyeur I don't see anything wrong with a woman as an art object.

DS: Philip Johnson made a famous statement about one of those magazines that photographs the extravagant homes, sumptuous apartments and unbelievable furniture of the wealthy. He said the magazines were pornography for architects. When you think about it, almost everything in American life is pornography for some special group, whether it's car buffs or house buffs or buff buffs. Everything in American life is about offering something unattainable in a commercially pack-aged way. That is American cultural life. But we're talking about the deliberate, unfettered use of things which are sexual and voyeuristic or just physiological or anatomical. The interconnection of all those things usually doesn't result in some-thing resembling commercial pornography. That's why the audience for commer-cial pornography probably doesn't know Jack's work and doesn't know my work. Because it's not packaged in quite the right way, even if it has some of the identical images, fascinations and fixations.

JH: The word "pornography" is pejorative to almost everybody. I've been read-ing a book by Walter Kendrick called *The Secret Museum: Pornography in Modern Culture*. Now what could be more desirable than a secret museum? The gist of the book is that the hatred and fear of pornography, at the outset, was really the fear of chaos. And what is art if not the necessity of creating chaos, of creating the possibility of chaos and then threatening us with it. But I want to know more about voyeurism, because, I think at heart I'm a kind of pornographer. I've never been able to give voice to it, but one of the first and most important images in my life was one I saw at the very late age of fifteen. In New York I saw what would be called a dirty postcard. It was a little black and white picture fading to yellow, with a man and a woman on a bed. They were both stark naked and the man was facing the camera. They seemed about half an inch high and they looked like little maggots. The woman was performing oral sex on the man. I had never seen a more frightening image, full of pathos and desperation. It was awkward because they weren't professionals and didn't know how to act for the camera. Implicit in the photograph was the need to view sexuality and the shame and ineptness in not being able to do so. The drama was overwhelming.

RE: What interests me is how you approach the notion of being a voyeur, why you choose certain images in the paintings, and whether they give you a charge. Do you assume that there will be an equivalent charge for the viewer? When you bring the naked buttocks of a woman as forcibly forward as you do in so many of the paintings, David, you must know you're dealing with a fairly provocative area?

DS: Of course it's charged. I'm sure that's why I'm attracted to it and use it so much. The premise is, simply, that you want to be able to see what you see in your mind's eye. You want to be able to externalize it so that you can see it again, so that you can then re-internalize it. I think that's a fairly common artistic method. Recently I saw a Matisse show at the National Gallery in Washington called *The Nice Years*. It looks at the period when he left Paris and moved his family into two or three adjoining apartments in the south of France. One of the great revelations was what it told me about the interiors—the ones with black and white tile and black grout lines—which served as a background for all the feminine guises that Matisse was fascinated with—the voluptuous nudes or odalisques or sylphides. They were stage sets that had been specifically built so that Matisse could then paint them as fragments of real life. They were totally manufactured. The sylphide was almost always his daughter; the violin player was almost always his daughter's best girl-friend, with whom he was passionately in love. Everything was partly from his life and partly an invented aspect of his life that existed in his imagination. But he externalized it so that he could paint it in order to re-internalize it.

RE: So Matisse was "an actor in the theatre of sex," to borrow a phrase from Jack's fiction?

DS: No question about it. And of course the sub-text of all these paintings is the bourgeois family man's conflict at being totally obsessed with this subject matter. Not just being superficially attracted to it but actually obsessively curious about the daughter, the daughter's best friend, the woman viewed on the beach through the window, the maid, and the guilt about moving the wife into an adjoining apartment so that the mistress could come into the master bedroom. You felt these things from the paintings before knowing anything about how they were made, but then seeing how they were made and seeing the paintings again—the transparency of the story, the tale being told—is like a great classical drama.

RE: Do you have any of those anxieties? You talk about the bourgeois Matisse bringing those desires to the surface. As an American artist in the latter part of the twentieth century do you have to have any of those reservations? Does society give you permissions that he didn't have?

DS: I think that the reservations are of a very different order and have nothing to do with respectability and middle-class family life. When I was growing up and becoming infatuated with serious art, it thoroughly excluded anything personal, let alone anything as transitory, subjective and common as sexuality. Art was really to do with something much more formal and much more verifiable. The hesitancy I feel doesn't have anything to do with social reprobation but has to do with baggage about a lack of intellectual seriousness. Exploring one's voyeuristic nature or one's inexplicable identification with female stand-ins is something that, apart from a few certifiably crazy cases who are allowed to be eccentric and auto-erotic, is just not the territory of serious art.

RE: But Picasso could get away with showing the twinkling sphincter of his lover, Marie-Thérèse Walter?

DS: Yes, and Picasso represents Europe and everything that American artists are not supposed to have anything to do with. There's no question that the approach to the visual arts is one of the mini-reflections of the Puritan culture which is still the dominant culture in this country. Having visited art schools recently, the first thing that I noticed is how morally uptight the students are. They're the most rabid little moralists—so full of anger and hatred for anything they view as a politically incorrect representation of the world. Particularly the world of men and women. They're desperate for the moral correctness which will give their work a direction and a feeling of legitimacy. You could say that this is just a cover for the uncertainty and anxiety of being an artist in the first place, since it is a completely rudderless, insecure thing to do in the world. So it's perfectly natural for these people to be terrified but their reaction to that terror is to moralize.

JH: What is moral correctness? What does it look like?

DS: I'll tell you what it doesn't look like. It doesn't have naked women in it. That's pretty clear. Beyond that I don't think it matters much.

RE: Feminist critics would ask both of you about the way in which you objectify certain parts of the body. Their argument is that you fetishize the female form.

DS: Is that the argument or does it go further? I think the argument is because it's so recognizable in this culture, the presentation of a naked woman in a picture, is helping to promote a fiction about who women are and what they do and think and feel. And this is helping to prolong their oppression in the culture. It might be true, in which case it would be unfortunate. If it's true, in my case, I think it's true in the short run and not in the long run. But we're talking about how a work is used in the world, which is something artists have very little control over. Part of the moralist's argument in art is precisely that it's something an artist should endeavour to correct. A serious artist does not leave the interpretation of a work to chance. You insure that the politically correct reading of your work will follow because you leave no other possibility open. The fact that I've left another possibility open in my work makes it damnable to feminists. I'm sure some women are horrified and offended. But I've done what I can to make the work emotionally honest. If the transgressional aspect is still the only thing one can feel from it, then I probably haven't done a very good job.

JH: It would be impossible to look at these paintings and think that the transgressional aspect is dominant and essential. That would be absurd. I want to tell a story, though. Last weekend, quite by chance, a young man who was Canadian came to visit me to talk about *Travesty*. He brought his friend with him, a young female undergraduate at a Canadian university. She was an art student. It turned out that she had a book on David's work in the car. She sat silently during most of the conversation and I was much concerned about what she thought, though if she had spoken, I think it would have been a serious attack. At any rate, this man and I talked about *The Passion Artist*, in which I had attempted to write about the worst male I possibly could, who was a version of my father and myself. The novel poses one of the crudest clichés of maleness and masculinity against a range of femaleness from mother to girl. And it performs violence on women. The protagonist causes the death of a glorious young woman who he sees bathing in an old wreck of a mill pond. There is one scene in it that is probably as close as I could come to real pornography, though when I was writing it that's not what I had in mind. It's a scene where the father goes to fetch his daughter from school, meets her young companion, a girl fourteen or fifteen, learns from her that his daughter is a prostitute and then has sex with the girl. It's an extraordinary scene where the fear of women, the terrifying anxiety, shame and hatred on the part of that man give way to an experience which is totally of the imagination. A child who has been destroyed herself for mere money happens to provide a male, who is really a criminal, with a moment of the joy of life. I think it's glorious. There's another scene in the novel where this man wanders through a swamp and the imagery, unintentionally, is all filigrees and lace droplets of water. It's a timeless thing. He's walking through the world of women. He's really an alien in a world where men have all the women imprisoned. At the end of the novel the women revolted and took over the prison and the male protagonist is, of course, executed. At any rate, the young man said he thought it was a great novel. The girl wouldn't buy it. And I said, in a moment of extreme irresponsibility, if this novel were pornographic, if it were contributing still more to the sometime horror of being a woman in contemporary life, I would have to say that as a work of art, it was valuable enough to justify even that.

RE: David, a number of critics have commented on the fact that your work seems distant and that you use all of the material and the approaches at your disposal to remove yourself and the viewer from a direct apprehension of the work. The use of photography which is then painted rather than used directly, also tends to do that because it's already two generations removed from reality. How do you react to the notion that you are distancing yourself from the work?

DS: I don't think it matters. It's not the ultimate criteria. The means you use to get there don't matter very much to me.

JH: I don't think I would even use the word "distanced" in referring to your work. I would say detached. I'm talking about the creative psychic state, the process out of which the work might come. I'm a very detached writer. I'm sure we would probably agree, for example, that filmmaker Peter Greenaway is detached in his work. He's not so emotionally involved that his formal imagination is obstructed or inhibited in any way. There is, as well, a detached quality in these paintings. I'm interested in *Symphony Concertante II*, with its two women and military officer. The little inset, the not-quite nude, is a photograph. She's black-and-white. But she's where the colour lies because she was real. I think one can't help but look at a black and white photograph and have it resonate with what was there or would have been there. Whereas I think the obvious colours in this painting—the reds and yellows—are used comically and, in this case, they reduce the man. The military officer is an interesting comic spoof in a world of looking and of artistry. But your colour puts itself in darkness, in shadow, in unattainability. What comes to my mind is an image from *The Cannibal*. The pea-green pit of stench. It's colour that is antithetical to humanness and human desire.

RE: Can you remember how this painting was made. I'd like you to talk about the process of composition.

DS: All the paintings are made the same way. It's completely intuitive. I never have a working drawing or a maquette. I start with one image typically, as I did, in the case of *Symphony Concertante II*. I started with a photograph of my model, a woman I have worked with for ten years. I'd take pictures of her doing different things, like holding a violin. I never know what's going to come out of them, if anything. Then months later I have the photographs and decide which one could be a painting. That's how it starts. One image necessitates the second and the two together necessitate a third and the three together necessitate a fourth and so on until it reaches a point of fullness and complication. To go any further would make it a different picture; to go less far would seem undercooked. I've made many, many paintings which, when I look at them today, seem undercooked.

RE: Not enough amplitude, there should have been more there?

DS: They're too vague, the frequency is not high enough, didn't reach the right pitch, too much bass and not enough something else. But that just means that I was wrong and didn't judge them correctly. Obviously, all those images are like characters who have a dramatic weight and making the pictures is simply arranging dramatic weights in the right way. It's about proportion, rhythm and syncopation. I think one reason why I'm so involved with choreography is that it is the physical literalization of exactly those concerns. So it doesn't feel detached to me in the least. It's just what it is. I think what people mean when they say it's detached is that it doesn't feel life-affirming in the way that say, Matisse or Picasso feel life-affirming and I would have to agree. It's just a completely different sensibility.

JH: Don't you think there is some difference though between being detached and being distanced? I'm talking about the psychic state of the artist when he's working and that simply means that the artist finds a distance. Certainly this is true in writing. You have to have a distance between yourself and the material and you have to have a set distance between yourself and the person who's going to be hearing or speaking the work. In my case, I can be extremely detached as I produce images of extreme violence, having old people shot, lying dead like punched cows in a field.

RE: Are we talking about differences between the way the art forms themselves work?

JH: I think we've been talking about looking at the work and saying: in this work, this artist is detached or he's not passionate or whatever. You can't shape without being detached. If you were totally feeling the emotion of the piece or of the materials, that's all you'd be doing. Imagine Shakespeare as he's writing about some horrendous thing.

DS: I think there are two things here. "Does the work give a feeling of detachment?" is one thing, and it's different from "Is the artist detached?" I wish my work were more detached. I think it would be better if it were less personal and more objective. I think the reason people say it's detached is because, in fact, it's hyper-personal and they have a hard time entering into it. They feel shut out so they react by saying that I'm detached, when it's quite the opposite. Art always operates by paradox. Think about the artists to whom you could apply the word passionate: artists who in the most conventional, clichéd sense would be engaged with the process of painting and very passionate. I think of their work as just completely sloppy. Work that looks as though it were made by someone in a passionate frenzy is always slightly embarrassing to look at. Not that my work is not embarrassing to look at but it's embarrassing in a different way. If I see a painting that was made in a way that's totally convincing, I feel elated for that person and in a siphoned-off way, I feel elated for myself for having had that experience as well. That is an ideal in art and I think it happens very seldom.

RE: Is there anything you won't paint?

DS: I think it's clear that I actually have a very narrow, specific range of images. The conceit in the work, though, what the work seems to say as a battle cry or modus operandi, is that anything can be used, anything is material. I believe that's generally true.

RE: So there's nothing you won't use?

DS: No, I'm saying the opposite. It's actually a very small range, it's a depressingly small range if you think about it. There are very few things that I use and I tend to use them over and over again.

RE: But that's because of a conscious choice, not because you feel any moral or ethical compulsion either way?

DS: The point is that I can't really think of how to use any other thing. For ten years I couldn't really imagine how to use a group of figures or a male figure. I'm really only just beginning to think about it now. There are whole ranges of experience that I can't even imagine using. So the critical cliché that everything is in the paintings, including the kitchen sink, is a misconception. The most common critical description of my work is that it's like watching television and flipping through channels. I can't imagine how anyone could say that. It's totally inappropriate. A simple, objective analysis shows that the work is a very specific orchestration of a handful of imagistic themes. I really have no idea how that came to resemble twenty-five channels on television.

RE: Do you have taboos, Jack? Are there things you won't write about?

JH: It never occurred to me not to write about something. No, I think the only task is to find what to write about. I'm now trying to write a novel about an old race horse who is telling his life story in the first person. It's a big risk.

DS: I'm amazed by your ability to have such a wide range of subjects. That's what is really interesting about this discussion—that you could invent this character, a race horse, and then go through with it and create the tone and the type of language this character will use. It's a great feat of imagination and so thrilling. I love the way you set your books in these mythic places which, in fact, are always real places. I remember when we first met you wanted to do some research on fashion attire. You hadn't started riding yet, you were just thinking about it. I'd promised to set up a meeting between you and Helmut Newton but that didn't work out.

RE: Did you use anybody in particular as a model for Michael, the photographer, in *Whistlejacket*?

JH: I think that book was explicitly prompted by Peter Greenaway's *The Draughtsman's Contract*. Seeing that film was like being in the closed space of a fiction that I myself had created. My affinities with the film were certainly as strong as the affinities I felt immediately upon first seeing David's work. What happened was— and I've never done such a thing before and I probably won't again—I wanted to make it mine. I wanted to have a share in that work. I didn't understand *The Draughtsman's Contract*. I'd seen it only once. I understood the general idea but I wanted to re-do it in my way, in my language. It had to be contemporary. It was impossible to use an artist or a painter. But David was always in the back of my mind because I had been in his studio and seen his work; we had talked; he had given me catalogues. I was much aware of him as an artist. I think there was also a photograph that David showed me of Karole Armitage sitting in an automobile.

DS: It was a Bruce Weber photograph.

JH: So that was in my mind. I knew my photographer had to work in fashion. And I knew that the analogous world to Greenaway's eighteenth century was the horse world. I tried to put the two together. Then David sent me some George Stubbs catalogues without which I simply couldn't have written *Whistlejacket*. Certainly the little section in the middle, probably the best part, is the heart of the book. But that novel tries to confront more directly my own concern with the business of being voyeuristic. I think there is nothing shameful about voyeurism.

I think without voyeurism there would be no life. I think that the hard thing these days is to preserve shame. Shame is an emotion we're in danger of losing. Anxiety and shame are inseparable to me; and they're both inseparable from the word "secret." I think all art must have something to do with the secretive.

RE: Eric Fischl told me that his work was sexual but not erotic because it wasn't freed from anxiety. He thought of your work as being erotic because he felt it was free from anxiety.

DS: It's a different kind of anxiety. Our subjects are really not similar. Ultimately his subject is the social and my subject is something else. I don't know what to call it but I know it's not that. So of course any depiction of sexuality in Eric's work is loaded in the way that it's loaded in the social realm. In my work it's loaded in a mostly personal way. But it's uncoded as much as it's coded and that's probably what people find baffling about it. Eric's work has never been attacked because the sexuality depicted in the paintings is exactly congruent with the sexuality in society. The codes of sexuality are the social codes.

RE: I want to ask you about your reaction to *Whistlejacket*, David. I want to get your sense of how it works.

DS: Well, I like it in the same way that I like many of Jack's other books. It seems to me that the way the novels are made is different from other writers; it's this thing about creating images in a purely imaginary space. Once they're created they become like fixtures in a landscape. The more amazing thing is that then they become conflated with other images which are equally a product of pure invention. It's the malleability in the text that has always struck me. There's a great deal of difference between *Whistlejacket* and *The Blood Oranges*, for example, but they're more the same kind of book than different kinds of books. They're more like each other than they are like anyone else's work. They give rise to a feeling of the utter malleability of the entire world, which is a pretty extreme feeling.

RE: Is the fluidity of composition, the play with time, something you respond to because of the nature of your work?

DS: I don't know why I respond to it but I find it appealing, remarkable, seductive and a little scary too. It's a high risk venture because if you're not saying something that's ultimately palpable people don't get it.

RE: Jack, you say in one of the books that true language is always precious and treacherous at the same time. And whenever I hear you talk about your work, you always seem to operate along a line that frames with those outer edges and then moves inside them.

JH: I think of language as the very substance of existence, let alone of art. Without it, there's really nothing. I love the sound and the taste of the language, the space the language fills, along with its rhythms and its cadences. It's the means of being and creating and I would like all my work to be thought of as erotic. I know that it is, ultimately, even though it may come out of nightmares, out of hostility, it may come out of extreme detachment toward all that's ugly and unpleasant. Each one of those fictions is an act of love in that they resonate with the uniqueness of life itself.

RE: I want to talk about desire and love—and intention. The Canadian poet and novelist Michael Ondaatje has a character in one of his poems say, "I could tell stories that would give erections around the room." Clearly what he's playing with is a very direct way of inviting the audience into a kind of erotic space. Does that notion make any sense of your work?

DS: I'm not looking for that kind of participatory response. I'm just imagining what a viewer is or does or sees. It's a work of fiction on my part. The process is more like the viewer watching my engagement with certain things in a stand-in kind of way. If I think about it—and this just now occurred to me—it's analogous to what's interesting to me about looking at pornography. What's interesting isn't just its functional intent, that is, to get erections in the room. What's interesting is that you're looking at someone who is posed in a certain way so that they can be looked at. In looking at paintings I never like to lose sight of the fact that what you're seeing is something someone did so that it could be seen. In my mind's eye I think that's what I see as the relationship between my work and the audience. One is an amplification of the other. If it has the function that Michael Ondaatje claims for his work, I would say that's just a fringe benefit.

RE: Why do you pose your models the way you do?

DS: The way the models appear in my work, and it's completely consistent with how I work with them as people, is completely sympathetic. There's an engagement almost to the point of their being stand-ins for me, which doesn't necessarily deny or refute the problem of their still being objectified for the male gaze. That's exactly what they are. But there are so many different levels within that general rubric that it doesn't go very far in explaining the specificity of the experience. It's just like there's good seduction and bad seduction. All these things are very mechanical and have nothing to do with the actual experience of the work because they don't address quality.

RE: So you're not talking as a distanced creator who has no relationship at all to the components of the painting. In fact you're talking about them in a very personal way.

DS: I think the idea of a distanced creator who has no relationship to the things he's creating has absolutely nothing to do with anything that actually exists in the world. It doesn't exist. It's a polemical fiction.

JH: I don't think there can be any serious work, painting or otherwise, that doesn't take into account our deepest dilemmas and desires and our actual identification with our criminal selves. The desire to cause arousal is interesting but that's not really the purpose of anything I write, although as I keep insisting, I think what I write is erotic. Of course, in my work the antithesis of sexuality is the erotic. Punched cows in the field are as erotic as the owl's eye or when Stubbs is painting the portrait of that woman and they have a coal grate behind them, and she's sitting in the sunlight and she draws up her skirt and one piece of almost thoroughly burned coal slips and you hear that little whoosh … that is all the eroticism I could ever ask for.

RE: David, what do you you think is erotic?

DS: I don't think my work is particularly erotic. It's not something I'm really going for or feel disappointed if I don't have. The erotic is purely a matter of complicity between someone who gives a signal and someone who notices the signal. The signal could be anything. It's just a question of style and intent. The intent might not even be conscious, and often isn't.

RE: If the work's an invention then you're not duplicating anything out there. You're inventing something in the studio.

DS: That's a given for everybody. There's no art that's like something in the world.

RE: What keeps you interested in an image? Why have you so persistently stayed with the woman's buttocks? Or with the Walter Kuhn images? Why now do Mr. and Mrs. Woodman hold your interest? Do you know?

DS: I'm not being disingenuous in saying this but sometimes it's the way the light falls on something and it's not the thing. That's often the first mistake critics make in writing about my work. It's never the thing. It's not about categorizing things in the world. It's about attitude, presence, presentation, framing, complicity, selection and reflection. And to have all of those qualities focus on an image is not easy. But I think that's what I've done. When someone looks at what I've done and says, "He fetishizes this girl's ass," for example, I don't think that's necessarily unfair because it's a certain way of looking and thinking. But that wouldn't take me very far in my studio in terms of how to make a picture. I'm not asking people to make that distinction; it's not their problem. But if someone were asking that question, they'd go into the studio with that as a kit of instructions—fetishize a girl's ass—and they'd say, okay, here we go, we're going to make a painting now. All of a sudden they'd realize it doesn't tell you very much about what's in the painting, or about what to put in the painting. So clearly that kind of categorizing hasn't quite covered it. Anyway, I'm not comfortable with the word fetish. I don't really know anything about it and in my mind I've stayed away from it.

JH: I've got to hear more about complicity because I'm not sure what that really is. To me, it connotes some kind of partnership in a secret enterprise. It suggests togetherness in the process of a taboo event. "Fetishist" is a word that I love dearly. I probably am a fetishist. I have a great feeling about feet, shoes, boots, Helmut Newton's riding boots, whatever. I don't, however, like the word "ass." And "girl," that's probably a difficult word. But I like the word "girl," so we'll save it. There must be infinite ways to fetishize a woman's buttocks? My narrator in *Whistlejacket* already said this but it is interesting to my mind that this shape is a part of the human anatomy common to both genders. Still, I'm only interested in women's mid-bodies. And the rear mid-body is to me utterly gorgeous because it is the totemic centre of the rest of the body from the genitalia to the breasts, from the shoulders to the thighs; it's the centre of gravity. I love all that.

RE: Tell us more about how the idea of complicity operates as a fulcrum for your notion of aesthetics?

DS: When something's interesting you feel that the maker of it is performing a kind of stand-in operation for the viewer. I just think that's something that happens when you encounter a work that is deeply involving. It certainly doesn't happen cruising through a museum or flipping pages in a book, but when you encounter something that really gets to you I think there's always a point where the maker is performing a stand-in, undergoing something you don't have to undergo, or that you're not capable of undergoing. Take the case of listening to Glenn Gould play a Bach sonata; it seems out of the question that anyone in the history of the earth could do that. It's something that goes further than mere playing. It's something else, some other level of playing. It's the difference between a really communicative dancer and a technically perfect one.

RE: I think complicity is a perfect way to describe what constitutes the erotic. It is that signal between two people.

DS: I think in the case of painting—certainly in the case of realist painting—and probably also in the case of writing, the viewer posits the existence of the painter's world which is somehow above the world that's seen in the painting. That's a sophisticated viewing. It could happen in a naïve way, too. You look at something and you posit the existence of the person who made something visible, even if it's a totally objective geometric abstraction. It's the only reason to look at anything. I'm certainly not going to look at a geometric abstraction in order to talk about how beautiful the formal qualities are. I'm only interested in positing the existence of the guy who made that and why did he think that was an important thing to make. Everything else, as they say in Hollywood, is just conversation.

RE: Do you have obsessions in the work?

DS: I have themes. I have ideas that recur rhythmically. I don't know if any of those things are obsessions. I don't think I have a good enough memory to even have obsessions.

JH: I am obsessed. I think that's safe to say. I don't know what the difference is between thematic insistence and an obsession, but I am obsessed. It's interesting to me in hearing you talk, David, that two people who have something in common can sound so different. You sound abstract and theoretical and highly formal, whereas I sound marvelously emotional. But my work is not marvelously emotional. I'll bet you anything that sometimes in the chaos of my conversation that I'm giving voice to some chaos that you transform in the way you do. At any rate, maybe I'm doing you a real injustice and maybe you are as dispassionate as you sound, but I don't think so.

RE: I want to ask you if love enters into the work? Karole Armitage says, for instance, that sex is everything in her work and she goes on to say that her work and her relationship with you are integrally combined. I'm assuming that somewhere in that mix is some notion of love. She has also fed your work by being a subject you've painted.

DS: I don't know if it has to be love. Let's just say that if it doesn't in some way reflect something like love for a person, for people, for light, or love for the past, then it probably is a rather superficial or empty work.

JH: That word would never cross my mind while trying to write something, but I certainly agree with what David just said, especially about the love of light. I can understand the love of light or of a word but I might really be writing about the love of death. Why not? But love is such a general word that I don't think it has much to do with the actual creative process except the drive to make something. It's simply one way of being alive. I think the artist creates the world; I don't think the artist reflects the world. I was thinking while you were talking about complicity that a very serious relationship exists between the artist and whoever is capable of complicity with that artist. Think of a single man in a dark, shabby theatre, watching a pornographic film; an isolated, deprived, disadvantaged person who has no humanity left. He's surely in complicity with a life that he doesn't have. Now that may not be a justification for the odiousness of pornography but it is an interesting fact. Or the person in prison experiencing some totally appalling debased form of desire is surely closer to artistic impulse than somebody who is just happily strumming the guitar in praise of life. My point is that we have a whole scale of valuable things and I don't want to deny anything that has to do with trying to get from one state to another or with any kind of desire.

RE: Can you have eroticism without shame?

JH: I don't know. I've been thinking about that. I'm not sure you can. You can't have eroticism without secrecy and you can't have eroticism without withholding. Eroticism is illusion. It's the signal sent. It's these signals going back and forth without the actual act.

RE: Is eroticism the secret revealed? Does it operate by gradually unlayering the secret?

JH: Well, it's the secret embodied, or it's the desire embodied. It's the fact that we're capable of desire at all. If you were denied desire, you would be denied eroticism. According to my mentor, Nabokov, if you are denied eroticism, then you're denied purpose. The only kind of fiction he was interested in was the kind that transports us from someplace we are to someplace we've never been. That's what complicity is: to experience something worthwhile that we haven't experienced.

DS: Yes, the only thing worth doing is what's never been done.

Jeff Koons
& Ilona Stoller

The Material Boy and
the Femme Fidele

Jeff Koons and Ilona Stoller were, by all reports, the show-stealers at the 1990 Venice Biennale. The issue of their collaboration, included in the "Aperto" section, was composed of billboard-sized paintings and a larger-than-life-sized polychromed wood sculpture of the lovers memorialized in an erotic swoon. Coiling around their rocky bed and threatening to swallow them up in a fatally attractive embrace was a huge, golden snake. Desire curled up with doom in a post-lapserian, postmodern tableau.

Viewers either loved it or hated it. Critics predicted Koons would be *the* artist of the '90s or they condemned him for going so far beyond the fringe that aesthetic salvation was impossible. There are those who think that in wrapping himself in the arms of Ilona Stoller, a.k.a. Cicciolina, porn-star and sometime Deputy of the Italian Parliament, that Jeff Koons—irrevocably and deservedly—has sealed his fate.

Prior to his collaboration with Stoller, Koons had already established a reputation as one of the bright lights of American art. His earlier work, which included store-bought inflatables, wall appliances, flotation tanks, life jackets and snorkels cast in bronze, and stainless steel rabbits, was a respectful and delightful ransacking of a universe already inhabited by Pop Art, Minimalism and Duchampian readymades. These diverse objects—which Koons has called his "Banality" work—were included in a succession of career-altering exhibitions beginning with The New in 1980 at the Museum of Contemporary Art in New York and coming to a head (all puns are on) in his partnership with Stoller in the late '80s. His polychromed, porcelain portraits of real life and cartoon characters, as different as Michael Jackson and the Pink Panther (although they didn't seem so different in Koon's versions of them), could be read as a good deal of fun and an even goodlier deal of kitsch.

While *Michael Jackson and Bubbles* (referring to his chimpanzee) made up the largest porcelain object in the world and offered its maker a shot at the *Guinness Book of Records*, it wasn't scale that gave this piece its undeniable presence. Koons shares with Andy Warhol an uncanny gift for selection and transformation: he picks the right object and he re-makes it even better. But for Koons, as it was for Warhol, the impulse is not towards a levelling down and the banal (despite the title of one of his most successful exhibitions) but towards a kind of Ur-glitter, a state that partakes variously of glamour, sentimentality, bathos and terror. *Pink Panther* takes the famous cartoon character and drapes him across the upper body of a woman transferred from the pages of a skin magazine; the limp hang of his pink fur and his sad countenance make him seem like a flaccid lawn ornament. The intercourse of these two icons of popular culture—an anthropomorphised panther and a "pet" (or a "playmate")—has a visual charge that quickly ignites the more rambunctious corners of our imagination.

Playing around has a lot to do with Jeff Koon's artistic production, although he is reluctant to engage that issue. This is partially a question of positioning: Koons is the grandchild in the art tribe begat by Duchamp and his first-born, Warhol, and like most members of the third generation, he is determined to appear more serious than he actually is. It's also a question of style: Jeff is so sincere that he's in danger of reversing Ezra Pond's declaration, so that it reads something like "sincerity is the test of a man's technique." His conversation is peppered with words like manipulation, seduction and propaganda and he is given to pronouncements like, "my work will do anything to communicate."

Part of the measure of his current seriousness—not to mention outrageousness—are paintings, billboards, sculptures and ultimately, a film, which take their life from the relationship he enjoys with Ilona Stoller. Together they are documenting their physical life—he calls it his "biological fascination with Ilona"—in what can only be described as "Big Attack Sex." A recent soft-core example of these cheeky mis-en-scene is called, *Ilona With Ass Up (Blue Background)*. Koons, as he often does, stares dreamily out at the viewer while Cicciolina, with her horizon-flat eyebrows and over-ripe lips, throws back a pout that could stop your heart. You needn't ask if the earth moved; all you have to notice is that the sea behind the lovers is in the throes of a Blakean turbulence that has had the added effect of angering a large monitor lizard (is this a stage set for "*Knight of the Iguana*"?) who wanders in from the left. Whatever garden these two lovers find themselves in, there always seems to be a reptile of some sort lurking in the background.

The following interview with Jeff Koons took place on two separate occasions: part one was done in May 1989 after Koons had given a lecture on his work at the Chicago International Art Exposition; part two was conducted by telephone in December, 1990 when he was working in his Munich studio. Part three, the conversation with Ilona Stoller, was recorded (with the help of a translator) in Winnipeg in September, 1990 when she was performing as "Cicciolina" at Centrefold's Showbar. Both Mr. Koons and Ms. Stoller were patient, accommodating and charming. Separately and together they are in the process of creating an entertaining and bewildering combination of art, arrogance and social interrogation. At this stage it may be that their collaboration embodies a series of questions: at what point does innocence become indulgent adolescence; what's the connection between art and getting your rocks off; what is the line of tolerance between privacy and publicity; how do we decide when one person's romance becomes another person's pornography; who is more sinned against than sinning; are these two for real? And so on … Koons may not be offering answers to these questions; so far he may simply be the Material Boy, giving us the stuff to ask them in the first place.

Part One

ROBERT ENRIGHT: I can't recall in recent memory an artist who has generated as much controversy as you. Critics don't know what to do with your work. When you started making the most recent pieces did you have any idea they were going to involve you in a heated debate about the validity and nature of the work you do?

JEFF KOONS: I never started with the intention of making work that would be scandalous or create turmoil. What I specifically did do was to try and create a body of work that removed the options for the viewer. Somewhere, whether through the sexuality, the spirituality, its colour, or maybe its romanticism—somewhere the viewer would just put his guard down and embrace the work and let the work communicate.

RE: You say embrace the work. The other possibility is that they'll reject it entirely, finding it grotesque or outrageous or irreverent.

JK: The only thing I'm trying to accomplish is to have my work communicate. I am not even being specific about the information. My work will do absolutely anything to communicate. What is being communicated is not important at this time. I just want to make art be as strong a vehicle as possible for manipulation, seduction and propaganda.

RE: Those are pretty loaded words. Are you suggesting that you really do control the reins of the viewer's reaction?

JK: Any response that's taking place is intentional. If there's a sense of vulgarity in my work, I've placed it there. Artists were always the masters but they gave up the great tools of being able to seduce and manipulate. Other industries—advertising and entertainment—have gained these tools and continue to exploit them. As a result, they have a very strong power base. Somebody working for an advertising firm or in the entertainment industry is in a position to be much more politically effective than the artist. Art has become impotent and I would like to change that.

RE: You talk a lot about sexuality in the work and you clearly exploit icons of sexuality. You'll appropriate an image from German *Penthouse* and collage it onto the Pink Panther. How much emphasis do you want to put on the question of seduction?

JK: The work in my Banality show is based on my viewing the Masaccio painting called *Expulsion from Eden*. I tried to remove bourgeois guilt and shame in responding to banality and dislocated imagery. The best vehicle for me to be able to do that is to operate on the level of sexuality.

RE: How do you want the viewer to respond to a work like *Pink Panther*?

JK: The work wants to meet their needs. It wants to meet their needs and create new needs which they would then be dependent upon art to meet. I am trying to make art be competitive in our contemporary society.

RE: How much will you push it? The images are fairly tame. There's no real raunch, no real exploitation of sexuality. Why haven't you gone further with it?

JK: What I've tried to do is recognize my limitations. I am trying to exploit myself and I also have to accept the responsibility of exploiting my audience. Artists over centuries have totally lost the responsibility of communicating and exploiting. They have to accept that they must first be a victim of society in order to absorb society and to interact with it, to break down the barriers. Then they must grab the responsibility to victimize others.

RE: Can you compete with the fashion and advertising industries? They have all the vehicles, they have the persistence and presence that your work—in limited editions in gallery spaces and even in publications—is not likely to have?

JK: You don't penetrate the mainstream through distribution; you penetrate the mainstream with ideas. Artists are the masters. If we want to be politically effective in the world we can do it.

RE: I'm reminded of a notion from Romantic poetry that artists are the unacknowledged legislators of the world. But they've remained unrecognized. Do you actually think artists are the masters and that what you're introducing is an age in which they will have gained new respect from a much larger audience?

JK: I'm not interested in positioning or in self-righteousness. But I am interested in political power and in the possibilities of art to manipulate. What communicative forum is left for art? What can it be? It can never compete with computer systems; it can't compete as a system for the storage of information. The only thing left for art to do is to be the most manipulative industry possible.

RE: Are you saying that right now it doesn't matter what the content is? Ultimately a message is going to have to be given. How do you decide what that message is going to be?

JK: I have a certain moral position on content, but that's not the most important thing. Effectiveness is. I'm an optimist. I believe things that are positive for mankind will survive and that negative things will be destroyed. If art gains this position and uses its great tools improperly, then other industries will compete and will destroy. But if art uses these tools positively for mankind, it will survive.

RE: It's a kind of aesthetic Darwinism?

JK: Yes.

RE: How do you decide what it is you want to use as subject matter, though? Michael Jackson turns up, images from soft-core porn magazines turn up, as does a whole range of popular icons. What attracts you to certain things?

JK: I go through a period of letting things resonate within myself. I end up using what I see as able to meet the public's needs.

RE: One of the images you ran as an advertisement in selected art magazines contained the message, "exploit the masses," as if you were a glitzy Jenny Holzer.

JK: My statement "exploit the masses" was part of an ad for *Artforum* magazine. The image shows me in front of a classroom of kindergarten children from different ethnic backgrounds and I am indoctrinating them into my political philosophy of art: exploit the masses, increase the power base. That ad was targeted at the audience of *Artforum*, and it was saying that if they couldn't absorb the idea that art must be more effective, then they were just like the children in the room with me. Also I felt that the people who already hated Jeff Koons or hated my ideas would just grit their teeth because I was stealing their future.

RE: I'm a bit puzzled. You talk as if your personality or ego has been subsumed by some kind of system of generosity.

JK: I believe in generosity. Artists must give, must reach deep and give everything they have. I also believe that I can be impetuous and run off in certain areas that are different from what my personal tastes may be. But this is because my work is separate from Jeff Koons. Jeff Koons is a person who has a private life.

RE: Do they overlap?

JK: In some areas they do; in some areas they don't. One area that I've always tried to keep distant is when art becomes a masturbative process. That's where I can get lost, indulge in something and go down the wrong path.

RE: Let's talk about another of your advertisements. What kind of play was going on in the piece in which you're surrounded by a clutch of bikini-clad girls?

JK: *Art in America* did the ad. I'm on a live, miniature pony and the pony is baying. I have one girl giving me a cake and another holding the head of the pony. It could be a symbol of the aristocracy offering me all its riches: "Yes, Jeff, you're clever, we want you, we can use you." But I'm looking off in the distance, still interested in love or something. The idea was to place myself as the saviour. Even though I wasn't on a donkey, I tried to place myself in a Christ-like manner.

RE: The inversion of religious iconography comes up a lot in your work. What is its source?

JK: I want to give a sense of security and a sense of authority in trying to meet people's needs. One of my favourite pieces is *St. John the Baptist*, which is taken from Leonardo's *St. John*. But mine has a pig in one arm and a penguin in the other. He's there to baptize in banality; he's an authoritarian figure there to remove the guilt and shame. I did another ad in *Arts Magazine* that I'm also proud of. I'm sitting beside a pool flanked by two live seals and they have flowered lais around their necks. Behind me is a cabana very similar to Caesar's tent and I have on a black robe with a Napoleon style "N" monogram. This ad was also targeted to the specific audience of the magazine in which it appeared. *Arts Magazine* has always been a vehicle in which young artists have been able to participate in the commercial art world; it's here where people first see their work and where they get their first reviews. What I tried to accomplish with this ad was to assume the responsibility of leadership of the art world. I declared myself King, even though my subjects may just be these seals.

RE: How much fun are you having in the process of making these pieces and setting yourself in these theatrical *mises en scène*?

JK: I enjoy creating and participating in the ads. These are my ideas and I enjoy the total coordination of things. I believe in using the tools. Why don't we use the entertainment industry; why aren't we using Hollywood more? I know that sexuality is effective. I'm going to use sexuality. The girls in bikinis are effective.

RE: You're not worried about questionable means justifying questioning ends? You're prepared to use anything in your work?

JK: My work will use absolutely anything. It cares only for the end.

RE: What about a startling little piece like *Naked*? It has two young children—they look like Hummel figures—who are both nude and the young boy is holding a bouquet which includes a fairly sexual flower. It seems entirely to have absorbed the young girl's attention. What is it that you're getting at in that particular figure? How does it free the viewer from guilt?

JK: They're also sitting on a heart which has flowers on it. The boy has the bouquet in front of him and is gazing slightly above it; the girl is looking past the bouquet. She's actually looking down directly at his penis. I was dealing with the concept of original sin and with sex.

RE: You talk about vulnerability on the one hand and authoritarian control on the other. I sense in those two positions an irreconcilable contradiction.

JK: My work enjoys contradiction. My work is totally involved in negotiation. You may think it appears to be very black and white but if you look more closely the work deals totally within the grey.

RE: Let's talk about where the grey is in the Michael Jackson piece.

JK: Part of the grey is that it's the largest porcelain piece in the world. So I'll get in the *Guinness Book of World Records*. The technology used in creating that piece is also part of the grey. For me to be able to place Michael and Bubbles in a baroque, rococco setting where he is truly white, is wonderful. Again I'm just exploiting the information that Michael works with.

RE: Are you worried about the question of taste? A lot of your sources are classical paintings and they are asked to be part of a dialogue that contains some pretty low objects.

JK: I don't see a Hummel figurine as tasteless. I see it as beautiful and respond to it. I truly love the sentimentality in the work. I love the finish, how simple the colour green can be painted. I like things just being seen for what they are. It's like laying in the grass and taking a deep breath. That's all my work is trying to do, to be as enjoyable as that breath.

RE: Do you pay much attention to the critical responses to your work?

JK: I do pay attention to the writing. Some of my favourite lines have been negative. Hilton Kramer, as an example, has said, "This is the lowest of the low, things are at an all-time bottom." But then he goes on to associate me with my great heroes, saying this was inevitable because Jasper Johns painted the flag and Warhol painted Marilyn, so of course Jeff Koons will come along and do Michael Jackson. I am also very interested in the idea of the teflon coating: no matter how much you're attacked, it can only help. This is something that artists have to be able to develop so that we can move forward and be as strong as possible.

RE: Just spell my name right, even if it's critical?

JK: Well, it's not just the promotion. It's the dialogue. I'm not interested in Jeff Koons being famous; I'm interested in Jeff Koons being able to communicate. If fame is part of that, then it's a necessary requirement for me as a professional. It's important that a dialogue about the art take place. I don't even know if what I'm doing is valid. I have my own doubts. But I'm moving forward and giving as much as I can give. I know my limitations and I feel strong because of that knowledge.

Part Two

ROBERT ENRIGHT: In the December issue of *Vanity Fair* you and Cicciolina were chosen as part of the 1990 Hall of Fame. The photographs were taken by Annie Leibovitz and in one you look like an image out of *Goldfinger*. You're naked and you look positively fourteen carat. How did that photograph come about?

JEFF KOONS: Ilona and I were doing matrimonial shots underneath some wedding flowers and then Annie got the idea to have us painted gold. It was really quite an ordeal and after a while both Ilona and I became a little sick from the fumes. So she stopped being photographed and I continued. I was just clowning around, more or less making art photos.

RE: So having your red tongue sticking out so that you look like a serpent being tossed out of a lucrative garden of Eden was just a sense of play on your part?

JK: I remember looking at Ilona and noticing that her eyes were very very pink, simply because of the nature of the skin there. Then I looked at her mouth and could see the pink on the inside. It was all just to heighten the pink.

RE: The other photograph in the magazine has the two of you embracing and you have a look of contentment on your face that is almost goofy. You're completely charmed and you look positively youthful.

JK: I'm usually smiling when I'm in the presence of Ilona because I love her very much. But I've also been working out now for a little over a year; I spend two hours a day in training and I do free weights and aerobics. I'm thirty-five at this moment and will be thirty-six in January. I imagine one of the reasons for the youthful presence is the working out. It's just that my physique can be a little baroque. So when I make the film or when I'm in my photo sessions and somebody looks at my body, I want my back not to be boring. It also enhances sexual pleasure tremendously. It heightens your endurance.

RE: So your motivation is double-barrelled—aesthetic and romantic?

JK: That's correct. It's for my own self-esteem and for my own pleasure. It's very hedonistic.

RE: How far along is the *Made in Heaven* film?

JK: Everything's still in pre-production and there hasn't been any shooting. It's been a slower process than I anticipated because I've run into a lot of difficulties with the production of my sculptures and my paintings. These difficulties have set me back financially to the point where I'm producing the work so that I can have the freedom to make the film.

RE: Do you have a pretty clear outline of what's going to be in the film?

JK: I have an outline but as far as having every word finished and every "i" dotted, no. The actual script does not exist. But the concept, what wants to be communicated, the basic settings for the film—all that has been taken care of. Ilona and I have already done several photo shoots in the line of fantasy we plan to take the film. I would say to a *maximum* in that direction. So we've performed sexually together well in advance of the film.

RE: What is it that wants to be communicated in the film and is being communicated in the completed photo-works?

JK: I think the main information is that people do not have to live with frustrated desire, that if they remove guilt and shame from their lives, they'll find fear has been removed as well. And when people remove fear, they're able to be effective in the world because they're in the moment. And when one's in the moment, one can come in contact with the objective, can come in contact with love. They also start to listen to their environment and learn that they can manipulate their environment and find beauty in the most simple things in life.

RE: They're almost billboard-sized paintings. They look like updated advertisements for 1940s romantic movies. But how far are you prepared to go with regard to documenting explicit sex?

JK: I showed soft ones in Venice, and the reason I showed soft was because I wanted to give only a tip of the iceberg as far as my vocabulary goes. But Ilona and I have done hard photo sessions. We started to work together in the very beginning of '89, drew up agreements for the shoots and did our first photo session in the early fall. I've shown some of them—the cover of *Art Press* had a hard photo on the cover and people who have visited my studios have seen a range, including *Glass Dildo*, which is a beautiful image of me penetrating Ilona with a glass dildo. You can see all the way up inside Ilona because light travels through it, so you see her inner skin which is absolutely beautiful. I like that photo. I was concerned that it might be a little too subjective, too tied to masturbation, but the realm of the objective does come through and it turned out to be one of my most successful ones.

RE: Ilona has described you as her private porno star. I gather the effect of *Made in Heaven* will be to somehow make you less than private in that regard. You'll have become a public figure in quite a graphic way?

JK: Well, I've always been interested in communicating to the public. Ever since my Equilibrium show in 1985 I've become more of a public figure and that has continued into the Banality exhibition. I would imagine that will continue on a greater scale. But to jump back to Ilona saying I'm a porno star: we really do have wonderful shared sexual moments together. I have always felt extremely confident with Ilona, always felt biologically connected to her. As a result I've had the confidence to go to my inner depths and to be generous with Ilona in return.

RE: You've said that she's managed to help you do away with any residue of shame that you may have had.

JK: I think that Ilona and I help each other. Ilona has helped me share beauty in the most simple things and I enjoy that. She shows beauty to me every moment. But I think that we've really been able to give gifts to each other. She's given me the low and I've been able to give her the high. People have been able to look at Ilona and say this woman is fantastic. I guess she is one of the greatest artists in the world. The articulation of the genitalia is a very accurate and precise vocabulary.

RE: She has a rather touching way of describing herself. She feels she's the eternal virgin. On the surface of things you wouldn't assume that to be an apt self-description.

JK: Ilona has always seemed like the eternal virgin to me. I stated that during the Banality show.

RE: So she borrowed the description from you?

JK: Well, no. Ilona told me she had always felt that way. You see, she carries no guilt and no shame and because of that she is eternally pure. Sexually pure.

RE: The polychromed piece that you included in the Biennale call *Jeff and Ilona: Made in Heaven*, has a rather prominent crucifix that tips back into the curve of her neck. I wonder how you mean the viewer to read that? Do you intend to provoke a sense of violation or outrage? What people see is a woman wearing a crucifix engaged in the abandoned afterglow of a sexual act. Do you want a sense of transgression? Transgression, by the way, is a word that Ilona uses a fair amount when she describes her own performances.

JK: I've always looked at everything as a ready-made. When I originally became interested in Ilona just on an artistic level, it was because things were already ready-made. She was already wearing the cross on her neck. I wanted to be sure to use it when we did our photo session, but she wore it naturally. I think she stopped wearing it about six months ago because she chose to give the cross to her mother. But because it highlighted a spiritual element in the work, it interested me very much. I'm interested in communicating and revealing beauty to people, but I'm not really interested in shocking them.

RE: So you wouldn't consider what you're doing as pornographic?

JK: No. The origin of pornography is tied to the act of prostitution. My definition of pornography is alienation. I find things that alienate one from life pornographic. And my work has never, in any manner, tried to alienate people from life itself. If anything, I've tried to show the beauty in life. I would never show an image of a cherry dripping honey because that would be alienating. I would much rather show the beauty of a closeup of the genitalia. It's absolutely beautiful, like a closeup of a flower.

RE: You cross over quite easily then between what you call soft- and hard-core in your collaboration?

JK: I found making the first photo session to be one of the most liberating experiences of my life. When you make a hard photo session there are normally at least seven people present, sometimes as many as ten. It's hard to explain why it's so liberating but making this hidden act in a public manner is quite good for self-esteem. When you make a hard session you feel able to make many other actions in life.

RE: It's a challenging time to be making art like this. While you don't consider the work pornographic in any way, I assume Jessie Helms and his moral carpet-baggers wouldn't agree. Are you at all concerned about the climate in America and the fact that you're going head on—if that's not an inappropriate pun—against the mores of middle America?

JK: The environment that I've worked in has never really changed. I've been dealing with the eternal virgin since I displayed The New with my vacuum cleaner. The Equilibrium show dealt more with the biological side of consumerism and social existence, but then in Banality the imagery was more sexual. I had Ilona with bare breasts; I had the pink panther naked and the two naked kids. I was using sexuality as the most direct reference to guilt and shame in the Banality show, but I'm really not interested in getting too caught up in the pornography debate. I'm interested in communicating beauty, and I will never stop participating in that dialogue. I really don't want to get involved in specific, political aspects of making the work.

RE: *Woman in Tub* was included in the Banality show as well. It has a Wesselman quality about it. The open mouth and the cheeky high-lustre sexuality of the bather makes me think more of Pop Art than the Duchampian tradition you come out of.

JK: The piece comes from a postcard and the woman is cut right where the postcard is cut. Her mouth is open in the postcard, too. I played on that also because it was a reference to how we confuse the victim and the victimizer: you look at the scene, you see that she's being victimized but as a viewer you want to participate. One of the things I like about Ilona's performances too, especially when she pee-pees on the audience, is that the audience is there enjoying their own kind of subversiveness in watching one of her "spectaculars of love." You must really love an audience to be able to abandon physical barriers. Ilona has tremendous capacity for love, but when she pee-pees on the stage all of a sudden the audience becomes her victim. It's really quite a beautiful sharing experience.

RE: She wouldn't have been able to do anything that radical in Canada but what she did do when she performed in Winnipeg was to insinuate homosexual relationships between male members of the audience. Suddenly what had been light banter took on a slightly more sinister cast. Is that strategic on her part?

JK: I think Ilona is very, very intelligent and she knows how to create the best environment for her ideas to be communicated.

RE: How often do you two meet?

JK: It's difficult right now in that Ilona cannot enter the United States, despite our vigorous attempts. We were just in Rome together but I had to come to Munich and Ilona stayed in Rome. We both have our professional lives which we continue. But we are going to be married in February, on St. Valentine's Day. That's why we were just in Rome. We finished our paperwork, handed everything in and gave the official announcement.

RE: Is it going to be a huge wedding or a discreet one?

JK: No, relatively small. I think that we plan to have about 150 people.

RE: As a couple you've managed to attract much more than your allotted fifteen minutes of fame.

JK: I'm going to bypass that comment: Ilona is part of my life and I'm part of her life and we have a continuing discourse with the world around us. The way I've chosen to go about intermixing my personal life and my professional life is something I've enjoyed very much. I'm excited about it because I enjoy life.

RE: How do you view your professional relationship with Ilona?

JK: I think of us as collaborators. There's a certain territory of product which is hers and a certain territory which is mine and then there's this cross-territory. I've appeared in *Diva Futura*—a hard-core Italian publication and Ilona has appeared in art magazines.

RE: When we first talked I remember that you said your work was separate from Jeff Koons, that Jeff Koons is a person who has a private life. It occurs to me that the relationship that you have with Ilona has made it more difficult to keep the two Jeff Koons separate?

JK: I don't know that there is much of the *personal* person left anymore. Only because I haven't chosen to keep my identity there. In the beginning it had to do with trying, in the face of all this cynicism, to let people know that I believed you could create something unique and new. I think the Equilibrium exhibition showed that to the public and I think the public really caught on when they saw the Banality show. It was a creative effort in spite of all the postmodern skepticism and cynicism.

RE: Did you find that people are still skeptical about the relationship between you and Ilona?

JK: I find in general that a lot of people are skeptical about me. I think people have been very skeptical about Ilona, but if anybody gets close enough they can see the beauty that she's able to generate. Not only is she physically the most beautiful woman in the world but intellectually and spiritually she's one of the most pure people I've ever met. She has a lot of confidence and very little fear.

RE: Do you still have fear and insecurity?

JK: I think that everyone carries fear and insecurity. While it's very difficult to remove I am enjoying life to a greater extent than I ever have. I've come to realize the things that are necessary to be in the moment. I also took acting lessons for about six months and the experience was very beneficial. I stopped about six months ago, only because I got tied down in the creation of the work for the Banality exhibition and had to spend more time in Europe.

RE: Were the acting lessons a way of preparing yourself for the film work?

JK: They were in preparation for the film but I also found them therapeutic in that they taught me to deal with just the self and to respond to things naturally. It's really very much about being in the moment.

RE: Is it also about discipline?

JK: I don't know about discipline.

RE: Can you recall your first meeting with Ilona? She said you sent her a fax to arrange it.

JK: I probably did first send a fax. Or I had my translator call. At first our communication was on very shaky ground, so everything had to be handled through a translator. I faxed her at the very end of 1988. I was already speaking about Ilona on the videotapes of my Banality show and in interviews I was saying that she was one of the greatest artists in the world, an artist who used her genitalia the way other artists use paintbrushes. Michael Jackson and Ilona were my two favourite artists. So we met in January of 1989 and decided we were going to make up a photo session together. I thought they would be very beautiful and magical.

RE: When you first saw her performance she wasn't aware you were in the audience. She says she actually sat on your lap, not knowing it was you?

JK: Well, I went backstage even before the performance. But when she sat on my lap I didn't respond too strongly because I really didn't want to abuse Ilona in any way. I didn't know how to respond so I gave her a cute smile.

RE: Her recollection is that you very gently touched her breasts, that you seemed very much a gentleman, or maybe coy.

JK: I think I touched her ass.

RE: So much for coyness.

JK: I was developing a fascination for my biological connection to Ilona. I think I'd been interested in her since 1988. When we made our first hard photo session she enjoyed the sex very much and fell in love with me then. We continued to make sex even when the photographer, Riccardo Schicchi, was rewinding his camera, or changing the lights, or when he left the room for a half hour on some other project or other. It was really quite beautiful.

RE: Do you consider yourself a romantic? Apart from the physical attraction I'm trying to get a sense of what made things click before you even met her.

JK: I responded to her sexuality, her desire and her creativeness in sex. I would look at her and feel that she was my biological mate. I would look at Ilona's feet. Do you know that Ilona's feet are beautiful and these are the feet I envision when we have a child? And we look forward to having a child next year.

RE: And you've never been married before? That's romantic, too.

JK: I gave a talk at Sotheby's about a month ago and Yoko Ono came up to me afterwards and said she thought it was very, very beautiful and that it reminded her very much of she and John. I thought it was a beautiful compliment and it meant a lot to me.

RE: There is one final thing. Ilona's most famous statement is her offer to go to bed with Saddam Hussein as a way of securing some peace in the Persian Gulf. How did you react to that declaration? I guess I'm asking an old-fashioned question about jealousy.

JK: I thought it was really quite beautiful and it had a tremendous amount of penetration. Johnny Carson spoke about it on the *Tonight Show*, it was on CNN, it hit the world media. Ilona was able to release some of the tension in the air. It was a very sincere statement and if she had been able to participate and be able to help in any manner, I would have been behind her one hundred percent.

RE: So the notion of being faithful to one another is not something that's part of your relationship?

JK: I think that we are both very *fidele* with each other. But these areas are really in the mind and aren't based on any type of physicality.

RE: Do you see an endless potential for art-making in your collaboration? Are there places still to go in your artistic relationship?

JK: I think Ilona and I have a tremendous amount of beauty to find in life. Areas of interest continue to change and I would imagine just as my work has changed in the last decade, it will continue to change in the future. The vocabulary will change, the medium will change. But I believe that Ilona and I are going to share and communicate and work directly for the rest of our lives.

Part Three

ILONA STOLLER: I met Jeff in 1988. He sent me a fax because he wanted to collaborate with me.

ROBERT ENRIGHT: Was it on the basis of your performances that he wanted to collaborate?

IS: When he sent the fax he simply stated that he wanted to meet me in order to introduce himself as a sculptor and painter. He wanted to make a sculpture of me so my manager, Riccardo Schicchi, invited him to Milan where I was working. Jeff came to the show and he sat down in the front row. I didn't know he was there. And while I was singing a song, I sat on his knees. He didn't touch me oddly like the rest of the people in the audience. He just very gently felt my breasts. Then he left while I was performing. I didn't know who he was.

RE: If you'd known who he was, would you have acted differently?

IS: I would have done exactly the same thing.

RE: Describe one of your performances.

IS: It's a special show. I sing and talk about the problems of drugs and AIDS, about prostitution, about the freedoms of sexuality and gay rights with respect to both sexes.

RE: So while you discuss these serious social subjects you also fondle yourself?

IS: Yes, of course. I apply those freedoms literally.

RE: Is there a point to the performances? Do they have a shape—a beginning, a middle and end? Are they choreographed or are they spontaneous?

IS: Mostly improvised. It depends on the audience.

RE: Do you actually make love during a performance?

IS: I've never made love on stage. It's very transgressive to do and it's also against Italian law. Even touching and fondling is a transgression against the law. But going back to the first encounter with Jeff: we were alone with Jeff's secretary, Marina. After a deep exchange of opinions he expressed the fact that he was very in love with me.

RE: So quickly?

IS: Si, yes, very much. I found him very attractive and also very intelligent and very talented.

RE: Jeff is a protestant, middle-class American. You were raised Catholic in Europe and you have a completely different attitude towards sexuality than most North Americans. Where was the sympathy between you?

IS: I went with Jeff and the photographer to shoot some nude photographs and perhaps to find out how deep the understanding was between us. From the outset Jeff had in mind to do this sculpture of the two of us because of the upcoming Venice Biennale. The next step was to take hard-core pictures in the very act of love. This is for an exhibition being planned for 1991 in New York. Of course, the real spark was the sex itself. Jeff's a very, very sensitive person and he likes very much to make love.

RE: So he's a good lover?

IS: He's an incredible lover. We make love under the eyes of the camera and it's very intense, very involved. Since then we have established this rapport and we meet whenever we can—in Argentina, in Canada, everywhere. And of course, I can now say that love is born.

RE: Was the filmmaking with Jeff different from the filmmaking you did when you made pornographic films?

IS: Yes. The difference is in the artistic roots and the love and attraction that is between us. Jeff and I feel that the movie will not simply be restricted to the porno audience but will touch people at large. And I have to say that Jeff is not a porno star, even though he's a good lover. Without diminishing his great porno star capabilities, he's my private porno star. He does have a very strong penis, a beautiful penis. In itself it is a sculpture. And he knows how to use it.

RE: Do you consider your earlier film work as pornographic?

IS: No. I was very well-known in Italy five years ago. I'd already appeared in about fifteen erotic movies, but certainly not pornographic ones. Pornography is a small part of Cicciolina. Cicciolina is made up of many things: she sings, she dances, she does interviews. And politics.

RE: Do you think of yourself as Jeff's muse, as his source of inspiration?

IS: I think that Jeff takes me very seriously and he is very much in love with me and with my artistic expression. Jeff's explanation is very simple. "He," being the artist that he is, expresses himself through sculptures or paintings. "I," being the actress I am, express myself by genitalia. Always quoting Jeff, I became a piece of art and I am so very happy that I could be a source of inspiration for him. According to various newspapers, Cicciolino has her own place in the mythology of the world.

RE: Jeff says that together you two represent the contemporary Adam and Eve. He says your spiritual and sexual union makes you not just close to God, but God-like. Do you agree with those kinds of declarations?

IS: Yes. I agree with Jeff. We are Adam and Eve in the terrestrial paradise.

RE: Is it your intention to take the message of the film *Made in Heaven*, along with the paintings and sculpture that come out of it, and use them as a platform to declare the need for open sexuality in the world?

IS: I think that the film will play a good part in allowing humanity to free itself from today's taboos about sex. By doing so hopefully we'll be helping everyone with sexuality and self-expression. That's the reason why there is no pornography within the film.

RE: It's not an explicit film? No ejaculation, no orgasm.

IS: Ejaculation, yes.

RE: So would it be considered hard-core pornography in America?

IS: No. Nevertheless it goes to the fullest of expression. Being true love it would be considered a normal expression of the senses.

RE: Are you a good actress?

IS: I like to be judged by the people.

RE: But what do you feel about your ability to act?

IS: I have been working for sixteen years and I have been in crescendo. I can tell you now that I am really landing in paradise with Jeff.

RE: So you believe in romance?

IS: Yes. I'm a very romantic person, I receive flowers from all over the world from many admirers. I like people who are also romantic and of course Jeff fits that.

RE: Do you have any conception of shame? One of the things that Jeff said you helped him with was removing all shame or anxiety from sex.

IS: I am the eternal virgin. What Jeff has done is to confirm what I really am. I always maintained that my various movies were the expression of my innocence.

RE: How did you become so free in your attitudes?

IS: My emancipation started very early. My father and my mother walked naked in our household and never felt shame. In Budapest at the age of thirteen, I was a photo model and I was naked. I appeared naked for the first time in Italian discotheques, naturally breaking new ground about sexuality. I have always been the object of attacks from conservatives and have been arrested various times by the police. They charged that my shows were obscene because I was avant-garde. Recently, I made an application to enter the United States and they rejected me. I think they might be afraid that I would be a prophet, the Messiah of liberated sex.

Christo
& Jeanne-Claude

Now You See It,
Now You Don't

Anyone foolish enough to attempt pinning a categorical tail on the extraordinary donkey of the art of Christo and Jeanne-Claude is bound to make an ass of himself. *Valley Curtain*, *Running Fence*, *The Pont-Neuf*, *Wrapped Coast*, *Surrounded Islands*—what are these magnificent, improbable projects: environmental art, public relations gambits, process art, lyric interventions in the landscape, clever variations on the commodification of art, or large-scale continuations of the tradition of drapery painting?

Enthusiasts and detractors have lined both sides of the aesthetic boulevard to comment throughout the almost thirty-five years during which Christo—and since 1961 his wife Jeanne-Claude—have been variously packaging, wrapping, surrounding and redefining their unique objects, places and environments.

It has been an unparalleled activity. From the time of their first high-profile project—*Wrapped Coast* in 1969—in which a million square feet of erosion control fabric and thirty-six miles of rope were used to "wrap" a section of Little Bay outside Sydney, Australia, they have been collaborative artists of apparently limitless imagination and defiant achievement.

I know of few artists in this century—or any other for that matter—who have so thoroughly challenged our notions of what it is that constitutes a work of art. Their art is essentialist, reducing whatever they deal with to its definitive elements. In wrapping things, they effect a surprising paradox: the subject is not so much obscured as more clearly defined; the Pont-Neuf was never so much a bridge as when they orchestrated its respectful bondage; *Valley Curtain*, 1970–72, with its 200,000 square feet of bright orange fabric made the landscape of Colorado an improbably dramatic stage set; *Running Fence*, 1972–76, became a dazzling line that perfectly highlighted the undulating hill country of Sonoma and Marin counties in California; it was as if they took drawing for a light walk. There is something magical about the look of their projects: in the act of obliterating the distinction between process and product, they have been able to make art of exquisite beauty; *Running Fence, Surrounded Islands*, 1980–83, and *The Umbrellas*, 1984–91 have been gorgeous manifestations—there's no other way to describe them.

The Umbrellas, Japan–USA was their first project for two countries, a sort of international diptych in a startling palette of blue and yellow that was also a commentary on the way people of different cultures inhabit space. As usual, we're back in the universe of polyglot definition: it was a space painting; an urban development project; a meditation on the functional elegance of the umbrella; a dialogue between artist and landscape; a simple indulgence in the blueness and yellowness of being. Christo and Jeanne-Claude give us the presence of their sensibility and what a rare gift it continues to be.

A section from the following interview with Christo was broadcast on the CBC Radio program "The Arts Tonight" in October of 1991, just a few days before *The Umbrellas* blossomed.

ROBERT ENRIGHT: I want to talk about wrapping. What effect does wrapping objects have on our overall perception of them?

CHRISTO: Basically wrapping gave the essential dimensions and proportions of the object. For example, in 1985 when we finally wrapped the Pont-Neuf in Paris, the bridge became the essence of a bridge and everything around it became ethereal. All the details, the figures and the elements of the original Pont-Neuf disappeared and what became visible were the principal proportions, the arches, the volume of the towers. This applies only to wrapped projects. It's important not to confuse projects like the *Surrounded Islands* and certainly not *The Umbrellas* with wrapping. They have a completely different dimension.

RE: But you've wrapped everything from typewriters to telephones; you've wrapped newspapers, storefronts, armchairs, you've even wrapped women. What makes you decide what it is you're going to use? Is it capriciousness, is it a passion for the object?

CH: These objects that you mention are all works from 1958 to the middle of 1960 and I don't do this kind of thing anymore. When that work was done it certainly had meaning for me, including the humble bottle, a can, a woman, a wrapped tree. They always had elements which were personally very inspiring.

RE: So these are autobiographical elements from your life then?

CH: Artists always do something very personal to them. Not only in our case.

RE: So when we look at the larger projects—like Pont-Neuf in Paris or your ongoing attempts to try and wrap the Reichstag—what is it about those particular monuments that is so personally appealing to you?

CH: We do all these projects to challenge our notions about art, to enlarge and continually pose the fundamental question, "What is art?" In the case of Pont-Neuf you can view it as a large sculpture—a three-hundred-metre-long sculpture that has a classical form. But the Pont-Neuf was also a bridge. It functioned as a bridge, people were walking over it, boats were passing underneath. What we were really trying to do was to borrow space which had never been part of the art experience. A classical modern sculpture like a Calder has its own space, we can walk around inside, we can play with the form but the space Calder created belongs to the sculpture. What we're doing with this project is to borrow the space of architecture, urban planning and urban design and make them become an intricate part of the art experience. Of course, we did not choose just any bridge in Paris. We precisely chose the Pont-Neuf because it was one of the most successful urban designs in Paris, designed four hundred years ago by the same architect who built the Louvre. A very unusual bridge with intricate designs but with a tremendous magnetic power of movement. When the Pont-Neuf became a temporary work of art for those two weeks all the energy of the people who lived in Paris and who used the bridge became part of the art experience.

RE: Where do the ideas come from? What makes you want to do one thing and not another?

CH: In all of our projects we are slow thinkers. In the particular case of Pont-Neuf you must remember that I lived in Paris for six years and that my wife is French. We only emigrated to the United States in 1964 and we had done a small project in Paris in 1962 called *The Iron Curtain*, which was a wall of oil barrels closing off the Rue Visconti. We had always contemplated returning to Paris and we were looking for something to do which was much more meaningful to us. From a distance we could see that one of the principal elements of the city is that silver line of the river. When the Romans arrived they discovered people living on the island and the city grew from that little island. After the bridge was built in the sixteenth century it immediately became the subject of inspiration for thousands of artists. For four hundred years right up through the Impressionists and the Cubists, the Pont-Neuf has inspired paintings and engravings and drawings but it had never been a work of art itself. This was what we were trying to do: to close that circle of four hundred years of inspiration and art. Of course we purposely tried to find a cultural subject because Paris is not a military or a religious city; it's not a financial centre; it's a city of culture and art. So it was essential to find a focal point that was intimately related to art. This is why we didn't wrap the Eiffel Tower or L'Arc de Triomphe or Sacre Coeur, because they are not part of the deep texture of living in Paris.

RE: Let's shift continents and talk about a pair of projects—*Surrounded Islands* and that miraculous project you did in Sonoma and Marin Counties in California, *Running Fence*. What was it about them that appealed to you? Neither have the kind of artistic or historical pedigree that inspired Pont-Neuf.

CH: All of our projects really do come from very unusual inspirations. In 1970 I was invited to lecture in Dade Country for the first time and we were surprised by the flatness of the landscape. We went several times to Miami and the flatness and the pastel colours were very curious and very inspiring. This project was Jeanne-

Claude's idea. So when I designed the first sketches in 1980 I did it as a very flat project involving this calm, shallow water and tropical vegetation. This flatness was designed as an essential part of the work. Basically it was like a giant painting, almost like a shaped canvas painting. In a way *Surrounded Islands* was our most painterly project.

RE: It's your idea of an early Kenneth Noland is it?

CH: We played with the colour. We took our cue from the marvelous variety of colour in Biscayne Bay—from light green to very deep blue. And then we artificially injected that very shocking, very powerful pink—which is not a natural colour at all—knowing that it would clash with the tremendous richness of natural colour. And of course that pink was also inspired by the Latin presence in Miami. We were very eager to do a project without an Anglo Saxon sensibility, a project which leans toward the Latin and Hispanic people living in Southern Florida.

RE: I was surprised to read that one of the few things you cherish about your early work experience in Bulgaria is that it taught you to work with people and to appreciate space. What kind of work were you assigned when you went to art school there?

CH: I hated that education when I was very young thirty-eight years ago. Art school in Bulgaria was extremely conservative and academic. You go seven years to become a painter or sculptor. Architecture was part of the art department, which was very good. I even had four semesters of medicine cutting the human body. Of course, this was happening at the height of the Cold War. Stalin was still alive, and many of the young students were obliged to do a variety of propoganda activities. On weekends we were sent to the cooperative farms to advise the farmers to park their trucks and their combines near the railroad tracks because the Orient Express included western passengers who would see the countryside of Bulgaria.

RE: So this was a way of showing the richness and the diversity of the country?

CH: Yes. It was to demonstrate the energy of mechanical work and agricultural activity. We were to tell the farmers to park their combines in a row near the tracks as a way of showing how much mechanization was going into agriculture. I hated those terrible autumn weekends but I did start to develop a flavour for talking to people outside the academic world. At that time I also started to develop a sense of the physicality of space which was something you couldn't learn at school. Of course there was another part to that schooling. Bulgaria is actually very close to the Soviet Union. Many professors who came from the Soviet Union to teach were part of the great Russian experience before Stalin put a stop to everything. It was illegal to tell us about their art and to give us information about that romantic period when art was really very imaginative, very idealistic, when it challenged the bourgeois dimensions of art in the Soviet Union. Between 1918 and 1929 this kind of art was done by many people who were not even artists—industrial designers, movie directors and architects—all of whom were doing temporary installations to create a revolutionary spirit and excitement. While it wasn't always very stimulating visually, it was exciting that artists were going beyond the walls of the musuem and beyond the idea that art should be "things." They were using the railroad stations, the streets, the farms—all that was part of the romantic excitement which was certainly an important element in my education.

RE: Your projects seem to ask you to spend the majority of your time dealing with people, persuading them, negotiating with them. Did you learn what seems to be a limitless sense of patience trying to convince farmers to move their machines closer to the tracks?

CH: Let me try to make an analogy. Take the case of a normal painter working in his studio; he can prepare orange by mixing together red and yellow pigment. It's pure chemistry at this stage; if he puts in more turpentine, the pigment will become more liquid. Finally he applies the colour to the canvas.If he's not successful, he will never have the right orange. Our case is the same; our colours are the farmers, the politicians, the variety of governmental agencies, the people who own the land. We need to mix these colours to get the chemistry right. If we fail, we'll never realize our project. This is why many art historians have difficulty with our work because they want to simply classify it as a painting or a sculpture. But it has an architectural dimension, even an urban planning dimension. If you are an urban planner, if you like to build new highways, an airport or a bridge, then you have to involve a tremendous number of elements quite similar to those in our work. It's just inevitable that the work carry these elements.

RE: Do you have a life outside of art, or does everything focus on the project that you're working on?

CH: I don't think any artists have outside lives. For us art is twenty-four hours. But it's pleasure, not work. It gives us enormous pleasure, enormous excitement and we enjoy it tremendously.

RE: But you can't tell me that your life has been one long serendipity. Surely there have been times when you've been frustrated by the ongoing process of getting a project completed?

CH: Of course. But how can I put this? All our projects have two distinct periods, the software and the hardware period. The first is when the project is in my drawings and in our heads, and in the heads of hundreds of people who are for or against it. This period is very unpredictable. Nobody knows how the project will go. We know how to build a running fence but we will never again build a running fence. We now know how to surround islands but we will never again surround islands. Each project is a new adventure, an exploration, and each project is a revelation. For me and Jeanne-Claude, and a number of friends who work with us, it's like a great university. So the joy and the moments of frustration and angst are all part of the enormous satisfaction that doing something unique gives to you, something that nobody else knows how to do. We don't even know how to do it ourselves. We don't know how *The Umbrellas* will look.

RE: Do you feel a sense of elation when a project is completed?

CH: We always profoundly believe that all of our projects will be very beautiful things. They will be sites of beauty and enormous visual exhilaration. It would have been very boring if *Running Fence* were dull. Fortunately, until now no drawings of mine have been able to match the magnitude of visual complexity of our projects.

RE: Do you dream as well about the unfinished projects? Do you have nightmares about the ones that you haven't been able to do?

CH: They're not nightmares, they're works-in-progress. Now there are some projects we've abandoned because we've lost interest in them. But there are still projects that we hope to do. We have been working for twenty-one years on the Reichstag project in Berlin and we hope that with the results of the *Umbrella Project* we can revive negotiations to wrap the Reichstag.

RE: Is there a possibility that you can get trapped by the enormity of your projects. *The Umbrellas* will have been the largest and most expensive project you've ever done and I wonder where you go from here. The projects seem to get bigger and bigger?

CH: The project seems big only because it is a work of art. Men do much bigger things—build airports, highways, cities—bigger than any of our projects. There is simply no comparison. The umbrellas are quite large, but they're not something impossible. The point is that all the energy and all the vision are only brought together to become art, not for any other reason. They are not even commissions. The only reason for their existence is because we decided to realize the project. So the most profound dimension of the work is its freedom. I don't think the work becomes bigger and bigger, I think it becomes richer and more complex. And each time we do a new project we try to add a new dimension to it. This is why we'll never wrap a bridge again. With *The Umbrellas* we purposely engaged the project on two sides, very much like a diptych where you compare similarities and differences in two places.

RE: So what have you found so far about the distinctions between Japan and the United States—two countries that, on the surface at least, are remarkably different?

CH: There are a great number of differences and also very great similarities. We really started to contemplate a work for Japan and the western world twenty-one years ago. Finally we came up with the scheme for *The Umbrellas* drawings at the end of 1984. We choose the umbrella because basically what we are doing is some kind of poetical colonization of the space. We found that the upper part of the umbrella looked very much like the roof of a house. Actually we were building houses without walls, building a new settlement. And of course the height of the umbrella—twenty feet tall, six metres—is the average height of a two-storey house in Japan and California.

RE: So you've become developers?

CH: Very much like that. We come to this inland valley with small villages and towns and suddenly where there were fifteen houses there will be hundreds of umbrellas taking over and building these incredible shelters. And of course the configuration of *The Umbrellas* in California and Japan relfect the availability of the space. In Japan space is very precious: 124,000,000 Japanese live on only eight percent of the country's surface. The other parts are very steep, volcanic mountains. So every square metre is used for something. The configuration of the blue umbrella in Japan will reflect that controlled and geometric space. The umbrellas will be much closer together, much more intimate. Sometimes they will even overlap one another in the terraces of the rice field. Whereas the configuration of the yellow umbrellas in California will reflect the immensity of the space and the possibilities of living in such an immense, open space. They will be much more capricious, much more arbitrary, expanding in all directions, very much like the branches of trees. Because the land is so available it is possible to do anything.

RE: What do you hope to discover when the umbrellas open up in the two countries?

CH: No project has been so difficult to visualize. It was impossible to see—in our head or otherwise—how this umbrella would look in the landscape. But I can tell you that these are not simple umbrellas. Actually, they are Rolls Royce umbrellas. Each triangle of fabric is sewn in a special way. It's not normal umbrella fabric; it's very luminous and will become like crystal diamonds of light in the landscape. Of course, all that is very difficult to visualize. Each umbrella will open in forty-five seconds, opened by nearly two thousand workers in Japan and California. I expect the project will have tremendous dynamic presence, that it will bloom like flowers on the landscape.

RE: There's something I've always wanted to ask you. Do you feel a sense of loss when you complete one of these magnificent projects? Have you ever wished that they could stay around for a couple of years so that more and more people could see them?

CH: This is a very good question. The temporariness is an esthetic decision. The project was designed to challenge our notion of the immortality of art, our arrogance in believing that we are immortal. So we build in stone, steel, concrete and marble to be remembered forever. These projects have a profound self-effacement because it takes much greater courage to go away than to stay. Of course, they occupy a continuous presence of missing, very much like flowers that have grown. So the project translates some urgency and sympathy to be seen because tomorrow it will be gone. This is all part of the aesthetics of the project.

RE: But flowers come back every year ...

CH: But the same flowers don't come back every year. Like our childhood or when we are in love once in a lifetime. So the project considers the question of whether or not art can be forever. That question goes to the very bottom of our project because it is about freedom. This is why nobody can purchase or control these projects, or charge tickets to see them. The reason why they cannot exist longer is because possession is equal to permanence and permanence is the enemy of freedom.

RE: You're the last great romantic.

254 Peregrinations

CH: I'm not a great romantic but we profoundly believe that the art discusses these issues. Even the economics of the project is about that. That's the reason we don't do commissions; it's the reason we do not permit anybody to commercialize our work. We want to challenge our materialistic society, to pull off-balance the way we think. In this so-called capitalistic society we try and justify ourselves all the time. All we do is make money for our children and our grandchildren; it's so boring and so unpoetic. Of course, at its bottom these projects address one of the missing and most important elements of late twentieth century culture: uniqueness. We're surrounded with banal and trivial things; we have the Olympics and the World's Fair every four years, we have Walt Disney exhibitions around the world, we have travelling blockbuster exhibitions. We need desperately to present something that is once-in-a-lifetime. There will never again be *The Umbrellas*; and there will never again be the *Running Fence*, or the *Valley Curtain* or the *Surrounded Islands*. That's why when these projects disappear they have some kind of legendary character. Their presence is felt much more because they are not here than if they were.

Photographies

Photographies

In 1990, in the slipstream of the celebrations surrounding the 150th anniversary of the invention of photography, I conducted a handful of short interviews which acted like snapshots of different photographic practices: documentary, fashion, landscape and portrait. My intention was to cover a lot of territory in a little space and while I knew that each of the photographers could easily sustain a longer interview, I concentrated on focussing our conversation. The five photographers were among the most accomplished in their particular genre and although there was some degree of overlapping, by and large, their individual categories held.

In this series of conversations you'll find a number of photographers testifying to the personal dimensions of what they do. For Sheila Metzner photography was a refuge from a grim and indifferent world; it was a place of romance and exoticism, a place where everyone was beautiful and handsome. It's not hard to read into her luscious, graceful images an alternative to the world in which she reluctantly lives. In the disturbing images of Joel-Peter Witkin you find an altogether different world, one in which the photographer's identification with his subjects is complete and uncompromising. "If they're crippled," he says about the actors in his tableaux of dark marvels, "I'm also a cripple. I like to start with things that are broken and then put them together."

The world as Humpty-Dumpty is not far from the sense that informs much contemporary photography. The elegantly perplexing garden photographs of Montrealer Geoffrey James are exquisite reminders that in the photographic garden, Adam and Eve are one-part taker and two-parts maker. Photographers are asking the same questions about the intersections of fiction and fact being posed by contemporary artists in other art forms. So Mary Ellen Mark, whose penetrating records of the lives of outsiders—from street kids in Seattle to prostitutes in Bombay—have made her one of the world's most sought-after photographers, discusses the limits of documentary, limits that are variously practical and ethical. And finally, Yousuf Karsh talks about the fun-house of portraiture, where the encounters are of an unusually close, not to mention abbreviated, kind.

All these photographers, whatever their genre, are after the same thing; they take the world at face value and then set about to re-make it. "The beauty of the marvellous is absolutely my need," is the way Joel-Peter Witkin explains his fascination with the art of photography, and while all five photographers take very different pictures, I think they might agree with his sense of absolute desire. It is a satisfying fact that photography, an art form governed by technology, remains inflexibly personal.

Sheila Metzner

Light Essentials

ROBERT ENRIGHT: I'm interested in genesis. So I want to ask if you can remember when you first began to look at or take photographs.

SHEILA METZNER: It began with my family photo album. I particularly loved pictures of my mother. I think I got to know her better through photographs when she was young, pictures of her in a waterfall and the waterfall would come to life and so would she.

RE: Did the photographs seem exotic to you at the time?

SM: Oh, absolutely. And mysterious. I had an uncle who had disappeared and there was a photograph of him in the album. He was surrounded by half-naked pygmies—women, of course. And there were men in army uniforms with hats and all kinds of brass and everybody looked handsome and beautiful. It had marvellous light. I looked at it again and again.

RE: That's a lovely notion that everybody looked beautiful. Do you think there's a residual effect of that in your work today? You've created one of the most consistently beautiful worlds in contemporary photography.

SM: Possibly. But my life when I was growing up in Brooklyn was very grim. Beautiful life was more in pictures than in reality. Reality was rather harsh. I liked staying inside much more than going outside. The summers were really hot and the heat used to burn up through your shoes. The kids were rough. Nobody ever seemed to know what I was talking about or be interested in anything I was interested in, except my mother. She was very fine and very quiet and used to read. So I liked being at home and I liked drawing. I always just liked pictures.

RE: Were you too sensitive for that world?

SM: I heard today that I'm still too sensitive for this world. I don't know which world I should have been in. I guess the invented worlds are the ones that are fascinating to me. I even came armed today with a Steichen book so as not to travel alone between my studio and here.

RE: So photography is a constant companion for you, whether in your imagination or in fact?

SM: In fact. Whenever I travel I bring a whole Haliburton case full of photography books. If I'm going to the Southwest I'll take Edward Curtis with me. I'll bring Georgia O'keefe along and try to track down locations and people and places out of those images.

RE: Is there a way in which your photographs have come out of other photographs? You have an image in your book *Objects of Desire* which is an homage to Man Ray. Is he particularly important to you?

SM: I think he's become important in the past four or five years. I look at his work often. I look at photography often, probably in the same way that I looked at my mother's album. It's a refuge for me. Whenever the advertising world gets too tough or the demands seem to be insurmountable, I open a book of photography and say, "Well, that's where it is, that's really important, this is really art, this is really fine, this is really beauty, this is really truth, this is what I'm trying to do."

RE: You studied at the Pratt Institute but you started out in television art-direction.

SM: I wanted to be an artist but I was told I couldn't because artists don't make any money. So I began by studying art-teacher education and then I realized that one couldn't teach anything until one became that thing. So I decided I had to find out something about art before I could teach it. I went into commercial art but my teachers at Pratt were people like Jack Tworkov. It was really more of a fine art education. We learned drawing and painting. And then most of my friends when I became an art director in the '60s and early '70s were photographers.

RE: I'm not surprised to hear that you studied painting and drawing because one of the things that strikes the viewer right away is how composed your work is. There's not a single object or person in your photographs that isn't there for a very appropriate reason. Was pictorial composition part of what you learned at Pratt?

SM: I think that came just from studying painting, mostly van Gogh. Also I had a very good friend, a photographer, who made it clear to me that a photograph wasn't complete unless every corner of it was considered—top to bottom, left to right. It had to fulfill itself completely. The image was a whole image, it was the whole space. But, yes, probably Pratt had something to do with it. We even studied a bit of architecture. I remember making constructions in space. It was an excellent formal education.

RE: What's your interest in fashion photography?

SM: I was very interested to photograph its structure and form. Before I was asked to photograph fashion I saw that a lot of the work was very surfacy. The best of fashion has art and its own craft and deserves to be respected. So I wanted to photograph fashion in a proper light so it could be seen as a construction. I always hope that I'm going to be asked to photograph something that's worth doing. I made a vow that I wouldn't enhance things that didn't deserve to be enhanced, that if I really couldn't believe in what I was photographing, it would be better not to document it at all. Because the photographs are as much a document of our time as they are of the article that's being sold.

RE: Has that choice ever been damaging for you?

SM: It's just the right direction for me. I think to do anything else would be more damaging, so I'm very careful about the people I work for. I always ask them if they're sure they know what they're getting themselves into when they choose to work with me.

RE: One of the things that struck me looking through some of the earlier work was how you were able to take simple objects and make them significant. I'm thinking of a photograph you did in 1981 of three plums. Out of that simple fruit you compose an almost monumentally beautiful thing.

SM: Those things are monumental to me. In the same way I look out the window and see a tree and it helps me to go on in life. These things have their moment just as we do. I had an apple we called the Cézanne apple that I photographed in Italy. You could be looking at hundreds of apples and then you come across one and it has a different life and something seems important about it. It just seemed essential to get it down one way or another—to draw it or photograph it before you ate it, before it disappeared.

RE: I want to pick up on the idea of simplicity. There's a photograph of one of your daughters wearing a plastic hat in which she looks like a vision out of Ingres.

SM: It's a baggie. That was what was so wonderful. She was going to take a shower and she had to tell me something. She just walked out with that baggie wrapped around her head, as you say, like an Ingres painting. It was an extraordinary moment.

RE: Did you just happen to have a 35mm camera with you at the time? That photograph is too well lit for you to have just snapped it off.

SM: They run away from me when they see the camera, but I rarely have a camera with me. I keep it packed away and I only take it out when I'm about to work. I consider it work. It takes a long time and there was a lot involved in that photograph. She probably got a little chill before she ran back into the hot shower.

RE: Now what about that photograph *Stella by Starlight*? It looks like a Klimt with vulnerability. It's an absolutely gorgeous photograph.

SM: I was actually working on a series of still lifes—potatoes—for *Cuisine* magazine at the moment when Stella came by. I think the original title was *Stella Galaxy*. It was a very exquisite moment in time—the cloth with the spinning things, the stars and the sky and then Stella, who's a little star. The beauty of photography is the truth of it. In a way, to compare it to painting diminishes the magic of photography because photography has a truth to it that painting can never have. Painting is always an interpretation, but photography is interpreted through life itself. It's direct.

RE: So you don't believe that photography is a fiction, even though you'll spend days setting up movie lights to get the proper mood?

SM: It's always truth because the fact is it's a photograph. It's real. It's life transformed. It's even the light of life on a surface of silver. It's very, very strange. I was reading something the other day about its being light fixed on paper. Light fixed—just the idea is mind-boggling.

RE: You talk about it as if it's a kind of alchemy. I guess for you it is magic?

SM: It is. You have the negative which is this tiny thing and you place it in a machine, put light through it, it projects onto the paper, you shut the light, you have an absolutely blank white paper. Then you dip the paper into some liquid and slowly, slowly the image appears. If you turn the light on it will go black, but if you put it in a fix, the acid stops it right there. You stop it at a certain point and there you have it: what was in front of you as real life is then fixed on a piece of paper. It's just extraordinary and always will be.

RE: What is your interest in the mask? You use masks a fair amount in photographs.

SM: The next picture I'm doing is of a woman holding a mask. I don't know what the interest is, but I guess there is one. I never know what the magnetism is of things, but I do follow it. As soon as I notice that I look at something too long, then I know I'd better either buy it or follow it. I do that with people too. I went to see a Bruce Weber film and there was a young man with a hat sitting in the audience. He got out of the theatre before I did. I left my husband, ran out of the theatre, grabbed him by the shoulder, gave him my card and asked him to come to my studio. He showed up and it turned out that he was a theatre student from Vermont. I'll probably get to photograph him one day. I found my best assistant that way. He was sweeping a stall in the barn where I keep my horses, and didn't know anything about photography. He stayed with me four and a half years.

RE: Does anybody ever refuse you when you ask?

SM: Yes. Warren Beatty's been totally elusive. There have been other people but from time to time someone doesn't want to be photographed or something escapes me.

RE: Mark Strand has a beautiful line in the introduction to your book *Objects of Desire*. He talks about "decor that hints at the erotic." A photograph like *Jill in Our Bedroom* has a sensuous quality that perhaps pushes through to the erotic. Do you seek that tone in the photograph?

SM: I don't know if I seek it directly but I'm aware of eroticism in life. I'm seeking the ideal of so many aspects of life and the sensual is as much a study as any other. It has so much to do with finding out what it is to be a woman, what it is to be a human being, and I see the sensual in so many things that on the surface are not sensual. For example, I think Egyptian art is very erotic, even warriors, bowls of fruit. I don't know if it's my own view but obviously it's in Chinese, Indian, and Japanese art. It's a fascinating side. One of the sides of life that I haven't really explored is evil, the dark side, but I think there are enough people covering that area in life right now.

RE: I'm looking at a photograph of the Mondrian orchid, an exquisite flower that is dreamily sexual and it seems to me to be inescapably female. You mentioned that you're figuring out what it is to be a woman. Do you think of yourself as a female photographer? Could a man do the kind of work you do?

SM: I don't think of myself as a female photographer. I think of myself as a photographer and I always try to be pretty clear about that, not wanting to be in women's exhibitions or books about women. I don't like the whole idea of that kind of segregation or discrimination. I'd rather think of it as human work. I definitely think women and men are different but the work is the proof of the difference rather than the other way around.

RE: I was thinking about you in connection with photographers like Sarah Moon and Deborah Turbeville, photographers who have done still lifes of flowers. Robert Mapplethorpe has photographed flowers as well, but his pictures look a lot different from yours. They have an edge.

SM: There are very essential differences in our views. I think that what he tried to express had a different aim than my own work. What I'm trying to leave or transmit has to do with a certain kind of ideal. This is not a criticism of Robert because I've always been a fan of his. I spent a week interviewing him and photographing him and his life. Although I always felt we were at opposite ends of the spectrum. If there is a spectrum, he's infrared and I'm ultra-violet. And his flowers always had an innate evil to me. They were on the dark side. If my work is heading in any direction, it's toward light, toward good, toward a certain kind of responsibility to life on earth.

RE: So photography can bring tranquillity, a serenity?

SM: Absolutely. I have found myself on my knees to things that I'm photographing. I'm actually physically brought to my knees. Photography is a very difficult process. I've just been working on landscapes in the Southwest and in ten days we drove three thousand miles to destinations that were like Mars and Jupiter, right into the very heart of the earth, into canyons, into Indian cave dwellings, to just stand there with a camera in front of something that you're questioning.

RE: You still bring questions to your subject matter, not answers, then?

SM: Always. It's really the unknown that fascinates me. The longer I live the more I appreciate that I don't know anything. That I can never read all the books, that I can never see all the landscapes, that I can never meet all the people who are worth meeting. It's a bit frustrating because life is so short. I try to do as much as I can.

Joel-Peter Witkin

Bringing Attic Thoughts to Light

ROBERT ENRIGHT: Do you remember the first photograph you ever made?

JOEL-PETER WITKIN: It was actually of a rabbi who, according to the *New York Daily News*, had seen God. My father used to come and visit us because he and my mother were separated. When I was three years old I thought my father's name was "Al Moany." Anyway, I had purchased my first camera just a week before and I needed something magical, and he told me about this rabbi. I was about seventeen. You should know that I was raised as a Roman Catholic. My father's being Jewish was the reason for the separation. So I was very anxious to photograph this person who had seen God because I thought that in photographing him I would see the visage of God. I was shocked that permission would be given to me. I thought that he would look like Charlton Heston. I walked into this library and there was this little, old, humble man. I was disappointed in a way because I was expecting somebody who had been sparked by lightning. I decided to go ahead with the project and photograph him anyway because I felt that if I didn't see the magic then perhaps I would see it in the resulting photograph. It turned out to be a very beautiful photograph but it was empty of the meaning I wanted to see. Still, it was the beginning of a need to do two things: to stop time and celebrate that time in printing. I think that combination is what gives my work a signature style.

RE: You manipulate the images don't you?

JPW: Yeah, exactly. I was thirty-seven when I went to New Mexico in 1975 to do graduate work. I had been making photographs for twenty years but they were basically straight photographs. The picture plane was sacrosanct, it was black and white work, pure photography. I would use only the exact frame in the camera. I was always interested in fairly strange characters and so I put ads in newspapers to photograph people who lived as comic-strip heroes. I decided early on, too, that it would be better to have people work with me in a collaborative way.

RE: What's the sense of fascination or wonder you have with characters who operate on the margins of sexual practice?

JPW: My interest in them is specifically that they are myself in a very real way. If they're unformed, I'm that way too; if they're crippled, I'm also a cripple.

RE: Do you mean because you're part of the human race or because you enter into this collaborative event with them?

JPW: Both things. I'm alive and I'm in need, that's the condition of all our lives. But I can only relate to certain people. I've always felt that everyone could be photographed in a masterpiece of photography. But I have to concentrate on the people I'm interested in. When I do finalize a photograph it's like looking in a mirror and it's not a reverse image. It's a very internalized image, an aspect of all the thoughts, the feelings and emotions that went into my day-to-day existence.

RE: Do you think of this work then as a kind of surrogate autobiography?

JPW: Absolutely. I think that we're all given gifts and we're given the means to evolve towards a higher sense of the self. In my case it's been photography. I've had that notion since I was a child. I didn't know the means then; now I think I do. But that doesn't mean that I have to be a photographer all my life. If tomorrow I find that I'm washing dishes or working to help people then I'll be satisfied with that. I do think, however, that the medium of photography as I approach it has always been something of a challenge. Recently, my ten-year-old asked me if I could be anything what would I be and I said I'd be doing exactly what I'm doing right now. Myself, being with you, trying to create images.

RE: Do you show your son all of the work you do?

JPW: In fact, he's been in one of my photographs, *The Capitulation of France*.

RE: It's an extraordinary photograph. Where do the two figures come from?

JPW: There's a story behind how each photograph is generated. I had everything set up, the background, the lighting. I spent the whole day making the connection of the tubes between the mask my son wears and this large naked woman in the background. It was about three o'clock and I positioned her and my wife took my son's clothes off and we put the mask on him and he basically just freaked out. He was screaming and ready to walk off the set and I ran behind the camera—the strobe was set but wasn't on—and I took this photograph. Only one exposure. I respected the fact that he didn't want to be in the photograph any more. It was only the next day in the set, without any model, that I actually stood some pieces of cardboard up to know exactly what the right exposure was without strobe and then I processed this one frame and the one frame was the photograph which you see.

RE: Then you scratched out the hands and head of the woman?

JPW: I scratch the negative to extend the mystification of things that I can't change physically when I first look into the camera. The process is that I'll construct a set and before that I'll relate with people whom I want to photograph. I'll show them other photographs I've made, sketches of things that I want to do, and tell them very earnestly and frankly that I can't make the photograph without them and their belief and their life and their consciousness. And that the reason I'm with them is that I've been given an opportunity to make a very unusual image of them, one that will be very honest and true and maybe different from anything they can imagine.

RE: There's a photograph from 1984 called *Entrail Lust* in which a man and the floor around him are covered by the entrails of some animal and he's masturbating. What relationship did you have with him that would give him the permission to enact that particular fantasy?

JPW: I made that image in San Francisco of a chap I've known for years. I've photographed him seventeen times. Since he was a close friend I could use him and his energy. In *Entrail Lust*, I addressed the concept of an externalization of something very internal. This thing about masturbating on meat is what unfeeling sexuality is about. In the process I was recording something special for him because he was excited about being an exhibitionist.

RE: Are these things therapy for the people involved as collaborators with you?

JPW: I wouldn't say they were therapy in all cases, but I'd say in this particular case therapy was involved.

RE: A lot of the photographs parody aspects of Roman Catholicism, in that there are a number of crucifixion scenes in which a rhesus monkey is tied to a cross. One is called *The Saviour of the Primates*. What's your relationship to the tradition you were raised within? Is it legitimate to throw at you the accusation of blasphemy or sacrilege or something worse?

JPW: I'm a practising Catholic in the sense that I believe in the essence of that faith. I don't go to church because it basically bores me. I think the sacrilege of the Catholic religion is that so little of the purity exists. We're not getting the essence of what was seen and felt and talked about; what we're getting is something that is very, very confused and has damaged people more than it's helped. More people have died in the name of faith than have lived it.

RE: From a Catholic point of view your involvement with these photographs would be an occasion of sin?

JPW: I'm concerned about the honesty of my own response in making the photographs. Religious iconography has basically been the starting point of my work. Two things happen for me: the fact that the key icon of my life has been Christ and the icon of beauty has been woman, the giver of life. The latter is finite, the former infinite. What I want to realize through photography is what it would have been like to believe—or attempt to believe—in the passion.

RE: Oftentimes the photographs look as if a poltergeist has run amok across the surface of the print. I think of *The Sins of Joan Miró*, it looks like it's been damaged by something impish at best and perverse at worst.

JPW: I normally attack the print with different chemistry. In the case of *The Sins of Joan Miró* I'm actually throwing and sponging a bleach onto the print which actually changes its colour. I was able to make shapes occur in the printing which of course didn't exist in reality. My photographs look like old photographs that have been hidden in someone's attic and are suddenly brought to light.

RE: Do you want the photograph to be beautiful? Is the expression of an aesthetic something that interests you?

JPW: Absolutely. That's the first criterion. The beauty of the marvellous is absolutely my need. The second aspect of that need is to show the person I'm about to photograph as wonderfully posed and as beautiful as I can make them. An odd thing happens: when I send a print as payment I generally get letters back that say, "I didn't know I looked this way." And sometimes in a gallery my collaborators can walk in front of their photograph and won't make a connection between themselves and reality.

RE: Do you find the process of photographing these people sexually exciting as well? Are you involved at that level?

JPW: Oh, yes. There's a multiple aspect of my association with the people I photograph. At one time early on I was engaged sexually after the photographic session but I decided not to do it again because I realized I couldn't hold the energy, the profoundness of what I wanted to create, unless I made myself photographically celibate.

RE: So the energy is about voyeurism for you and for the audience?

JPW: I really think so. I don't think there's anything wrong with that. I think it's a form of fantasy and association and projection.

RE: I was thinking of Robert Mapplethorpe who has done some celebrated and controversial leather photographs. His approach was one of clarity and as a result he sought out conventionally beautiful subjects. You have gone to people who wouldn't be considered beautiful in any conventional sense of the term.

JPW: You're making a very good point. I think of Helmut Newton, too. I mean if I were to photograph a seven-foot-tall magnificent woman it would be pretty difficult not to create a wonderful photograph. Not that Helmut isn't wonderful; he's a fantastic photographer. And Robert, whom I knew quite well, engaged in the beauty of skin and movement and form. I make it harder for myself in that I like to start with things that are broken and then put them together. To the majority of people they'd be outcasts but to me they're as wonderful as any other known form of beauty. What is that anyway? It's very subjective to say that this is more beautiful than that. I think there's nothing to hold that opinion.

RE: Is there anything you won't photograph?

JPW: I won't photograph people who I know are principally about demeaning another person. But if their activities are about their own sense of wonder and purpose on the earth and if I can agree and sense in them a dialogue and a challenge, then, yes, I'm interested.

Mary Ellen Mark

The Limits of Documentary

ROBERT ENRIGHT: One of the central questions for any documentary photographer is this issue of ethics. What's your take on it?

MARY ELLEN MARK: It's something I think all photographers have to come to terms with, whether they do fashion or whether they do documentary work. It's a form of voyeurism. I try not to exploit people; I really feel that the act of taking someone's picture is in a sense exploitive. No matter what. But I think—I hope—that the people I've dealt with have wanted their stories told.

RE: They're complicit, they go along with you?

MEM: Of course. It's very difficult when people don't go along with you. I think when you're photographing a major event, like a war, then you're a fly on the wall. You can say you're there and people don't know you're there. But where it's a photographer among people and there's not a catastrophe or major event going on, then *you're* the major event. So they know you're there. They go along with you. If someone says "no," I try never to push it. Of course, I think one of the most important things is access and that's something I really do try to get.

RE: Let's talk about that astonishing series of photographs you did of the Bombay prostitutes. I want to know how you got there and how they let you into that intimate world.

MEM: Of all the stories I've worked on, that was probably the most difficult project in terms of access. It's something that I'd thought about for ten years and finally decided I was going to do, and I went to Bombay. The first ten days or so I thought it was going to be hopeless, but I just stuck on that street. I had a camera around my neck all the time and the people got used to seeing me there. Finally, I knew that just being out on the street wasn't enough, that I wanted to go inside those brothels. The first few times I tried to get in people would scream and run into their rooms and I'd get chased out. Then, one day I went back to the same brothel. Again, people screamed and ran up to another floor. But one woman invited me in for tea and I made friends with her and then I started to work. And when she accepted me, everyone else in that building accepted me too. When the

267

people in other buildings saw that those in this building had accepted me, then they accepted me and one thing led to another. I think emotionally that was the most difficult story to leave. When I think about the runaway kids in Seattle and stories like that, I always knew I could have continuing contact with the people. With these women I knew that we were so far away and, even though I was going to come back to India, their lives were so transient and changing that I would probably never see any of them again. That was true. Many of those women I've lost forever.

RE: I'm fascinated by this idea that you go in as an empathetic human being and people get used to you, and then the real matter of your being there comes out.

MEM: I never let people get used to me and *then* bring in the camera. I always immediately start to photograph, and I started immediately on that street in Bombay and in the mental hospital. The first day I arrived I had my camera out. But I agree with you. I think it would be very difficult to make friends and then bring out your camera. I make it totally clear from the beginning why I'm there. I'm not there to be a social worker or an analyst or a best friend, I'm there to record their lives.

RE: One of the photographers you admire a lot is Robert Frank, and Frank is best known for that magnificent document of American culture called *The Americans*. I mention him because I wonder if you have a feeling that your work is adding up to a series of documents on culture. Is it the big picture that you're involved with?

MEM: I'm interested in a series of documents on culture, definitely. And when I go into cultures that are foreign I'm interested in looking at aspects that are universal. Prostitution is universal. Street kids are universal and poverty is universal. It's a thread.

RE: I want to talk a little bit about the art of chance, because you said earlier that things happen, and then you caught yourself and said, "Well, in a way you make them happen." I'm thinking of a photograph you took in Seattle of a kid, I think it was a boy but I'm not sure, it could be a girl, smoking a cigarette or a joint, I'm not sure about that, either.

MEM: It was a cigarette. The thing is, that kid saw we were filming every day on the street. Her name was Lilly and one day she showed up with a doll. I don't know whether she showed up with a doll because she thought it would appeal to us, or whether she just really showed up with a doll, but in a way that's chance. She's in the film. You see her walking across the street with a doll. I also took a picture of her. She was smoking a cigarette. She would never smoke a joint on the street. But it is luck, in a sense. It's also spending a long time in one place, getting to know all the characters, knowing what it all means, and then things just happen. But I also feel that being a photographer, being a photo-journalist or documentary photographer, encourages you to develop another sense. You develop an intuition as to which corner to turn, almost about where to go.

RE: What about the portrait of Marlon Brando from *Apocalypse Now*? The one where he has a shaved head and beetles play a significant role. You brought the jar of beetles.

MEM: I brought the jar of beetles because I thought that would make a great picture. But then I didn't put it on his head because he might have said "no." He understood exactly what to do, but that was chance. I could have said, "Listen Mr. Brando, do you think you could put that beetle on your head?" and he would have said "yes" or "no," or I could just have handed him the jar and he might have looked at it and put it away. But then he didn't.

RE: It increases the odds, though. In a sense you shape reality. The traditional notion of documentary is that it's the thing you find there rather than the thing you orchestrate.

MEM: It depends. Someone like Robert Frank, say, is a street photographer and observer. I'm different from that in the sense that I go into a situation where people are very aware of me and then work the situation from there. I do both. But I'm not as good a street photographer as I am someone who can go into a situation where people just unfold their lives for me. That's what I'm better at.

RE: Are there limits to what you'll photograph?

MEM: I wouldn't photograph something where I thought I was putting someone in a terribly compromising position. I would photograph a certain brutality or violence if I felt it was real and touched people in a way, but I wouldn't compromise somebody. If I saw someone in a situation that I really wanted to shoot but understood that they felt it was bad for them, I guess I couldn't do it.

RE: So when the autistic child had an epileptic fit, you wouldn't photograph it?

MEM: I didn't photograph it. It probably would have been all right with the family but I just felt that it was such a tragic moment I couldn't bring myself to do it. Suddenly I saw the amazing depths of tragedy this family was enduring with this kid, I saw how the kid felt and I couldn't do it.

RE: One of the photographers you've been influenced by is Diane Arbus. An astonishing thing that has emerged about her is how intimately involved she was with her subjects. Even in a sexual way.

MEM: I think that's another rumour. I'm not sure that's even true. I think she was intimately involved and obsessed with people in the sense that she would spend a lot of time with them.

RE: But she liked the rough trade.

MEM: I'm not interested in her that way. If you want to talk about those kind of tough photographs, then we can talk about Mapplethorpe's photographs with people in leather. For me they're his most interesting photographs because they document a life that people would ordinarily never get to see. I'm not interested myself in the rough trade. I'm more of a voyeur, maybe. I lead a normal life. I'm very straight and safe when it comes to this heavy-duty stuff. It's not my trip.

Geoffrey James

Gardening Utopia

ROBERT ENRIGHT: Is there something special about landscape photography that distinguishes it from portraiture or documentary or any other form of photography?

GEOFFREY JAMES: I think one thing that it probably can do is indicate attitudes different generations had towards nature and to what was around them. I think people tend to photograph the landscape according to conventions that exist at the time. I mean, the first photographers in the 1850s in France encountered lots of things they simply couldn't cope with. They tended to go into the forest and take photographs that looked like Barbizon paintings. In North America, with the whole continent opening up, there were photographers who tried to deal with this totally new landscape. What do you do in the prairies for example, where you just have a sky and an horizon?

RE: You try to get through it as quickly as you can in order to get to British Columbia.

GJ: But they had to photograph it. They were commissioned to photograph the railway or expedition routes, and they went to enormous trouble to make beautiful photographs. They were carrying these huge glass plates which they had to cover with treacle. They had to coat them just before they took the photograph. The equipment was heavy, unwieldy, prone to breakage and dust and all sorts of problems. And they had to climb the mountains to find the best views. They didn't just knock off a snap. So a lot of photographs that are thought of as utilitarian because they were commissioned are really the product of a number of carefully considered aesthetic choices.

RE: Does the landscape photographer always want to make a beautiful photograph?

GJ: Certainly not all landscape photographers. Think of the two Adamses. Obviously Ansel Adams, whom everybody knows, could really only deal with nature untouched. He tried to present a picture of the world before we were banished from the Garden of Eden. Everything is perfect. Then there's a younger

American photographer, Robert Adams, who lives in the Midwest. All his photographs have some human trace, sometimes very subtle. Instead of trying to pretend that there's a great untouched wilderness out there, he shows how we've marked nature. So, not all photographers try to make photographs with those conventional ideas about the sublime in their heads.

RE: Robert Adams's photographs are extremely beautiful. Not in a grandiose, monumental Ansel Adams way, but they're beautiful nonetheless. Is it just because he's a good photographer? I guess I'm asking if after 150 years of looking at photographs, have we now a bias towards finding beauty in what may actually be ugly?

GJ: I think that's absolutely true of photography. It has this sometimes rather frightening capacity to transform things which when viewed directly are not that beautiful. The side of a logged hill can be extremely beautiful in black and white—with pristine and extraordinary textures. But faced directly, when it's smoking away, it's really not that great.

RE: Is there something moral that landscape photographers should be looking at if they want to document the intervention of culture into nature?

GJ: I think it's a healthy corrective. I think most landscape photography that gets published in Canada is idealized and calendar-like with special effects and pretty patterns. I never see that landscape when I'm out.

RE: It doesn't show the pulp mill or the smelting plant in the middle of the Rockies?

GJ: Exactly. I think one has to try to have some understanding of a picture bigger than merely the picturesque.

RE: Don't we want to confront our place in landscape? As Canadians, we have the second largest country in the world, but haven't done a terribly good job of coming to terms with it in photography.

GJ: Well, I think it's extremely hard. Simply because of the scale and the endlessness of it. How do you deal with that photographically? A lot of it doesn't have picturesque qualities, it's just miles and miles of trees with miles and miles of lakes and trees. And all the conventions of painting simply don't apply.

RE: Is photography even suited to capturing landscape?

GJ: Yeah, I think so. It can make sense of things, especially in book form where there are groups of images rather than individual images.

RE: In light of that, your newest project is an intriguing one. You're documenting Mount Royal in Montreal, the mountain in the city. What's your interest in it?

GJ: Well, I didn't exactly stumble on Mount Royal. I live almost in its shadow. I started to photograph it because I'm still doing a large project on the work of Frederick Law Olmsted, the great nineteenth-century American designer of parks. He was a landscape architect, really, and he had a hand in Mount Royal. When I started to photograph it, I realized that it's very hard to put your finger on something that he actually did, even though his name's up there on the side of the mountain. So I quickly recognized that Mount Royal was a lot more than Olmsted.

It's an absolutely central part of the city of Montreal. It's a very rich place, it has very private places and very public places. The cemeteries are extraordinarily rich, for example.

RE: You're using the project as a way of understanding the place in which you live, then?

GJ: Absolutely. It's different from travelling. I do a lot of travelling and even if you're somewhere for three or four months there's a terrible pressure to work. But in Montreal I've got a couple of years so I just work when the light feels good or when it looks interesting or different.

RE: Does the studio call you every day?

GJ: Some days it's awful. Some days it's simply too cold to photograph. My camera won't photograph when it's forty below and my union doesn't allow it either.

RE: You're doing another project too. You're also working on the alleys of Montreal. Is this very different from the mountain and the city?

GJ: Totally. Where I live is all alleys. They seem to be an integral part of Montreal life. I didn't grow up in Montreal but all my friends say that your first interesting experiences happen in alleys if you live in the east end of Montreal. What's fascinating is the way that people create gardens and the way the alleys frame all kinds of important buildings. You get a kind of unauthorized view of the city and you also get a really good look at how people create their own environments. My street is largely Portuguese and they have a real way of doing gardens.

RE: One of the things that runs throughout your work is an interest in gardens of one sort or another, whether nurtured or natural. What's been your fascination with them?

GJ: It's really hard to say. Obviously, I find them interesting. On one level, I'm interested in investigating people's aspirations because when you build a garden, especially a big one, you're building an ideal world. Each generation has gardens which reflect the aspirations of that age, so there are different styles. It goes from one to the other. It's an extraordinarily rich subject. Also, I'm amazed at the continued existence of these places in this world. It seems miraculous that some have survived. They're very strange, they're like time capsules, complete environments which take you back into another world. They're fascinating places and there are not that many of them.

RE: There's a positively delightful photograph you did back in 1984 of the Villa Medici. It includes a whole collection of statues—people staring at the sky and horses rearing up—in what looks like an Arcadian forest.

GJ: It's an odd place, the Villa Medici in Rome. It's run by the French Academy and the director at the time was the painter Balthus. The statues are from a revenge myth about Niobe and her daughters and in it they're all wiped out. The stuff was stolen from Hadrian's villa by the Medicis and then it was rearranged under Balthus in this completely surreal setting. It's in a little room which I didn't really know was there. I had bribed my way into the Villa Medici and stumbled across this garden room completely enclosed by hedges. It's virtually the only Renaissance garden left in Rome.

RE: There's also a photograph of the Villa Brenzone in which it's virtually impossible to tell the difference between the garden and what looks to be the side of the building. Everything is so lusciously overgrown. I find it a very elegant photograph.

GJ: It's rather a private place and I had very little time. A gardener was sent to accompany me and so I had to work at great speed. And I really don't like photographing when there's someone looking over my shoulder. But it's very old and the bushes and the rocks in black and white photography do become identical. It's an astonishing, wonderful place.

RE: One of the things that emerges in a lot of your photographs is a particular interest in levels of perception which seem to open out onto one another. There are all kinds of ways in and out of the photographs.

GJ: I am really interested in a poetics of space. I like to work in places that are very complex and that have many entrances and exits, because the visual game is more fun as it gets more complicated. You've got to load the film with all that information.

RE: Are you improving on nature?

GJ: I don't know about improving. Certainly changing it. The photographs are almost totally fictional.

RE: You talk about a place yielding up a photograph. Is there something you can take from every place or are there some that don't give you what you need as a photographer?

GJ: There are lots of places I have been unable to photograph, even some very famous gardens in Italy. They've either been too overrun or they're one-dimensional. There's only a prescribed view. There's the Villa Garzoni in Collodi, one of the great baroque gardens which goes up the side of a hill. I've never been able to figure out how to photograph it. Some places are more propitious than others.

RE: As I think about what you do, I realize how complex a process it is. The gardens were an attempt to make a perfect world, which you enter as an artist set on creating your own reading of that perfect world. Upping the utopian ante in a way. So you create your own ideal world within this other ideal world. Is that the way the process works?

GJ: I think it is. Sometimes I feel I should be dealing with political problems, or with the dark side of life. People ask me why I don't photograph a little squalor. And it crosses my mind. But it comes down to a metaphysical question about the purpose of life. I'm interested in these places because they seem to be about certain aspirations. The people who built them had no material problems except when they bankrupted themselves building the gardens. They're utopian and they always fail. They're symbols of mortality and I find them poignant.

Karsh

A Portrait of Our Time

ROBERT ENRIGHT: If I asked you to tell me what the Karsh style is, could you come up with the general principles that make one of your photographs different from the work of any other portrait photographer?

KARSH: Yes, I can tell you that. It is really like reading biography or autobiography, you come to know the person through the writing. For a picture to be significant, it has to be complete in itself, a consummation of the many moods of that one person in a single photograph—some of that person's frailties, some of his or her good qualities, what has made that man or woman tick. You should be aware of all that as you look at the photograph.

RE: I know you don't always have that long a period of time with any subject. How do you get anyone to reveal his or her personality in that single image?

KA: Really, you don't try, except to approach the task with a great deal of dedication. You know these people very well through the media; you read a great deal about them. Only a few days ago I photographed Benazir Bhutto, the Prime Minister of Pakistan, and when I read her book *The Daughter of Destiny* it was so tragic I couldn't even finish it. I had photographed her father and we all know the sad ending he came to. I photographed Prime Minister Bhutto in Washington a few minutes before she went to join President Bush at a state dinner, and so the time was very exacting. When she came in, her eyes spoke. We had to do something worthwhile, which we were able to do because there was an immediate meeting of minds.

RE: But does that always happen? Can you always take that meeting of hearts and minds for granted?

KA: No, if you took it for granted you wouldn't accomplish it. But if you approach the task with all your dedication, it has to come. I think of some of the many photographs I have made: with Winston Churchill I had two minutes, with Charles de Gaulle half a minute. With others, like Helen Keller—which is one of my favourite photographs—I had two hours.

RE: Have you ever panicked when you realized how little time you had? With de Gaulle did your fingers suddenly begin to shake?

KA: I never panic because I can bring enough energy to bear in five minutes instead of spreading it around for two hours if I know beforehand the time limitations.

RE: Do you have a methodology where you begin that process of focussing your energy hours or days beforehand?

KA: If there were a method life would be simple. I am always mentally prepared; it is second nature for me. I'm always ready because this is my calling.

RE: Don't you ever get personally involved? Is it possible for you to know too much about the character?

KA: Yes, it is. I try to control that as much as I can because it would colour my thought, it would colour my interpretation, and I always try to be objective.

RE: I assume the sitter must give something back, as well. How much of these portraits are collaborations between the subject and the photographer?

KA: I think always to be a success there is a collaboration. That's why I feel it's very stimulating because I'm often given all kinds of emotional support from the person I photograph.

RE: What about your portrait of Grey Owl? Grey Owl always has puzzled me because he invented his persona. He was an English gentleman who fabricated a life as a native. How much of what you're getting through the camera is the invention of the person's life?

KA: I think in that case you hit a very sensitive chord. I photographed him as a North American Indian who was devoted to the conservation of Canada's national symbol, the beaver. I only knew that he was not an authentic Indian when I realized the juggling he did. He had four wives and one did not know one from the other. He fooled everyone. It was only later on when I photographed Governor General Tweedsmuir (John Buchan) that he said Grey Owl was a totally deceptive person. But everything about his Indian identity seemed authentic. He nurtured the characteristics of an Indian, his hair was long and somewhat lustrous. He affected their manners completely. I had just arrived in Ottawa so I invited our most distinguished poet, Duncan Campbell Scott, and other people from the Little Theatre for dinner in his honour. Everyone showed up except Grey Owl. I ultimately discovered he had lost himself in a bar in one of the hotels.

RE: You've done photographs of photographers too—Steichen and Ansel Adams come to mind. I always think of the cliché that doctors make the worst patients and wonder if, similarly, photographers make the worst subjects?

KA: Well, they are very much more difficult to photograph. Man Ray was among them, but he was very much easier. At one point I asked him, "What is the most serious problem you have ever had?" He said, "My dear sir, I never have problems, I only have solutions." Photographers of that calibre are accomplished and they end up collaborating. But in some ways it's more difficult to photograph someone who knows what is going on.

RE: So there are no tricks? You can't get away with anything when you're photographing a photographer?

KA: You can get away with a lot if they hold you in some affection.

RE: Did Ansel Adams and Steichen feel that way about you?

KA: I think Steichen did. With Ansel Adams—although I'm not a landscape or a nature photographer—we had great personal respect and affection for each other.

RE: You talk about a certain kind of truth coming through in the portrait. You did a series of portraits of Ernest Hemingway and among the best known is one where he looks out at the world with a slight degree of unease. The other portraits that you did at the same time show a much more withdrawn man, a man who shows fear *of* the world rather than one who causes fear *in* it.

KA: You read in the picture what is there exactly. When we met Hemingway was in agony physically, because it was soon after the fourth African safari and he had a wooden support for his back. John F. Kennedy had some support like this as well. But the moment I photographed Hemingway he was in agony, so I nodded to my wife to please leave us alone; I asked his wife—Miss Mary—to leave as well and then I offered him a glass of his favourite wine. It was on the table beside us for that very purpose. He took a good gulp of it and said, "This is dreadful, I feel like crying. You're very sensitive to let me cry from the excessive pain." He was a giant to photograph and he was very shy. The shyness came because he did not want to be seen crying in front of a stranger.

RE: On the subject of vulnerability, unless I'm wrong, you haven't done nude photography in your career, have you?

KA: I did a few but my upbringing was wrong to do them. I was born in the wrong era for it, the wrong culture. In my puritanical upbringing that was not encouraged at all. It was one of the taboo things. Even currently I find it difficult, but maybe I will still make them because I think the human figure is very beautiful.

RE: I want to talk about some specific images. I hadn't seen the photograph of Christian Dior before. I imagined him as an outgoing man, whereas you photograph him in such a way that the shade around him extends his image. His one eye comes through lit, while the eye that's in shadow emerges as much whiter. It's an extremely affecting photograph, but I'm not quite sure what it is I'm reacting to.

KA: That was just one hour before he presented his show to the world in Paris. There was so much secrecy that even I couldn't see any of his new gowns before I took the photograph. That's what prompted me to record him with his fingers on his lips, concealing much from the world.

RE: Now, what about the photograph of John Paul Getty? He doesn't look entirely pleased with the experience. He even looks hostile.

KA: We spent seven hours in Getty's home, one of the most magnificent mansions I've ever seen. Everything in it was a work of art. We were a group of people—the writer, his assistant, my wife and my assistant—and no hospitality was offered during the entire time. When we left, I saw this immensely wealthy person, sitting at a long refractory table with three dogs around him, eating all alone. The loneliness shows in the photograph. We made some marvellous photographs of him that are now in several museums, including the Getty. That day was a red-letter day for him. He told us he had bought a painting for twenty-eight pounds at auction some years ago which he had put in storage. Only when he gave the painting to be cleaned was he told it was a Raphael.

RE: I want to talk about the art of composition. Among the photographs of yours that I've always admired is one of Jacob Epstein, the sculptor. In it his hand mimics the structure of the sculptured hand behind him. And there's another of Zadkine in which his hand exfoliates just the way a floral sculpture does in the photograph. Are those deliberate compositional choices that you make?

KA: Jacob Epstein was short a model, so he sculpted his own hand and I photographed him in front of that sculpture. Only after I developed the negative did I realize he had unconsciously assumed that gesture. Zadkine made a sculpture to look like the atom bomb exploding. It was an attempt, perhaps a frivolous attempt. But he was very serious about that work. It has since been acquired by some museum.

RE: Did the portrait of Churchill actually make your career? It's taken on an almost legendary status. How significant was it?

KA: Very significant. It changed my life and I have had no rest ever since. It happened to be the right picture of the right man of history.

Musicalities

John Corigliano

Notes from Rebelground

John Corigliano is a kind of musical Midas; everything he touches turns to aural gold. The praise shines from all quarters: Aaron Copland described him as "the real thing, one of the most talented composers on the scene today"; in the sometimes parsimonious musical pages of the *New York Times* he is "one of American's most important composers"; and the *Boston Globe* registers his status as "the most performed and most admired of young American composers." The compositions have received significant awards as well: his opera, *The Ghosts of Versailles*, won the 1991 International Classical Music Award; Symphony no. 1 won a pair of Grammys; the score for Ken Russell's 1980 sci-fi film, *Altered States*, received an Academy Award nomination; and he himself has won the Grawemeyer Award, the music world's equivalent of the Nobel Prize. Corigliano has written a wide range of music—orchestral, choral, chamber and solo—for a distinguished number of orchestras, including the Boston and Chicago Symphonies, the New York Philharmonic and the Metropolitan Opera, for which venerable institution he was asked to write an opera to celebrate its hundredth anniversary.

John Corigliano was born on February 16, 1938 into a musical family; his mother was a pianist and his father the Concert Master of the New York Philharmonic, a position he held for twenty-three years. John was educated at Columbia and at the Manhattan School of Music but it was winning first prize at the 1964 Spoleto Festival Chamber Music Competition for his Sonata for Violin and Piano that initially established his reputation as a composer to watch. We've been all ears since.

Corigliano's influences are as various as the kinds of music he writes. A Moroccan Rheita serenading a mesmerized cobra in Marrakech turns up in his Oboe Concerto; the profound emotion of seeing that massive interwoven memory blanket for AIDS victims, *The Quilt*, provokes his Symphony no. 1; a meditation on the technical perfection of the clarinet informs his Concerto for Clarinet and Orchestra; and his sensitive readings of the poetry of Charles Baudelaire, Robert Browning and Dylan Thomas are re-articulated in the *Voyage for Flute and String*, the *Pied*

Piper Fantasy and *Poem in October*. These last two compositions have been played by flutist James Galway and clarinetist Richard Stoltzman, respectively, virtuoso musicians for whom Corigliano has a special attachment. After all, he is himself a virtuoso composer, pushing both the instruments and their players in new and demanding directions.

There is a good deal of the rebel in Corigliano, a predisposition he is quick to acknowledge. He composes music for under-appreciated instruments, he resists fashion and he sets for himself a musical agenda that refuses to become predictable. Corigliano is also something of a musical architect, building out of a disparate range of influences and musical intelligence a body of work as complex and moving as any in contemporary music.

John Corigliano was the Distinguished Artist-in-Residence for the Winnipeg Symphony Orchestra's second annual New Music Festival in February of 1993. He contributed a fair amount to the tone of the festival; the genuine enthusiasm and indefatigable energy he displayed during his ten-day stay in Winnipeg are evident throughout the following conversation which took place on the final day of the festival.

ROBERT ENRIGHT: Does the aesthetic language of the twentieth century necessarily involve a dialogue between the primitive and the sophisticated? When you compose, are you able to run a much wider gamut than did previous composers?

JOHN CORIGLIANO: Yes, today we have no rules. We make our own. Certainly in my music—like the "Arabic Rheita Dance" in the Oboe Concerto—the primitive is actually primitive. In the old days—even in Stravinsky and Bartok—the primitive was still orchestrally sophisticated. It was highly sophisticated primitivism. When I did the score for *Altered States* an interesting problem came up. As they always do in films, they put music behind the pictures for the executives. Even though it doesn't link up, they get an aura of sound. Ken Russell had picked selections from *The Rite of Spring* and *The Miraculous Mandarin* as background for his movie. I didn't think this was a good idea because it was dated, sophisticated primitivism. I mean, it was great stuff but when you put it in back of a film it becomes a little creature-featuresey. A lot of horror movies have taken off on exactly those pieces.

RE: The makers of *Jaws* must have lifted a few bars from Stravinsky's *Rite of Spring* for the moment when the shark is on his way.

JC: Actually, that's partly an earlier Stravinsky neo-classical piece. But if you look at the horror movie genre you'll notice it uses a lot of those techniques. I wanted to use much less realistic and much more primitive techniques. I was worried a little bit that Ken wouldn't like it. But he did and everything turned out fine. We have the ability in this age to use all techniques, and as a result we can get very primitive and then very refined in the blink of an eyelash. The palette is very great. And just as I love it in my home, I love music that puts a carved mask that was used for ritual worship right up against something very long and clean-lined and contemporary.

RE: Do you think of this as pastiche?

JC: I think the difference between eclecticism and pastiche has to do with architecture and inevitability. In the passage of the piece something happens that is inevitable and yet divergent from what you might think it would be. The justification has to do with thinking of the big shape and the big structure and not just sticking something in on a whim. That's not the way I work, even though it's fun to do. There is something delightful about the irreverence of a pastiche. Cage did that a lot. But my feeling of surprise in music is it should be something that seemed like you could never think of it but was inevitable after it happened. Beethoven always does that; it's marvellous to see how inevitable his surprises really are.

RE: So it's not something that you can whimsically introduce; the element of surprise is actually part of the larger structure of your thinking? When do you feel something is right for you?

JC: The "Turkomania" scene in *The Ghosts of Versailles* is something I planned right from the beginning. I wanted to end act one that way, partly because it was a grand *opera buffa* and to me the great *buffa* are things like Rossini and Mozart. In the Turkomania works they were reproducing a whole other culture. That was a great surprise to audiences in those days. At the end of act one of *The Italian Woman in Algiers*, Rossini not only surprises us with the music and the orientalisms, but also goes into nonsense verse and into people imitating animals. It's the most amazing digression from reality in a time where that was not done. Paisiello had a sneezing quartet in his *Barber of Seville* in 1782. These are wonderful moments but I think Rossini's are planned on a big scale. He's a wonderful theatrical planner. When he did these things he really did think about what was happening twenty minutes down the road. He also wrote so fast that twenty minutes down the road wasn't that far away for him. For me it's quite another matter.

RE: You've talked about parodying Parisien orientalisms, as well. It isn't just that you use those musical styles or accents but you can also parody them.

JC: Yes, like in the last movement of the Oboe Concerto. The idea of adding a kazoo provides the nasal quality many Arabic instruments get by sympathetic string vibrations and playing the oboe with the lips on the reed produces a seemingly authentic Rheita sound, rather than the refined oboe sound—all that is very pungent. So in the subsection, after all that rough-sounding stuff it's like the seventh veil suddenly goes over everything and we're into Sheherazade-land and Orientalism via the elegance of Paris in the nineteenth and early twentieth centuries. Then we're back into the primitive dance. I enjoyed the idea of it becoming a fantasy seen through the eyes of an elegant orchestra, which was then carried back into the rawness of the dance.

RE: You're attracted to that kind of layering aren't you? Are these multiple perspectives things you deliberately go after, or are they just an inescapable part of your musical consciousness?

JC: A friend of mine labelled my music three-dimensional. What he meant was that there are many things happening—sometimes at the same time and sometimes very divergently—which together make a general panorama. It's essential that each of these things be rather simple; otherwise you get total confusion. Each one relates to the other and yet is independent and harmonically different. In the last scene of act one of my opera there are three or four different things happening at the same time and all of them have to be clear. There are Arab instruments serenading a group of dancing maidens around this twenty-six-foot pasha. In addition there's a formal recitative with harpsichord (you've got players in a play discussing various elements), and ghosts watching the play accompanied by a full pit orchestra. It's a very three-dimensional, multi-layered approach. It's like Charles Ives except I tend to want to control more of it, like *when* these things rise and fall. But I love the idea—in his *Three Places in New England*—of the concept of two bands coming to town the same day and each playing different music. If you've ever gone to a parade you have that wonderful moment of hearing the band coming towards you and being in the centre and moving away, as the next band plays in its own key and at its own rhythm. They make a music together and this multiplicity is part of the excitement of our lives.

RE: You talk about composition as a state of being in control. Are there no accidents in your work?

JC: There are small bits of control one gives up. Just writing notes down and not playing it yourself is giving up control because notes are subject to interpretation. Then there are other areas of control you can give up in an aleatoric way. They're limited control. When Cage does it, it's basically unrestricted. He gives the players something like a star map or very few sets of signs and the performers have much more control than the composer. In the Baroque days the performer was expected to improvise around the theme of the composer. The composer provided a good deal of information and then each performance would differ, as does jazz. As he gained more and more control we saw less of this, until, at the beginning of the twentieth century, the composer basically controlled everything. Now it's a balancing act; we have ways of giving up and keeping control. Part of the act of composition is deciding how to do that, how to give certain areas back to the performers so that they have a sense of life and vitality, and yet not give over so much that you don't have any control left. I think we're always playing a seesaw game because notation has become so perfect that we can write out the performer if we choose. We can make the performance so specified that the performer is an automaton who obeys orders and has nothing else to contribute. Since that's now available to us, we have to decide how much of that specificity we want to use.

RE: Because you grew up around orchestras and musicians, I assume that writing out the performer would be anathema to you?

JC: Yes. It's also a lifeless thing to do. The idea of going to a concert to hear things done so exactly means you want to hear the same thing at each performance. What's the point of doing it again? Just do it once, record it and listen to it.

RE: You've been relentless in your condemnation of composers who don't believe in communication. You don't seem very fond of the idea that music is something outside of life.

JC: Well, obviously I'm a composer and I happen to have opinions. If I liked everything I wouldn't be able to write anything. I do feel the purpose of art is to reach people and to say something. You can say all the things you want but if it's in an empty room, then you're not reaching anybody. I have no objection to people who don't want to communicate as long as they don't mind the fact that no one wants to listen. If people are not speaking to the concert audience they shouldn't expect the concert audience to listen and they shouldn't intimidate them into listening. A Pulitzer Prize-winning composer told me that he considered a concert "a private communication through public means." And I answered him, "Well, that's all very nice but why should the public support that?" And he said, "Because it's art." And I said, "Not for them, you're not speaking to them. Let the people you're speaking to support it. That seems fair, doesn't it?" The only part that bothers me is that it's pushed on people who don't want it. I like adventurous things and I think this week we've seen a lot of adventure here in Winnipeg. I don't think adventurous things alienate people. I think what they really don't like is feeling they're not being spoken to. I resent being cut out of the process.

RE: There is another side to this, though. I remember reading a comment James Joyce made when someone complained about the difficulty of reading *Finnegan's Wake*. He said it took him seventeen years to write the book and it ought to take the reader as long to read and understand it. Would you say that Joyce is entirely off base? Are his expectations not appropriate?

JC: That's ridiculous. Why should I read it? Joyce has no right to expect me to read his book unless I'm interested in it. That's my right. If you want me to listen, show me why I should, not through bawling me out, not through making me feel guilty, not through making me feel stupid. Simply provide me with something I'm interested in. Like Shakespeare did. Or Beethoven. Or Picasso.

RE: Since you know how important it is to get the audience initially interested, do you compose strategically?

JC: It's not thought out like that, although I do believe in clarifying music at all times. I love complexity but I don't believe in obscurity for its own sake. Many people, especially in the German Romantic tradition, seem to believe that incomprehensibility and art are inseparable, and that something becomes a work of art when we don't understand it. I don't believe that's true and I don't think Mozart would have thought that, either. That's the MGM movie view of art, where the tortured, misunderstood composer writes a symphony overnight after seeing dancing girls on the quais. No one understands it and that means it's a masterpiece.

RE: Obviously music has also got to be a part of life for you. In Symphony no. 1, you addressed the highly significant public issue of the AIDS crisis. I'm wondering how much you feel the composer is obliged to respond to the political aspects of the time in which he lives?

JC: I don't think it's an obligation. I think that composers reflect their society by composing in their lifetimes. It's not so obvious as saying I'm going to compose a piece about this or about that. But certain pieces do take on a shape because of specific things the composer wants to address. I would say a composer like Shostakovich in his *Leningrad* Symphony or a painter like Picasso in *Guernica* did that. Every statement of Picasso's is not a statement about politics, yet he reflects the world around him by his very actions. Whereas Shostakovich's Eighth or Ninth Symphonies have nothing to do with politics. Actually, the Ninth is a joyous and rather funny piece. So I think the creative person is going to sit down and write a piece on something that fascinates him. It might be purely musical; it might be political; it might be a message; it might be a feeling. Whatever it is, it's a jumping-off point for the imagination.

RE: But let me ask you about the historical and personal origins of Symphony no. 1.

JC: Actually, it wasn't written as a political piece; it was written for my friends. I wrote it as a personal piece and then it became political because of the subject. Although I must say that the rage in the first movement is amplified beyond personal rage because of political issues.

RE: It strikes me that a lot of your work has been very personal?

JC: I write for people I know. That's one thing. I wrote my *Pied Piper* Fantasy for James Galway because he commissioned it; my Clarinet Concerto was an elegy for my father who was Concert Master of the New York Philharmonic, the orchestra that premièred it. Whether these things are known by the audience really doesn't matter. One of the great things about music, perhaps its greatest attribute, is its non-specificness. When people came up to Stravinsky after a performance of *The Rite of Spring* describing the various animals they heard his response was, "There are no elephants in my music." He also said, "Music means absolutely nothing," which was his way of debunking the tendency of listeners to attach something to music as a way of compensating for its abstraction. It's like looking at abstract art as a Rorschach test, picking out figures that the creator never saw and distorting it into a realistic piece. You can do it, the artist might not object, but he certainly didn't think of that. He wanted you to sense the abstraction of it, rather than the specificity of it.

RE: I want to talk about American composers for a bit. When I first heard Aaron Copland's *Rodeo*, for instance, I thought of it as a quintessentially American piece. Is there something about music that is particularly American? What makes a composer American?

JC: I can give you the simple answer by quoting Virgil Thomson, who defines an American composer as an American who composes. But that won't do, will it? I think that, first of all, American composers are the least Germanic of twentieth-century composers. German Romanticism really turned out to be a frightening thing. Benjamin Britten said the rot began with Beethoven. He was referring to the alienation of music from its audience that grew out of the philosophies inherent in German Romanticism: the composer as prophet, the idea that misunderstanding is a virtue, the notion that the composer really had to satisfy himself and no one else, the excesses of length and breadth that were really about ego satisfaction—all these horrifying things come out of distorted Romanticism. Also, I always associate World War II and the extreme elegance with which Haydn serenades were played on the way to the gas chambers with a kind of super-Romanticism. I'm sure Hitler thought of himself as an artist and a visionary who was doing something beautiful in cleansing the world.

RE: Actually, there's a brilliant and unsettling film about that very attitude called *The Architecture of Doom*. It's a kind of film essay and meditation on Nazi aesthetics which looks at everything from Hitler's sentimental water-colours to his obsession with Wagner.

JC: Yes, Wagner laid it all out. If you want to see the ground work for the Third Reich, you just have to read Wagner's treatise on Jews. He was a monster and it's no accident that Hitler loved him. If you look at the *Ring* you see these dwarf-like creatures with big noses running around and then you see the beautiful German gods. I've always been upset that Levine and Bernstein conduct Wagner because I find his repugnant ideas implicit in his art. So one of the things I loved about American music—and why I feel myself an American composer—is because I think we rejected that. We stripped it clean. It isn't tortured and angst-filled. Now, my Symphony no. 1 is the closest thing I've ever written to German music because I was writing about something that was very angst-filled—the idea of death and horror. Whereas the opera or my concertos are very American in their mentality. You know, Thomson and the idea of simple hymn tunes. I don't think a twentieth-century German composer would know what the phrase "with simplicity" means. Yet, American scores are full of words like "understated," "with simplicity." I think what I love about American music is its sense of optimism, its sense of clarity and purpose, its need to strip away all the excess notes; its sense of rhythmic drive and rhythmic pulse.

RE: Velocity is something that you often refer to in speaking about your music.

JC: Yes. Velocity, excitement and direction of kinetic energy are something that North American music has. I think we have a lot of things that make our music healthy, wonderful and outreaching. Even now, I think modern German composers are lost. I think Europe's enormously behind the times when it comes to composition.

RE: But isn't history something that demands attention? If your history is loaded and oppressive, like German history, then it's almost impossible to escape. I see this especially in contemporary German visual art. Now, because in North America we believe in velocity and speed and openness—not to mention a certain degree of aggression—does that become the pattern from which we must work? Does it lock us in?

JC: I think we have matured into a world in which all kinds of music are being played. It's not a question of which one is the most modern because there is no more avant-garde. In a sense the avant-garde is dead in music. It's an old idea. Now there's still music being written with an avant-garde approach. And it should be. All these musics should be written. Fashion changes a lot, but now there are a multiplicity of fashions. There are well-known people writing in a variety of languages in this country and I think that's great.

RE: So that eclecticism is healthy as far as you're concerned?

JC: I think free speech is healthy. And these composers should find their audiences. I'm all for real democracy in music. I don't like it when there's only one language that can be spoken or one kind of technique. I think we should simply open up the floodgates. Young composers can write one piece and take a whole new direction in their next piece if they want to experiment. They can be as curious as the listener.

RE: I could accuse you of being naïve. As public arts support is increasingly being reduced in both our countries, there's a driving necessity to make music that's accessible. Because that's the only way we're going to survive. What do we do about the fact that we're living in an economic climate that is not going to be very responsive to the kind of openness you talk about?

JC: I don't think that's true. First of all, I said that everyone should find his audience; I didn't say everyone should have an audience. I can understand that people in universities are getting tired of playing serial music [the contemporary mode of composition popularized by Schoenberg's twelve-tone system]. Then they shouldn't play it. Someone else will play it; or no one else will play it. It's Darwinian but it's true. We cannot make a species survive because we think it should. We can encourage it, but we can't—and we shouldn't—legislate it. I'm not advocating total populism. I mean, I think some pretty phony pieces got played here during the [New Music] Festival. But we have to change people's attitudes. I think the biggest problem with audiences, aside from being confounded by things, was that their right *not* to like things was taken away from them. People have a right not to like things. Maybe audiences have to be more demanding. But this isn't just populism; this is the way art has always existed. I mean, Beethoven existed that way, Mozart, Handel and Bach all existed that way. I just don't see why all of a sudden in the twentieth century we have to have an entirely different set of rules about how a person should approach a work of art.

RE: Mozart and Beethoven were obsessed with audiences.

JC: Exactly. Mozart would go from town to town and change the movements of his symphonies to please audiences. I just think that as soon as we understand how old-fashioned and nineteenth century Joyce's idea is, the better. It's like people who talk about modern music and mention Schoenberg. Do they realize Schoenberg's been dead for a long time, and the pieces they're talking about are eighty years old? That's not modern music; that's old music. Modern music is music being written now and I can assure you that somebody who says they don't like modern music hasn't got any idea what they're talking about. You know what they mean by modern? They mean dissonant and incomprehensible. They wouldn't consider a John Adams piece modern music because it's not dissonant or incomprehensible, but they would consider Schoenberg modern music.

RE: I was struck by the fact that one of the first pieces you were really taken by was *Billy the Kid*. Billy the Kid was a bandit, someone outside society. Did you decide that you wanted to be an outsider? You've been the first person to do a lot of things and it seems to me that you've always been pushing the edges a little bit. Is that a conscious choice that comes out of your personality?

JC: I really picked up *Billy the Kid* because of the bass drum making all that sound on my hi-fi. It had nothing to do with banditry. What occurred to me is that I could make this incredible sound with a fifteen-inch woofer that made my stomach churn. The truth is that I probably became a composer because my father was a violinist and discouraged me from going into music and I'm a very rebellious person. He said, "You'll never make it, you can't do it," and I did it. That's part of the reason I'm also a very rebellious composer. I started composing right at the high point of the age of serial music and no one would look at my music. My publisher just called and wanted to know why *Tournaments* was written in 1965 and premièred in 1980 and I said because nobody would play it then. It wasn't the right kind of music. In those days only one kind of music got played and commissioned. Everybody hated contemporary music in the '50s; audiences just fled from concert halls. So both my parents were against my becoming a musician. I actually wrote a violin and piano sonata for them both and my father never looked at it. It got played and won the first prize in the 1964 Spoleto Festival Competition. My mother did go to Spoleto to hear it but my father never even congratulated me. And then it was played by the Concert Master at the London Symphony and still he never said anything, and then it came closer to New York when it was played by Roman Totenberg in Boston. Finally my father had to take it out and learn it. And he played it and recorded it. Until then he never said a word to me about it. But he did go to other musicians to try to get them to say things that were negative so that he could report back to me. He showed it to George Szell, David Diamond and Morton Gould, saying, "My son wants to be a composer, isn't that ridiculous?" They all told him I knew what I was doing and to leave me alone. I guess he thought he had the answer for me because he had found music to be a very tough life. He was being protective but he said the wrong things. He should have said, "I *want* you to become a composer."

RE: The old "Don't throw me in the briar patch" strategy.

JC: Exactly. Anyway, all this contributed to my sense of being a rebel. Today, things are different. Now that music is getting more and more tonal and simple, my music is getting wilder. I'm going to turn into a Modernist soon, only because it's going to be so out of fashion. In my mind I'm so incredibly out of fashion that the idea of being in fashion appalls me.

RE: But in fact you're a very popular composer.

JC: But they don't know what I'm going to do next. It's not like a Glass or a Babbitt piece. I don't want to be predictable to myself and when I write a new piece, I don't know what I'm going to write. I don't know what techniques I'm going to use or the world I'm going to be in. I don't want to get locked into my last piece. Because I start with a clean slate I think it's very hard for me to be in fashion. I'm constantly changing my vocabulary from piece to piece. It really invigorates me; it's what gives me a sense of excitement.

RE: If you're not interested, then you can't expect an audience to be either?

JC: It begins with the discovery of things I haven't done. Twenty-five years ago when the Beatles were writing all those wonderful songs—*The Magical Mystery Tour* and all that stuff—everybody in the classical music world was very impressed with their sophistication. They did mixed meters, they did modes, they did polyrhythms, they combined Oriental instruments with Western ones. But they weren't doing anything that hadn't been done. It wasn't new, it's just that *they* were discovering it. The trick was in their discovery. Every time they discovered wonderful things—like having seven-bar phrases or when they did something in a modal way—they got excited by it. The music has a sense of inner excitement. The things they did were musically very subtle and beautiful.

RE: So you can reinvent the wheel and keep the interest of both the inventor and the audience?

JC: But you can't come in knowing everything. You have to discover. If a composer is so equipped at the age of twenty that he knows everything—harmonically, rhythmically, etc.—then he's either got to find a whole new world to discover or he's going to start sounding tired. I always discover new things. I don't know anything about the guitar, so I'm going to write a guitar concerto.

RE: But you're musically saturated. You're by no means naïve?

JC: I'm absolutely naïve in some areas. In opera, for instance. I'm not an opera lover, I don't go to the opera very much. When I wrote *The Ghosts of Versailles*, it was from the vantage point of an outsider.

RE: Why would the Metropolitan pick you to do the first opera in twenty-five years by an American if you weren't an opera enthusiast?

JC: That's why Levine did it. He said he didn't want someone who had solutions. He wanted someone from outside who would come in and shake things up. He felt that an opera by theatrical people who were not opera people was the most exciting thing.

RE: Weren't you terrified, though?

JC: I was physically ill. It's the scariest thing in the world to write your first opera for the hundredth anniversary of the Met. In those days I went to exercise at the Sixty-third Street Y, which is right near Lincoln Center. I couldn't look at the building, so I would take my bicycle and drive it all the way to Central Park West and then I would avoid looking down sixty-third street in order not to see even a piece of Lincoln Centre. I didn't want to know that building existed. It was very scary, but I do get scared when I write. I always get scared because I don't know what I'm doing until I get an idea.

RE: Do you need that edge? Don't you ever want to settle back into the comfort of knowing what you're doing at some point, just to give yourself a breathing space?

JC: I'd love to but it doesn't work out that way. When I write a piece, I have no technique and no imagination for a good part of the beginning process. I put my subconscious into overdrive; I make it come up with answers. I feed it more and more information because I don't know how and when the synapses will come out with the answer. So what I ask myself is, "Why are you writing this piece? Who are you writing this for? What is going to happen there? What do you want to see? Why are you writing music in the first place?"

RE: You constantly question yourself?

JC: Absolutely. So with the Guitar Concerto I ask, "What does a guitar mean to you? What are the problems?" And of course the biggest problem is hearing the damn thing. Can you write a guitar concerto where the orchestra is playing and the guitar plays and you actually hear a guitar rather than something in a distance? I'm talking about a natural acoustic guitar versus orchestra. It's not a viable combination, so I'm writing for the smallest possible group.

RE: One of the things that has fascinated me about you is that you have deliberately chosen instruments—like the oboe, the clarinet and flute—that have been under-valued or under composed for in the symphonic repertoire. Clearly that has been a conscious political choice?

JC: I wouldn't call it political. The composer has to look at the modern orchestra and ask, "What am I doing here, what's my part in this?" Either he says, "My part is to illuminate the world with my greatness," or he says, "I'd love to find a useful way to be a part of this." For me one of the best ways is to write concertos for instruments that have limited repertoire and great performers. I don't see that I need to write a violin concerto. But look at Richard Stoltzman. He's got very limited repertoire to play. He plays my Clarinet Concerto all over the place because once he finishes with Mozart, Weber and a few others, he's finished. The same is true with flute, oboe, french horn and guitar.

RE: I gather you also compose for certain instruments in order to take advantage of the properties of the instruments themselves. Would that consideration be as important as who might play it?

JC: In the case of the oboe the fascination for me was taking an instrument I have only seen exhibited lyrically and asking myself, can I write a piece in which the traditions, mechanism, qualities and the whole aspect of the oboe is reflected in the concerto? So it was a different kind of challenge. When I write a piece I set up goals and challenges for myself. In that case it had to do with an instrument that I found fascinating.

RE: You like tension in your composing, don't you?

JC: What I like is tension and release. I like movements that set up a need for each other. But Baroque was the same; every age has been the same. They had preludes and fugues. If there was an aggressive prelude they didn't have an aggressive fugue after it, they had a lyrical fugue and vice versa. Things set up things. You have a big fast movement first, then you have a slow movement. These just set up the human needs of excitement versus relaxation, of chromatic versus diatonic, of loud and soft. The opposites of life, the yin and yangs of music.

RE: Are you a musical Manichaean then, systematically orchestrating balanced tensions?

JC: It's satisfying my own need. Human need is like that. Too much repetition and it's boring. Balance keeps people happy. This is not a conscious thought, any more than the Beatles when they composed "Yesterday" had consciously thought of using the same three note motive that Mozart used in his Fortieth Symphony. Do you think they thought of those things? No. The reason they did that is they were making an idea change, presenting it at the same time they were letting it metamorphosize. Did they intellectualize that? No. It was the need to hear it again— familiarity—and the need to change it—variety. Those things are part of human sensibility and people acknowledge them when they compose.

RE: There are people who want music to be a ritual of repetition and there are also people who say that art must constantly put pressure on the edges, that it must challenge the audience. Is finding a workable relationship between those two tendencies a fairly delicate road to walk much of the time?

JC: I'm more of an in-between person. But different people do different things; different cultures do different things. You can look at the difference between the sense of order in the Classical period and the Romantic period with its sense of change and excess. There's also order and chaos. Because everyday life represents order—we make our beds, clean up, put on a tie, go to work—John Cage said that art should represent chaos. He has a valid point. I don't think the music itself works but I understand what he's after. Of course, the thing about his concerts is that the performers have great fun because they're delighting in confusion, chaos and the joy involved in just doing anything. They're not worried about missing a trill or an octave run because there are no such things to miss. So there is a high spirit about a concert of that kind of music. And Satie's whole point was to make fun of the seriousness of concerts. That's why he writes "flabby preludes," or a piece in the shape of a pear. He was the first person who really had very little craft who was basically philosophical.

RE: A Duchampian composer?

JC: Very similar.

RE: I want to just briefly turn now to what's been happening here in Winnipeg. Has this been a significant week for you personally?

JC: It's been a wonderful week. First of all I've heard a lot of new music, as well as Canadian music I didn't know before, and I've met a lot of extraordinarily wonderful people. But the best thing was the attitude. I was very moved by how thrilled everyone is—the orchestra, conductor and audience—about New Music. Let me give you an example. During the last rehearsal of my symphony we ran into overtime and I still hadn't finished giving my notes. I had ten more minutes but they had to dismiss the orchestra. Bramwell Tovy announced that although we were out of time, I wanted to finish. The entire orchestra stayed and listened to me. I was floored. There's no way you'd get that in New York. Nor, by the way, would you get what happened last night. The orchestra was backstage under the curtain and when the five young composers whose music they just played took their bows and were applauded by the audience, there was stomping in the back from the orchestra as well. I thought, my God, here's an orchestra wanting to pay tribute to the composers of pieces they had just played. I've got to tell you that was worth the whole trip right there.

RE: So you get some sense of genuine musical excitement here in Winnipeg?

JC: Yes, I really do, I get a sense of passion from the audience. Passion, care, excitement and joy. I've had a wonderful time. It's been one of the only times I've seen real health radiating at concerts. Maybe there's a magical environment here but it makes me feel good about writing music again. Sometimes when the cynical, hard line thing goes on for a long time, it's hard to stay in love with music. But here I feel rejuvenated.

Gavin Bryars

Musical Constructions

Gavin Bryars has patched together a fascinating life in music. A gifted double-bass player, he worked with jazz improvisers like Derek Bailey and Tony Oxley in the mid 1960s, while sustaining an interest in everything from Beat poetry and prose, to the music of John Cage and the philosophy of Wittgenstein.

His life is a series of conjunctions, so many "ands." This range of interests has sustained his composition and has led him to construct a piece on the sinking of the Titanic, on the Jules Verne short story called "The Green Ray," as well as to work with the brilliantly mercurial Robert Wilson on the opera *Medea* and on a section of *the CIVIL warS*. He has also taught university courses on Marcel Duchamp and Jasper Johns, and has been taught by William Empson, the English poet and author of *Seven Types of Ambiguity* (one of modern literature's most influential texts).

Still, there has been nothing ambiguous about Bryars's omnivorous eclecticism. He started the famous Portsmouth Sinfonia, a group of thirteen musicians who achieved cult status for their performances and recordings of classical music, played with what has been generously described as "minimal music skills." Bryars has also performed with popular artists, including Tom Jones, Sammy Davis Jr., Dusty Springfield and Petula Clark; he regards the Beach Boys as "one of the supreme musical groups" and is sufficiently a fan of Tiny Tim's that he joined his fan club in 1968. "I appreciate voices which are outside the norm," he says with a fox-like naïveté.

What holds together this disparate range of interests is his search for "some kind of middle ground" between the intellectual rigour which informs each piece and a quality of apparent simplicity which he hopes describes that same piece.

I say apparent because Bryars compositions can be astonishingly complicated in their conception and construction. He has the attitude of a conceptual artist when he begins, and the thoroughness of a researcher when he works. With *The Sinking of the Titanic*, for example, he operated like a detective. He found out who were the musicians on board, what instruments they played, what songs they likely performed as the ship went down, and then after conducting all this research and writing the music, was content to let the piece exist in the mind only and not be played in time. We shouldn't forget that he is a member of the College of Pataphysics, the "science of imaginary solutions."

The Sinking of the Titanic was written in 1969 and since then Bryars has been composing pieces which are getting a considerable amount of play. Certainly the most successful has been *Jesus' Blood Never Failed Me Yet*, a four-line hymn fragment sung by a London tramp Bryars recorded as part of a documentary film on England's homeless. The section wasn't included in the documentary but Bryars had other and more ambitious uses for it. He took the voice and added a layered instrumentation that elevates the tramp's voice to an almost mantric transcendence. He thinks of the most recent recording of *Jesus' Blood*, a seventy-five-minute-long version which includes the splendidly ragged voice of Tom Waits, as an "assisted ready-made" in the tradition of Duchamp, one of the modern periods greatest risk-takers and one of Bryars's most profound influences. It's in a piece like *Jesus' Blood* where you become aware of the myriad cultural and aesthetic experiences playing through the music. Bryars's fascination with Duchamp and minimal music are all mixed in with a persistent social conscience, and an abiding and essential humanity.

Gavin Bryars was invited to be the Distinguished Artist-in-Residence for the Winnipeg Symphony Orchestra's 1994 New Music Festival. The following interview was conducted after the evening performance on February 2, and then again, three days later, after Bryars had taken part in a panel discussion called "The Contemporary Composer: An Endangered Species." Bryars's vitality, range and success with audiences seem to make his extinction an unlikely proposition.

GAVIN BRYARS: My mother is an amateur cellist; she's eighty-seven and every Monday night she still plays string quartets. My father died when I was nine, but he was a good amateur baritone who sang in the church choir. I did too and my uncle played the church organ.

ROBERT ENRIGHT: So you grew up in a world where music was as natural as breathing?

GB: Mostly making music rather than listening to it. We didn't have a record player. We listened to the radio, usually the classical station. Then when I was a teenager I began to get interested in jazz and pretty soon I was playing on an amateur level with a few friends in town.

RE: When did you begin to take music seriously as something you might want to do?

GB: I guess that was probably during the time I was at university. I started teaching myself the double-bass and little by little I found myself playing in the university jazz scene. And when I became reasonably good as a bass player, I moved more into the local jazz community which turned out to have two or three really quite exceptional and, ultimately, internationally famous players. At the time I also had a girlfriend who was in the local art college. That was my first encounter with the visual arts. I actively started to look at painting. But I guess the only thing I was really passionately interested in at that time was jazz and some areas of contemporary music. I used to do a lot of poetry in jazz. I had all the records of people like Kenneth Rexroth and Lawrence Ferlinghetti.

RE: I don't mean this as a naïve question, but what was it that initially attracted you to jazz? I'm asking in light of your later observation that jazz was a tyranny because you carried to it what you already knew. So in some senses it wasn't improvisational at all.

GB: When I first started getting interested in jazz, I'd also started reading people like Kerouac. So there was a jazz life which I knew about. But also there were some players who earned respect in the classical world. People like Dave Brubeck, Jerry Mulligan and the Modern Jazz Quartet. There were academic musicians who respected that music and even talked about it favourably. I remember one of my tutors in music at Sheffield, a guy called Roger Bullivant, who wrote one of the standard academic works on the fugue. He was completely steeped in the baroque. Music for him probably stopped with the death of Bach, except for the Modern Jazz Quartet because he enjoyed the way they came to terms with the baroque in the controlled area of jazz. Eventually, what I found most interesting as a teenager were the early recordings of Ornette Coleman. The music was so wild and strange, and one of the reasons I was determined to like it was because the people announcing it on the radio were actually putting down the music. I thought, if they're putting it down, there must be something in this stuff.

RE: Almost all of the influences you've mentioned were American. Did you have a sense of being British in any of this? Or were you already edging towards some notion of an international community of music?

GB: Certainly most of the things that we listened to in jazz would have been American. Also the contemporary music which interested me was also American. It was Cage, Christian Wolff and Morton Feldman.

RE: Did you make a fairly good living playing double-bass?

GB: Yeah. I was a very serious bass player. At that time I started to take lessons so I developed my technique more and more. I used to practice on average between six and seven hours a day. And then I'd be playing two or three hours a night too. My hands were in fantastic shape and I developed a very fast technique.

RE: You were a good double-bass player, then?

GB: I was probably the best in the country. But I didn't play much outside Sheffield, mainly because the people I was working with—Derek Bailey and Tony Oxley—were so good. We had an experimental attitude to jazz and later a free improvisation which was way ahead of the rest of the country. And this went on for maybe two or three years. I abandoned it in the summer of 1966.

RE: Abandoned is a big word. Do you mean you consciously said I don't want to do this anymore and decided to do something else?

GB: More than that. I developed an almost pathological aversion to jazz and all improvised music. So in the early part of 1967, I put my bass in its case and didn't take it out again until 1983.

RE: Why the aversion? What happened that would have made you turn your back on what had been the most vital thing in your life for over ten years?

GB: There were some things within the music itself which gradually changed for me. At the same time as I was playing jazz I was studying composition and had even started to compose a bit. Sometimes I would compose things for the jazz group, trying to find ways to structure improvisation. And I began to get more and more interested in John Cage. I bought *Silence* in hardback when it first came out in 1962. I was very struck by his writings. Eventually I found an imbalance between the kind of aesthetic I was admiring, and beginning to understand, and the work I was doing. Also, as a philosophy student I'd gotten more and more interested in Oriental philosophy, especially in Zen. So when you combined that with Cage it seemed to me that conceptually I was moving into a territory other than hedonistic self-gratification, which is the territory occupied by jazz. I admired the cool, objective way of thinking about music that Cage seemed to represent.

RE: Was part of your aversion to jazz that you had discovered it wasn't free?

GB: That's right. There was a certain formal pattern which had begun to impose itself in our overall search for improvisation. It seemed almost intrinsic to the discipline and a limitation. The second thing happened when we went down to London to play in a club. I remember at the end of this session a London bass player came up and started talking about instruments. I had a particularly fine, old, English bass, a couple of hundred years old, very beautiful. It had a lovely clean sound; you'd get a nice ground on the bottom and it would sing at the top. And he said, "Could I do something with your bass?" So I passed it to him and he started playing. I watched him and listened to what he was doing and I could see that he hadn't any idea where his hands were going. But it sounded sensational. To the people who were listening, this man was a tremendous bass player, someone revered in the London jazz community. I thought, if he can do that and get away with it, what's the point of spending ten hours a day. I think I was probably rather naïve, and probably my response was a bit adolescent and emotional, but it was a real response at the time. I felt very discouraged. So I decided I would stop being a professional musician and that I would teach. I got a job teaching contemporary music in a technical college, which had a small art college attached. The students were welders, hairdressers and bricklayers, and teaching them was pretty damn impossible. I generally thought I could talk to people about music but in the end I was banging my head against a brick wall. In fact, I had a nervous breakdown and found myself retiring as an out-patient in a mental hospital for close on a year. It cracks you up a bit, but if you come out the other side you do see life in a much more healthy way. You're aware of human fragility, of your own personal limits and you also become skeptical about chemical medicine. Around that time some friends were doing a dance program at the University of Illinois and they had asked me for some music. I sent a tape to them and they said if I could get there, they'd put me up for as long as it was necessary to get the piece together. It was better than being in the nut house, so my aunt paid my air fare and I flew to New York. I had these boxes of pills—antidepressants, antihallucinatories, all kinds of stuff—and I was taking seventeen a day. But after three days in New York I flushed the whole lot down the toilet. I was a bit shaky for a day or two, but I never touched them again and I ended up staying in Illinois for about eight months. Cage happened to be there on a fellowship. I'd met him briefly in London and he actually remembered me, which I was very surprised by. He's a remarkable man. He knew I was in America on a tourist visa so that I was not allowed to work, and that I didn't have much money. Occasionally I would borrow a bass to play in a roadside diner. But Cage gave me work, doing some copying and preparing material for *HPSCHD*. This was in 1968, the year of Nixon's election. I was there when Martin Luther King was killed; Bobby Kennedy, too. People like Paul Newman and Dustin Hoffman came and spoke at the campus. So I became much more aware politically than I had been in England. When I came back I got a job teaching one day a week at an art college, doing music projects with art students. That was at Portsmouth, where we made the Portsmouth Sinfonia.

RE: What were you trying to accomplish with the Sinfonia?

GB: Well, none of the players were musically trained, so all we could work on were things other than conventional music notations. Some of the Fluxus pieces— La Monte Young, Christian Wolff—those kind of things. So they became adept at the territory of indeterminate music.

RE: Did you know the Fluxus people because of your connection with Cage in America?

GB: That was the first encounter. I also came to know them in connection with the performance art tradition. And George Brecht was living in England at the time and his work was quite well-known. I remember we had this idea to have an event based on the TV-show *Opportunity Knocks*. It was a talent show where different acts would come forward and do whatever they did. Then at the end of the show there was a "clapometer" and the best act would come onto the next show. Some people would tell jokes, there was a rock band, a conjurer, a ventriloquist and we decided to form an orchestra. There were about thirteen of us. We were interested in classical music as a popular phenomenon. But of course we had no knowledge of music history outside of popular culture. So the only music we could possibly play was stuff which they'd heard through popular sources. We chose the *William Tell* Overture because of *The Lone Ranger*. We had to acquire instruments, so I went out and I bought a euphonium at a bicycle shop. Other guys got saxophones. We had about three days to sort out the basics of our instruments, then we got a photocopy of Rossini's piano score and we underlined those notes we needed to know. It was all done on a beautiful, sunny May afternoon in the quadrangle of the college.

RE: Did you realize that what you were up to was performance art? That's what we'd call it now?

GB: And that's what it was, but we didn't think of it like that. We played the *William Tell* Overture, and then we put down our instruments and sang "The Lord is My Shepherd," and we became the Pontypridd Voice Choir. We were also a group of acrobats called the Pyrotechnic from the Pyrenees. We did all this stuff. Anyway, at the end of the afternoon the Portsmouth Sinfonia was the winner and so we had to perform again. We were hopeless. I mean our lips had gone and we were tired. But we did it anyway. There was quite a strong documentary film department in the college and it had a sound recording studio. So we decided we'd make a recording; we taped it and had it manufactured as one of those floppy singles, the kind you get with a magazine. And we sent copies through the College Post to people we admired all over the world. We sent one to Leonard Bernstein; one to the English prime minister, Edward Heath. Boulez got one; we sent one to our English soccer hero, Rodney Marsh; we even sent one to Mao Tse-tung. We didn't hear much back. Although, we were told later that Bernstein found it really very interesting.

RE: Today that looks like a piece of mail art. Without knowing it, you were plugging into the Fluxus notion of the devaluation of the precious art object. Were you aware of what you were doing in an art context, or were you just having fun?

GB: I suppose we were having fun. But we were aware of those values because we had done a lot of work on Brecht's Fluxus boxes, which included ideas about deconstruction. But when we were playing for the Sinfonia—although it was objectively hilarious—we were absolutely straight-faced. We were not trying to be funny. Humour was a by-product of what we did. I think later in that same year there were loads of very serious concerts in England because it was the Bicentennial of Beethoven's birth. The Scratch Orchestra had formed by then and had organ-ized a concert at the Purcell Room in London—a kind of rethinking of Beethoven. We did Beethoven's Fifth there by invitation. Eventually we found we had a whole concert. I think by about '72–73 we were in a position to make our first album which Brian Eno produced. He'd been an art student at Winchester, which was just down the road from Portsmouth, so he knew of our existence.

RE: When did the art and thinking of Marcel Duchamp begin to play into what you were doing?

GB: Slightly later. I left Portsmouth in the summer of '70 and went to Leicester to teach. I was doing some tutorial work with individual students who were making performance pieces and time-based video pieces. An art historian named Fred Orton asked me if I would contribute some lectures to his program. He thought I might be interested in talking about Jasper Johns. Now, I had never really thought about Johns but I looked at the work, and started thinking about Johns and Wittgenstein and their connection to meaning; you know, all these numbers and letters in Johns, and how they related to some particular areas of Wittgenstein. I don't think it was very good but I did try very hard and Fred enjoyed it. He gave me a few tips on how to make it better and then he asked me to do some others. Little by little I enlarged my repertoire. Then he asked me if I'd do one on Duchamp and I remember I was going to try and cover the whole of Duchamp in a two-hour lecture. By the end of the lecture I'd only just got up to the *Large Glass*. So Fred and I decided to offer a course just on Duchamp. Every Wednesday afternoon we'd meet for four hours; the first half either Fred or myself would do a paper on some aspect of Duchamp and the second half one of the students would do a paper. The students did some very interesting work. I remember a guy called Reg Wilmer who started to make practical reconstructions of Duchamp's works. We also used to go down to visit Richard Hamilton and he would talk to us about his remake of the *Large Glass*. It was very serious. This went on for about two years and during that time I stopped writing music. It wasn't a crisis; I just felt I was actually learning more from the Duchamp research. I wrote no music at all between 1972–1975.

RE: Your life has had strange patterns of abdication.

GB: That's true, actually. I never thought about it like that. I guess I've had my ups and downs.

RE: But to borrow a line from the '60s, you've always found a way to feed your head, even in what you call the down times.

GB: Absolutely, I never really had a time when I was away from it. Even when I was in the mental hospital I used to go down to London weekends and play for dance classes. So I found things to do. Certainly at that time the Duchamp thing was very important because it got me in touch with a whole lot of artistic ideas. They were mostly French, especially the writings of Raymond Roussel. So when I started writing music again I was thinking in a different way. Up to that point I'd done things like *The Sinking of the Titanic* and *Jesus' Blood*, which in a way relate to aspects of art college culture. In fact, the first sketch of the Titanic piece was written for an exhibition to support students who were under attack from more traditional painters. I was thinking if we've got conceptual art, what could conceptual music be? And so I tried to make a piece which would just be research material, which didn't have to exist as music. I wrote it in 1969 and the first performance wasn't until the end of '72.

RE: You really had been strongly influenced by Duchamp and by conceptual art. It's a pretty radical notion to compose music that needs only to be thought and not played.

GB: That's right. A lot of the pieces that I did at that time were prose notations. I did this very silly piece, which actually got recorded, called "One Two, One Two Three Four." It related to my cabaret days where each performer had a pair of headphones and a cassette machine containing identical material. On a given signal, you'd go "One, two, one two three four," as if you were counting at the beginning of a big band number. Then you'd press the start button. When you heard the music you'd play along. So what the player heard was this very beautiful hi-fi recording. It was rather like a karioke. But what the audience heard was everyone playing part of this music slightly out of time because obviously there was a certain error built in about the exact starting point. So it was a conceptual piece, a systems piece and a kind of deconstruction. It also could be performance art.

RE: By this time you seem to be operating very easily within a hybrid world. You're not making distinctions between performance art or music or visual art. Did blurring the boundaries make a lot of sense to you, then?

GB: Sure, I tended not to go to conventional concerts. The places where most of this stuff went on was usually an art gallery or a college. It would also take place where there were other kinds of art events which were not necessarily music but were similarly not so clearly defined or focussed.

RE: Were you conscious of being part of anything that could be called a movement?

GB: I never thought of it as a movement. Although we were developing a strong sense of this rather strange English experimental music through the Scratch and composers like myself who were on the fringe. There was also a strong connection with Cage in America. But then Cage found himself ostracized by some of the English people, especially when Scratch moved to an extreme Maoist position. But we also had strong connections with people like Philip Glass and Steve Reich, both of whom came to England in 1971. They would play to an audience of maybe a dozen at the Royal College of Art canteen. I remember on consecutive days Philip and Steve came out to Leicester to give lectures. They were paid ten pounds and their return rail fare. The Japanese group, The Taj Mahal Travellers came up as well. Then we started an organization called Experimental Music Catalogue. Because there was so much going on in London we decided to pool all this stuff and make the pieces available to people who wanted to buy them. In 1972, I became editor of the catalogue and ran it until it folded in 1981. People would write to my address to find out how to get individual pieces by London-based composers. We also started to anthologize pieces. It wasn't real publishing in the sense that we got royalties or anything. I simply printed the stuff, paid for the photocopying and got back a cheque. But I started to develop correspondence and connections with people abroad. For example John Adams got in touch with me in 1972 and started to buy things when he was teaching at the San Francisco Conservatory. He invited me over in 1973 or 1974 and we did the first American performance of *Jesus' Blood*. In fact, probably the only one until this weekend.

RE: Were there other differences between the kind of experimental music you were doing in England and what was happening in America? Was the distinction largely political rather than musical?

GB: A combination. Beginning in 1972 English experimental music became polarized between those who developed a strong political line, and those who wanted to keep politics and music separate. So the Scratch split. But there was also an artistic difference in that there was none of the self-aggrandizement that we felt the Americans had. One of the things which illustrates the difference for me was the Steve Reich Group—it would have four high-powered, state-of-the-art electronic organs, highly amplified and with sound technicians. In England there was a group called PTO—short for the Promenade Theatre Orchestra—run by a very interesting composer named John White. PTO also played four identical organs, but theirs were little battery-operated machines bought from Woolworth's. And they were playing rigorous systemic music, often based on found material. They made reworkings of seventeenth-century keyboard pieces. They'd also make silly arrangements of pop songs. There was the same kind of rigour, but it was more like a gentlemen's club. And there was no interest in promotion or in making recordings. The question for PTO was simply—what can we do with this material? They had a self-deprecating sense of humour. The Americans had no sense of irony at all. We could see how damn stupid the whole thing was. Within ourselves we'd put it down at the same time that we'd defend it to the hilt against the philistines.

RE: I want to talk now about your work as a composer. We'll start below the surface. What was it in the Titanic that attracted you as a subject?

GB: The description that touched me most came from one of the heroes of the Titanic, the wireless operator, Harold Bride. He was floating in the sea with a life belt on 150 feet away as the ship went down. He said that the band was still playing and that he heard this hymn floating across the sea. My first reaction was to ask what would have happened physically with people trying to play music as they go under water. What if you were to transform the sound by treating it in an aquatic way? I became interested in the whole acoustic idea because one of the participants in the whole Titanic drama was Marconi. It was one of the first instances of using wireless telegraphy in ocean rescue. Marconi became intrigued toward the end of his life by the idea that, once generated, sounds never die. They simply get fainter and fainter because other sounds start to obliterate them. But if you had fine-tuning equipment you could go back to the sounds and recover them. Ultimately, Marconi was interested in hearing Christ speak his Sermon on the Mount. Now, I wasn't going to try and do that, but at the same time his idea that sounds never die had a resonance. I knew that sound is treated in a much more efficient way under water than in the air; it travels four times as fast and it is actually more secure. We know from recordings of whale songs, that sound can travel great distances under water; the sound bounces up and down from the water's surface which acts as a kind of seal. This fact probably explains the myth of the Sirens. Sailors would sleep with their heads against the hull of the ship, and the wood acted as a transducer between them and the water. What they actually heard were the sounds of porpoises and dolphins.

RE: So they weren't seduced by beautiful women, but rather by the properties of wood and some creatures swimming underneath?

GB: That's the theory and it seems perfectly rational to me. But I found I was researching more and more about the Titanic, and I based anything I composed on facts. I invented nothing. I may have made some extreme piece of reasoning but it originated in a fact. What I wanted was to find the tune they were playing, the instruments they were playing it on, where were they when they played it, what key did they play it in—all those kinds of things. I found there were eight musicians: three violins, two cellos, one little bass and two pianists. I got their names, photographs, even where they lived before they were killed. I thought of it all as detective work.

RE: So you weren't concerned about the upper-class people on board. You were interested only in the musicians?

GB: I was interested in the musicians only but I was eventually interested in their relationship to everybody else on the ship. Obviously the musicians had a social function; to play during dinner; to accompany the church service on Sunday, to play for dancing. They had very specific roles. As the water came through the decks, everyone naturally moved towards the surface, and eventually the musicians found themselves on the boat deck playing in the open air against the gymnasium wall. I have descriptions from different witnesses of what was happening as the ship went down and during that time they played light ragtime tunes to give a sense that life was perfectly normal. But when it became clear that all the lifeboats were gone and everyone was going to die, they stopped and they played this hymn. I'm almost certain the hymn is called "Autumn," which sounds a little bit like one version of "Nearer My God to Thee." But it has no connotations with anything funereal. It has lines like, "See the whitening harvest languish." It's an autumnal thing about the end of the harvest, about winter coming and the need to gather the grain. They probably didn't have music with them, so the song had to be something they knew. And it probably wasn't played very well. So what I did with my arrangement was simply stretch this hymn tune to last for five minutes, the time it had taken for the ship to sink. Then I took the tape to the Physics Laboratory at Cardiff University and subjected it to a number of treatments. I gave the physical description of what was going on to the acoustic physicist and he worked out what would have happened at different depths in terms of deflection. We were trying to work out all kinds of scientific ideas, many of which were probably totally absurd. In a way I've always thought of it as an open piece because there isn't a definitive score. I add to it each time I find out new information about the Titanic. I found out, for example, that there was a Scottish bagpipe player on board who played for dancing classes. So when I did the new version of the *Titanic* in 1990 I added a traditional Scottish horn lament. I didn't have pipes but I had a bass clarinet, which was a metaphor for the bagpipes. And I'm doing a new version to which I'm going to add an ensemble of young girl cellos. Both my daughters—who are eleven and thirteen—play the cello and every Saturday they play in a cello group of a dozen girls aged six to fourteen. And then I'm also working with a group of very beautiful boy trebles. So everything I'm adding to this recording will pick up on the idea of women and children first. Things are still factual but the metaphor grows and the resonance changes.

RE: I want to describe you as a romantic in the way you see music operating in the world. I'm thinking of pieces like *After the Requiem* and *The Sinking of the Ti-*

tanic. These works are elegies which not only measure our recognition of loss, but also register a fundamental hope.

GB: Quite a lot of the things I've done certainly have that connotation and even that specific content. I don't think of it in a religious way but in a broadly human-ist way. The *Jesus' Blood* piece, for me, had nothing to do with the Christianity of the man. It was his voice; it had to do with human dignity.

RE: Which is implicit in the band playing while the Titanic goes down. Maybe there was nothing else they could do, but the point is they didn't scream and yell and cry "God save me." They played music.

GB: One of the things we used to read a lot was Maoist talks on art and litera-ture at the Yenan Forum. And one of the central questions was what should be the function of art in a society. It seemed to me that if music does have a social func-tion, then it became clear to me when those musicians decided that they had a relationship to the other people on the ship. As you say, they could have run for the lifeboats at the first opportunity, just as musicians today would run for the bar at the first opportunity. They could have tried something crazy, strapping the cellos and the bass together to make a raft and row to Canada. But they didn't. They realized that while everything else was gone, they had one thing that nobody else had, and they chose collectively to use that skill.

RE: That's the spirit you must bring to *Jesus' Blood* then. Because you're open to accusations of everything from appropriation to sentimentality. His life was prob-ably disastrous and Jesus's blood probably failed him at every turn. Did you ever worry about how you were using this unknown singer's voice?

GB: It was an issue. I could be accused of that but there were several other things that I was doing. One was almost a Duchampian idea about an assisted ready-made, where you've found something that you don't do anything to, but you add something to it. That was the conceptual idea. Added to that was the emotional dimension: this man's voice alone, without me doing anything, had an extraordinary power and force. What I wanted to do was to see if I could reinforce that voice, give it greater strength and even increase its emotional force.

RE: Did you think of yourself as a collaborator, then, from the beginning?

GB: Yeah. For me he was the starting point. The piece didn't exist without him. I wouldn't be interested at all in someone else singing the piece. Another thing is that the song was something I didn't know. If he'd sung "Rock of Ages" or "The Lord is My Shepherd," that would have been the end of it. But this song was mysterious.

RE: Did you ever locate its tradition?

GB: Never. I was brought up a congregationalist Christian and I never came across it, and no one's pointed it out to me.

RE: Could they have been his own lyrics and melody?

GB: That's perfectly possible. I'd be delighted if that was the case. So the fact that it was a bit enigmatic—in a sort of scholarly way—was something which I also found fascinating. But ultimately it was the cumulative power of this man's voice alone.

RE: You've got this romantic, humanist side but you also seem to set problems for yourself as well? Your approach to composition is conceptual?

GB: Yeah, that's right. Sometimes I even invent the problem. In 1988 I was doing this commissioned project for the opening of the Liverpool Tate Gallery with Bill Cadman. I created problems for myself just by the scale. I decided that I would use both the Anglican and the Catholic organs from their cathedrals, which were each about a mile away from the site where we were playing. Then the way in which I wanted to collaborate with local musicians created additional problems. I found out who would be interested and that became the basis for the orchestration. You then have to reconcile all those problems.

RE: I'm intrigued to hear you talk because conceptual composers are often accused of arrogant intellectualism and the most obvious thing about your music is its essential humanity.

GB: Well, it's perfectly possible for someone to write a piece which is humanly touching but which is conceptually vacuous. Many pop songs are like that. There's nothing wrong with them but they don't last very long.

RE: Like "MacArthur Park." "I left my cake out in the rain and I'll never find that recipe again." It's bizarre.

GB: I love that song. But similarly there are things which intellectually regress, that you wouldn't want to hear a second time because they're totally unattractive. So I've always tried to find a middle ground between things which actually have rigour—involving some notion of craft and technique, and musical and intellectual skills—and things which are capable of being taken at a simple, direct level by someone who is not a specialized music listener.

RE: Has that been a conscious search for you?

GB: Yeah. One of the things I find hardest to do is to write music about music. For example, I couldn't even begin to write a piano sonata. Now I could maybe find out something about the piano's history or about some performer and then I'd make a piano piece. But I couldn't do it in the abstract way. I had a project two or three years ago where I was commissioned to write a saxophone concerto. Fortunately, this particular organization, The Bournemouth Sinfonia, made a rule that none of the three commissioned composers were allowed to call the piece anything with "saxophone" in it. It had to have a title which was more attractive so they could market it.

RE: And I guess the Sexy Sax Concerto just wouldn't cut it?

GB: No. I wrote a piece called "The Green Ray," based on the Jules Verne story. I found a connection between the saxophone's history and the setting of that particular story, which has always been one of my favourites. At one moment in certain latitudes as the sun sets it touches the horizon and emits a green ray. When two people see that at the same time, their love is sealed. I actually saw the Green

Ray once in California. Then I looked at the area of West Scotland. I knew it was the home of one of the pipe traditions. It occurred to me that the chanter is not a million miles from the soprano saxophone. There's a similar tone; it has an abrasive, nasty sound; in the wrong house it can sound damn unpleasant. Then I thought is there anything that connects the pipes and the Green Ray. When I was researching the history on the west coast of Scotland I found there were two locations where people used to practice the pipes. One was called the Pipers Cave where male pipers used to practice; and there was another called the Pigeons Cave where the females used to practice. So I decided that maybe these two people practice the saxophone at the same time and the Green Ray happens. They both see it and it makes a connection between them. So that became my title.

RE: You think like a writer. The connections you make come out of a writerly imagination.

GB: One of the people I've admired most has been the writer Raymond Roussel and his artificial techniques of making literature. Duchamp said that Roussel is responsible for his life's work. And similarly Roussel helped me begin to write music again. I made pieces which involved word play and puns. Like "The Cross Channel Ferry," which was the first piece I ever played in France. The person who best explained Roussel to me was the French writer Jean Ferry. So he was the ferry across the channel. And Ferry's favourite composer is Palestrina, whose name ends with an "A," so that gave me the key of the piece. But the Cross Channel Ferry is also the way I get to France.

RE: You're beginning to sound more and more like Peter Greenaway.

GB: I'm sorry. I apologize. I can get quite obsessive. Sometimes I find myself justifying everything so much that it's actually uninteresting. It can become so cryptic that it gets pretty damned opaque. I actually wrote pieces at the time where every single note had to be justified. Anyway, I went down that route, found the cul-de-sac, bounced back and said, okay there's a middle ground. By the mid '80s I realized that was the line to take. I think I've become a far better composer since then.

RE: Let's talk about some of the work made by this better composer. Tell me about *Medea*, the piece you worked on with Robert Wilson.

GB: It was produced at the Lyon Opera. We did six performances there and five at the Paris Opera. It sold out every night. And no one from any of the English opera houses came to see it. Now there's some interest in reviving it. The problem is it would be looking back at a ten-year-old piece and frankly, I made some mistakes.

RE: You wouldn't want to see it resurrected?

GB: I would but I would modify it. I would probably change the entire prelude section. Bob misled me on that. He said we didn't need any music, but everything was happening so damn slow that he needed music to support it. I actually have an audio recording of the dress rehearsal and some of it still strikes me as being very powerful. It's curious that no one was interested in Britain because the response at the Lyon Opera House was fantastic. They still talk about it in reverential terms. When I go into the opera house in Lyon now there are some people in the orchestra from those days. As I walk into the building they'll stand up and applaud. It's incredible. I would never have gotten a reaction like that in England.

RE: Why *Medea* by the way? It's a grotesque and terrifying story.

GB: It wasn't my choice, certainly. Bob had already committed himself to it. He was doing a play version in the original Greek and he started sketching this piece, working with a New York composer but it wasn't working out. One of Wilson's representatives in France had been to my performances in Paris where I had done this "Cross Channel Ferry" thing and she told Bob that I was a possible collaborator. She felt that he actually needed a musical collaborator after working with Philip Glass on *Einstein on the Beach*. So Bob came to London at Easter, in 1981, and we spent three days together looking at material. He talked about projects he had in the future and one of these was *Medea*. He showed me some of the videos he'd sketched in Washington. And he actually had an opening date for a play with music at La Fenice in Venice for September 1982. What he needed was an idea of how this piece would sound because he couldn't imagine it. So I sketched an aria for the soprano Medea, an aria for Jason, a chorus and an instrumental piece. I did these two or three-minute long sketches on a synthesizer with a couple of singers and he liked those. He'd already thought that the chorus should be sung rather than spoken. He asked me to go through the play and analyze where there could be singing and where there would be speaking. I did that and by August our play with music had become an opera with a few spoken lines. The problem was that the September opening date in Venice still stood. Here it was August of '81 and I had a September '82 performance of an opera which I realized was going to last over four hours. Then almost immediately after Bob left he phoned me from Munich to ask could I come over because he was starting rehearsals on *the CIVIL warS* and he needed a musician. I went to those first sketch rehearsals and was immediately thrown into Bob's world.

RE: Anyone I've talked to about Wilson gets involved in a bigger world than they're prepared for.

GB: Absolutely. I was just completely sucked in because I was pleased to be taken seriously. In January of '82, I'd written virtually half the opera and sketched some of the remaining material. We had a month in New York working that material, and then I went away and wrote the rest. I worked very hard and by the end of June had finished the opera. I actually learned a lot.

RE: So *Medea* was finished but *the CIVIL warS* was also percolating?

GB: Simultaneously. In June we had a production meeting in Venice to see where things were. It lasted for thirteen hours. And in the course of this meeting it became clear that a lot of things weren't ready. There were problems with the production music; they hadn't contracted the costume designer and the whole of the Italian workshops were going to be closed for August. So we had to cancel. I had busted my gut for a year writing this damn music and it was cancelled. I felt very low. Anyway I picked myself up and went on working with *the CIVIL warS*. Eventually *Medea* was produced in 1984, at which point I made a couple of changes. When we first did it, we had the idea that Medea would be black. And we had in mind Wilhemenia Fernandez, who was in *Diva*. A beautiful woman and a terrific singer. Now because Medea was black, Aegeus had to be black. So I wrote this whole thing almost as a jazz scene with two black characters singing in a very gentle, relaxed way. But when we produced it Medea was an Australian white singer, Yvonne Kenny. It was absolutely stupid to have her singing this stuff. So I had to completely rewrite the scene. It was very hard work and Bob and I fell out a few times. We had a big fight at the dress rehearsal, but the thing was done and it was a big success.

RE: It sounds like working with Wilson broke any notions you might have had of conceptually thinking through the piece. Were you flying by the seat of your musical pants?

GB: To a certain extent. But I did also take some time to research Greek music.

RE: You love this whole aspect of research, don't you? I mean learning is something that matters to you?

GB: Immensely. The problem with *Medea* was that I could do that to a certain extent but finally I had to write a lot of notes in a short time. I had to develop my skills very fast because it was the first thing I'd written for voices, as well as the first thing I'd written for orchestra. It was a hell of a job.

RE: Tell me about how the work proceeded on *the CIVIL warS*.

GB: Bob had been sketching the whole structure of the piece at the Munich Opera House. He was working with opera singers and he just felt he would be more comfortable with a composer there. And as the structure developed, I was given one section of music to write—the French section. It was to be act 2, scene b; act 3, scene a; and act 3, scene b. We recorded the percussion music for 2-b at a Baden-Baden radio station. It was the first thing that was done and I remember Bob felt very happy that we actually had some sounds on tape. It wasn't just phone calls and letters. A lot of the singers were going to be put out on fly wires and it would have been prohibitively expensive. You needed four technicians per fly wire and that gave us fifty-six technicians just for the flying. So it was dropped. But it was never clear how we were going to develop the sections I was involved with. It started very late. We worked for a two-week period in February of 1984 in a monastery in the hills about fifty kilometers from Versailles, the monastery where Mary Magdalene is supposed to have come to in France. It was a multi-faith religious retreat but it was closed during January and February. There were writers already there, the Lebanese writer Etel Adnan and then later Heiner Müller came over from Germany. I was given a grand piano and I'd be fed pieces of the libretto, then I'd write my stuff and send it through to this rehearsal room a couple of doors away and then carry on writing. Eventually it would come back with some comments or a blue pencil through it and I'd try again. It was a very intense two weeks. It also caused one of the worst moments of my life. I wrote an aria to a text called "The Queen of the Sea," by Etel Adnan. This was a scene where Jessye Norman arrives in the underwater kingdom of the Queen of the Sea and Bob's idea was that it was some kind of crazy part. I didn't know that was his idea and I set the aria as a beautiful, rather rhapsodic poem. I was writing something else when the baritone rushed in and said, "Quick, you've got to stop them, they're ruining this beautiful aria. He's cutting it up, he's breaking it into little fragments. It's one of the most beautiful things I've ever heard. Come and stop them." I said, "No I'll carry on here and we'll discuss it when it comes lunch time." Bob had a bit of a revolution on his hands. The cast said they wouldn't let this happen to this piece of music. So it provoked a crisis and we realized that we had to make some changes. It was to Bob's credit that we had this meeting which went on most of the night with Etel and Müller. We restructured things and started again. That was when I realized the enormity of what we had to do. We had about five or six days to completely sketch operatic material which was probably going to be about two hours in duration. I would then have to complete it within the space of two months, have it fully orchestrated, printed and ready to be sent to Los Angeles. I remember feeling absolutely dead at that moment.

RE: Because this is mid January and the piece was supposed to be performed at the L.A. Olympics in June or July?

GB: Yeah. This also happened at a time when I had decided to leave my wife and family so there were all kinds of personal, domestic and artistic pressures happening at the same time. Anyway the next day I just thought: Snap out of it you fool, you're just going to have to do it. So I got down to it and we completed some very interesting work. Unfortunately, the cancellation in Los Angeles happened before I was able to complete the opera. But I think it would have been pretty extraordinary stuff.

RE: Is Wilson difficult to work with? His imagination seems limitless but his lack of resources and time seem eventually to catch up to him.

GB: There is that aspect. Bob does have an extraordinary imagination and vision. But he's also equally single-minded. And so you get a sense of collaboration, but it's not necessarily the reality. I know that when we did *Medea*, Bob found it difficult to understand that once you've actually written out stuff for orchestras, it's rather hard to stretch or compress it. It's not like the Philip Glass Ensemble with *Einstein*, where you can simply cut out or double a few repetitions to make it fit. I remember one particular crisis towards the end of *Medea*. When we came to the final dress rehearsal it was the first time we'd actually gone from act 5, scenes b to c, the penultimate to the final scene. At the end of 5-b and at the beginning of 5-c you have Jason singing on stage. But between those two moments he has a costume change as well as the whole scenery changes. So we needed some extra music. Here it is an hour before the dress rehearsal and I had to write a minute and a half or two minutes of music for orchestra, put in the parts, and have it sight read by the musicians on opening night. Actually, I wrote a little interlude just for wind.

RE: Do you like Wilson? His demands seem almost inhuman at times.

GB: Yeah, that does happen. We had a couple of fights. But in general Bob and I got on very well. And I like him very much personally. If the opportunity came up to work together again, I would embrace the possibility.

RE: You know you're loaded with culture. Does that ever become an impediment?

GB: I've never found it a problem. I think in cultural terms.

RE: The reason I ask is because one of the things you admire about Duchamp is that he was always on the margin of things. Your respect for him has to do with risk-taking. And I wonder if you can run risks when you're so tradition-laden?

GB: I'm not sure about that. To a certain extent there are expectations when you work within particular traditions. If you're writing an orchestra piece for example, the musicians have certain expectations. And I must confess that I actually do try to give them things that fit onto their fingers, things which they actually feel will be suitable to play; so that their instruments do the things they feel they should be doing. But at the same time I'm giving them music which they actually haven't played before.

RE: Do you want them to stretch? Or do you just want them to be alienated?

GB: Not necessarily to stretch, either technically or conceptually. For example *Jesus' Blood* is incredibly easy for an orchestra to play. We had a first read-through just to make sure the notes fit. But I know the orchestra is going to have problems with it because it's so slow and so easy. The stretching is actually *not* having to play something very difficult. Playing something incredibly easy is very hard.

RE: I'm interested in the connection with Tom Waits. I saw a video where he tells you about hearing *Jesus' Blood* at his wife's birthday party and how much he admired it. How did you finally get him to perform?

GB: I actually sent him a plan of the whole seventy-five-minute-long piece and where the instruments come in and where he would be in that structure. He could see the rationale and he accepted it. So in November '92 we started recording all the instruments because Tom was still in Hamburg doing *Alice in Wonderland* with Bob Wilson. The idea was that he was going to be back in California for Christmas, for a holiday break with his family, and that in the new year we would finish the mix. So we came back in the new year and Tom had disappeared; his manager didn't know where he was; no one knew where he was. He wasn't answering the phone, he didn't reply to letters. This went on for three months. Anyway, he finally called and apologized saying he'd never done anything like that before, that he'd just been through some personal difficulty and that he'd intended no disrespect to me or to the project. But he wanted to work with his own engineer, with me and with nobody else. So I had to fly from New York to California with this master tape, rent a car and drive north to this studio in Northern California. Tom performed in real time. He was the only thing which isn't playing as a loop. He's actually following the journey of the man. The length of tape reel we could use was a maximum of fifteen minutes, so what we did was three different passes of fifteen minutes each.

RE: In all that time he never gets it.

GB: Never once. He never gets it right. But all the variations are fascinating. What I did was categorize the ways in which he sang it and put them into different groups. Ones which were closest to "Ruby's Eyes," one of his own songs; other ones where he omits certain words, or where he omits certain notes. Then I edited those into a particular sequence. Sometimes I'd keep four or eight groups together, then I'd pull in another one. And I created an artificial sequence of his perform- ance—a constructed sequence—to match the line of the orchestration.

RE: It's haunting. It also strikes me that it was very risky?

GB: Yeah, I think it is risky and it could have gone very wrong. But I also had to make sure that the piece was coherent without Tom. One of the partners in this whole deal was The Frankfurt Ballet and they weren't sure whether they wanted him or not, so I had to do a separate mix. It was almost like making a karioke version. Tom could be in or not. The first time I heard the whole piece was when we were actually transferring it to the CD master.

RE: The reason I said, "risky" is because Waits's voice almost blows the lid off the back end of the piece.

GB: The risk was probably one I constructed. For example, the coda is not that soft in his performance. He's singing in a very spacy room but I deliberately took out all the instruments and made him even more distant. There was something in his vocal performance that sounded to me as if he was slowly disappearing. I made a kind of imaginary narrative in the piece.

RE: Then the danger is more interesting because you create the sense of risk in the piece. What the tramp's voice didn't have was a sense of edge. His narrative is one of acceptance. Then Waits comes along and introduces a raw, almost outraged quality to this delicate, mesmeric pattern of transcendent hope. That's a risky thing to do.

GB: That's right. And one of the things which made me aware of that was ac- tually in the live recording. We worked in the room where he records all his current albums, it's actually called "The Waiting Room." The place is like a series of con- verted chicken shacks but it's very beautifully done. One houses all of Tom's in- struments; it's a rough-and-ready room, not acoustically sealed but it has an inter- esting ambiance. For this fifteen-minute period there were only two of us in there. He was standing in front of what looked like an old rock-and-roll microphone with his eyes closed, swaying and singing. He could hear the tramp; I could hear the tramp. And he began to construct sequences. On some of them he was singing in a lyrical, slightly whimsical way. Then he'd move into an area where he was singing with real anger and pain; his eyes were closed and he started to clench his fists and his fists would come down as he sang each phrase; then he started to stamp his foot and he was swaying. It was one of the most extraordinary things

I've ever seen a performer do. I was within a few feet of it. It was just incredibly moving.

Louis Andriessen

The Terrifying Twenty-first Century Composer

"Every piece should be a new experiment," says Louis Andriessen. The Dutch New Music composer is talking about an approach to music-making that is his personal, unwavering credo. "The only concern for a composer, really, is to do something he has never done before." Andriessen's career has been a series of radical shifts in theme and approach that he has sustained right from his earliest compositions. Born in Utrecht in 1939 into a musical family (his father was a composer and his brother wrote the first opera for Dutch television, as well as a piece based on the *trompe l'oeil* prints of M. C. Escher), Andriessen studied at the Conservatory in the Hague and later with Luciano Berio in Berlin and Milan. But even within this relatively conventional education, Andriessen found ideas and activities that would set him apart; he was asked to leave a Jesuit school at the age of twelve, became one of Holland's first serial composers in the late '50s and was deeply involved in the politics of dissent in the '60s. In the early years of the following decade he systematically studied Marxism and from that point on all of his work has been sensitive to the complicated relationship between music and society.

It has led him to investigate styles outside the orbit of traditional symphonic music and to gather around him musicians more readily adaptable to what he felt compelled to say. When *De Staat* was given its first performance outside of Holland in Warsaw in 1977, Andriessen had to sing every note to the symphony players "because they articulated the piece like Bruckner and Mahler and it should be articulated like Count Basie and Stan Kenton!" To avoid the trap of convention, in the '70s Andriessen started two avant-garde musical groups in Holland: De Volharding (Perseverance) in 1972, an assortment of irreverent players who were closer to jazz than to classical repertoire; and then four years later he organized Hoketus—"just young dogs" as Andriessen described them, who brought to his music the muscular presence of rock. In each of these groups, Andriessen's intention was to break down the lines separating high and low culture, an approach evident in the range of venues De Volharding and Hoketus played; they seemed to perform for street demonstrations and in abandoned buildings as often as in anything remotely resembling a concert hall. In the mid '80s he wrote a piece called *De Stijl* (named after the Dutch Utopian movement in art and architecture of which Mondrian was a member) for some thirty musicians from De Volharding and Hoketus, an assemblage of players he anointed "the terrifying twenty-first-century orchestra."

While Andriessen's music may not be millennial, it is anything but conventional in its sound and inspiration. You're as likely to hear echoes of Charlie Parker, Dizzy Gillespie and Miles Davis, or scales and pitches from Indonesian music, in an Andriessen composition as you are to pick up hints of American Minimalism or of Stravinsky. (Andriessen is a Stravinsky devotee and has co-authored a book on the twentieth-century composer called *The Apollonian Clockwork*.) But even with this posse of influences, when Andriessen finally gives a piece its legs, the run is entirely his own: loud, aggressive, dissonant and decidedly in the vernacular. These are qualities that he admires equally in the performance of his work; his reaction to the Winnipeg Symphony Orchestra's playing of De Staat was to describe it approvingly as, "very rough and noisy and majestic."

Andriessen's compositions have come from the most disparate sources: *De Snelheid* (Velocity), 1982–1983, set out to explore the idea of speed in musical terms; *De Tijd* (Time), 1980–1981, was a meditation on eternity that came out of his reading of *The Confessions of St. Augustine*; *De Materie*, 1989, was a response to Dutch shipbuilding in the seventeenth century; *De Staat*, 1972–1976, answered a notion in Plato's *Republic* about banning dulcimers from the perfect state; and *Facing Death*, 1991, was an homage to jazz great Charlie Parker. But perhaps no piece is as curious in its formation as Andriessen's more recent collaboration with filmmaker and painter Peter Greenaway. *Rosa* is a horse opera that was performed at the Netherlands Opera in November 1994 with music by Andriessen, and libretto and design by Greenaway. At one point, an assistant to the Investigatrix (who is attempting to solve the murder of the composer who lends the opera his name) says, "Let us perform some unnatural practices."

They do. *Rosa* is a visceral, splendid and thoroughly charged collaboration that is something of a musical murder mystery tour. What it makes clear is that Louis Andriessen has no intention of coming away from the edge, which is where all his ladders seem to start. *Rosa* gives us clues, but no real answers and in that incomplete form it is a perfect metaphor for Andriessen's rich imagination. He is fond of quoting the French poet Valéry who said, "what is finished is not made." In Andriessen's provocative world the opposite is no less true: what is made is never finished.

The first thing you notice about Louis Andriessen is his infectious enthusiasm and openness to people and events. We initially met on a punishingly cold and windy Manitoba morning, and he was so impressed with the weather that it became a thread running through our entire conversation. Andriessen is consummately alive to the place in which he finds himself. He was in Winnipeg as the Distinguished Artist-in-Residence for the 1995 New Music Festival, during which two of his compositions were performed: De Staat at the opening gala, and later in the week, *Facing Death*, performed by the Kronos Quartet who had commissioned the piece. We met twice during his stay in Winnipeg and recorded the following interview which has been edited as a continuous conversation.

ROBERT ENRIGHT: Both your father and a brother were composers. You've described your background as classical: precise and French, and devoid of German romanticism. How much did that environment influence your own musical tastes?

LOUIS ANDRIESSEN: I would say ninety percent. I simply imitated my brother and my father. You start learning by imitating. I have a friend, a playwright in Amsterdam, who started copying one of the large Dostoevski novels and halfway through became bored by the copy. He finished up by writing his own Dostoevski novel. I think that's a very good way to start learning to make art.

RE: That's what painters used to do; they learned by copying the masters. Did you feel that's what you were doing early on when you began composing?

LA: Yes, certainly. I had no idea—and still have no idea—what my voice is at all. People will now say that something is typically Andriessen, but what I attempt in every piece is to research a totally different aspect of composing. In a way, I always try to be somebody else. I think that having a personal style has much more to do with your limitations, with the things you are *not* able to do. And since you're not able to do a lot of things, when you try something different you fall back on what is closest to your ability. I would like to be as good as Bach for instance, but when I try I don't come much further than what's in my hands. I have the feeling that all we can do is listen as well as we can, and then we reproduce what we hear. This sounds very depersonalized, but what I learned from my father is that the product of what we do is far more important than what we ourselves are. And that is probably what you call my anti-romanticism. I have a very strong feeling that I am only a medium.

RE: I suppose it's also a Marxist position, in that it recognizes the individual as part of some collective harmony?

LA: I agree completely with that. I studied Marxism quite profoundly in the '70s, but I had this feeling long before I had any idea who Marx was.

RE: Did your father approve of what you did as a composer?

LA: In the beginning he took an extremely positive approach. However, he was very critical. Especially when I was a kid, everything was wrong all the time: "I hope he will find this good enough now." Of course, this is not true anymore, and I think I'm a better composer than my father now. I can say that rationally but that's not what's in my subconscious. In a way he was a guide in being extremely critical all the time. But he was also a very open, positive, funny and intelligent person.

RE: You've used Stravinsky as a way of saying you're not interested in expressing your emotions in music, that you just want to get the right notes. Are you saying that your music has no personality?

LA: I think your question is somewhat better than my answer will be. I do agree with that idea about personality. For a composer there are only two important things: composing and love. When I feel extremely close to or fall in love with somebody I have this same feeling of depersonalization. There is a strange discrepancy between the closeness you feel and the recognition that you'll never understand her at all. I have the feeling that it would still be useless and uninteresting to try to realize myself in what I compose. That's not what I'm dealing with. But hiding is not really the right word, either. Sometimes, such as when I worked with Peter Greenaway on *Rosa*, I had the feeling that I had to show off, which I found very painful and difficult.

RE: Were you trying to counter the work he was doing as a designer and librettist?

LA: Yes, with the script for *Rosa* I had to do something which I would not have dared to do ten years ago. In Greenaway's scripts in general, I find exactly the characteristics which I described in the woman before; this deep emotion combined with intellectual distance. This tendency to hide behind formalism is something that I consider very important to the way art works.

RE: As you describe the sources of *De Stijl*, your composition about Mondrian, you list not only the geometric and formal quality of his work, but also that he was a man strongly influenced by theosophy and unusual religions. I wonder if art then becomes a way we can avoid the chaos of our emotions; is it a way of giving form to possible chaos?

LA: I totally agree. I think every psychiatrist will agree—and Freud in the first place—that artists seem to need less help than other people. I'm sure art is a way of helping you *not* become mad. Of course, there are numerous examples where this does not work, specifically in the Romantic period. That's why I find the second half of the nineteenth century a dark period in history in general, and certainly in the arts. It's very typical for the nineteenth century to cross the border into the dark side. I am more of a classicist and like the attitude that distance accounts for at least half the energy.

RE: So, it's a question of finding a form within which you can play inside?

LA: When I write long pieces for large ensembles I have a vision which is metaphysical, and that's something you can't control. What you have to do first of all is to find a way to formalize this vision. You have to come up with an idea about form. Just as in the visual arts, conceptualism has been very important for me. In the '70s I was dealing quite intensely with people in Amsterdam who were involved in conceptual art, body art, and land art. Most of them were Dutch, although Lawrence Weiner was also around.

RE: You said that Mozart is the most ironic composer. What did you mean by that?

LA: I don't think of it as referring to a nice little joke or teasing somebody, which is the lower side of irony. For me it's a profound philosophical approach that goes back to the original meaning of the word, to the idea of saying something which has another meaning. All the art I like has this combination of passion and distance. That's the philosophical use of the word irony. You may call it dialecticism. I use almost one word for the other.

RE: Some of the people you've worked with—Greenaway certainly, and Robert Wilson to some extent—have liked the idea of the arcane and of patterns. I'm thinking here of *Rosa* in which clues are given throughout. Do you yourself like the idea of there being some sense of mystery or pattern inside the piece that allows you to give it shape?

LA: I hope so. All the time you're dealing with totally uncontrollable material. That's the interesting thing with music; there are so many times where you have no idea what you're doing. So the formalist side only captures half of what is happening. I'm sure that intuition and uncontrollable things and hidden laws are operating. There are chaotic elements which we don't know. We can't even really analyze why a certain Mozart symphony is much more beautiful than another one. Beauty cannot be analyzed because it always has a hidden, dark side.

RE: Are you interested in that dark side? I'm talking here about the human sensibility. The relentless energy of your music seems to be concerned with the darker side of human expression.

LA: The large, aggressive side in *De Staat* for instance, doesn't have anything to do with the dark. Literally, I see very clear colours—white, blue, yellow.

RE: The primary colours, the colours Mondrian loved.

LA: Yes. It's more about enthusiasm, or energy or power or passion. There's no perverse side in that. However, darkness and perversity are probably not the same. Now, I have done less accessible pieces where I get into unknown territory in which I get lost. There is a strange piece I did for the Schoenberg Ensemble which is called *Neitzsche Speaks*. There's this guy who starts talking and he's quoting Neitzsche's texts—so it's Neitzsche—and there are quotations where he explains why Bizet's *Carmen* is much better than all of Wagner, which was, of course, a polemic with the Schoenberg Ensemble. But when he talks there's this ensemble playing all kinds of harmonies in exactly the same rhythm. It's a very unpretty piece, I must say. First of all you can't hear the music very well and then you can't hear the voice very well either. It's a very strange mixture of the two different disciplines. I have seldom heard about people who really like the piece.

RE: You seem to be a master of composing for ensemble and voice. I thought *De Staat* a beautiful use of those two musical components. Are you particularly interested in the human voice as an instrument?

LA: Don't you think that voice is the most important instrument we have? I certainly think that. It started for me in the theatre in which I wrote funny dialectical songs for strange anarchist plays in the '60s. I felt it was an advantage that I didn't start with classically trained singers. Instead, I started with jazz singers and actresses and actors. What that meant was that I had a limit in the register of the voice but my approach to singing is that I like every sort except classically trained singing. It was a problem for a long time, but since the '70s I've just written what I want and hope to find singers who understand how to do it. Nowadays, it works out because you can work on two levels, with jazz singers and with baroque singers. I have the same problem with the instruments. Except knowing the technology of their instrument, I think what I ask from players has very little to do with what they learned at the Conservatory.

RE: You were known as the Bad Boy of Dutch music when you first went to the Conservatory in the Hague. Were you a trouble-maker?

LA: Yeah, but I had a bunch of friends who were very radical. I always did things which I wasn't supposed to do. I had been kicked out of Jesuit College when I was twelve years old. I consider it one of my first victories. But at the Conservatory I met a group of composers who were angry young men. The real political action came much later in the late '60s.

RE: Were you always political? You said you systematically studied Marxism in the '70s. I'm wondering where the political consciousness and conscience came from?

LA: I'm not sure. I remember when I was studying in Berlin in 1964 I crossed the border into East Berlin, for the first time I had a feeling that there was something totally wrong in the world.

RE: Was there a connection between your political views and the kind of music you wanted to make?

LA: It probably had to do with the difference between how people who played in symphony orchestras looked and how jazz musicians looked.

RE: But there must have been more to it than a goatee versus a tuxedo?

LA: No, no, it's as simple as that. Why shouldn't we be very clear? I felt this total difference in my attitude towards life at that time.

RE: I'm interested in the way you were always able to find ensembles that suited the kind of music you wanted to make. I'm thinking of De Volharding and then later on Hoketus. Has that been a compulsion of yours all along?

LA: I think it has to do with what we've been talking about. I wanted to be surrounded by musicians who I also liked as persons. We liked the same films, read the same papers, we had the same dreams.

RE: Was De Volharding as democratic as it's been described? Was it actually a group of people making decisions among themselves, or did you emerge as the leader and major figure inside the group?

LA: It was the other way around. You should realize that the late '60s were totally different from any period in this whole century. I started the group so that did make a sort of hierarchy. Those kids were extremely bold and blunt but they had no idea how to rehearse. So I had to teach them. Then I think I taught them to organize discussions. This is also very difficult when you have no training. Now I really sound like a communist, don't I? But I did this to make myself unnecessary. So after five years I quit the group as a pianist, and they continued on and it went very well. They are still very difficult people. They ask composers to write for them and then they say, "This is bullshit, we don't play it." That's really terrible.

RE: Do you consider yourself a Dutch composer? Are there characteristics that set you apart from, say, an American composer?

LA: My first answer is that we should fight all levels of nationalism, all the time, but Holland is somewhere between Europe and America, right. More than all the countries in Europe, Holland has been very closely related to North America— and Canada also. So I can talk a long time about those things in relation to the kind of music I've written. But I shall tell you an anecdote. There was somebody visiting me in Amsterdam and we had a morning off. I said I wanted to take her to some place near Amsterdam. We drove to a little isle which is quite authentically Dutch, a tourist place—all wooden houses and things. It was a very cold winter day. There was sun and a very cold wind, which you understand very well living in Winnipeg. Then when you walk around the village, you come onto the other side of the isle and you see this enormous amount of water and then this very sharp horizon. It was so violent and at the same time so empty, so hard and blunt. I almost started getting tears in my eyes and I said to the person I was with, I think you understand my music better now.

RE: I heard you say that there's not enough angst in American music. I wanted to get you to elaborate a little bit on what you meant by that. You find Glass and Reich too pretty, too cosmic?

LA: They are very different I think. I mean most of the time they are different. What makes my music different from a lot of Minimalists from the '70s is that I use much more earthy and chromatic material. I'm not sure that has anything to do with angst, but it's somewhat more outspoken and aggressive. I'm not talking about Glass or Reich, whom I esteem very highly, but all the minor people who interpret this as nice background music for television advertisements. So, there's not enough angst generally—instead, music is meant to calm nervous passengers at airports.

RE: You talk with pride about being Dutch because in the seventeenth century the culture stood up against Spanish imperialism; ship-building was so important to this, and that is what you loved about it. That was part of why I asked the question about nationalism. Not as a way of condoning the kind of nationalism we see in Bosnia, but rather as a way of positively distinguishing yourself from another culture.

LA: Oh, that's certainly true. I would not seriously think of emigrating. Venice or Prague are very beautiful cities but Amsterdam has the same kind of charm. It's almost a female charm, if I may say. And Amsterdam's charm is very cold also. It has to do with the light and the clouds and the weather.

RE: There's a telling moment in Steve Martland's documentary film about you where the camera pans across the room and you see a figure at a harpsichord. I think of Vermeer.

LA: Yeah, I also liked that very much. What I play on the harpsichord is an English piece as a gesture of homage to Steve, and Peter West, the cinematographer. But the whole thing was a reproduction of a Vermeer painting, which is exactly right because he was one of my heroes. Again, he has that combination of tenderness and chilliness.

RE: The film also has an extended scene where you and your friends are having dinner and drinking. It puts me in mind of Dutch painting. Was that intended?

LA: Sure. I remember telling the singer in the first part of *De Materie* about the atom physicist who had discovered the smallest particles. What I imagined was a drunken guy in a bar explaining this theory while thinking of the paintings of Frans Hals with characters red-nosed from drinking all that beer. That's where the enthusiasm in the music comes from.

RE: In *De Stijl* the singers are wearing bright red and they're lined up very precisely. Is that also a comment on the painterly origins of the piece, which was Mondrian's *Composition with Red, Yellow and Blue* from 1927?

LA: I think the piece is somewhat more complicated. It doesn't really describe the paintings of Mondrian at all. It describes the darkness of his mind, with his solitude and all his metaphysical writers behind him.

RE: But the *Broadway Boogie Woogie* side is there too, isn't it?

LA: Yes, and he was quite happy in New York during the last years of his life. However he was a boogie woogie fan already in the '20s. He had records, that only real connoisseurs know, by Jimmy Yancey, the inventor of boogie woogie. Mondrian had those seventy-eights and this little record-player in his atelier all the time.

RE: Do you feel closer to pop and jazz and rock than to traditional classical music?

LA: I'm not sure, but I certainly have more in common with this kind of music than with a lot of so-called avant-garde music over the last thirty years. However, I am the first serial composer in Holland, so I have my own history. When you talk about traditional classical music, I remember that when my father took me to concerts I was extremely bored with Beethoven and Schumann, and was really waiting until there was a piece by Bartok or Stravinsky. Then I started to listen and be interested.

RE: Was it a lack of respect? You already knew what they had done and therefore were uninterested in what they were doing?

LA: At that time that is true. Nowadays I'm intelligent enough to realize the revolutionary elements of the symphonies of Beethoven, for instance, but when you are a fourteen-year-old kid you're not worried about that. So we shouldn't worry about youth; they'll develop their taste later and almost everybody who really loves music will find out that history has already had all these Mick Jaggers. That's a good approach to history I think: to see it as a continuation of subversive leads in music.

RE: So you don't have a favourite kind of music? I mean, you do jazz and bebop and classical—you seem to run the whole range.

LA: I have a lot of heroes but at the highest level are Stravinsky and Bach. They're almost the same kind of person. I see a lot in common with those two composers and I try to do the same thing.

RE: Is Stravinsky a kind of friendly ghost who haunts you? You said that he's in your consciousness almost all the time. Does he sit on your shoulder?

LA: We talked about my father before, right?

RE: He's on the other shoulder?

LA: That makes my life very heavy! Seriously, they're all dead, so they're not really present. But it changes during your life. I remember that I was unfaithful to Stravinsky for a period in the '60s. I didn't really need him then. But I cannot remember a time when I did not love the music of Stravinsky. And it has always been a real love—there was invariably something in the music that irritated me. He hid things, or he did something different from what you expected. And this love-hate thing—although that may be a little strong—this discrepancy, is exactly what I liked in his music. That is a good example of how I try to continue composing myself. I've never said this before but it is very true. Of course my relationship with my father is another book. But Bach gets more and more important, I must say. When we talk about Bach I should mention the development of authentic baroque practice. This whole question of how we deal with music and the authentic commitment of the musicians who do it is very important, and interests me very much. So Bach in Holland is different than in a lot of other countries. He's a very alive, modern composer and that has also helped me to reinvent the quality of Bach.

RE: I want to talk for a minute about music and social change. Rock music has altered the world. I wonder if you believe that art—to contradict W. H. Auden's lament—can make something happen?

LA: I simply don't know. I knew everything when I was thirty; now I don't know anymore. More and more I seem to be worrying about writing the right notes. It sounds very silly, but it's so difficult to do that, I can't tell you. And it takes so much concentration.

RE: Do you find it more difficult to be a composer now than you did thirty years ago?

LA: Yes, because when you want to do what I want you always have to go into new territory. And the more you have discovered, the more difficult it is to find new territory. And as soon as you work only on your experience, you are lost. Here's the dilemma. During your life you get experience, so I am probably better than before at writing an opera like *Rosa*. I wrote it in one year, which is not bad. But it deals a lot with known material. And, of course I wrote *Rosa* leaning upon a lot of my experiences, so that's the other side. I could not have written *Rosa* twenty years ago, I was not technically able. You have to keep the people there for one hundred minutes and now I am technically able to do that. I could make my life very easy and continue to write nice, accessible, aggressive, ironic, fast, interesting music. I am able to do that and I may sometimes do it. But I should not do it all the time.

RE: How do you keep yourself on edge enough to always reinvent your own sense of what music is? Is that difficult to maintain?

LA: I try to change my sense and my taste and my ideas all the time. Or at least to develop—maybe that's a better word. And to do that means simply to have an open mind. First of all, I get a lot of cassettes from young composers from all kinds of strange countries. Then I go to a lot of concerts in Amsterdam—as many as I can. I try to read a lot. I'm very interested in architecture, in the visual arts and in photography. I try to find many things around me which could be important for my development as a composer.

RE: I think of architecture as being a building in which things happen. Is that the way you think of music also—that composition is an object within which all kinds of things can happen?

LA: Absolutely. In fact you almost quote Goethe who says that architecture is petrified music. And it's absolutely true. When I write big pieces, I even design a sort of building where I plan what kind of things are happening at that moment. And I use simple numbers to calculate things, which architects do all the time. Mostly simple numbers, but I use irrational numbers and square root numbers as well.

RE: The music of *De Staat* seemed to me to be like a sculpture, as if it were an object. In a way, you make sculptural music. Does that observation make sense to you?

LA: In fact I myself use that kind of metaphor all the time. I remember having said several times when I was writing *De Staat* that what I wanted to do was to create this large stone wall which falls over you.

RE: It has that feeling. It's as if it had no centre, but it was everywhere.

LA: I think I understand what you mean. It reminds me also that there is something behind, which is hidden. And that's what I call classicism in art. The other thing is what Valéry observed when he said, "What is finished has not been made."

RE: Do you really believe that your life work is an unfinished thing and should always be? You seem to love this idea of the incomplete. The Martland film picks up that metaphor because at the end, it's still going on. Then in *Rosa* the investigatrix doesn't really have all the answers.

LA: Yeah. Having "the answer" makes your life small. I consider it stupid and reactionary. If you can't ask questions anymore, if you have answers to all the questions, then you are lost.

RE: You're still an anarchist.

LA: I consider this a compliment.

Looking at Matisse

Looking at Matisse

Henri Matisse: A Retrospective was on exhibition at the Museum of Modern Art in New York from September 24, 1992, to January 12, 1993. Organized by John Elderfield, this dazzling exhibition of some 425 works (275 paintings as well as 150 works in other media, including drawings, prints, sculptures, cut-outs and a single theatrical costume) was the largest Matisse exhibition ever mounted. It offered a unique opportunity to appreciate the combination of the audacious and the magisterial that earned him a place in the painterly pantheon. While Matisse claimed that Cézanne was "like a god" and that the work of Giotto operated at a level to which he aspired during his own lifetime, he himself seemed to take on an Olympian character.

Born in 1869, Matisse would be twenty-one years old before he made his first paintings. At his death sixty-four years later, he was working on the cut-outs, works that were to astonish the art world and make him, in the words of Alex Katz, "the newest artist alive." Matisse was one of the great innovators in modern art but above all else he remains a painter's painter. With that recognition in mind, I spoke to five contemporary artists to get their insights into his achievement and significance. The artists I chose cover a wide range of current art activity: Alex Katz has emerged as one of the most significant figurative painters of the last forty years, while Nancy Graves occupies a similar place in sculpture through her own colourful, three-dimensional arabesqueing. April Gornik and Eric Fischl are two of America's most looked-at painters: Fischl continues to paint edgy *mises en scène* that present the real and the gothic character of middle America; while Gornik is the architect of the most precisely evocative landscapes being made in the United States today. And Nancy Spero gazes back at Matisse from outside his social and sexual orbit, and finds there a radically different painter from the one we thought we knew. Taken together these five artists offer insights into a range of issues from Matisse's palette to his sense of isolated theatre, and in the process come up with unique and revealing readings of many of his most familiar paintings. All five artists live in New York, a "marvellous city" as Matisse described it in a letter written to Bonnard in 1930, a city which made him feel "thirty years younger."

The following interviews (except with Nancy Graves, who was interviewed by phone) were conducted in New York in December, 1992.

Alex Katz

Looking at Matisse

ROBERT ENRIGHT: Was Matisse an early influence on you? His name keeps cropping up in critical writing about your work.

ALEX KATZ: Yeah. I saw an exhibition in 1948 at the Pierre Matisse Gallery when I was an art student. Morris Kantor, who was my teacher at the time, said, "Go up and take a look at these paintings. The guy's an old man but he's good." And I went up there and I fainted. I didn't hit the floor but I lost consciousness. I couldn't believe anyone could paint that well.

RE: You actually passed out?

AK: Yeah. I passed out and caught myself just before I hit the floor. The paintings still look that good to me. You see, after four years of painting School of Paris, doing Cubism and everything else, you could appreciate how skillful he was plastically. It was that fantastic surface, the way he could control everything with the line. It was so perfect. I once looked at a Raphael when it came over on a German loan show and again I couldn't figure out how a human being could paint that well.

RE: I guess it's naïve to ask whether it was liberating to see work like Matisse's as a young painter?

AK: Well, it was inspirational. You had to get away from him and that took a while, but he did set a standard.

RE: What were you able to take from Matisse?

AK: I think it was colours and weights and pushes and pulls and how to make a surface.

RE: Was your attitude towards him commonly held? How was he viewed by American painters at the time?

AK: Matisse barely got accepted. He was put down because of the New York School. Picasso was a much larger influence in New York then. The other problem was that most of the people who were influenced by Matisse painted like him and that really looked awful. For me it was like with any other artist I've looked at. There are things you like about them and things you don't like. There are things they can do and things they can't do. Picasso can't paint a landscape to save his soul, and he can't paint large paintings very well, either. So that's the way out of Picasso.

RE: Do you mean that in order *not* to compete you find things the modern masters couldn't do?

AK: You go into other areas. I started to paint directly from nature and so it was a whole different thing. Matisse became one of my indirect influences at the time. He popped up intermittently in my stuff in the '50s. By the time I started doing the collages I had already broken away and by the time I got to the figures-on-ground around 1957, I was on my own.

RE: What are the things about him that you don't like?

AK: I didn't like the decorative quality and the fact that he liked Islamic art. I never liked pattern and that claustrophobic thing of his; it's a little too close to everything. I like open spaces better. Also, he dealt with absolute tones and absolute colours and didn't go in for half tones much. I went in for a lot of tones.

RE: You said Picasso couldn't make a big painting. What about Matisse's handling of scale?

AK: He was dynamite on large paintings. I think the paintings like the *Dancers*—most of the paintings in Russia—are the benchmark for the century. Those large interiors are just incredible paintings.

RE: Does he close off avenues of pictorial invention because he's so good?

AK: I never felt that way; I felt he opened things up, really. He didn't do enough large paintings to exhaust it; he just dipped into it. *Bathers by a River*—the one from the Art Institute of Chicago—is an incredible, complicated painting. It's like a movie in that it seems to be in different sections of time. Space and time.

RE: Can you still go back and learn things from him?

AK: Well, I bought a couple of his sugar-lift aquatints. They've been hanging around and I think I've gotten something from just looking at them. He uses a big line and it doesn't get fussy. A de Kooning line is fussy, for instance; he wants to show you he's a good painter all the time. But Matisse's line, and Picasso's too, is almost uninflected and it still seems able to do a great many things at once. It's very complicated and very simple at the same time. It's not a fancy surface line. Matisse is a real virtuoso painter because he can do twenty things with a line. I also like his restraint on the big gesture.

RE: The line is ubiquitous in Matisse, isn't it; it's everywhere in the drawings and paintings?

AK: The line is the whole thing. Line and edge.

RE: Does this show change your view of Matisse? What do you make of him now that you've seen all this work together?

AK: Matisse had one eye on fashion all the time. He never was out of it and he was a conscious stylist. Usually artists have one three-year period where they're connected to fashion, but Matisse had two real big ones, one in the early teens before he gets into the Cubist stuff and then again with the paper cutouts at the end. When he was doing those cutouts, he was the newest artist alive. He made Jackson Pollock into an old artist. That's very interesting. Picasso just had one blast. With early Cubism, Picasso's on top of the world. But he just had one three-year shot at being a fashionable artist.

RE: Are you surprised at the painting he did early on, just after he decided to stop studying law?

AK: Those early paintings were fantastically talented. He was in one of these dull studios with all these people painting these dreary paintings and he was cutting out tons of stuff. The early paintings were extremely impressive. It was a marvellous start. He was really trying to do things.

RE: Your sense is that he recognizes early on what to leave out of the painting?

AK: Right away he was organizing and leaving things out. It wasn't until he got to the Fauve period that he trusted himself enough to break wind anywhere he wanted. Then, for the rest of his life he had—what do you call it—rough French manners. A nice rough quality like Balzac. He's sticking it to the bourgeoisie and being an animal. So the Fauve paintings are kind of interesting but I don't think he gets to the great paintings until a little later.

RE: You mentioned earlier that sculpture gets minimized in this exhibition. What's your overall estimation of his achievement in the medium?

AK: I don't think he's much of a sculptor. He's okay but he's nowhere near Picasso or Brancusi or Giacometti.

RE: What about *Two Women*, a piece he did in the summer of 1907? When you look down the linked arms it's like visually traversing a long landscape. His attenuation of the limb is really intriguing. Is it also about line for him?

AK: I think his line comes from Michelangelo. The line is the whole arm, the whole mass of the whole arm. Michelangelo does it but he doesn't show it to you. With him you just have the bumps, but if you put a line on top of the bumps you'd have a great big line all the time. I think Matisse looked at Michelangelo a lot.

RE: Matisse does that too, doesn't he? He makes the line and you see the shadows, you see the erasures.

AK: Bumps and lumps, trying to find a line. Yeah.

RE: So Matisse is a painter in search of a line?

AK: He searches for the line. But the line is the traditional idea of an edge and volume, something moving in space. So it's natural that it go back to sculpture. But somehow the sculpture just seems heavy-headed. The *Backs* are fake profound.

RE: Those pieces are much admired.

AK: Everyone likes them but I think they're like lead. They're nowhere close to the paintings. I mean, the best collages—when he had the figures bending backwards—are totally, totally thrilling. So with the sculptures, you say, this is very good, this is very nice. But I don't think they're as good as de Kooning's sculptures.

RE: Are you moved by the pictures of Matisse drawing from his bed, working with huge scissors to make the pieces you describe as his second major breakthrough?

AK: It doesn't matter at all how he made it. He could do it on one leg, pounding his chest and it wouldn't matter to me.

RE: One of the criticisms of this show is that we learn so little about the man from it, that he remains mysterious despite the size and scope of the exhibition.

AK: Yeah, it bothers some people. I think he gives us enough. What do they want? I mean, we don't know anything about Velasquez, either. I don't think it's really that important, especially if you have enough art to take the place of it.

RE: By the time he's working in Nice he has been able to invent his own world and populate it with women over whom he seems to have complete control.

AK: Yeah, the whole thing is internal. If Picasso is a social realist, Matisse is an escapist. With Picasso all the issues are in the paintings. But Matisse's eye is on aesthetics; he's not interested in the rest of the world. It's an idea of beauty as removed.

RE: That would be appealing to you as well?

AK: Yeah, I seem to go that way.

RE: There's a small painting done in 1935 called *The Blue Eyes*. It's a woman resting her head on her arms and it made me think of your work.

AK: Well, I must have been influenced by it. I liked that whole series with his Russian lady. He got some great drawings from her.

RE: You've studiously avoided the notion of psychology in your work. You say your work is simply about style, that it isn't about psychology. What do you think when you look at some of the loaded paintings Matisse came up with?

AK: I don't think my work is minimal. There are all kinds of things lurking down in the bottom of it, but they're not what I'm interested in. Somehow if you get in contact with your work a lot more gets into it than you know about. I don't know how conscious Matisse was about all of what got into his paintings, either.

RE: His work just ends up being so incredibly self-referential.

AK: Well, he can layer things so nicely. You look at the painting and it's this, and then you look again and it's that. Or you can look at the painting and see that the colours are so pretty and then you say, that looks just like flesh, and it's a wash of orange; and that looks just like silk and it's nothing but blue and a little bit of turp. You go through the whole painting and you realize how great he is at getting the overall colour and he's also great at getting specific colours. If you look at a lot of detailed, realistic painting, they often don't get the surfaces that well. So his skill is fantastic just at the level of the light of the all-over to the light of the specific thing. It's enough to keep you occupied. Then you look at the way he pushes and pulls everything on the surfaces—every line, every shape is going in several directions at once, and then all of a sudden they become very spatial and you realize how terrific the spatial architecture is.

RE: He uses light structurally, doesn't he?

AK: It becomes a form. It's a light *and* it's a shape.

RE: You've done a similar thing in *Luna Park*, a piece done in 1960.

AK: I also did some interiors at the same time that dealt with those ideas, with work pulling that way.

RE: Does the dialogue between the interior and exterior space interest you?

AK: Oh yeah. I did a lot of those window paintings. First it was interiors and then window paintings. And they're brought to an American place and they're abstracted.

RE: When you do that, do you think to yourself, "Thanks, Henri"? Do you nod in his direction, aware that you're carrying on a dialogue?

AK: Well, I knew it when I was doing interiors and then the interiors changed to windows. So by the time I was doing windows, it was "Bye bye, Henri."

RE: Do you still think about Matisse?

AK: I enjoyed looking at this show and I went and saw it twice. I didn't think I had to see it three times. I was very happy to get out from under some of his influences. I feel I've gone off in another direction. He never worked much with tones or with really specific details and both those things have interested me. He's not involved with the issue of painting a modern, realistic painting, which seemed to me an interesting issue. He has a tendency toward generalization and what I did was to go simultaneously towards more specific and more abstract elements. Then I also went into half tones. And I'm dealing with an American space, which is more open.

RE: Do you sometimes find his palette bizarre?

AK: No, his palette is never bizarre because it's always readable.

RE: What do you mean by readable? That you could make it if you wanted?

AK: His palette's always plausible. You can see that one colour is transposed from another colour. Like *Harmony in Red*. To me it's summertime, it's very green, you walk into a room and there's a red flash. He painted the red flash. That's only one thing. There are a lot of colours that are transposed, so if a dark grey doesn't do it, you turn it into a dark, bright red.

RE: Does he instinctively know that?

AK: I would think he got it more intellectually. But I learned about transposing colour from him. Like with my painting called *The Red Smile*. It has a grey background that has a different light than on the face. The grey was dull and I transposed it to red, but it had the exact pitch of a grey background. That's something I learned from Matisse. So when you look at his things, some of the colours are real and others are transposed. When you get the effect right, it's the sensation of what you're looking at. All those paintings have that. It's all optical.

RE: In one sense you're saying there are no mysteries in Matisse.

AK: I don't think there are any mysteries there at all.

April Gornik

Looking at Matisse

APRIL GORNIK: There was not one point where the exhibition disappointed me. Even though Matisse's work is so different from mine, he's still my favourite painter. There's a point of absolute serendipity for me when you come to the work just before and just after Morocco. It's more than I could ever have hoped to see in one room. When he first goes to Collioure and St. Tropez he's clearly fascinated by the outside colour and he begins to interiorize the experience and then all the paintings start to be suffused by that. Everything seems to come together and there's this kind of colour orgasm that must be—lucky for us and lucky for him—the longest colour orgasm anybody ever had. It's such an extraordinary body of work, so unbridled. That's the only point in his work where I feel I'm seeing him really happy too. There is a lot of work—like *Bathers by a River* and *Conversation*—that has an existential weight about it. But those other paintings are so perfect in their transporting joy. It's like Molly Bloom's "yes" at the end of *Ulysses*. To me there's a point where he's just coasting on that yes. I'm moved even thinking about it now because it's the most extraordinary achievement. It's something that my work's not about and I don't really deal with colour that way but I know it when I see it. I frankly can't imagine anybody dealing with colour the way Matisse did.

ROBERT ENRIGHT: Is it about the end of something, about closing off certain possibilities?

AG: Not at all. I think he's very much about interstices in art history. He doesn't come close to finalizing anything but he comes so close to being perfectly particular about something. He's absolutely particular about his use of colour. Even very great artists don't achieve the idiosyncratic use of colour that he does. Can you think of anyone?

RE: He startles you all the time, then?

AG: Yeah. And it really is about colour more than anything else. The way that he reduces drawing is remarkable but it's not startling. But the way he manages to make the plane of a painting be as complex as he does defies my notions of space and frontality. Somehow it doesn't seem to be simply about either of them. Most other artists deal with one or the other but Matisse seems always to be able to warp them in a truly multidimensional way. He's like a sea creature that you come upon that has its own little world and its own way of doing something. You can see it function and you can understand how it's getting through the water and absorbing nutrients; you can see it by the way it looks and by the way it does things, but how it got to be that way is a problem for comprehension.

RE: Does this exhibition make him seem more superlative a painter than you had thought before?

AG: It verifies it more than anything else. But I have a lot of thoughts about him that I hadn't had before. I see him now as the perfect voyeur. He doesn't make you aware of being the voyeur. You just happen upon what you're looking at. I mean, his odalisques are so perfectly sexual and sensual but so unemphatic in the way they're rendered. He doesn't make you get hot under the collar, or start having some physical response. But they're completely sexy and the distance between himself and his subject is just perfect.

RE: In all his self-portraits where he's actually painting he looks off to the side, towards the model. He's not looking at the model as an object of desire, but as a thing to paint. He's actually *making* the painting. Is that part of where the distance comes from?

AG: I would imagine. I think with him it's really painting first or maybe painting is so sexy that everything gets absorbed by that.

RE: So as a woman you find these sexy paintings? He's been attacked as a monster of the male ego. Does that enter into your estimation of him?

AG: No. I look at the painting first and at the potential sexism second. But it's period painting, whether we like it or not. Plus, I think that women have a real power in his painting. He honours their sexuality more than Picasso. If you think about some of the portraits of Dora Maar—split up with tears and being hysterical—they feel much more misogynistic than an odalisque that looks out at you from half-closed, completely satisfied and self-contained eyes. That's a whole different experience. Again, it's that Molly Bloom thing; it's a heightened affirmation of sexuality and sensuality as life. Matisse always kicks up the volume in some way that doesn't leave the painting as a simple portrait of a person. His odalisques don't look like people, anyway, except for a couple of portraits of Madame Matisse and Marguerite and some family members. Most of the models that he used don't look like people per se. They're coalescences of people and sexuality.

RE: But even when he renders Marguerite's nose, it has a beautiful, linear sense. It's actually a description of what she looks like, not merely a trademark schematization as I'd previously thought.

AG: To tell you the truth, I don't really care about that. I'm not interested in what he really saw. I look at those paintings as being absolutes, so I don't look at them as a way of measuring how he got from point A to point B, because he's already left me in the dust.

RE: Can you figure out how he got from point A to point B?

AG: To a certain extent. But it doesn't interest me how he got there. It's that he got there and then what he did once he arrived.

RE: You say that the women have power in his paintings. A work like *Conversation* is a standoff; it's like the domestic gunfight at the O.K. Corral. Nobody's going to win that one. The solidity of the woman's arm as it curls on that chair is something you don't mess with. You get a sense that these domestic interiors are very often about a pretty frightening psychology. How much do we read these paintings as measures of anxiety?

AG: I don't get the impression that he's happy in most of the work. Except for this brief thing around the Morocco period where he's really painting out of his mind. I think that a lot of the paintings show a deliberate, intense decision to go ahead and make something that's extremely beautiful, extremely sensuous. But he's fighting something in himself to do it. You feel a darkness at the base of some of them.

RE: Do you want to know anything more about him?

AG: I really am not that interested in his life. I'm curious about how the cutouts happened, and I'm curious about that depression or sadness lurking under the work. But it seems so basic. I mean isn't any sensitive person beset by a certain amount of existential anxiety? It makes sense that it comes out; what amazes me more is that sometimes he actually left it behind.

RE: I was surprised by the early landscape paintings, the ones that are brooding and dark and rather reduced. What do you make of them as a landscape painter?

AG: My first reaction was to think, Oh, his are a little like mine, we do have something specifically in common and if I keep painting my landscapes a little longer maybe they'll grow into something like Matisse's. I was surprised to see *Large Grey Seascape*, that very Munch-like composition. I'd never seen these landscapes reproduced so I was completely taken aback.

RE: But when we get to the Fauve paintings—like *Red Beach*—I read them as a rendering and interpretation of colour. What do you think when you look at those paintings?

AG: I think all his paintings ground themselves in their subject matter. I think there's a point where landscape and the kind of light that he's experiencing get interiorized for him. There's something really essential about his having done the Collioure and St. Tropez landscapes which gave him a license to deal with light in a certain way. He brings it indoors and definitely starts to suffuse the interior light that he's working with.

RE: In his window paintings he doesn't seem to distinguish between the interior and the exterior?

AG: His still lifes, too, tend to emanate light and colour rather than having colour fall on them in the picture plane. No matter what he's looking at—we've been to his house in Nice and he has the things you see in the paintings, the old *fauteuil* and stuff—the sum of the parts doesn't in any way equal the totality of the way he actually paints. So there's this leap that he's always making. He has a vision of colour and of form and of the dissolution of form into colour, into line and into the plane of the picture itself that gets them to emanate, gets them to vibrate.

RE: Can you take things away from this exhibition that you can then use?

AG: There's one portrait that he does of a woman called Olga Merson where this black curved line cuts through the figure. It's weird because it's a painting that a painter was thinking about and then made an absolutely radical decision to leave it where it is. As a painter you've probably made these kinds of decisions too and you're startled that someone actually went ahead and left it at that point. So the evidence of decision-making in his work is a license for me to experiment. It's an affirmation more than anything else.

RE: Because of decisions like that, because of the sheer will to make the painting, he ends up being a more radical painter than I had thought before.

AG: You see, I've always thought he was the most radical painter ever because his vision is so completely idiosyncratic. I can understand Monet; I can completely understand Picasso. Matisse's drawings are understandable; many of the paintings aren't. It's astonishing to me how he gets a certain colour going or how he reduces something. There's so much versatility within a single painting.

RE: Do you think he's ever tentative?

AG: Within certain paintings, yes. There are lots of Nice period paintings, for instance, that are definitely tentative and struggling. He has faults, he's not perfect. He painted his share of dogs too. It's just that when he's good, he's so much the best.

RE: What do you make of *Bathers with a Turtle*?

AG: It's interesting to me that he would have these dumb bands of colour in the background—the dumb greyish blue, then this richer blue, then this greenish blue. The way they're painted is so rich that I've often come to think of cobalt plus a smidge of ultramarine as particularly Matisse blue. It's a colour which has a lot of weight to it. He has a way of working with colours where he gives them weights and a lack of gravity that I find fascinating. Actually, I remember thinking about the weight of colour in his work in school and it had a huge influence on my work. Obviously, I don't mean in terms of the work looking like that or even using colour like that, but when I'm painting the bottom part of a painting with a lot of water, what I think about is not how to make it look wet but how to make it look heavy. And with such a fast surface that it's just barely staying still. Even though it's a big expanse it would have this nervous speed to it.

RE: And that has nothing to do with mimeticism, with making water look like water?

AG: Nothing at all. I just realized this is exactly the way Matisse has influenced me. When you look at the middle blue in the background of *Bathers with a Turtle*, it is of such an absolutely particular weight. It holds her torso and her head inside it in a certain way, right on the edge. The head of the middle woman sits so precariously against that edge and the blonde bent head is so far beneath it and the woman on the right is so contained within it. You can't do that with any old blue. I don't know how intuitive all this is for him but you can tell this is a worked colour, not a one-shot colour. And then compositionally it's such an amazing painting. These woman are pretty loaded up in the picture plane but they're so completely apart from each other too because of their shyness and also by the way they're bent into their own spaces and silhouetted. I think that's completely right. And the green the third woman is sitting on is nothing. It's preposterous. She's sitting on a wall with a little shadow. To make the decision to put a shadow underneath her, so that the green suddenly bends outward and comes toward you, so that *she* comes toward you, so that her curve occupies the right side of the painting in a dimensional way, which makes the figure on the left be silhouetted, removed and pushed into the painting—to make that decision is extraordinary.

RE: One of the things you notice throughout the show is his use of shadow. It has nothing to do with what a body would actually cast; it has to do with some totally different notion of composition.

AG: I think he's so much more about mass. Mass in some sort of absolute way, body as mass, the way that mass will work in space. I think his sculptures are extraordinary and so bizarre. They're serpentine in an unserpentine way. There is this inner grace that's just wild because it's grace that seems to have moved through the hip socket of an elephant, or something like that. This beautiful biology comes through that's not really about the way it literally looks.

RE: It's also about improbable distances. Those small sculptures are like landscapes, like the *Two Women*.

AG: There is an infinitude of possibilities in that piece. I love it. If there is one piece that I can think of that has a whimsical quality, but in a serious way, it's that one.

RE: Serious whimsy is an interesting way of describing Matisse's work.

AG: It's happy existentialism or something. There is this sense that they're together and apart, grasping and letting go. It also has to do with that cross shape: they come up vertically and horizontally at the same time.

RE: What do you make of his use of black? Is it a way of weighting the painting as well?

AG: He uses black all different ways. Sometimes he uses it as a hole, sometimes he uses it as a gravity force, almost like a piece of iron, a structural thing—and sometimes he uses it as a shadow. He uses it for weightlessness too.

RE: There's a very early painting called *Still Life with Black Knives* which has an insistent knife on the bottom that does become a structural thing. It's not an element of still life, it's a way of building the painting.

AG: I think everything that's in Matisse is in the early work, save that disintegration of structure by colour and then the rebuilding of it by his own sense of colour. Drawing with colour in a painting in order to completely restructure the weights and gravities and balances of a pictorial scene happens later. It happens later but it's really a pretty smooth evolution.

RE: So there's nothing apocalyptic in his development? It's not about ruptures; it's about subtle continuity?

AG: Yeah, I think so. It's a subtle continuity that nevertheless defies logic.

RE: I haven't asked you how good a drawer he is.

AG: Oh, he's the best drawer. He and Rodin. Astonishing. I mean, besides the simple line drawings and the charcoal drawings, he gets this push into the space of the paper. The paper becomes like cloth or something, it gets this dense texture. I start to see the white of the paper in a different way because of the way he's smudged the charcoal. When he goes back into it and the thing takes form, I don't see it just as the finished thing. For some reason I see that in a time lapse.

RE: As a sequence of things that happen?

AG: Yeah, I think it exists. I sometimes think that if you do a good job when you paint paintings it's like a machine. It's like you've made this machine which generates various kinds of evocative responses in people. When you look at a really great painting there's a sense that it's still forming itself. The paintings of mine I like best feel that way. When I look at them I feel as if I can't quite see the whole thing at once. There's a bit of a shift that's built into the painting. Matisse does that when he paints and draws. I'm talking about a final thing that somehow keeps generating its own creation. It makes it more rich and more elusive.

Nancy Spero

Looking at Matisse

NANCY SPERO: I'm skeptical about blockbuster shows. I think all the hype is just that—hype! An artist friend said they were scalping tickets outside the show for about fifty dollars. It sounded like a sporting event. Now, if you look at it in a positive way it's great that art might be appreciated and of interest to huge segments of the population.

ROBERT ENRIGHT: Even if we accept the fact that the hype has been incredible, why is there so much interest in Matisse?

NS: The paintings are easy to take. After the early radical and innovative paintings the work gets increasingly relaxed and ultimately flaccid. I think they become bourgeois. If I understand Matisse's history correctly, while this was not a deliberate agenda, it was a protective cocoon in which he enclosed his responses to nature and possibility. I am still thrilled by the *Dance* paintings and the smaller works that were done subsequently, which were influenced by Cézanne. He remains experimental even if the early vitality is largely missing. But by the 1920s he is recycling decorative formulae.

RE: I'm interested to hear you say you are still thrilled by the *Dance* piece because your own art has often used attenuated, moving figures as well. Do you think part of your response to *Dance I* and *Dance II* is because of that?

NS: These were bold, liberating canvasses, without backgrounds or any attendant details. The figures are unfettered, stylized in a way that looks forward to the machine age. I have always appreciated *Dance* at MOMA and it's great getting the second version from Russia.

RE: What do you make of the early work?

NS: Well, he was very adept—a prodigy—and they're beautiful paintings. But had he continued in this conservative vein his work would never have been remarked.

RE: Does he start to become a better painter in the Fauve period when colour becomes the issue?

NS: He breaks away from tradition and goes along with a Modernist sensibility. He gets rid of a lot of the classical easel techniques that had been prevalent since the Renaissance. Breaking up spaces and flattening things out, they're more experimental. There's an abandon to the large paintings, a sense of freedom of movement, of possibility. And they aren't yet clichéd or trapped in a recurrent rhythm or regime.

RE: Do you sense that Matisse gets caught in a trap of his own formal making?

NS: Yes. To give him credit, he very brilliantly does what he does. *Conversation* is quite daring and stylized and I find it strong. Although not as moving as the early ones.

RE: One of the obvious questions to ask a painter like yourself, committed to social and feminist issues, is what you make of the relationship between Matisse, his wife and his models? What do you make of the whole surrogate world he invented for himself?

NS: He deliberately chose to stay away from politics in his art. His wife and daughter were in the Resistance but he also stayed away from that. His daughter was tortured by the Nazis. His later works were done during the war when he was in the south of France. This was a deliberate political act—to eschew politics, to think about colour, beauty, a certain decor, and how they transport one into another space and idea. That was his agenda.

RE: Does it bother you that he becomes the great painter of the bourgeoisie?

NS: It didn't bother me. I thought the museum looked better since its revamping. I have never really been fond of MOMA since they enlarged it—somehow the rooms became greyer, the ceilings lower, the whole space more monotonous. It doesn't have the sense of lightness and openness that it had previously. But there was something about the Matisse show—the comfortable size of his canvasses and these paintings flowing from one room to another—that made the museum look good. He had a deliberate agenda to beautify. But I want to pick up your question about art and politics. I respond more to art that's on the edge, political art or an art that's confrontational, like the Constructivists, Dadaists, etc. What some people call beautiful in Matisse I call bland or decoratively exotic.

RE: What does Matisse have to teach painters today? Are there lessons to be learned from this show?

NS: Well, his heritage is recognizable in lots of contemporary artists' work, certainly in his way of breaking up flat space. Perhaps in colour-field painting.

RE: Matisse's influence turns up in surprising places. There's a drawing by Joseph Beuys that is extremely similar to Matisse's cutout of the acrobat. It seems as much an appropriation as an homage. Have the cutouts influenced you at all?

NS: The use of scissors is not a sufficient connection! I am critical of a cursory, decorative quality. It's interesting that Matisse made the shift to the cutouts because of his arthritis. Maybe they worked well in their intended settings but I think they're an addendum to the show. Scanty examples. Perhaps the concept and execution are liberating, but they do not possess the remarkable avant-garde quality of the early works.

RE: But when you started doing cutouts Matisse wasn't in your mind?

NS: No. I derive more from examples like the Bayeux Tapestry or the *Egyptian Book of the Dead* than Matissean collage.

RE: I want to get your estimation of the quality of the drawing and what it tells us about Matisse as an artist.

NS: It was just so evident in those early sombre paintings that he was masterful and that he honed his skills over and over again. Perhaps too masterful, too suave.

RE: Do you remember the first time you saw a Matisse?

NS: As an art student at the school of the Art Institute of Chicago. I liked the work more then than I do now. But you can't help appreciating the consistency and the production of the man, the overwhelming abundance. I have a friend, an art historian, who has critiqued Matisse from a feminist viewpoint. She illustrated how he presents himself in some of these canvasses as the scientist. He's there in his white smock and glasses with his paint brush, which of course is interpreted as this phallic gesture, and then the odalisque is reduced to an object with no character whatsoever. In most cases it's accomplished with very swift, undifferentiated lines and tones, plopped there for bourgeois delectation. He set up a hotel room, hired models and recreated this memory of exoticism. I think these paintings echo the falsity of the set-up.

RE: Is there a uniformity to the way the women look?

NS: Much of the time.

RE: The argument is made that when Manet paints *Olympia*, her forthright stare *out* at the audience changes the relationship between the woman as object consumed by the male gaze into something more aggressive. Do you buy that argument and can it also be used to "defend" Matisse and the way he uses the female?

NS: Manet did paint another "reality," and many women in his works do challenge the viewer, become less objectified. There are no such confrontations in Matisse.

RE: So this show doesn't in any way cut him down to size; it actually amplifies the popular conception of Matisse as a Modernist master?

NS: People love the show because they find a pleasing, perfumed ambiance with no nastiness. This is a world deliberately removed from reality, that particular kind of modernism which provides a screen covering the world, through which few humans filter. They're suave surfaces which block out the grit and ugliness, the misfits and the untamed. It's like this pseudo-perfect, utopian vision. Matisse blocks out all the blemishes, angst, he blocks out any realities except these models plopped in a chair.

RE: There are paintings that strike me as being rather more menacing than you seem to suggest. I take your point that there's all kinds of beauty—overwhelming beauty at times—but there are also troubling relationships in the paintings between men and women. He comes at it indirectly in *Nymph and Satyr* with the male figure bending over a woman. She's in for trouble. I guess I'm sensing an aggression in the piece that speaks to something other than comfort.

NS: Perhaps.

RE: When he introduces some degree of tension in the paintings, do they then begin to interest you?

NS: Yeah, I think so. Which he did at first, and arguably at the very end of his life. There are also periods when the imaging is heightened. But his is largely a contained world, a sealed bubble.

RE: When you criticize MOMA for putting on this show, it makes me want to ask whether you think there is a place for these major retrospectives? Should museums be doing these shows; how can they do them better? I'm thinking of the Picasso retrospective as well as the Matisse.

NS: I think my objection comes to this. It started in the '50s with the hyper media exposure of the Abstract Expressionists. After the war these artists were named as purveyors of the idea of freedom, and the notion developed that modern art was a breakthrough, a signal to the world. Artists like Matisse and Picasso came to be considered masters but here American artists were more like rock stars. Everything becomes inflated and this includes Matisse and Picasso. MOMA, by installing acres of bland Matisses, shows an amazing visual blindness.

RE: But even if we don't want a painter like Matisse today we're still obliged to deal with the facts of history. We're caught in this bind because he's such a fabulously good painter.

NS: I don't think they're fabulously painted. All that monotonous and glib repetition.

Eric Fischl

Looking at Matisse

ERIC FISCHL: I've seen the exhibition two times and I still haven't seen the whole thing. It's vast, it's exhaustive, it's a spectacle. It's probably too big. There are too many paintings that don't deserve to get elevated and some masterpieces get diminished a bit. There are some paintings that, taken alone, I would have thought higher of.

ROBERT ENRIGHT: Let's talk about a work I assume you would like, *Bathers with a Turtle*, an unusual painting done in 1908. The girl in the middle looks as if you could have painted her face.

EF: I do find that painting very strange. I don't know what's going on; it seems as if there are some symbolic relationships taking place as well as some measure of social innocence—just three naked people out in nature. But then the head of the woman in the middle is so bizarre, so grotesque.

RE: It's rendered differently from the others, isn't it?

EF: Yeah. It's very neanderthal, very primitive. It reminds me of Picasso's *Demoiselles* where the African masks on a couple of the women get hideous and distorted. The painting is also strange because she's so perplexed. Perplexed and she looks as if she's flossing. What I also love about this painting is the gesture of the woman who's enticing the turtle. The way she's holding the piece of leaf or lettuce, or whatever it is, is so specific; it's not between the thumb and the forefinger, it's between the other two. It's delicate and specific and I find it stunning that he's able to carry that over in the midst of all that simplification. Matisse is so much the painter's painter. It's his directness. He makes decisions you can follow but it blows your mind that he made them. His technique is not complex; his vision is complex. I'm interested in how he abstracts something. I mean, it must have been so much fun to paint the towel or toga or whatever it is that surrounds this one boy in *The Game of Bowls*. It's such a great abstract shape but he also included a little indication of the leg and the fold which gives it this wonderful, sensuous and naturalist quality. It's so delicately balanced between the flat abstract, non-objective thing and real observation. There's a painting in the show of an interior in which light coming through hits an ashtray or a bowl in the foreground that's filled with water. The bowl is done in four colours. You see the light skimming across the surface of the water and the rim of the bowl as well. His observation of that phenomena is so dead on and yet so simple and abstract. Just these four colours and this simple pattern.

RE: His play between abstraction and truth to observation has a number of other painterly nooks and crannies. When I look at paintings like *View of Notre Dame* or *French Window at Collioure* I can't help but think of Diebenkorn.

EF: Yeah, except the *View of Notre Dame* is done sixty years earlier and Diebenkorn doesn't take it any farther than Matisse did. He took out the bush but that's it. And somehow it's better with the bush in because it gives you yet another way of referencing. You see, I think there's three kinds of abstraction. There's abstraction which is pure, that is derived from geometry or mathematics; then there's abstraction which moves away from reality and the experience of it is the measured distance between what is retained and what has been transformed; and then there is abstraction which moves from the outside toward reference. Here the measure is what you associate with a form, when something organic reminds you of a leaf. Matisse's abstraction is the middle one; it moves away from reality and you measure the space between. And what you're measuring is inspiration and vision and, in his case, genius. That space is so simplified but it includes geometry, light, colour, it includes the gestures of painting itself, it includes this spontaneous reacting to what paint does, that also reacts to what you've seen. So it's not one thing that makes him stand out among others, it's all that. It's how dense his space is. With some artists you can measure the space between but the distance is not that interesting. I've always found, for example, Picasso's abstraction of the bull to be uninteresting because it's so didactic. It follows a certain kind of logic, so that by the second one you already know how far it's going to go. Whereas with Matisse you never know what the result of his distancing is going to be, how far away from reality it's going to get or how close it's going to get.

RE: So he constantly surprises you when you look at the work?

EF: Painting to painting. Plus he does things you just cannot explain. My favourite Matisse painting is *Bathers by a River* and it's interesting that this show didn't change my mind. I lived with this painting in Chicago for several years; I would make weekly pilgrimages to see it because it always surprised me. So many things in there are unexplained but evocative. There's a shape that comes in from the bottom that's like a tail or a snake or some kind of serpent. What's it doing there? The people in the water don't seem particularly surprised by its presence. And I love the blocky forms of the figures, with grey moving toward pink flesh. It's like humans being formed. It feels like this river is Eden, it's the primordial garden and it's early in evolutionary time. And so the figures and what they're doing are just at the beginning. They're just becoming. I think that's very beautifully realized. Then there's this one figure on the shore that has an insert where the head would be; it shows shapes that mimic the flattened shapes of the bodies. It isn't specific and you don't know what it is; you never will know what it is or why it's there and yet it completely works. It reminds me of the sculptures that were taken from Rodin's studio, plaster sculptures that had never been seen and that nobody really knew what to do with. There were these back-to-back, three-foot versions of Eve and then tied on top of them was the sculpture of the flattened-out woman, who's sitting squat with her knees up to her shoulders. She's flipped up and laid on top of the two Eves and they're tied together. And this was found in his studio. It's so weird you can't explain it at all. What occurred to me is that the Eve sculpture by itself shows a woman just after she's been caught by God and expelled. She's in a state of shame but the event has already occurred. By going one step back to the moment just as it's happening, Rodin delivers a more unresolved, frenetic and chaotic moment, right?

RE: And that's Matisse's moment in *Bathers by a River*?

EF: Well, this one figure you can't explain has something to do with that. It's not as frantic, but it's a figure that is both crouching and stepping into the blackness. You assume it's the river but it's also the void, and at the moment this happens the head has been replaced by some kind of repeating image that is not a head. And while you'll never figure it out, it doesn't seem wrong, which is what's so amazing. It does *not* seem like it doesn't belong there; it seems like it's at a different state of being. In the same way the Rodin thing represents an unresolved moment.

RE: Let's talk about something that seems more resolved—Matisse's eroticism. Do you find that these paintings are about a kind of eroticism?

EF: Some are *all* about eroticism. You definitely get that sense, especially during the Nice period. There's actually two paintings where you can see that the model has become a lot more relaxed: one's called *Lorette Reclining* and the other *The Studio, quai Saint-Michel*. You sense that he painted her and then he had sex with her and then she was laying there so happy and relaxed that he just painted her again. It's very funny.

RE: Do you feel that the world he's created by the time we get to the Nice period doesn't have anything to do with the outside world, that it's almost hermetically sealed?

EF: That was the strategy most artists were using at the time and it's one I greatly admire. But if you go to Giverny you'll see the same closure where Monet made this world of beauty out of flowers and gardens and stuff.

RE: Except that Matisse constructs an exotic world that has nothing to do with the place in which he finds himself.

EF: Yeah, it doesn't surprise me as a way of working but the quality of his closure is pretty interesting.

RE: That world has been criticized as unforgivably bourgeois. It comes up all the time—Matisse's comment about a painting being as comfortable as an armchair is the focal point for this kind of criticism.

EF: There's a story about Matisse that always struck me as extraordinary and as a way of explaining how powerful his work really is. During the war his wife and daughter were picked up by the Gestapo for questioning and he was informed about it. He was working at the time so you assume there is a painting that corresponds with that moment but you don't know what painting it is. Because he did not let the trauma of daily life come into the vision he had about art. I think that transcends a bourgeois sense of denial. It certainly includes the need to control the world and to isolate yourself from it in some way. But who cares about that? What it's about is somebody whose sense of beauty, simplicity and dialogue with the world and with himself is the stuff of his work. When I see it, especially when I'm oppressed by the weight of the world, it inspires me. What more could you ask for? And it's not like you don't sense that he suffered, but he chose to leave that outside the work. There are paintings where you see that there's an edge. Think of *Conversation*, that's a tough moment between him and his wife. There are paintings he does of women where there's a real aggression; there are others where it's nothing but pure erotic delight. I just think that you don't look to Matisse if you want to express the Holocaust.

RE: How good a drawer is he?

EF: He's one of the best. Within the modern vernacular, he is certainly *the* best; his sense of process and line, his sensuous material, beautiful stylization and directness, the nice combination of flat and linear type of thing with volume—all these are delicate balances.

RE: Does he extend the pictorial language?

EF: I don't think he extended it; I think he invented it. He and Picasso. Those of us who come after haven't been able to do much more. Nobody comes to mind, at any rate. Some people have freed up the line to do its own thing and have taken the sensuous, smudgy stuff with it, but I don't think much more has been done. Every artist who's come after Matisse wonders what to do with the smudge. They make drawings just to make the smudge. Matisse's drawings look as if he were trying to find the form and everybody else's looks as if they were trying to find the smudges because they already knew what the form was.

RE: What about the sculpture? I'm interested to get your sense of what he does with three-dimensional space, now that you've become a sculptor as well.

EF: It's incredible but I don't really know what to say about it. Somebody told me that he did it at night, which interests me. He would paint during the day with light and then at night he would get into the feeling thing.

RE: I know you're interested in Bonnard, so I wanted to know if you're aware of the correspondence between them?

EF: I heard a funny story in connection with them when they were both living in the south of France. Actually, it involves three painters. Apparently, Bonnard wanted to use Aristide Maillol's model, Dina Vierny, but his wife, Marthe, is insanely jealous. So there's this big negotiation with three artists involved. It turns out Matisse has used her as a model as well, so he's part of it. They have to write letters to Madame Bonnard to get permission and to assure her this is on the up and up. Matisse tells this one artist, who was the go-between, that Marthe shouldn't worry because Dina Vierny looks like a wet noodle. Of course she doesn't; she's this incredibly voluptuous teenage girl. Apparently, when she came to model— and I got this directly from Dina—Marthe locked herself in her room and wouldn't come out for the entire time. She just absolutely couldn't deal with it at all. If you ever go to Bonnard's house you'll see it's very small, so that even if she locked the door, the vibes coming through that wall would have been absolutely ferocious. It must have been quite a situation.

Nancy Graves

Looking at Matisse

NANCY GRAVES: The first time I ever saw a Matisse painting was at the Museum of Modern Art here in New York. I was twelve years old and I guess you could say it was an epiphany. I didn't live in New York. I was visiting with my parents and it was probably the first time I had been in the museum. My father was employed in an arts and science museum so I had an understanding of venerable institutions.

ROBERT ENRIGHT: And venerable artists. Can you remember what it was that attracted you initially?

NG: It's hard to say how things affect you because that operates on some kind of unconscious level. Certainly the colour and I would say the composition and the daring, the limited amount of line and form.

RE: Has he stayed with you?

NG: Well, when I was a painting student we all had the Alfred Barr book—it was one of the bibles of the time—and I knew everything in it. So there were only three or four paintings that were surprises in the Matisse exhibition. The rest I either had seen on travels or was familiar with through reproduction. The surprises were *Open Door, Brittany* of 1896 that predicates everything from the open windows of 1905 to *Violinist at the Window* of 1918; and then the Cubist landscape from 1917, the *Garden at Issy*. I hadn't recognized the power of that painting, which really has two viewpoints: from a window looking down, and then looking up, which would be typical of the way Braque and Picasso painted houses in landscape prior to that. I was unaware of *Open Door, Brittany* altogether. It has that elliptical, amorphous centre. This notion of the open window and how one could create interior and exterior space was the type of thing for which Matisse had an unconsciously strong predilection.

RE: He must have quickly realized that the interior and exterior literally gave him all kinds of space in which to play around.

NG: Absolutely. And then think about all the studio pieces he did with Notre Dame out the window; then he moved to Nice and there were any number of window focusses, and then how he played with Islamic art with the painting in the painting in the painting. My point is that as an artist you have certain innate predilections. It's important to know that, although at the time you make those initial forays you may not be certain where they're going to lead. This was the way in which I was looking at *Open Door, Brittany*, seeing the raw substance Matisse had to deal with and then seeing what he did with it.

RE: What about the earlier paintings? I'm thinking of a strange work called *Studio Under the Eaves* from 1901–02. It's very spare, more like an interior by Eric Fischl than by Matisse.

NG: It's an extraordinary painting because of the sparseness; I mean, the way in which things are played with, the forms, the kind of composition, and then everything that's going on in the exterior. It's the first time where he used the window and put in so much information.

RE: In fact, there's more going on outside the window than inside the studio.

NG: In that sense it's very like Fischl, it's true.

RE: Since you knew all the work, I assume you weren't surprised by the overall achievement that emerges from the exhibition?

NG: No. Whereas with Picasso, I was. And interestingly, I had thought somehow that the number of works in the exhibition would bring new insights. I must say that for me the strongest work is from the Cubist period and to see that room with *Bathers by a River*, *Piano Lesson* and *The Moroccans* in it—paintings that are normally stretched across the world—was the most compelling reason to keep returning to the show. And to have some of the Hermitage paintings from St. Petersberg neck and neck with the others was thrilling.

RE: In the *Village Voice,* Peter Schjeldahl said he'd like to make a trade with the Russians for their version of *Dance*. How do you think the two big paintings stack up one against the other?

NG: The two *Dance* paintings have never been as meaningful for me as they are to some other people. I do recognize the quality of the line and the form. Yes, the Russian painting is more complete and more expressionist in its sense of colour. It probably is the better painting.

RE: Have there been occasions when you've found yourself aware that Matisse handled space in a particular way and that maybe you could borrow his ideas? Has he ever been that directly functional?

NG: Well, as a student I was very much influenced and then I tried to throw that out and start afresh. But, of course, everything that you've ever done is part of your history, whether it's obvious or not. He certainly made me aware—along with the course that Josef Albers put into being at Yale—that pure colour needed nothing to recommend it other than a paint brush and the pigment itself on the canvas. And so I was definitely affected by that colour sense. By comparison, of course, Picasso is a black and white artist. When he uses colour it's always with a graphic concern. He never was able to make the leap Matisse made and that's one of the major distinctions between the two.

RE: Are Picasso and Matisse the two giants striding across the landscape of twentieth-century painting?

NG: Well, certainly for the first half and possibly beyond that. The issues are changing so rapidly that whether this will be true down the road is really hard to say. But I do go back to Matisse. It's like reading a good novel or listening to a great symphony. You learn what magnitude is and it gives you contact with what can be. You may have to do something with completely different attitudes and means but it's a levelling. So it's very significant from that standpoint. There's also always rigour there. I can say that the paintings of the '30s and the '40s are less interesting, but on the other hand, the amount of detail and the way in which the composition varies have benefited me a great deal. Still, when all is said and done, I come back to Cubism; those are the quintessential works. Some of the portraits are magnificent as well.

RE: I want to get your reaction to one of the portraits. It's of Olga Merson, done in 1911. It would be a traditional portrait were it not for the heavy black lines that he puts in to abstract the body. It's as if he were seeing into his own future and anticipating his own drawings. It leads me to ask you whether you feel it was already all in his head, so that his career was just a working out of things about which he was already aware?

NG: Not at all. I think there's tremendous struggle in Matisse. With Picasso you don't see that. In the beginning with Matisse you wonder, Can this guy really get there? But he had such determination and obviously so many untapped resources which could not be defined in terms of what had been necessary for art-making in the past. He was able not only to bring them to bear but to persevere as well. I can remember seeing a show of early drawings in the mid '80s in Paris, a beautiful drawing show on the Left Bank in the School of Architecture. Most of the loans were from Paris collections. A lot of them were quite extraordinary after-the-masters type of thing, and you could see the tremendous struggle. On the other hand, the necessity to equal the past masters gave him a technique and discipline that served him well when he branched into his own style.

RE: What do you make of the sculptures in the show?

NG: I would prefer there were more of them. In one sense they're an accent, which I think is good, but I don't feel there's enough of a statement made by them. They seem parenthetical and they're not. He was a great sculptor. I saw an exhibition at the Hayward in London about ten years ago of almost every piece of sculpture he'd ever done. There is not a huge number of them but the growth is incredible. I think John Elderfield probably limited the number out of necessity. I don't think he could do it all, so I assume he tried to deal with as many themes and parallels as possible.

RE: In the sculptures he creates a dialogue between painting and sculpture. When you look down the line of the linked arms in *Two Women*, it suddenly becomes topographical. In a strange way those figures are imagining themselves as landscapes.

NG: That's very typical of him to move something from one system into another through line and colour, to transform our boundaries of expectation. And then, of course, there's the way he included his own works in his canvasses and drawings, so that his own paintings and sculpture became transformed or metamorphosed as part of subsequent works.

RE: So they're meta-paintings?

NG: Yes. And he's concerned with breaking down the barriers between painting and sculpture, which is a very typical stance today. And that's something that I think a great deal about: where are the boundaries between sculpture and painting? I'm constantly attempting to redefine them in my own work.

RE: When you said earlier that Matisse had struggled tremendously, are you referring to aesthetics or psychology?

NG: Well, let me answer in this way. Picasso more or less came full-blown so you didn't see that struggle. When he's in Barcelona in the 1890s he's making paintings that were very typical of that time, in which black became the dominant and the most opulent colour one could possibly imagine. There was a whole school of painters and he could have stayed there.

RE: And been one of the best of that kind of painter?

NG: Exactly. But that lasted maybe five minutes for him and then he went on and did *The Absinthe Drinker* and the two *Saltimbanques* and all that. He never lacked an ability to absorb whatever was in the air and then transform it.

RE: So he's a quick study and Matisse is comparatively laboured?

NG: Early on he is. It took him longer to get off the ground but once he did, his acuity and his technique took over. But it did take him longer. His paintings are definitely fewer in number and more time-consuming than those of Picasso. He wasn't versatile.

RE: What do you make of his palette? Can you make anything of it as a practising painter?

NG: I'd love to have his palette.

RE: Is it unusual?

NG: The use of pure colour at that time was genius. He was aware of chevreul and other colour theories and kept colour as planar and as pure as one could at the same time. Colour was light, was form, was air. Awesome.

Acknowledgements

If acknowledgements were honest carriers of indebtedness, they could easily rival the length of the books to which they're attached. These acknowledgements attempt thoroughness and conciseness, hoping that my aim at the latter won't lead me to miss entirely the former.

In Canada, cultural journalists are cobblers, patching together a life of writing about the arts from a number of different places. My interviewing began in the early 1980s, when Anne Gibson, the executive producer of the CBC program "Stereo Morning," sent me to New York to interview Robert Motherwell as part of a documentary on his art and life. She had faith when I had enthusiasm and little talent, and I'm grateful for the confidence she gave me.

More recently, Arthur Danto offered valuable encouragement and Mary Ann Caws made a suggestion that vastly improved the way I ordered the various gazings at Matisse in this book. Geoffrey Hayes kindly read all three interviews from the Musicalities section and saved me from repeating any embarrassing errors. Peter Atwood was scrupulous in his attention to the manuscript and helped clear away the fog from my sometimes impenetrable thinking.

A dozen of these interviews exist because Renate Ponsold, the photographer and wife of Robert Motherwell, allowed us the use of her apartment in New York. How rare must it be to have as a base of operations a place in which you are surrounded by the art of one of the twentieth century's greatest painters, and by Renate's own photographic portraits, sometimes of the artists included in this collection. Her apartment, like her being, is filled with elegance and grace, and her friendship has helped make this book possible.

All of the interviews originally appeared in the pages of *Border Crossings* magazine and sections from "Making a World from Scratch" have subsequently been published in the June 1996 issue of *Harper's* and in the November 1996 issue of the German edition of *GEO*. "Regendering the Garden" won the Gold Medal for the best Profile at the Western Magazine Awards in 1993, and the Matisse miscellany won the Silver medal for Editorial Excellence at the National Magazine Awards in 1994. Three of the interviews were first published with different introductions.

I'd like to thank Richard Rhodes for his insights on Tony Cragg, and Meeka Walsh for the invention and lyric precision of her assessments of Maria Fernanda Cardoso and Jim Dine. The gratitude I owe Meeka—as my colleague and editor—is almost sinful in its scope. Her involvement with *Border Crossings* has been as intense as my own and these interviews would not have happened without her encouragement and intelligence. She talked with me about all of them before they were done; sat through a number while they were being done; and did the initial shaping after they were completed. At every stage her suggestions were what my other mind would have wanted to ask and these spoken interviews and their written introductions are stronger for her discriminating attention.

Finally, I want to thank the artists themselves, who agreed to talk to an unknown editor from a small Canadian magazine, and then had to put up with what must have seemed like endless, sometimes impertinent questions. They not only consented to the original conversation, but were unanimous in their agreement to be included in this book as well, often reading the interviews and clearing up any inaccuracies or inconsistencies. I consider it an honour that they have spoken so candidly and with such attention about the art we see together as a passionate, necessary pursuit.

ROBERT ENRIGHT is an art and film critic who is recognized as one of Canada's leading arts journalists. He has been interviewing international artists for many years and has published widely on issues in contemporary culture, art and film, as well as having lectured extensively in Canada, the United States, and Europe. At present, he is Editor-at-Large for the arts magazine *Border Crossings*, film critic for CBC Television, regular arts commentator for CBC Radio, and regular contributor on the arts to *The Globe and Mail*. His reputation as an informed and unobtrusive interviewer has won him access to the most interesting artists of our time.